THE RISE OF RAIL-POWER
IN WAR AND CONQUEST
1833—1914

THE RISE OF RAIL-POWER

IN WAR AND CONQUEST

1833—1914

WITH A BIBLIOGRAPHY

BY

EDWIN A. PRATT

Author of "A History of Inland Transport,"
"Railways and their Rates," etc.

The Naval & Military Press Ltd

Published by

The Naval & Military Press Ltd
Unit 5 Riverside, Brambleside
Bellbrook Industrial Estate
Uckfield, East Sussex
TN22 1QQ England

Tel: +44 (0)1825 749494

www.naval-military-press.com
www.nmarchive.com

In reprinting in facsimile from the original, any imperfections are inevitably reproduced and the quality may fall short of modern type and cartographic standards.

CONTENTS.

CHAP.		PAGE
I	A NEW FACTOR	1
II	RAILWAYS IN THE CIVIL WAR	14
III	RAILWAY DESTRUCTION IN WAR	26
IV	CONTROL OF RAILWAYS IN WAR	40
V	PROTECTION OF RAILWAYS IN WAR	54
VI	TROOPS AND SUPPLIES	62
VII	ARMOURED TRAINS	67
VIII	RAILWAY AMBULANCE TRANSPORT	81
IX	PREPARATION IN PEACE FOR WAR	98
X	ORGANISATION IN GERMANY	103
XI	RAILWAY TROOPS IN GERMANY	122
XII	FRANCE AND THE WAR OF 1870–71	138
XIII	ORGANISATION IN FRANCE	149
XIV	ORGANISATION IN ENGLAND	175
XV	MILITARY RAILWAYS	205
XVI	RAILWAYS IN THE BOER WAR	232
XVII	THE RUSSO-JAPANESE WAR	260
XVIII	STRATEGICAL RAILWAYS: GERMANY	277

CONTENTS.

CHAP.		PAGE
XIX	A German-African Empire	296
XX	Designs on Asiatic Turkey	331
XXI	Summary and Conclusions	345
	Appendix	
	Indian Frontier Railways	357
	The Defence of Australia	368
	Bibliography	376
	Index	398

PREFATORY NOTE.

THE extent to which railways are being used in the present War of the Nations has taken quite by surprise a world whose military historians, in their accounts of what armies have done or have failed to do on the battle-field in the past, have too often disregarded such matters of detail as to how the armies got there and the possible effect of good or defective transport conditions, including the maintenance of supplies and communications, on the whole course of a campaign.

In the gigantic struggle now proceeding, these matters of detail are found to be of transcendant importance. The part which railways are playing in the struggle has, indeed—in keeping with the magnitude of the struggle itself—assumed proportions unexampled in history. Whilst this is so it is, nevertheless, a remarkable fact that although much has been said as to the conditions of military unpreparedness in which the outbreak of hostilities in August, 1914, found the Allies, there has, so far as I am aware, been no suggestion of any inability on the part of the railways to meet, at once, from the very moment war was declared, all the requirements of military transport. In this respect, indeed, the organisation, the preparedness, and the efficiency throughout alike of the British and of the French railways have been fully equal to those of the German railways themselves.

As regards British conditions, especially, much interest attaches to some remarks made by Sir Charles Owens, formerly General Manager of the London and South Western Railway Company, in the course of an address delivered by him to students of the London School of Economics on

October 12, 1914. He told how, some five or six years ago, he had met at a social function the Secretary of State for War, who, after dinner, took him aside and asked, "Do you think in any emergency which might arise in this country the railways would be able to cope with it adequately?" To this question Sir Charles replied, "I will stake my reputation as a railway man that the country could not concentrate men and materials half so fast as the railways could deal with them; but the management of the railways must be left in the hands of railway men." We have here an affirmation and a proviso. That the affirmation was warranted has been abundantly proved by what the British railways have accomplished in the emergency that has arisen. The special significance of the proviso will be understood in the light of what I record in the present work concerning the control of railways in war.

Taking the railways of all the countries, whether friends or foes, concerned in the present World-War, and assuming, for the sake of argument, that all, without exception, have accomplished marvels in the way of military transport, one must, nevertheless, bear in mind two important considerations :—

(1) That, apart from the huge proportions of the scale upon which, in the aggregate, the railways are being required to serve military purposes, the present conflict, in spite of its magnitude, has thus far produced no absolutely new factor in the employment of railways for war except as regards the use of air-craft for their destruction.

(2) That when hostilities were declared in August, 1914, the subject of the employment of railways for the purposes of war had already been under the consideration of railway and military experts in different countries for no fewer than eighty years, during which period, and as the result of vast study, much experience, and many blunders in or between wars in various parts of the world, there had been slowly evolved certain fixed principles and, also, subject to constant amendments, a recognised and comprehensive organisation which, accepted more or less completely by the leading nations, with modifications to suit their national

circumstances and conditions, was designed to meet all contingencies, to provide, as far as human foresight could suggest, for all possible difficulties, and be capable of application instantly the need for it might arise.

The time has not yet come for telling all that the railways have thus far done during the war which has still to be fought out. That story, in the words of a railway man concerned therein, is at present "a sealed book." Meanwhile, however, it is desirable that the position as defined in the second of the two considerations given above should be fully realised, in order that what the railways and, so far as they have been aided by them, the combatants, have accomplished or are likely to accomplish may be better understood when the sealed book becomes an open one.

If, as suggested at the outset, the world has already been taken by surprise even by what the railways are known to have done, it may be still more surprised to learn (as the present work will show) that the construction of railways for strategical purposes was advocated in Germany as early as 1833; that in 1842 a scheme was elaborated for covering Germany with a network of strategical railways which, while serving the entire country, would more especially allow of war being conducted on two fronts—France and Russia—at the same time; and that in the same year (1842) attention was already being called in the French Chamber to the "aggressive lines" which Germany was building in the direction of France, while predictions were also being made that any new invasion of France by Germany would be between Metz and Strasburg.

If, again, it is found that a good deal of space is devoted in the present work to the War of Secession, criticism may, perhaps, be disarmed by the explanation that the American Civil War was practically the beginning of things as regards the scientific use of railways for war, and that many of the problems connected therewith were either started in the United States or were actually worked out there, precedents being established and examples being set which the rest of the world had simply to follow, adapt or perfect. The possibility of carrying on warfare at a great distance from the base of supplies by means of even a single line of single-track railway; the creation of an organised corps for the restoration, operation or destruction of railways; the control of railways in war by the railway or the military interests independently or jointly; the question as to when the railway could be used to advantage and when it would be better for the troops to march; the use of armoured trains; the evolution of the ambulance or the hospital train—all these, and many other matters besides, are to be traced back to the American Civil War of 1861-65, and are dealt with herein at what, it is hoped, will be found not undue length.

As for the building up of the subsequent organisation in Europe—Germany, France and England being the countries selected for special treatment in relation thereto—this, also, has had to be described with some regard for detail; and, incidentally, it is shown (1) that the alleged perfection of Germany's arrangements when she went to war with France in 1870-71 is merely one of the fictions of history, so far as her military rail-transport was concerned; (2) that France learned the bitter lesson taught her by the deplorable and undeniable imperfections of her own transport system—or no-system—on that occasion, and at once set about the creation of what was to become an organisation of the most complete and comprehensive character; and (3) that the "beginning of things" in England, in the way of employing railways for the purposes of war, was the direct outcome of the conditions of semi-panic created here in 1859 by what was regarded as the prospect of an early invasion of this country by France, coupled with the then recognised deficiencies of our means of national defence.

Military railways, as employed in the Crimean War, the Abyssinian Campaign, the Franco-German War, the Russo-Turkish War and the Sudan are described; a detailed account is given of the use of railways in the Boer War and the Russo-Japanese War; and this is followed by a description of the strategical railways constructed in Germany for the purpose of facilitating war on the possessions of her neighbours.

Chapters XIX and XX deal with the building of railways which, whether avowedly strategical or what I have described as "economic-political-strategical," are intended to effect the purposes of conquest, with or without the accompaniment of war. The former of these two chapters, which shows how, with the help of railways, Germany proposed to transform the African continent into an African Empire of her own, should be found deserving of notice, and especially so in view of the statements quoted (p. 311) as having been made by German officers in what was then German South-West Africa, to the effect that the main objective of Germany in going to war would be the conquest of Africa, "the smashing up of France and Great Britain" being regarded only as "incidents" which, followed by seizure of the possessions of the smaller Powers, would make Germany the supreme Power in Africa, and lead to the whole African continent becoming a German possession.

From Chapter XX the reader will learn how Germany proposed to employ railways for the furthering of her aims against, not only Asiatic Turkey, but Egypt and India, as well.

The subsidiary articles on "Indian Frontier Railways" and "The Defence of Australia" have no direct bearing on that *evolution* of rail-power in warfare with which it is the special purpose of the present volume to deal; but in the belief that they are of interest and importance in themselves, from the point of view of the general question, they have been given in an Appendix. The difficulties and other conditions under which the Sind-Pishin State Railway, designed to serve strategical purposes, was built to the frontiers of Afghanistan are unexampled in the history either of railways or of war. As regards Australia, the gravity of the position there was well indicated by Lord Kitchener when he wrote of the lines running inland that they were "of little use for defence, although possibly of considerable value to an enemy who would have temporary command of the sea."

At the end of the volume there is a Bibliography of books, pamphlets and review or other articles relating to the use of railways for the purposes of war. In the first instance this compilation was based on a "List of References" prepared by the American Bureau of Railway Economics; but, while many items on that list have here been omitted, a considerable number of others have been inserted from other sources. The Bibliography is not offered as being in any way complete, but it may, nevertheless, be of advantage to students desirous of making further researches into the matters of history here specially treated.

The assistance rendered in other ways by the American Bureau of Railway Economics in the preparation of the present work has been most helpful. In the writing of the chapters concerning German designs on Africa, Asia Minor, etc., the resources of the well-arranged and admirably-indexed library of the Royal Colonial Institute have been of great service. I have, also, to express cordial acknowledgments to the General Managers and other officers of various leading railway companies for information given respecting the organisation of railways in this country for military purposes.

November, 1915.

EDWIN A. PRATT.

The Rise of Rail-Power in War and Conquest

CHAPTER I

A NEW FACTOR

WHILE the original purpose of railways was to promote the arts of peace, the wide scope of their possibilities in the direction, also, of furthering the arts of war began to be realised at a very early date after their success in the former capacity had been assured in Great Britain.

Already the canal system had introduced an innovation which greatly impressed the British public. In December, 1806, a considerable body of troops went by barge on the Paddington Canal from London to Liverpool, *en route* for Dublin, relays of fresh horses for the canal boats being provided at all the stages in order to facilitate the transport; and in referring to this event *The Times* of December 19, 1806, remarked:—" By this mode of conveyance the men will be only seven days in reaching Liverpool, and with comparatively little fatigue, as it would take them above fourteen days to march that distance."

But when, on the opening of the Liverpool and Manchester Railway, in 1830, a British regiment was conveyed thereon, in two hours, a journey of thirty-four miles, which they would have required two days to accomplish on foot, far-seeing men became still more impressed, and began to realise that there had, indeed, been introduced a new factor destined to exercise a powerful influence on the future conduct of war.

The geographical position of the United Kingdom led, in those early days, to greater importance being attached to the conveniences of railways as a means of transport than to their actual strategical and tactical advantages; and the issue by the War Office, in 1846, of a "Regulation Relative to the Conveyance of Her Majesty's Forces, their Baggage and Stores, by Rail," may have appeared to meet the requirements of the immediate situation, so far as this country was concerned.

On the Continent of Europe, however, the rivalry of nations divided from one another only by a more or less uncertain or varying frontier, and still powerfully influenced by the recollection of recent conflicts, resulted in much greater attention being paid to the possibilities of the new development.

The first definite proposals for the use of railways for strategical purposes were advanced, as early as 1833, by Friedrich Wilhelm Harkort, a Westphalian worthy who came to be better known in his native land as "Der alte Harkort." A participant in the Napoleonic wars, he had subsequently shown great energy and enterprise in the development of steam engines, hydraulic presses, iron-making, and other important industries in Germany; he had been the first writer in that country to give an account— as he did in 1825—of the progress England was making in respect to railways and steamships; and he had, in 1826, placed a working model of a railway in the garden of the Elberfeld Museum. These various efforts he followed up, in 1833, by bringing forward in the Westphalian Landtag a scheme for the building of a railway to connect the Weser and the Lippe. Later in the same year he published "Die Eisenbahn von Minden nach Köln," in which he laid special stress on the value to Germany of the proposed line from a military point of view. With the help of such a railway, he argued, it would be possible to concentrate large bodies of troops at a given point much more speedily than if they marched by road; he made calculations as to what the actual saving in time, as well as in physical strain, would be in transporting Prussian troops from various specified centres to others; and he proceeded :—

Let us suppose that we had a railway and a telegraph line

on the right bank of the Rhine, from Mainz to Wesel. Any crossing of the Rhine by the French would then scarcely be possible, since we should be able to bring a strong defensive force on the spot before the attempt could be developed.

These things may appear very strange to-day; yet in the womb of the future there slumbers the seed of great developments in railways, the results of which it is, as yet, quite beyond our powers to foresee.

Harkort's proposals gave rise to much vigorous controversy in Germany. The official classes condemned as "nonsensical fancies" his ideas, not only as to the usefulness of railways for the conveyance of troops, but, also, as to the utility of railways for any practical purposes whatever; and contemporary newspapers and periodicals, in turn, made him the butt of their ridicule.

The pros and cons of the use of railways for military purposes were, none the less, actively discussed in numerous pamphlets and treatises. Just as, in France, General Rumigny, adjutant to Louis-Philippe, had already foreshadowed the possibility of a sudden invasion by a German army reaching the frontier by rail, so, also, in Germany, in the words of one writer at this period, "anxious spirits shudder at the thought that, some fine spring morning, a hundred thousand Frenchmen, thirsting for war, will suddenly invade our peaceful valleys at bird-like speed, thanks to the new means of locomotion, and begin their old game (*das alte Spiel*) over again." On the other hand there were military sceptics—such as the author of a pamphlet "Uber die Militärische Benutzung der Eisenbahnen" (Berlin, 1836)—who, basing their calculations on locomotive performances up to that date, asserted that, although the railway might be of service in the conveyance of supplies, guns and ammunition, it would be of no advantage in the transport of troops. These, they declared, would get to their destination sooner if they marched.[1]

[1] In 1847 one of the leading military writers in Germany published a pamphlet in which he sought to prove that the best-organised railway could not carry 10,000 Infantry a distance equal to sixty English miles in twenty-four hours. As for the conveyance of Cavalry and Artillery by train, he declared that this would be a sheer impossibility.

The most noticeable of the various publications issued in Germany at this period was a book by Carl Eduard Pönitz (" Pz."), which appeared at Adorf, Saxony, in 1842, under the title of " Die Eisenbahnen als militärische Operationslinien betrachtet, und dürch Beispiele erlaütert." The writer of this remarkable book (of which a second edition was issued in 1853) gave a comprehensive survey of the whole situation in regard to railways and war, so far as the subject could be dealt with in the light of railway developments and of actual experiences of troop movements by rail down to that time; and he argued strongly in favour of the advantages to be derived from the employment of railways for military purposes. He even suggested that, in the event of an inadequate supply of locomotives, or of operations having to be conducted in a mountainous country where locomotives could not be used for heavy traffic, the troops might still use their own horses to draw the coaches and wagons along the railway lines, so that the men would arrive fresh and fit for immediate fighting at the end of their journey.

Describing railways as the most powerful vehicle for the advancement of " Kultur " since the invention of printing, Pönitz showed how Belgium and Saxony were the two countries which had taken the initiative in railway construction on the Continent of Europe; and his references to the former country are especially deserving of being recalled, in view of recent events. He pointed to the good example which had been set by the " far-sighted and energetic " King of the Belgians, and continued :—

> Although, in a land torn asunder by revolutionary factions, many wounds were still bleeding; and although the newly-created kingdom was threatened by foes within and without and could organise means of resistance only with great difficulty, there was, nevertheless, taken in hand a scheme for the construction of a network of railways designed to extend over the entire country, while at the present moment the greater part of that scheme has, in fact, been carried out. In this way King Leopold has raised up for himself a memorial the full value and significance of which may, perhaps, be appreciated only by generations yet to come.

A NEW FACTOR.

While Belgium was thus shown to have been setting a good example, the only railways which Prussia then had in actual operation (apart from the Berlin-Stettin and the Berlin-Breslau lines, which had been begun, and others which had been projected) were the Berlin-Potsdam and the Berlin-Magdeburg-Leipzig lines; though Saxony had the Leipsig-Dresden line, and Bavaria the Nüremberg-Fürth and the Munich-Augsburg lines. Pönitz, however, excused the backwardness of Prussia on the ground that if her Government had refused, for a long time, to sanction various projected railways, or had imposed heavy obligations in regard to them, such action was due, not to prejudice, but to "a wise foresight"—meaning, presumably, that Prussia was waiting to profit by the experience that other countries were gaining at their own cost.

Having dealt with all the arguments he could advance in favour of the general principle of employing railways for military purposes, Pönitz proceeded to elaborate a scheme for the construction of a network of strategical lines serving the whole of Germany, though intended, more especially, to protect her frontiers against attack by either France or Russia. Without, he said, being in the secrets of international politics, he thought he might safely presume that Germany's only fear of attack was from one of these two directions; and, although the relations of the Great Powers of Europe were then peaceful, a continuance of those conditions could not, of course, be guaranteed. So, he proceeded—

We have to look to these two fronts; and, if we want to avoid the risk of heavy losses at the outset, we needs must—also at the outset—be prepared to meet the enemy there with an overwhelming force. Every one knows that the strength of an army is multiplied by movements which are rapid in themselves and allow of the troops arriving at the end of their journey without fatigue.

In a powerful appeal—based on motives alike of patriotism, of national defence and of economic advantage—that his fellow-countrymen should support the scheme he thus put forward, Pönitz once more pointed to Belgium, saying:—

6 THE RISE OF RAIL-POWER.

The youngest of all the European States has given us an example of what can be done by intelligence and good will. The network of Belgian railways will be of as much advantage in advancing the industries of that country as it will be in facilitating the defence of the land against attack by France. It will increase alike Belgium's prosperity and Belgium's security. And we Germans, who place so high a value on our intelligence, and are scarcely yet inclined to recognise the political independence of the Belgian people, shall we remain so blind as not to see what is needed for our own safety?

Pönitz could not, of course, anticipate in 1842 that the time would come when his country, acting to the full on the advice he was then giving, would have her strategic railways, not only to the French and the Russian, but, also, to the Belgian frontier, and would use those in the last-mentioned direction to crush remorselessly the little nation concerning which he himself was using words of such generous sympathy and approbation.

The ideas and proposals put forward by Pönitz (of whose work a French translation, under the title of "Essai sur les Chemins de Fer, considérés commes lignes d'opérations militaires," was published by L. A. Unger in Paris, in 1844) did much to stimulate the discussion of the general question, while the military authorities of Germany were moved to make investigations into it on their own account, there being issued in Berlin, about 1848 or 1850, a "Survey of the Traffic and Equipment of German and of neighbouring foreign Railways for military purposes, based on information collected by the Great General Staff."[1]

In France, also, there were those who, quite early in the days of the new means of transport, predicted the important service it was likely to render for the purposes of war no less than for those of peace.

General Lamarque declared in the French Chamber of Deputies in 1832, or 1833, that the strategical use of railways would lead to "a revolution in military science as

---

[1] "Uebersicht des Verkehrs und der Betriebsmittel auf den inländischen und den benachbarten ausländischen Eisenbahnen für militärischen Zwecke; nach dem beim grossen Generalstabe vorhanden Materialen zusammen gestellt."

great as that which had been brought about by the use of gunpowder."

At the sitting of the Chamber on May 25, 1833, M. de Bérigny, in urging the "incontestable" importance of railways, said:—

From the point of view of national defence, what advantages do they not present! An army, with all its material, could, in a few days, be transported from the north to the south, from the east to the west, of France. If a country could thus speedily carry considerable masses of troops to any given point on its frontiers, would it not become invincible, and would it not, also, be in a position to effect great economies in its military expenditure?

In a further debate on June 8, 1837, M. Dufaure declared that railways had a greater mission to fulfil than that of offering facilities to industry or than that of conferring benefits on private interests. Was it a matter of no account, he asked, that they should be able in one night to send troops to all the frontiers of France, from Paris to the banks of the Rhine, from Lyons to the foot of the Alps, with an assurance of their arriving fresh and ready for combat?

Then, in 1842, M. Marschall, advocating the construction of a line from Paris to Strasburg, predicted that any new invasion of France by Germany would most probably be attempted between Metz and Strasburg. He further said:—

It is there that the German Confederation is converging a formidable system of railways from Cologne, Mayence and Mannheim. . . . Twenty-four hours will suffice for our neighbours to concentrate on the Rhine the forces of Prussia, Austria and the Confederation, and on the morrow an army of 400,000 men could invade our territory by that breach of forty leagues between Thionville and Lauterburg, which are the outposts of Strasburg and Metz. Three months later, the reserve system organised in Prussia and in some of the other German States would allow of a second Army being sent of equal force to the other. The title of "aggressive lines" given by our neighbours to these railways leave us with no room for doubt as to their intentions. Studies for an expedition against Paris by way of Lorraine and Champagne can hardly be regarded as indicative of a sentiment of fraternity.

France, however, had no inclination at that time to build railways designed to serve military purposes, whether from the point of view of aggression or even from that of national defence ; so that in a letter to his brother Ludwig, written April 13, 1844, von Moltke, then a member of the General Staff of the Fourth Army Corps of the Prussian Army, declared that whilst Germany was building railways, the French Chamber was only discussing them. This was so far the case that when, later on, Germany had nearly 3,300 miles of railway France was operating only a little over 1,000 miles.

Apart from the experiences, on quite a small scale, which had been obtained on the Liverpool and Manchester Railway, the earliest example of what railways could do in the transport of large bodies of troops was afforded in 1846, when Prussia's Sixth Army Corps—consisting of over 12,000 men, together with horses, guns, road vehicles and ammunition—was moved by rail, upon two lines, to Cracow. In 1849 a Russian corps of 30,000 men, with all its equipment, was taken by rail from its cantonments in Poland to Göding, Moravia, whence it effected a junction with the Austrian army. There was, also, a certain movement of German troops by rail to Schleswig-Holstein in the troubles of 1848-50 ; but of greater importance than these other instances was the transport of an Austrian army of 75,000 men, 8,000 horses and 1,000 vehicles from Vienna and Hungary to the Silesian frontier in the early winter of 1850.

It is true that, owing to the combined disadvantages of single-line railways, inadequate staff and rolling stock, unfavourable weather, lack of previous preparations and of transport regulations, and delays from various unforeseen causes, no fewer than twenty-six days were occupied in the transport, although the journey was one of only about 150 miles. It was, also, admitted that the troops could have marched the distance in the same time. All the same, as told by Regierungsrat Wernekke,[1] the movement of so large a body of troops by rail at all was regarded as especially

---

[1] " Die Mitwirkung der Eisenbahn an den Kriegen in Mitteleuropa."
" Archiv für Eisenbahnwesen," Juli und August, 1912.

A NEW FACTOR. 9

instructive. It was the cause of greater attention being paid to the use of railways for military purposes, while it further led (1) to the drawing up, in May, 1851, of a scheme for the construction throughout the Austrian monarchy of railways from the special point of view of strategical requirements; and (2) to a reorganisation of the methods hitherto adopted for the transport of troops by rail, the result being that the next considerable movement in Austria—in the year 1853—was conducted with "unprecedented regularity and efficiency," and this, also, without any cessation of the ordinary traffic of the lines concerned.

In 1851 a further striking object lesson of the usefulness of railways was afforded by the moving of a division of 14,500 men, with nearly 2,000 horses, 48 guns and 464 vehicles, from Cracow to Hradish, a distance of 187 miles, in two days. Reckoning that a large column of troops, with all its impedimenta, would march twelve miles per day, and allowing for one day's rest in seven, the movement would, in this instance, have occupied fifteen days by road instead of two days by rail.

It was in the *Italian campaign of 1859* that railways first played a conspicuous part in actual warfare, both strategically and tactically. "In this campaign," said Major Millar, R.A., V.C., of the Topographical Staff, in two lectures delivered by him at the Royal United Service Institution in 1861 [1]—

Railways assisted the ordinary means of locomotion hitherto employed by armies. By them thousands of men were carried daily through France to Toulon, Marseilles, or the foot of Mont Cenis; by them troops were hastened up to the very fields of battle; and by them injured men were brought swiftly back to the hospitals, still groaning in the first agony of their wounds. Moreover, the railway cuttings, embankments and bridges presented features of importance equal or superior to the ordinary accidents of the ground, and the possession of which was hotly contested. If you go to Magenta you will see, close to the railway platform on which you alight, an excavation full of rough mounds and simple black crosses, erected to mark

[1] "Journal of the Royal United Service Institution," vol. v, pp. 269-308. London, 1861.

the resting-places of many hundred men who fell in the great fight. This first employment of railways in close connection with vast military operations would alone be enough to give a distinction to this campaign in military history.

The French railways, especially, attained a remarkable degree of success. In eighty-six days—from April 19 to July 15—they transported an aggregate of 604,000 men and over 129,000 horses, including nearly 228,000 men and 37,000 horses sent to Culox, Marseilles, Toulon, Grenoble and Aix by lines in the south-east. The greatest movements took place during the ten days from April 20 to April 30, when the Paris-Lyons Company, without interrupting the ordinary traffic, conveyed an average per day of 8,421 men and 512 horses. On April 25, a maximum of 12,138 men and 655 horses was attained. During the eighty-six days there were run on the lines of the same company a total of 2,636 trains, including 253 military specials. It was estimated that the 75,966 men and 4,469 horses transported by rail from Paris to the Mediterranean or to the frontiers of the Kingdom of Sardinia between April 20 and April 30 would have taken sixty days to make the journey by road. In effect, the rate of transit by rail was six times greater than the rate of progress by marching would have been, and this, again, was about double as fast as the best achievement recorded up to that time on the German railways. The Chasseurs de Vincennes are described as leaving the station at Turin full of vigour and activity, and with none of the fatigue or the reduction in numbers which would have occurred had they made the journey by road.

As against, however, the advantage thus gained by the quicker transport of the French troops to the seat of war, due to the successful manner in which the railways were operated, there had to be set some serious defects in administrative organisation. When the men got to the end of their rail journey there was a more or less prolonged waiting for the food and other necessaries which were to follow. There were grave deficiencies, also, in the dispatch of the subsequent supplies. On June 25, the day after the defeat of

A NEW FACTOR.

the Austrians, the French troops had no provisions at all for twenty-four hours, except some biscuits which were so mouldy that no one could eat them. Their horses, also, were without fodder. In these circumstances it was impossible to follow up the Austrians in their retreat beyond the Mincio.

Thus the efficiency of the French railways was to a large extent negatived by the inefficiency of the military administration; and in these respects France had a foretaste, in 1859, of experiences to be repeated on a much graver scale in the Franco-German War of 1870-71.

As regards the Austrians, they improved but little on their admittedly poor performance in 1850, in spite of the lessons they appeared to have learned as the result of their experiences on that occasion. Government and railways were alike unprepared. Little or no real attempt at organisation in time of peace had been made, and, in the result, trains were delayed or blocked, and stations got choked with masses of supplies which could not be forwarded. At Vienna there was such a deficiency of rolling stock—accelerated by great delays in the return of empties—that many of the troop trains for the South could not be made up until the last moment. Even then the average number of men they conveyed did not exceed about 360. At Laibach there was much congestion because troops had to wait there for instructions as to their actual destination. Other delays occurred because, owing to the heavy gradients of the Semmering Pass, each train had to be divided into three sections before it could proceed. Between, again, Innsbruck and Bozen the railway was still incomplete, and the First Corps (about 40,000 men and 10,000 horses) had to march between these two points on their journey from Prague to Verona. Notwithstanding this fact, it was estimated that they covered in fourteen days a journey which would have taken sixty-four days if they had marched all the way. From Vienna to Lombardy the Third Army Corps (20,000 men, 5,500 horses, with guns, ammunition and 300 wagons) was carried by rail in fourteen days, the rate of progress attained being four and a half times greater than by road marching, though still inferior by one and a half times to what the French troop-trains had accomplished.

On both sides important reinforcements were brought up at critical periods during the progress of the war. Referring to the attacks by the allies on Casteggio and Montebello, Count Gyulai, the Austrian General, wrote :—" The enemy soon displayed a superior force, which was continually increased by arrivals from the railway " ; and the special correspondent of *The Times*, writing from Pavia on May 21, 1859, said :—

From the heights of Montebello the Austrians beheld a novelty in the art of war. Train after train arrived by railway from Voghera, each train disgorging its hundreds of armed men and immediately hastening back for more. In vain Count Stadion endeavoured to crush the force behind him before it could be increased enough to overpower him.

Then, also, the good use made of the railways by the allies in carrying out their important flanking movement against the Austrians at Vercelli gave further evidence of the fact that rail-power was a new force which could be employed, not alone for the earlier concentration of troops at the seat of war, but, also, in support of strategic developments on the battle-field itself. Commenting on this fact the *Spectateur Militaire* said, in its issue for September, 1869 :—

Les chemins de fer ont joué un rôle immense dans cette concentration. C'est la première fois que, dans l'histoire militaire, ils servent d'une manière aussi merveilleuse et entrent dans les combinaisons strategiques.

While these observations were fully warranted by the results accomplished in regard to concentration, reinforcements and tactical movements by rail, the campaign also brought out more clearly than ever before the need, if railways were to fulfil their greatest possible measure of utility in time of war, of working out in advance all important details likely to arise in connection with the movement of troops, instead—as in the case of the Austrians, at least—of neglecting any serious attempt at organisation until the need arose for immediate action.

From all these various points of view the Italian campaign of 1859 marked a further important stage in the early development of that new factor which the employment of railways for the purposes of warfare represented ; though far greater results in the same direction were to be brought about, shortly afterwards, by the American Civil War of 1861–65. Not only does the real development of rail-power as a new arm in war date therefrom, but the War of Secession was to establish in a pre-eminent degree (1) the possibility, through the use of railways, of carrying on operations at a considerable distance from the base of supplies ; (2) the need of a special organisation to deal alike with restoration of railway lines destroyed by the enemy and with the interruption, in turn, of the enemy's own communications ; and (3) the difficulties that may arise as between the military element and the technical (railway) element in regard to the control and operation of railways during war. To each of these subjects it is proposed to devote a separate chapter.

CHAPTER II

Railways in the Civil War

Such were the conditions under which the War of Secession in the United States was fought that without the help of railways it could hardly have been fought at all.

The area of the military operations, from first to last, was equal in extent almost to the whole of Europe. The line of separation between the rival forces of North and South was fully 2,000 miles. Large portions of this region were then unexplored. Everywhere, except in the towns, it was but thinly populated. Civilisation had not yet progressed so far that an advancing army could always depend on being able to " live on the country." There were occasions when local supplies of food and forage were so difficult of attainment that an army might be wholly dependent on a base hundreds of miles distant from the scene of its operations.

Of roads and tracks throughout this vast area there were but few, and these were mostly either indifferent or bad, even if they did not become positively execrable in wet weather or after a considerable force of troops had passed along them. In the low-lying districts, especially, the alluvial undrained soil was speedily converted by the winter floods into swamps and lakes. Further difficulties in the movement of troops were offered by pathless forests as large as an English county ; and still others by the broad rivers or the mountain ranges it might be necessary to cross.

Apart from the deficient and defective roads and tracks, the transport facilities available for the combatants were those afforded by coastal services, navigable rivers, canals and railways. Of these it was the railways that played the most important rôle.

RAILWAYS IN THE CIVIL WAR. 15

The American railway lines of those days had, generally speaking, been constructed as cheaply as possible by the private enterprise which—though with liberal grants of land and other advantages—alone undertook their provision, the main idea being to supply a railway of some sort to satisfy immediate wants and to improve it later on, when population and traffic increased and more funds were available. The lines themselves were mostly single track; the ballasting was too often imperfect; iron rails of inadequate weight soon wore down and got out of shape; sleepers (otherwise " ties "), which consisted of logs of wood brought straight from the forests, speedily became rotten, especially in low-lying districts; while, in the early 'Sixties lumber, used either in the rough or smoothed on two sides, was still the customary material for the building of bridges and viaducts carrying the railways across narrow streams, broad rivers or wide-spread valleys.

All the same, these railways, while awaiting their later betterment, extended for long distances, served as a connecting link of inestimable advantage between the various centres of population and production, and offered in many instances the only practicable means by which troops and supplies could be moved. They fulfilled, in fact, purposes of such vital importance from a strategical point of view that many battles were fought primarily for the control of particular railways, for the safeguarding of lines of communication, or for the possession, more especially, of important junctions, some of which themselves became the base for more or less distant operations.

The North, bent not simply on invasion but on reconquest of the States which had seceeded, necessarily took the offensive; the South stood mostly on the defensive. Yet while the population in the North was far in excess of that in the South, the initial advantages from a transport point of view were in favour of the South, which found its principal ally in the railways. Generals in the North are, indeed, said to have been exceedingly chary, at first, in getting far away from the magazines they depended on for their supplies; though this uneasiness wore off in proportion as organised effort showed how successfully the lines of rail communication could be defended.

In these and other circumstances, and especially in view of the paramount importance the railway system was to assume in the conduct of the war, the Federal Government took possession of the Philadelphia, Wilmington and Baltimore Railway on March 31, 1861. This preliminary measure was followed by the passing, in January, 1862, by the United States House of Representatives, of "An Act to authorise the President of the United States in certain cases to take possession of railroad and telegraph lines, and for other purposes."

The President, "when in his judgment the public safety may require it," was "to take possession of any or all the telegraph lines in the United States; ... to take possession of any or all the railroad lines in the United States, their rolling stock, their offices, shops, buildings and all their appendages and appurtenances; to prescribe rules and regulations for the holding, using, and maintaining of the aforesaid telegraph and railroad lines, and to extend, repair and complete the same in the manner most conducive to the safety and interest of the Government; to place under military control all the officers, agents and employés belonging to the telegraph and railroad lines thus taken possession of by the President, so that they shall be considered as a post road and a part of the military establishment of the United States, subject to all the restrictions imposed by the Rules and Articles of War." Commissioners were to be appointed to assess and determine the damages suffered, or the compensation to which any railroad or telegraph company might be entitled by reason of such seizure of their property; and it was further enacted "that the transportation of troops, munitions of war, equipments, military property and stores, throughout the United States, should be under the immediate control and supervision of the Secretary of War and such agents as he might appoint."

Thus the Act in question established a precedent for a Government taking formal possession of, and exercising

RAILWAYS IN THE CIVIL WAR.

complete authority and control over, the whole of such railways as it might require to employ for the purposes of war; although, in point of fact, only such lines, or portions of lines, were so taken over by the War Department as were actually required. In each instance, also, the line or portion of line in question was given back to the owning company as soon as it was no longer required for military purposes; while at the conclusion of the war all the lines taken possession of by the Government were formally restored to their original owners by an Executive Order dated August 8, 1865.

Under the authority of the Act of January 31, 1862, the following order was sent to Mr. Daniel Craig McCallum, a native of Johnstone, Renfrewshire, Scotland, who had been taken to America by his parents when a youth, had joined the railway service, had held for many years the position of general superintendent of the Erie Railroad, and was one of the ablest and most experienced railway men then in the United States :—

WAR DEPARTMENT.
Washington Ctiy, D.C.,
February 11, 1862.

Ordered, That D. C. McCallum be, and he is hereby, appointed Military Director and Superintendent of Railroads in the United States, with authority to enter upon, take possession of, hold and use all railroads, engines, cars, locomotives, equipments, appendages and appurtenances that may be required for the transport of troops, arms, ammunition and military supplies of the United States, and to do and perform all acts and things that may be necessary and proper to be done for the safe and speedy transport aforesaid.

By order of the President, Commander-in-Chief of the Army and Navy of the United States.
EDWIN M. STANTON,
Secretary of War.

McCallum commenced his duties with the staff rank of Colonel, afterwards attaining to that of Brev.-Brig.-General. The scope of the authority conferred on him, under the War Department order of February 11, 1862, was widened a year later, when he was further appointed general manager of all railways in possession of the Federal Government, or that might from time to time be taken possession of by military authority, in the departments of the Cumberland, the Ohio, the Tennessee, and of Arkansas, forming the "Military Division of the Mississippi."

The total mileage of the lines taken over by the Federal Government during the course of the war was 2,105, namely, in Virginia, 611 miles; in the military division of the Mississippi, 1,201; and in North Carolina, 293. Much more was involved, however, for the Federal Government than a mere transfer to themselves of the ownership and operation of these lines for the duration of the war.

One of the greatest disadvantages of the American railways at the time of the Civil War lay in their differences of gauge. The various companies had built their lines with gauges chosen either to suit local conditions or according to the views of their own engineers, with little or no consideration for the running of through traffic on or from other lines. There were, in fact, at that time gauges of 6 ft., 5 ft. 6 in., 5 ft., 4 ft. 10 in., 4 ft. 9 in., 4 ft. 8½ in. (the standard English gauge), and various narrower gauges besides. These conditions prevailed until 1866, when the companies adopted a uniform gauge of 4 ft. 8½ in.

During the Civil War the lack of uniformity was in full force, and military transport by rail was greatly complicated in consequence. More than one-half of the lines taken over and operated had a gauge of 5 ft., and the remainder had a gauge of 4 ft. 8½ in., except in the case of one short line, which was 5 ft. 6 in. As locomotives and rolling stock adapted to one gauge were unsuited to any other, the obligations falling upon the Director and General Manager of the Federal Military Railways included that of taking up the lines of certain companies which had adopted the 5 ft. gauge, and relaying them with the 4 ft. 8½ in. gauge, so that the same rolling stock could be used as on lines connecting with them.

Incidentally, therefore, the Civil War in America taught the lesson that the actual value of rail-power as influencing warfare in one and the same country, or on one and the

RAILWAYS IN THE CIVIL WAR.

same continent, may vary materially according to whether there is uniformity or diversity of railway gauge.

In certain instances the lines taken possession of were in so defective a condition that it was imperatively necessary to relay them, apart altogether from any question of gauge. When McCallum was appointed General Manager of Military Railways for the Division of the Mississippi, the main army was at Chattanooga, Tennessee, and its supplies were being received from Nashville, 151 miles distant, over the Nashville and Chattanooga Railroad. This was necessarily the main line of supply during the subsequent campaigns from Chattanooga towards Atlanta, and from Knoxville towards South-western Virginia; yet McCallum says of it, in the Final Report he presented to the Secretary of War in 1866:—

The track was laid originally in a very imperfect manner, with a light U-rail on wooden stringers which were badly decayed and caused almost daily accidents by spreading apart and letting the engines and cars drop through them.

In still other instances, lines which, though begun, were not finished, had to be completed; in others new lines had to be constructed throughout, or extensive sidings provided; so that once more we see that it was not then simply a question of the Federal Government taking possession of and operating an existing complete and efficient system of railways.

Whatever, again, the condition of the lines when taken over, the railways of both combatants were subjected to constant attack by the other side with a view to the interruption of communications, the destruction of railway track, railway bridges, rolling stock and other railway property being enormous.

Reviewing the general situation at this time, McCallum says in his report:—

In the beginning of the war military railroads were an experiment; and though some light as to their management had been gleaned by the operations of 1862 and 1863, yet so little progress had been made that the attempt to supply the army of General Sherman in the field, construct and reconstruct the railroad in its rear, and keep pace with its march, was regarded by those who had the largest experience, and who had become most familiar with the subject, as the greatest experiment of all. The attempt to furnish an army of 100,000 men and 60,000 animals with supplies from a base 360 miles distant by one line of single-track railroad, located almost the entire distance through the country of an active and vindictive enemy, is without precedent in the history of warfare; and to make it successful required an enormous outlay for labour and a vast consumption of material, together with all the forethought, energy, patience and watchfulness of which men are capable.

To meet the various conditions which had thus arisen, McCallum was authorised by the Federal Government to create two distinct departments, destined to bring about a still further development in the application of rail-power to war by establishing precedents which the leading countries of the world were afterwards to follow more or less completely, according to their own circumstances and requirements.

The departments were known respectively as the "Transportation Department," embracing the operation and maintenance of all the lines brought under use by the army of the North; and the "Construction Corps," which was to repair the damage done by wrecking parties of the enemy, maintain lines of communication, and reconstruct, when necessary, railways captured from the enemy as the Federals advanced.

Concerning the Construction Corps, and the great work accomplished by it in keeping the lines open, details will be given in the chapter which follows.

In regard to the Transportation Department, it may be of interest to state that this was placed by McCallum in charge of a General Superintendent of Transportation on United States Railroads in the Military Division of the Mississippi. For each of the principal lines there was appointed a Superintendent of Transportation who, acting under the control of the General Superintendent, was held responsible for the movement of all trains and locomotives; and these superintendents, in turn, had under their direction one or more Masters of Transportation, whose business it was to be constantly moving about over the sections of line placed under their charge, and see that the railway employés were attending properly to their duties.

At each of the principal stations there was an Engine Dispatcher who was required to see that the locomotives were kept in good order and ready for immediate use whenever required, to exercise control over the drivers and firemen, and to assign the requisite " crew " to each engine sent out.

Maintenance of road and structures for each line (as distinct from the reconstruction work left to the Construction Department) was in charge of a Superintendent of Repairs, assisted by such supervisors, road-masters and foremen as he needed to control and direct his working staff; and maintenance of rolling stock was delegated to (1) a Master Machinist, responsible for repairs to locomotives, and (2) a Master of Car Repairs.

These various officers were independent of each other, and all of them reported direct to the General Superintendent. The maximum force employed at any one time in the Transportation Department of the Military Division of the Mississippi (as distinct from the military lines in Virginia and elsewhere) was about 12,000 men.

A sufficient staff of competent railwaymen for the operation of the Military Railways was difficult to get, partly because of the inadequate supply of such men in the United States at that period, and partly because those still at work on railways not taken over for military purposes were unwilling to give up what they found to be exceptionally good posts; but of the men whose services he was able to secure McCallum speaks in terms of the highest commendation.

Having got his Department and Construction Corps into working order, McCallum had next to turn his attention to ensuring an adequate supply of locomotives and cars, with the necessary shops, tools and materials for keeping them in working order. Here the Secretary of War again came to his help, issuing, on March 23, 1864, an Order addressed to locomotive manufacturers in which he stated that Colonel McCallum had been authorised by the War Department to procure locomotives without delay for the railways under his charge, and proceeded :—

In order to meet the wants of the Military Department of the Government, you will deliver to his order such engines as he may direct, whether building under orders for other parties or otherwise, the Government being accountable to you for the same. The urgent necessity of the Government for the immediate supply of our armies operating in Tennessee renders the engines indispensable for the equipment of the lines of communication, and it is hoped that this necessity will be recognised by you as a military necessity, paramount to all other considerations.—By order of the President.

In January, 1864, McCallum had estimated that he would require 200 locomotives and 3,000 cars for the lines to be operated from Nashville, and towards this number he then had only 47 locomotives and 437 cars available. There was thus a substantial shortage which had to be made good; but the manufacturers, inspired by "a spirit of zealous patriotism," responded heartily to the appeal made to them, putting their full force on to the completion of further supplies. These were furnished with a speed that surpassed all previous records.

Then, to maintain the locomotives and cars in good condition—more especially in view of the constant attempts made by the enemy to destroy them—extensive machine and car shops were built at Nashville and Chattanooga. Those at Nashville—the terminal station for 500 miles of railway running south, east or west—had, at times, as many as 100 engines and 1,000 cars awaiting repair.

Next to that insufficiency of engines and rolling stock which hampered the movements of both combatants came the difficulty in the way of obtaining further supplies of rails, whether for new lines or to take the place of those which had either worn out or been so bent and twisted by the enemy that they could not be used again without re-rolling. For the Confederates, cut off by the advance of General Grant to the south and west from their sources of supply, the want of iron for new rails was declared to be a worse evil than was the lack of gold for the Federals.

One expedient resorted to by the Federal Government, on finding they could not procure from the manufacturers all the rails they wanted, was to pull up the railway lines

RAILWAYS IN THE CIVIL WAR. 23

that were not wanted for military purposes and use their rails for relaying those that were. Altogether the rails on over 156 miles of track in Virginia and the Military Division of the Mississippi were thus taken up and utilised elsewhere. Later on the Federal Construction Corps erected at Chattanooga some " very superior " rolling mills, equipped with all the latest improvements in the way of machinery and mechanical appliances; though these mills did not actually get to work until April 1, 1865. Their production of new rails during the course of six months from that date was 3,818 tons, this supply being in addition to nearly 22,000 tons which the Federal Government obtained by purchase.

These details may convey some idea of all that was involved in the utilisation of rail-power in the American Civil War under such development of railway construction as had then been brought about. Great, however, as was the outlay, the forethought, the energy, the patience and the watchfulness spoken of by McCallum, the results were no less valuable from the point of view of the Federals, who could hardly have hoped to achieve the aim they set before themselves—that of saving the Union—but for the material advantages they derived from the use of the railways for the purposes of the campaign.

Some of the achievements accomplished in the movement of troops from one part of the theatre of war to another would have been creditable even in the most favourable of circumstances; but they were especially so in view alike of the physical conditions of many of the lines, the inadequate supply of rolling stock, and the risks and difficulties to be met or overcome.

One of these achievements, carried out in September, 1863, is thus narrated in an article on " Recollections of Secretary Stanton," published in the *Century Magazine* for March, 1887 :—

The defeat of Rosecrans, at Chickamauga, was believed at Washington to imperil East Tennessee, and the Secretary [of War] was urged to send a strong reinforcement there from the Army of the Potomac. General Halleck (General-in-Chief of the Army of the United States) contended that it was impossible to get an effective reinforcement there in time; and the President, after hearing both sides, accepted the judgment of Halleck. Mr. Stanton put off the decision till evening, when he and Halleck were to be ready with details to support their conclusions. The Secretary then sent for Colonel McCallum, who was neither a lawyer nor a strategist, but a master of railway science. He showed McCallum how many officers, men, horses, and pieces of artillery, and how much baggage, it was proposed to move from the Rapidan to the Tennessee, and asked him to name the shortest time he would undertake to do it in if his life depended on it. McCallum made some rapid calculations, jotted down some projects connected with the move, and named a time within that which Halleck had admitted would be soon enough if it were only possible; this time being conditioned on his being able to control everything that he could reach. The Secretary was delighted, told him that he would make him a Brigadier-General the day that the last train was safely unloaded; put him on his mettle by telling him of Halleck's assertion that the thing was beyond human power; told him to go and work out final calculations and projects and to begin preliminary measures, using his name and authority everywhere; and finally instructed him what to do and say when he should send for him by and by to come over to the department. When the conference was resumed and McCallum was introduced, his apparently spontaneous demonstration of how easily and surely the impossible thing could be done convinced the two sceptics, and the movement was ordered, and made, and figures now in military science as a grand piece of strategy.

The feat thus accomplished was that of conveying by rail 23,000 men, together with artillery, road vehicles, etc., a distance of about 1,200 miles in seven days. It was estimated that if the troops had had to march this distance, with all their impedimenta, along such roads as were then available, the journey would have taken them three months. By doing it in one week they saved the situation in East Tennessee, and they gave an especially convincing proof of the success with which "a grand piece of strategy" could be carried out through the employment of rail transport.

In December, 1864, General Schofield's corps of 15,000 men, after fighting at Nashville in the midst of ice and snow, was, on the conclusion of the campaign in the west, transferred from the valley of the Tennessee to the banks of the Potomac, moving by river and rail down the Tennessee, up the Ohio and across the snow-covered Alleghanies, a distance of 1,400 miles, accomplished in the short space of eleven days. In 1865 the moving of the Fourth Army Corps of the Federals from Carter's Station, East Tennessee, to Nashville, a distance of 373 miles, involved the employment of 1,498 cars.

What, in effect, the Civil War in America did in furthering the development of the rail-power principle in warfare was to show that, by the use of railways, (1) the fighting power of armies is increased; (2) strategical advantages unattainable but for the early arrival of reinforcements at threatened points may be assured; and (3) expeditions may be undertaken at distances from the base of supplies which would be prohibitive but for the control of lines of railway communication; though as against these advantages were to be put those considerations which also arose as to destruction and restoration, and as to the control of railways in their operation for military purposes.

CHAPTER III

RAILWAY DESTRUCTION IN WAR

ONE of the earliest and most obvious criticisms advanced against the use of railways in war was based on the vulnerability of the iron road. The destruction of a bridge, the tearing up of a few rails or the blocking of a tunnel would, it was argued, suffice to cause an interruption in the transport of troops or supplies which might be of serious consequence to the combatants prejudiced thereby, though of corresponding advantage to the other side. By means of such interruption the concentration of troops on the frontier might be delayed; an army might be divided into two or more parts, and exposed to the risk of defeat in detail; the arrival of reinforcements urgently wanted to meet a critical situation might be prevented until it was too late for them to afford the desired relief; a force advancing into an enemy's country might have its rail connection severed and be left to starve or to surrender at discretion; invaders would find that the force they were driving before them had taken the precaution to destroy their own railways as they retreated; or, alternatively, lines of railway constructed to the frontier, and depended upon to facilitate invasion of neighbouring territory, might—unless destroyed —be of material service to the enemy, should the latter become the invaders instead of the invaded.

While these and other possibilities—foreshadowed more especially in the controversies which the whole subject aroused in Germany in the 'Forties—were frankly admitted, it was argued that, however vulnerable railways might be as a line of communication, it should be quite possible either to defend them successfully or to carry out on them such speedy repairs or reconstruction as would, generally speaking, permit of an early resumption of traffic; though experience was to show that these safeguards could only be assured through a well-planned and thoroughly efficient organisation prepared to meet, with the utmost dispatch and the highest degree of efficiency, all the requirements in the way of railway repairs or railway rebuilding that were likely to arise.

The earliest instance of an attempt to delay the advance of an enemy by interrupting his rail communications was recorded in 1848, when the Venetians, threatened with bombardment by the Austrians, destroyed some of the arches in the railway viaduct connecting their island city with the mainland. Then in the *Italian campaign of 1859* the allies and the Austrians both resorted to the expedient of destroying railway bridges or tearing up the railway lines; although the allies were able, in various instances, to repair so speedily the damage done by the Austrians that the lines were ready for use again by the time they were wanted.

It was the *American Civil War* that was to elevate railway destruction and restoration into a science and to see the establishment, in the interests of such science, of an organisation which was to become a model for European countries and influence the whole subsequent course of modern warfare.

The destruction of railways likely to be used by the North for its projected invasion of the Confederate States was, from the first, a leading feature in the strategy of the South. Expeditions were undertaken and raids were made with no other object than that of burning down bridges, tearing up and bending rails, making bonfires of sleepers, wrecking stations, rendering engines, trucks and carriages unserviceable, cutting off the water supply for locomotives, or in various other ways seeking to check the advance of the Northerners. Later on the Federals, in turn, became no less energetic in resorting to similar tactics in order either to prevent pursuit by the Confederates or to interrupt their communications.

For the carrying out of these destructive tactics use was generally made either of cavalry, accompanied by civilians, or of bodies of civilians only; but in some instances, when it was considered desirable to destroy lengths of track extending to twenty or thirty miles, or more, the Confederates put the whole of their available forces on to the work.

At the outset the methods of destruction were somewhat primitive; but they were improved upon as the result of practice and experiment.

Thus, in the first instance, timber bridges or viaducts were destroyed by collecting brushwood, placing this around the arches, pouring tar or petroleum upon the pile, and then setting fire to the whole. Afterwards the Federals made use of a "torpedo," eight inches long, and charged with gunpowder, which was inserted in a hole bored in the main timbers of the bridge and exploded with a fuse. It was claimed that with two or three men working at each span the largest timber bridge could be thrown down in a few minutes.

Then the method generally adopted at first for destroying a railway track was to tear up sleepers and rails, place the sleepers in a heap, put the rails cross-ways over them, set fire to the sleepers, and heat the rails until they either fell out of shape or could be twisted around a tree with the help of chains and horses. But this process was found to require too much time and labour, while the results were not always satisfactory, since rails only slightly bent could be restored to their original shape, and made ready for use again, in much less time than it had taken for the fire to heat and bend them. A Federal expert accordingly invented an ingenious contrivance, in the form of iron U-shaped "claws," which, being turned up and over at each extremity, were inserted underneath each end of a rail, on opposite sides, and operated, with the help of a long wooden lever and rope, by half a dozen men. In this way a rail could be torn from the sleepers and not only bent but given such a spiral or corkscrew twist, while still in the cold state, that it could not be used again until it had gone through the rolling mills. By the adoption of this method,

RAILWAY DESTRUCTION IN WAR.

440 men could destroy one mile of track in an hour, or 2,200 men could, in the same time, destroy five miles.

The most effective method for rendering a locomotive unfit for service was found to be the firing of a cannon ball through the boiler. Carriages and wagons which might otherwise be used by the enemy, and could not be conveniently carried off, were easily destroyed by fire. In one period of six months the Federals disposed of 400 in this way. Stations, water-tanks, sleepers, fuel and telegraph poles were also destroyed or rendered useless by fire or otherwise.

In the first year of the war—1861—the Confederates gave the Federals a foretaste of much that was to come by destroying forty-eight locomotives on the Baltimore and Ohio Railroad, and making a complete wreck of 100 miles of the North Missouri Railroad track and everything thereon.

Much more serious than this, however, from a strategical point of view, was the wholesale destruction carried out by the Confederates, in April, 1862, on the Fredericksburg Railway, connecting Richmond and Washington, the immediate result of the mischief done being to prevent an impending combination between the Federal armies of the Potomac and the Rappahannock, neither of which could act without the other, while neither could join the other unless it could make use of rail communication. There was much that required to be done, for the Confederates had carried out their work in a most thorough-going fashion. Several indispensable railway bridges had been destroyed; three miles of track had been torn up, the rails being carried south and the sleepers burned; and wharves and buildings had been burned or wrecked. The whole transportation service, in fact, had been reduced to a state of chaos.

At the urgent request of the Secretary of War, the work of restoration was undertaken by Mr. Herman Haupt, a railway engineer who had already distinguished himself more especially as a builder of bridges, and was now to establish a further record as the pioneer of those Construction Corps of which so much was to be heard later on in connection with railways and war.

In carrying out the necessary repairs the only help which Haupt could obtain, at first, was that of soldiers detailed from the Federal ranks. Many of these men were entirely unaccustomed to physical labour; others were sickly, inefficient, or unwilling to undertake what they did not regard as a soldier's duties, while the Army officers sent in a fresh lot daily until Haupt's remonstrances led to their allotting certain men to form a "Construction Corps." Other difficulties which presented themselves included an insufficient supply of tools, occasional scarcity of food, and several days of wet weather; yet the work advanced so rapidly that the Akakeek bridge, a single span of 120 ft., at an elevation of 30 ft., was rebuilt in about fifteen working hours; the Potomac Creek bridge, 414 ft. long with an elevation of 82 ft. above the water, and requiring the use of as much roughly-hewn timber as would have extended a total length of six and a half miles, if put end to end, was completed in nine days;[1] and the three miles of track were relaid in three days, included in the work done in that time being the preparation of more than 3,000 sleepers from lumber cut down for the purpose in woods a mile and a half distant from the track. General McDowell subsequently said, concerning the Potomac bridge :—

When it is considered that in the campaigns of Napoleon trestle bridges of more than one story, even of moderate height, were regarded as impracticable, and that, too, for common military roads, it is not difficult to understand why distinguished Europeans should express surprise at so bold a specimen of American military engineering. It is a structure which ignores all rules and precedents of military science as laid down in the books. It is constructed chiefly of round sticks cut from the woods, and not even divested of bark; the legs of the trestles are braced with round poles. It is in four stories—three of trestle and one of crib work.

While constructed in so apparently primitive a fashion, the bridge was, General McDowell further said, carrying

---

[1] In May, 1864, when this bridge had been again destroyed, it was rebuilt, ready for trains to pass over, in forty working hours.

RAILWAY DESTRUCTION IN WAR.

every day from ten to twenty heavy railway trains in both directions, and had withstood several severe freshets and storms without injury.

Thus early, therefore, in the more active phases of the Civil War, evidence was being afforded that, although the railways on which so much depended might be readily destroyed, they could, also, be rapidly restored; and subsequent experience was to offer proofs still more remarkable in support of this fact.

On May 28, 1862, Haupt was appointed Chief of Construction and Transportation in the Department of the Rappahannock, with the rank of Colonel. He was raised to the rank of Brigadier-General in the following year, and did much excellent construction and other work for the Government, though mainly in Virginia, down to September, 1863. In his "Reminiscences" he relates that the supplies of repair or reconstruction materials, as kept on hand by the Federals, included the interchangeable parts of bridge trusses, in spans of 60 ft., and so prepared that, taken on flat cars, by ox-teams or otherwise, to the place where they were wanted, and hoisted into position by machinery arranged for the purpose, they could, without previous fitting, be put together with such rapidity that one of his foremen claimed to be able to build a bridge " about as fast as a dog could trot." When the Massaponix bridge, six miles from Fredericksburg, was burned down one Monday morning, a new one was put up in its place in half a day—a feat which, he says, led some of the onlookers to exclaim, " The Yankees can build bridges quicker than the Rebs can burn them down." In May, 1862, five bridges over Goose Creek which the "Rebs" had destroyed were reconstructed in a day and a half. In the following month five other bridges, each with a span of from 60 ft. to 120 ft., were renewed in one day. At the Battle of Gettysburg Lee's troops destroyed nineteen bridges on the Northern Central Railroad and did much havoc on the branch lines leading to Gettysburg; but the Construction Corps was hard at work on the repairs whilst the battle was still being waged, and rail communication with both Washington and

Baltimore had been re-established by noon of the day after Lee's retreat.

In some instances railway bridges underwent repeated destruction and reconstruction. By June, 1863, the bridge over Bull Run, for instance, had been burned down and built up again no fewer than seven times. Many of the bridges, also, were swept away by floods, and this even for a second or a third time after they had been rebuilt. Precautions thus had to be taken against the destructive forces of Nature no less than against those of man.

Haupt's pioneer Construction Corps in Virginia was succeeded by the one set up on much broader lines by McCallum when, in February, 1864, he became General Manager of railways in the Military Division of the Mississippi. This corps eventually reached a total of 10,000 men.

"The design of the corps," wrote McCallum, in his final report, "was to combine a body of skilled workmen in each department of railroad construction and repairs, under competent engineers, supplied with abundant materials, tools and mechanical appliances." The corps was formed into divisions the number of which varied from time to time, in different districts, according to requirements. In the military division of the Mississippi the corps comprised six divisions, under the general charge of the chief engineer of the United States military railroads for that military division, and consisted at its maximum strength of nearly 5,000 men. In order to give the corps entire mobility, and to enable it to move independently and undertake work at widely different points, each of the six divisions was made a complete unit, under the command of a divisional engineer, and was, in turn, divided into subdivisions or sections, with a supervisor in charge of each. The two largest and most important sub-divisions in any one division were those of the track-layers and the bridge-builders. A sub-division was, again, composed of gangs, each with a foreman, while the gangs were divided into squads, each with a sub-foreman.[1] Under this method of

[1] A division, completely organised, consisted of 777 officers and men, as follows:—Division engineer, assistant engineer, rodman,

organisation it was possible to move either the entire division or any section thereof, with its tools, camp requirements and field transport, in any direction, wherever and whenever needed, and by any mode of conveyance—rail, road, with teams and wagons, or on foot.

To facilitate the operations of the corps, supplies of materials were kept at points along or within a short distance of the railway lines, where they would be comparatively safe and speedily procurable in case of necessity. At places where there was special need for taking precautionary measures, detachments of the corps were stationed in readiness for immediate action, while on important lines of railway Federals and Confederates alike had, at each end thereof, construction trains loaded with every possible requisite, the locomotives attached to them keeping their steam up in order that the trains could be started off instantly on the receipt of a telegram announcing a further interruption of traffic.

At Nashville and Chattanooga the Federals built extensive storehouses where they kept on hand supplies of materials for the prompt carrying out of railway repairs of every kind to any extent and in whatever direction.

On the Nashville and Chattanooga Railway itself the Construction Corps, from February, 1864, to the close of the war, relaid 115 miles of track, put in nineteen miles of new sidings, eight miles apart and each capable of holding from five to eight long freight trains, and erected forty-five new water tanks.

clerk, and 2 messengers (6). Sub-division I : Supervisor of bridges and carpenters' work, clerk and time-keeper, commissionary (taking charge of transport and issue of rations), quartermaster (in charge of tools, camp equipment, etc.), surgeon, hospital steward, 6 foremen (1 for each 50 men), 30 sub-foremen (1 for each 10 men), 300 mechanics and labourers, blacksmith and helper, and 12 cooks (356). Sub-division II : Supervisor of track, and remainder of staff as in Sub-division I (356). Sub-division III : Supervisor of water stations, foreman, 12 mechanics and labourers, and cook (15). Sub-division IV : Supervisor of masonry, foreman, 10 masons and helpers, and cook (13). Sub-division V : Foreman of ox-brigade, 18 ox-drivers, and cook (20). Train crew : 2 conductors, 4 brakesmen, 2 locomotive engineers, 2 firemen, and cook (11).

The reconstruction of this particular line was more especially needed in connection with General Sherman's campaign in Georgia and the Carolinas—a campaign which afforded the greatest and most direct evidence up to that time alike of the possibilities of rail-power in warfare, of the risks by which its use was attended, and of the success with which those risks could be overcome by means of efficient organisation.

In that struggle for Atlanta which preceded his still more famous march to the sea, Sherman had with him a force of 100,000 men, together with 23,000 animals. His base of supplies, when he approached Atlanta, was 360 miles distant, and the continuance of his communications with that base, not only for the procuring of food, clothing, fodder, ammunition and every other requisite, but for the transport to the rear of sick and wounded, refugees, freedmen and prisoners, depended on what he afterwards described as " a poorly-constructed single-track railroad " passing for 120 miles of its length through the country of an extremely active enemy. Yet Sherman is said to have made his advance in perfect confidence that, although subject to interruptions, the railway in his rear would be " all right " ; and this confidence was fully warranted by the results accomplished.

Early in September, 1864, the Confederate General, Wheeler, destroyed seven miles of road between Nashville and Murfreesboro', on the Nashville and Chattanooga Railway, and in the following December Hood destroyed eight miles of track and 530 ft. of bridges between the same stations ; yet the arrangements of the Federal Construction Corps allowed of the repairs being carried out with such promptness that in each instance the trains were running again in a few days.

The Confederate attacks on the Western and Atlantic Railway, running from Chattanooga at Atlanta, a distance of 136 miles, were more continuous and more severe than on any other line of railway during the war ; but, thanks again to the speed with which the repair and reconstruction work was done, the delays occasioned were, as a rule, of only a few hours, or, at the most, a few days' duration. One especially remarkable feat accomplished on this line was the rebuilding, in four and a half days, of the Chattahochee bridge, near Atlanta—a structure 780 ft. long, and 92 ft. high. Hood, the Confederate General, thought still further to check Sherman's communications by passing round the Federal army and falling upon the railway in its rear. He succeeded in tearing up two lengths of track, one of ten miles, and another of twenty-five miles, in extent, and destroying 250 ft. of bridges; but once more the work of restoration was speedily carried out, McCallum saying in reference to it :—

Fortunately the detachments of the Construction Corps which escaped were so distributed that even before Hood had left the road two strong working parties were at work, one at each end of the break at Big Shanty, and this gap of ten miles was closed, and the force ready to move to the great break of twenty-five miles in length, north of Resaca, as soon as the enemy had left it. The destruction by Hood's army of our depôts of supplies compelled us to cut nearly all the cross-ties required to relay this track and to send a distance for rails. The cross-ties were cut near the line of the road and many of them carried by hand to the track, as the teams to be furnished for hauling them did not get to the work until it was nearly complete. The rails used on the southern end of the break had to be taken up and brought from the railroads south of Atlanta, and those for the northern end were mostly brought from Nashville, nearly 200 miles distant.

Notwithstanding all the disadvantages under which the labour was performed, this twenty-five miles of track was laid, and the trains were running over it in seven and a half days from the time the work was commenced.

Concluding, however, that it would be unwise to depend on the railway during his further march to the sea, Sherman collected at Atlanta, by means of the restored lines, the supplies he wanted for 600,000 men, sent to the rear all the men and material no longer required, and then, before starting for Savannah, destroyed sixty miles of track behind him in so effectual a manner that it would be impossible for the Confederates—especially in view of their own great lack, at this time, of rails, locomotives and rolling stock—to repair and utilise the lines again in any attempted pursuit. It was, in fact, as much to his advantage now to destroy the railways in his rear as it had previously been to repair and rebuild them.

All through Georgia, for the 300 miles from Atlanta to Savannah (where he was able to establish communications with the Federal fleet), Sherman continued the same tactics of railway destruction; and he resumed them when his army, now divided into three columns, turned northward to effect a junction with Grant at Richmond.

On this northward march, also, there was no need for Sherman to make a direct attack on Charleston. By destroying about sixty miles of track in and around Branchville—a village on the South Carolina Railroad which formed a junction where the line from Charleston branched off in the directions of Columbia and Augusta respectively—one of Sherman's columns severed Charleston from all its sources of supply in the interior, and left the garrison with no alternative but to surrender. Commenting on this event, Vigo-Rouissillon remarks, in his "Puissance Militaire des États-Unis d'Amérique":—

> Ainsi il avait suffi de la destruction ou de la possession de quelques kilomètres de chemin de fer pour amener la chute de ce boulevard de l'insurrection, qui avait si longtemps résisté aux plus puissantes flottes du Nord. Exemple frappant du rôle reservé dans nos guerres modernes à ce precieux et fragile moyen de communication.

In the aggregate, Sherman's troops destroyed hundreds of miles of railway track in their progress through what had previously been regarded as a veritable stronghold of the enemy's country; though meanwhile the Construction Corps had repaired and reopened nearly 300 miles of railway in North Carolina and had built a wharf, covering an area of 54,000 square feet, at the ocean terminus of the Atlantic and North Carolina Railroad in order both to facilitate Sherman's progress northwards, by the time of his reaching the lines in question, and to enable him to obtain supplies from the fleet. The railways, in fact, contributed greatly to the brilliant success of Sherman's cam-

RAILWAY DESTRUCTION IN WAR.

paign, and hence, also, to the final triumph of the Federal cause.

The total length of track laid or relaid by the Federal Construction Corps during the continuance of the war was 641 miles, and the lineal feet of bridges built or rebuilt was equal to twenty-six miles. The net expenditure, in respect alike to construction and transportation, incurred by the department in charge of the railways during their control by the Government for military purposes was close on $30,000,000.

From this time the interruption of railway communication became a recognised phase of warfare all the world over; and, not only have numerous treatises been written on the subject in various languages, but the creation of special forces to deal alike with the destruction and the restoration of railways has become an important and indispensable feature of military organisation. These matters will be dealt with more fully in subsequent chapters; but it may be of interest if reference is made here to the experiences of *Mexico*, as further illustrating the universality of practices with which, in her case, at least, no effective measures had been taken to deal.

"How Mexican Rebels Destroy Railways and Bridges" was told by Mr. G. E. Weekes in the *Scientific American* for September 13, 1913, and the subject was further dealt with by Major Charles Hine in a paper on "War Time Railroading in Mexico," read by him before the St. Louis Railway Club, on October 10, 1913. The term "rebels" applies, of course, in Mexico to the party that is against the particular President who is in office for the time being; and in the revolutionary period lasting from 1910 to 1913 the "rebels" of the moment found plenty to do in the way of destroying railways not only, as in other countries, in order to retard the advance of their pursuers, but, also, to spite the national Government, who control about two-thirds of the stock in the railways of the Republic.

Altogether, the mischief done by one party or the other during the period in question included the destruction of many hundreds of miles of track; the burning or the dynamiting of hundreds of bridges, according as these had been built of timber or of steel ; and the wrecking of many stations and over 50 per cent. of the rolling stock on the national lines.

Concerning the methods adopted in the carrying out of this work, Mr. Weekes, who had the opportunity of seeing track and bridge destruction in full progress, says :—

Up to the past six months track destruction had been accompanied either by the use of a wrecking crane, which lifted sections of rails and ties (sleepers) bodily and piled them up ready for burning, or by the slower process of the claw-bar, wrench and pick. But a Constitutionalist expert devised a new system.

A trench is dug between two ties, through which a heavy chain is passed around two opposite rails and made fast in the centre of the track. To this one end of a heavy steel cable is hooked, the other end being made fast to the coupling on the engine pilot. At the signal the engineman starts his locomotive slowly backward, and as they are huge 220-ton " consolidations," with 22-inch by 30-inch cylinders, one can easily imagine that something has to give. And it does ! The rails are torn loose from the spikes that hold them to the ties and are dragged closely together in the centre of the road bed. The ties are loosened from the ballast and dragged into piles, while in many cases the rails are badly bent and twisted by the force applied. A gang of men follows the engine, piling ties on top of the line and leaving others beneath them. These are then saturated with oil and a match applied. In a short time the ties are consumed and the rails left lying on the ground twisted and contorted into all sorts of shapes and of no further use until after they have been re-rolled.

As for the bridges, those of timber were saturated with oil and burned, while in the case of steel bridges rows of holes were bored horizontally in the lower part of the piers and charged with dynamite, which was then exploded by means of fuses connected with batteries of the type used in Mexican coal mines.

Another favourite method adopted for interfering with transportation by rail was that of attacking a train, compelling it to stop, taking possession of the locomotive, and burning the cars.

There is no suggestion by either of the authorities mentioned above of any well-organised Construction Corps in

RAILWAY DESTRUCTION IN WAR.

Mexico repairing damage done on the railway almost as quickly as it could be effected by the destroyers. Mr. Weekes believed, rather, that it would take years to restore the roads to the condition they were in before the rebellion against President Diaz, and he further declared that it would cost the national lines of Mexico many millions of dollars to replace the destroyed rolling stock, bridges, stations, etc.

CHAPTER IV

CONTROL OF RAILWAYS IN WAR

CURTAILMENT of the efficiency of railways during war may be due to friend no less than to foe ; and there have been occasions when, of the two, it is the friend who has caused the greater degree of trouble, hindrance and interruption.

These conditions have arisen mainly from three causes—(1) questions of control ; (2) irregularities in the employment of railway material ; and (3) absence or inadequacy of organisation for military rail-transport purposes.

When the use of railways becomes an essential factor in the conduct of war, it may appear only natural that the military authority charged with the duty of furthering or defending national interests should, through the Government concerned, have power to command the transport facilities of all railway lines the use of which may be necessary for the movement of troops or other military purposes.

Yet, while the soundness of the principle here involved is beyond dispute, there is much to be said as to the circumstances and conditions under which a military control of railways should be exercised.

It is, in the first place, especially necessary to bear in mind that the railway, as a means of transport, must needs be regarded from a point of view wholly different from that which would apply to ordinary roads. On the latter any sort of vehicle can be used, and there are, generally, alternative roads along which traffic can pass, in case of need. Railroads are not only available exclusively for vehicles constructed to run upon them, but the degree of their usefulness is limited by such considerations as the num-

CONTROL OF RAILWAYS IN WAR. 41

ber of separate routes to a given destination; the important matters of detail as to whether the lines are single track or double track and whether they are on the level or have heavy gradients; the number of locomotives and the amount of rolling stock available; the extent of the station and siding accommodation; the provision or non-provision of adequate facilities for loading and unloading; and, in war time, the damage or destruction of a particular line or lines by the enemy. The amount of traffic it is possible to convey between certain points in a given time may thus be wholly controlled by the physical conditions of the railway concerned, and such conditions may be incapable of modification by the railway staffs, in case of a sudden emergency, however great their desire to do everything that is in their power.

In the next place, all these physical conditions may vary on different railway systems, and even on different sections of the same system. It does not, therefore, necessarily follow that military requirements which can be complied with on one line or in one district can be responded to as readily, if at all, under another and totally different set of conditions elsewhere; though it is conceivable that a military commander or officer who fails to realise this fact may, if he is left to deal direct with the railway people, become very angry indeed at non-compliance with his demands, and resent protests that what he asks for cannot be done at one place although it may have been done at another.

Then a railway must be regarded as a delicate piece of transportation machinery which can easily be thrown out of order, and is capable of being worked only by railwaymen as skilled in the knowledge of its mechanism, and as experienced in the details of its complicated operation, as military officers themselves are assumed to be in the technicalities of their own particular duties. The Chief Goods Manager of a leading line of railway who offered to take the place of a General at the seat of war would arouse much mirth in the Army at his own expense. It is, nevertheless, quite conceivable that the General would himself not be a complete success as a Chief Goods Manager. In the earliest days of railways it was assumed that the men best qualified both to manage them and to control the large staffs to be employed would be retired Army officers. This policy was, in fact, adopted for a time, though it was abandoned, after a fair trial, in favour of appointing as responsible railway officers men who had undergone training in the railway service, and were practically acquainted alike with its fundamental principles and its technical details.

In the operation of this delicate and complicated piece of machinery dislocation of traffic may result from a variety of causes, even when such operation is conducted by men of the greatest experience in railway working; but the risk, alike of blocks and interruptions and of accidents involving loss of life or destruction of valuable property must needs be materially increased if military commanders, or officers, themselves having no practical knowledge of railway working, and influenced only by an otherwise praiseworthy zeal for the interests of their own service, should have power either to force a responsible railwayman to do something which he, with his greater technical knowledge, knows to be impracticable, or to hamper and interfere with the working of the line at a time of exceptional strain on its resources.

Under, again, a misapprehension of the exact bearing of the principle of military control of railways for military operations in time of war, there was developed in various campaigns a tendency on the part of commanders and subordinate officers (1) to look upon railways and railwaymen as subject to their personal command, if not, even, to their own will, pleasure and convenience, so long as the war lasted; (2) to consider that every order they themselves gave should be at once carried out, regardless either of orders from other directions or of any question as to the possibility of complying therewith; and (3) to indulge in merciless denunciations, even if not in measures still more vigorous, when their orders have not been obeyed.

Apart from other considerations, all these things have a direct bearing on the efficiency of the railway itself as an

CONTROL OF RAILWAYS IN WAR. 43

instrument in the carrying on of warfare; and it is, therefore, a matter of essential importance to our present study to see how the difficulties in question had their rise, the development they have undergone, and the steps that have been taken to overcome or to guard against them.

It was once more in the *American Civil War* that the control problem first arose in a really acute degree.

The fundamental principle adopted for the operation of the railways taken possession of by the Federal Government for military purposes was that they should be conducted under orders issued by the Secretary of War or by Army commanders in or out of the field. It was for the Quartermaster's department to load all material upon the cars, to direct where such material should be taken, and to arrange for unloading and delivery; but *because* the Government had taken possession of the railways; *because* the Quartermaster's department was to discharge the duties mentioned; and *because* the railways were to be used during the war for the transport of troops and of Army supplies, therefore certain of the officers came to the conclusion that the whole operation of the particular lines in which they were concerned should be left either to themselves individually or to the Quartermaster's department.

Among those holding this view was General Pope, who, on taking over the command of the Rappahannock Division, on June 26, 1862, disregarded the position held by Herman Haupt as "Chief of Construction and Transportation" in that Division, gave him no instructions, and left him to conclude that the Army could get on very well without his assistance as a mere railwayman. Thereupon Haupt went home. Ten days afterwards he received from the Assistant-Secretary of War a telegram which said:—" Come back immediately. Cannot get on without you. Not a wheel moving." Haupt went back, and he found that, what with mismanagement of the lines and the attacks made on them by Confederates, not a wheel was, indeed, moving in the Division. His own position strengthened by his now being put in " exclusive charge of all the railways within the limits of the Army of Virginia," he was soon able to set the wheels running again ; and from that time General Pope exercised a wise discretion in leaving the details of railway transportation to men who understood them.

Then there was a General Sturgis who, when Haupt called on him one day, received him with the intimation, " I have just sent a guard to your office to put you under arrest for disobedience of my orders in failing to transport my command." It was quite true. Haupt had failed to obey his orders. Sturgis wanted some special trains to convey 10,000 men, with horses and baggage, the short distance of eighteen miles. The railway was a single-track line ; it had only a limited equipment of engines and cars ; there was the prospect of further immediate requirements in other directions, and Haupt took the liberty of thinking that he had better keep his transportation for more pressing needs than a journey to a prospective battle-field only eighteen miles away—the more so as if the men were attacked whilst they were in the train they would be comparatively helpless, whereas if they were attacked when on the road —doing what amounted to no more than a single day's march—they would be ready for immediate defence. These considerations suggest that, of the two, the railwayman was a better strategist than the General.

Sturgis followed up his intimation to Haupt by taking military possession of the railway and issuing some orders which any one possessing the most elementary knowledge of railway operation would have known to be impracticable. Meanwhile Haupt appealed by telegraph to the Commander-in-Chief, who replied :—" No military officer has any authority to interfere with your control over railroad. Show this to General Sturgis, and, if he attempts to interfere, I will arrest him." Told what the Commander-in-Chief said in his message, Sturgis exclaimed, " He does, does he ? Well, then, take your damned railroad ! "

Haupt found it possible to put at the disposal of Sturgis, early the following morning, the transportation asked for ; but at two o'clock in the afternoon the cars were still unoccupied. On the attention of Sturgis being called to this fact he replied that he had given his orders but they had been disobeyed. Thereupon the cars were withdrawn for service elsewhere—the more so since no other traffic could pass until they had been cleared out of the way. The net results of the General's interference was that traffic on the lines was deranged for twenty-four hours, and 10,000 men were prevented from taking part in an engagement, as they might have done had they gone by road.

Of the varied and almost unending irregularities which occurred in the working of the lines as military railways during the progress of the same war a few other examples may be given.

One prolific source of trouble was the detention or appropriation of trains by officers who did not think it necessary to communicate first with the Superintendent of the Line. A certain General who did inform the Superintendent when he wanted a train was, nevertheless, in the habit of keeping it waiting for several hours before he made his appearance, traffic being meanwhile suspended, in consequence.

Special consideration was even claimed for officers' wives, as well as for the officers themselves. On one occasion Haupt was much disturbed by the non-arrival of a train bringing supplies which were urgently wanted for a body of troops starting on a march, and he went along the line to see what had happened. Coming at last to the train, which had pulled up, he made inquiries of the engine-driver, who told him that he had received instructions to stop at a certain point so that an officer's wife, who was coming in the train to see her husband on the eve of an engagement, could go to a neighbouring town to look out for rooms for herself. At that moment the lady put in an appearance. She took her seat again and the train then proceeded; but her side-trip in search of rooms meant a delay of three hours alike for this one train and for three others following behind.

The impression seems to have prevailed, also, that officers were at liberty to make any use of the trains they pleased for the conveyance of their own belongings. To check the abuses thus developed, Haupt was compelled to issue, on June 25, 1862, the following notice :—

Assistant Quartermasters and Commissaries are positively forbidden to load on to cars on any of the Military Railroads of the Department of the Rappahannock any freights which are not strictly and properly included in Quarter and Commissary stores. They shall not load or permit to be loaded any articles for the private use of officers, or other persons, whatever their rank or position.

Officers, again, there were who, regardless of all traffic considerations, would order a train to pull up at any point they thought fit along the main line in order that they could examine the passes and permits of the passengers, instead of doing this at a terminal or other station. In still another instance a paymaster adopted as his office a box car standing on a main line. He placed in it a table, some chairs, a money-chest and his papers—finding it either more comfortable or more convenient than a house alongside—and proceeded with the transaction of all his Army business in the car. Invited to withdraw, on the ground that he was holding up the traffic, he refused to leave, and he persisted in his refusal until troops were called up to remove his things for him.

Defective arrangements in regard to the forwarding of supplies were another cause of traffic disorganisation. The railwaymen made from time to time the most strenuous efforts in getting to the extreme front large consignments of articles either in excess of requirements or not wanted there at all. After blocking the line for some days, the still-loaded cars might be sent back again, no fewer than 142 of such cars being returned on the Orange and Alexandria Railroad in the course of a single day. If the excessive supplies so sent were unloaded at the front, they might have to be loaded into the cars again when the Army moved ; or, as was frequently the case in exposed positions, they might be seized or destroyed by the enemy. Under a well-organised system an adequate stock of supplies would, of course, have been kept in stores or on sidings at some

CONTROL OF RAILWAYS IN WAR.

point in the rear, only such quantities being forwarded to the advanced front as were really needed.

At the railway stations there were frequent disputes between the responsible officers as to which should have the first use of such troop trains as were available, and Haupt found it necessary to ask the Commander-in-Chief to delegate some one who would decide in what order the troops should be forwarded.

Much trouble arose because, in their anxiety to send off as many wounded as they could, medical officers detained their trains for such periods as dislocated the service, instead of despatching at schedule time the men they had ready, and then asking for an extra train for the remainder.

In other respects, also, the arrangements for the transport of the sick and wounded were defective. Telegraphing on this subject to the Assistant Secretary of War on August 22, 1862, Haupt said :—

I fear that I may be compelled to-night to do what may appear inhuman—turn out the sick in the street. Doctors will persist in sending sick, often without papers, to get them off their hands, and we cannot send forward the troops if we must run our trains to Washington with sick to stand for hours unloaded. My first care is to send forward troops, next forage and subsistence.

Still more serious were the irregularities due to delays in the unloading of trucks and the return of empties. The amount of rolling stock available was already inadequate to meet requirements; but the effect of the shortage was rendered still worse by reason of these delays, due, in part, to the too frequent insufficiency of the force available for unloading a train of supplies with the expedition that should have been shown, and in part to the retention of the cars for weeks together as storehouses; though the main cause, perhaps, was the inability of military men, inexperienced in railway working, to appreciate, as railwaymen would do, the need of getting the greatest possible use out of rolling stock in times of emergency, and not allowing it to stand idle longer than absolutely necessary.

How such delays interfered with the efficiency of the

railways was indicated in one of Haupt's oft-repeated protests, in which he wrote :—

If all cars on their arrival at a depôt are immediately loaded or unloaded and returned, and trains are run to schedule, a single-track road, in good order and properly equipped, may supply an army of 200,000 men when, if these conditions are not complied with, the same road will not supply 30,000.

On July 9, 1863, he telegraphed to General M. C. Meigs :—

I am on my way to Gettysburg again. Find things in great confusion. Road blocked ; cars not unloaded ; stores ordered to Gettysburg—where they stand for a long time, completely preventing all movement there—ordered back without unloading ; wounded lying for hours without ability to carry them off. All because the simple rule of promptly unloading and returning cars is violated.

As for the effect of all these conditions on the military situation as a whole, this is well shown in the following " Notice," which, replying to complaints that railwaymen had not treated the military officers with proper respect, Haupt addressed " To agents and other employés of the United States Military Railroad Department " :—

While conscious of no disposition to shield the employés or agents of the Military Railroads from any censure or punishment that is really merited, justice to them requires me to state that, so far, examination has shown that complaints against them have been generally without proper foundation, and, when demands were not promptly complied with, the cause has been inability, arising from want of proper notice, and not indisposition.

Officers at posts entrusted with the performance of certain local duties, and anxious, as they generally are, to discharge them efficiently, are not always able, or disposed, to look beyond their own particular spheres. They expect demands on railway agents to be promptly complied with, without considering that similar demands, at the same time, in addition to the regular train service and routine duties, may come from Quartermasters, Commissaries, medical directors, surgeons, ordnance officers, the Commanding General, the War Department and from other sources. The Military Railroads have utterly failed to furnish transportation to even one-fifth of their capacity when managed without a strict conformity to schedule and established rules. Punctuality and discipline are even more important to the operation of a railroad than to the movement of an army; and they are vital in both.

It is doubtful if even the Confederate raiders and wreckers had, by their destructive tactics, diminished the efficiency of the Union railways to the extent of the four-fifths here attributed to the irregularities and shortcomings of the Federals themselves. The clearest proof was thus afforded that, if the new arm in warfare which rail-power represented was to accomplish all it was capable of doing, it would have to be saved from friends quite as much as from foes.

Haupt, as we have seen, suffered much from officers during the time he was connected with the Military Railroads in Virginia. He had the sympathetic support of the Commander-in-Chief, who telegraphed to him on one occasion (August 23, 1862), " No military officer will give any orders to your subordinates except through you, nor will any of them attempt to interfere with the running of trains"; and, also, of the Assistant Secretary of War, who sought to soothe him in a message which said:—" Be patient as possible with the Generals. Some of them will trouble you more than they will the enemy." But the abuses which arose were so serious that, in the interest of the military position itself, they called for a drastic remedy; and this was provided for by the issue of the following Order:—

War Department,
Adjutant-General's Office,
Washington,
November 10, 1862.

SPECIAL ORDER.

Commanding officers of troops along the United States Military Railroads will give all facilities to the officers of the road and the Quartermasters for loading and unloading cars so as to prevent any delay. On arrival at depôts, whether in the day or night, the cars will be instantly unloaded, and working parties will always be in readiness for that duty, and sufficient to unload the whole train at once.

Commanding officers will be charged with guarding the track, sidings, wood, water tanks, etc., within their several commands, and will be held responsible for the result.

Any military officer who shall neglect his duty in this respect will be reported by the Quartermasters and officers of the railroad, and his name will be stricken from the rolls of the Army.

Depôts will be established at suitable points under the direction of the Commanding General of the Army of the Potomac, and properly guarded.

No officer, whatever may be his rank, will interfere with the running of the cars, as directed by the superintendent of the road. Any one who so interferes will be dismissed from the service for disobedience of orders.

By order of the Secretary of War.

J. C. KELTON.

Commenting on this Order, General McCallum says in his report that it was issued " in consequence of several attempts having been made to operate railroads by Army or departmental commanders which had, without exception, proved signal failures, disorganising in tendency and destructive of all discipline " ; and he proceeds :—

Having had a somewhat extensive railroad experience, both before and since the rebellion, I consider this Order of the Secretary of War to have been the very foundation of success; without it the whole railroad system, which had proved an important element in conducting military movements, would have been, not only a costly but ludicrous failure. The fact should be understood that the management of railroads is just as much a distinct profession as is that of the art of war, and should be so regarded.

In *Europe*, Germany and Austria-Hungary were the first countries to attempt to solve problems that seemed to go to the very foundations of the practical usefulness of rail-transport in war. Various exhaustive studies thereon were written by railway or military authorities, and it may be of interest here to refer, more especially, to the views expressed by an eminent German authority, Baron M. M. von Weber, in " Die Schulung der Eisenbahnen," published in 1870.[1]

Railway irregularities peculiar to war service were stated by this writer to be mainly of three kinds :—(i) Delays from unsatisfactory arrangements of the service and from the misemployment of rolling stock ; (ii) temporary

[1] See Bibliography.

CONTROL OF RAILWAYS IN WAR. 51

interruption of traffic owing to the crowding of transport masses at the stations or sidings ; (iii) unsuitableness of the stations and conveyances for the required military services. The special reasons for the first of these causes he defined as (a) the absence of sufficient mutual comprehension between the military and the railway officials ; (b) the strict limitation of the efficiency of individual railway authorities to their own lines only ; (c) the ignorance of the entire staff of each line with regard to the details and service regulations of the neighbouring lines ; and (d) the impracticability of employing certain modes of carrying on business beyond the circuit to which they belong. It should, however, be borne in mind that these criticisms of authorities and their staffs relate to the conditions of the German railway system in 1870, at which time, as told by H. Budde, in " Die französischen Eisenbahnen im Kriege 1870–71," there were in Germany fifteen separate Directions for State railways ; five Directions of private railways operated by the State ; and thirty-one Directions of private railways operated by companies—a total of fifty-one controlling bodies which, on an average, operated only 210 miles of line each.

On the general question von Weber observed :—

The value in practice of mutual intelligence between military and railway officials has hitherto been far too slightly regarded.

Demands for services from military authorities, impracticable from the very nature of railways in general or the nature of the existing lines in particular, have occasioned confusion and ill-will on the part of the railway authorities and conductors. On the other hand the latter have frequently declared services to be impracticable which were really not so.

All this has arisen because the two parties in the transaction have too little insight into the nature and mechanism of their respective callings, and regard their powers more as contradictory than co-operative, so that they do not, and cannot, work together.

If, on the contrary, the nature of the railway service, with its modifications due to differences in the nature of the ground, the locality, and the organisation of transport requirements, is apparent to the military officer, even in a general way ; if he appreciates the fact that the same amount of transport must be differently performed when he passes from a level line to a mountain line, from a double line to a single line, from one where the signal and telegraph system are in use to one in which these organs of safety and intelligence are destroyed; if he can judge of the capability of stations, the length of track, and arrangements for the loading, ordering and passing of trains, etc., he will, with this knowledge, and his orders being framed in accordance with it, come much sooner and with greater facility to an understanding with the railway executives than if his commands had to be rectified by contradiction and assertion, frequently carried on under the influence of excited passions, or attempted to be enforced by violence.

The railway official, also, who has some acquaintance with military science, who understands from practical experience and inspection, not confined to his own line, the capabilities of lines and stations in a military point of view, will, at his first transaction with the military authorities, enter sooner into an understanding with them than if he were deficient in this knowledge, and will find himself in a position to co-operate, and not be coerced.

Here the suggestion seems to be that the individual Army officer and the individual railway executive, or railway official, should each become sufficiently acquainted with the technicalities of the other's business to be able to conduct their relations with mutual understanding. It would, however, be too much to expect that this plan could be carried out as regards either the military element in general or the railway element in general.

The real need of the situation was, rather, for some intermediary organisation which, including both elements, would provide the machinery for close co-operation between the Army on the one side and the railway on the other, guiding the Army as to the possibilities and limitations of the railway, and constituting the recognised and sole medium through which orders from the Army would be conveyed to the railway, no individual commander or officer having the right to give any direct order to the railway executives or staffs on his own responsibility, or to interfere in any way with the working of the railways, except in some such case of extreme emergency as an attack by the enemy on a railway station.

All these problems were to form the subject of much more controversy, together with much further practical experience, in various other countries—and notably in France during the war of 1870-71—before, as will be told in due course, they were solved by the adoption of elaborate systems of organisation designed to provide, as far as possible, for all contingencies.

CHAPTER V

PROTECTION OF RAILWAYS IN WAR

THE liability of railway lines to interruption or destruction—whether by bodies of cavalry sent across the frontier for that purpose, and aiming at damage on a large scale; by smaller raiding parties operating in the rear of an advancing army; or by individuals acting on their own account in a hostile country—rendered necessary from an early date in the railway era the adoption of protective measures of a type and character varying according to circumstances; while these, in turn, introduced some further new features into modern warfare.

Under the orders given by General McDowell for the guarding of railways in the Department of the Rappahannock, in the *American Civil War*, twelve sentinels were posted along each mile of track; block-houses were constructed at each bridge, at cross-roads, and at intervals along the track; pickets were thrown forward at various points; bushes and trees were cleared away from alongside the line, and the men at each post had flags and lanterns for signalling. General Sherman took similar measures to guard his rail communications between Nashville and Atlanta.

Precautions such as these were directed mainly against the enemy in the field; but an early example was to be afforded of how a civil population may either concern themselves or be concerned against their will in the maintenance of rail communication for military purposes. This position is well shown in the following proclamation, issued July 30, 1863, by Major-General G. G. Meade from the head-quarters of the Army of the Potomac at a time when attempts to

PROTECTION OF RAILWAYS IN WAR. 55

throw troop trains off the railway lines were a matter of daily occurrence :—

The numerous depredations committed by citizens or rebel soldiers in disguise, harboured and concealed by citizens, along the Orange and Alexandria Railroad, and within our lines, call for prompt and exemplary punishment. Under the instructions of the Government, therefore, every citizen against whom there is sufficient evidence of his having engaged in these practices will be arrested and confined for punishment, or put beyond the lines.

The people within ten miles of the railroad are notified that they will be held responsible, in their persons and property, for any injury done to the road, trains, depôts or stations by citizens, guerillas or persons in disguise ; and in case of such injury they will be impressed as labourers to repair all damages.

If these measures should not stop such depredations, it will become the unpleasant duty of the undersigned, in the execution of his instructions, to direct that the entire inhabitants of the district of country along the railroad be put across the lines, and their property taken for Government uses.

On the Manassas Gap Railway General Auger further sought to protect Federal army trains against guerilla attacks by placing in a conspicuous position in each of such trains some of the leading Confederates residing within Union lines, so that, should any accident happen to the train, they would run the risk of being among the victims.

In the *Austro-Prussian War of 1866* the principle of punishing the civil population for attacks on the railway lines underwent a further development. Captain Webber says in reference to the line through Turnau, Prague and Pardubitz to Brünn [1] : " The Prussians were fortunate in being able to preserve the line intact from injury by the inhabitants, partly by the number and strength of the guards posted along it, and partly from the terror of reprisals which they had inspired." Captain Webber suggests that, in the face of an active enemy, and in a country where the population was hostile, it would have been impossible to depend on the railway as a principal line of communication ; but

[1] "Notes on the Campaign in Bohemia in 1866." By Capt. Webber, R.E. Papers of the Corps of Royal Engineers, N.S., vol. xvi. Woolwich, 1868.

the significance of his expression, "the terror of reprisals," as denoting the policy adopted by Prussia so far back as 1866, will not be lost on those who are only too well acquainted with more recent developments of the same policy by the same country.

The number of men per mile required for guarding a line of rail communication is declared by Captain John Bigelow, in his "Principles of Strategy" (Philadelphia, 1894), to be exceedingly variable, depending as it does upon the tactical features of the country and the temper of the inhabitants. According, he says, to the estimate of the Germans for the conditions of European warfare, the number will average about 1,000 men for every stretch of fifteen miles. At this rate an army sixty miles from its base requires about 4,000 men for the protection of each line of communication.

With the help of figures such as these one may, perhaps, understand the more readily how it is that a Commander-in-Chief, of merciless disposition, and wanting to retain the active services of every soldier he possibly can in the interests of an early and successful advance will, by spreading a feeling of "terror" among the civil population, seek to reduce to as low a figure as circumstances will permit the number of men he must leave behind to guard his lines of rail communication.

These considerations will be found to apply with the greater force when it is remembered that in the *Franco-Prussian War of 1870-71* the Prussians had to adopt an especially elaborate system for safeguarding their lines of communication with Germany during the time they occupied French territory. At each railway station they placed a guard formed of detachments of the Landwehr, while small detachments were stationed in towns and villages in the neighbourhood. In each signal-box a detachment of troops was stationed, and the whole line of railway was patrolled from posts established along it at distances of every three or four miles. Altogether, the Germans are said to have employed, on over 2,000 miles of French railway lines controlled by them, as many as 100,000 troops for protective

PROTECTION OF RAILWAYS IN WAR. 57

purposes only; and even then the *franc-tireurs* were able to cause many interruptions.

Under a Prussian regulation dated May 2, 1867, it was laid down that after the restoration of any lines taken possession of in an enemy's territory, notice should be given that in the event of any further damage being done to the railway, the locality would be subject to a fine of at least 500 thalers, the belongings of the inhabitants would be liable to seizure, and the local authorities might be arrested.

As a further precautionary measure in the war of 1870-71, the Germans took a hint from the example of the Union Generals in the American Civil War by compelling a leading citizen of the district passed through to ride on the engine of each train run by them on French soil. In defence of this practice, the German General Staff say in their handbook on "The Usages of War"[1]:—

Since the lives of peaceable inhabitants were, without any fault on their part, thereby exposed to grave danger, every writer outside Germany has stigmatised this measure as contrary to the law of nations and as unjustified towards the inhabitants of the country. As against this unfavourable criticism it must be pointed out that this measure, which was also recognised on the German side as harsh and cruel, was only resorted to after declarations and instructions of the occupying authorities had proved ineffective, and that in the particular circumstances it was the only method which promised to be effective against the doubtless unauthorised, indeed the criminal, behaviour of a fanatical population. Herein lies its justification under the laws of war, but still more in the fact that it proved completely successful, and that wherever citizens were thus carried on the trains . . . the security of traffic was assured.

Writing under date December 16, 1870, Busch offered the following justification for the course adopted:—

They were taken, not to serve as a hindrance to French heroism, but as a precaution against treacherous crime. The railway does not carry merely soldiers, ammunition and other war material against which it may be allowable to use violent measures; it also conveys a great number of wounded, doctors,

---

[1] "The German War Book. Being the Usages of War on Land"; issued by the Great General Staff of the German Army. London, 1915.

hospital attendants, and other perfectly harmless persons. Is a peasant or *franc-tireur* to be allowed to endanger hundreds of those lives by removing a rail or laying a stone upon the line? Let the French see that the security of the railway trains is no longer threatened and the journeys made by those hostages will be merely outings, or our people may even be able to forgo such precautionary measures.

In the *South African War*, Field-Marshal Earl Roberts issued at Pretoria, on June 19, 1900, a proclamation one section of which authorised the placing of leading men among the Boers on the locomotives of the trains run by the British on the occupied territory; but this particular section was withdrawn eight days afterwards.

The English view of the practice in question is thus defined in the official "Manual of Military Law" (Chap. XIV, "The Laws and Usages of War," par. 463):—

Such measures expose the lives of inhabitants, not only to the illegitimate acts of train wrecking by private enemy individuals, but also to the lawful operations of raiding parties of the armed forces of the belligerent, and cannot, therefore, be considered a commendable practice.

To guard against the attacks made on the railway lines in the Orange Free State and the Transvaal during the British occupation, entrenched posts were placed at every bridge exceeding a 30-feet span; constant patrolling was maintained between these posts; and the block-houses introduced (in 1901) by Lord Kitchener were erected along all the railway lines, at distances of about 2,000 yards. Each block-house, also, was garrisoned by about ten men, and each was surrounded by wire entanglements which, together with various kinds of alarm fences, were also placed between the block-houses themselves in order both to impede the approach of the enemy and to warn the garrison thereof.

Block-houses are to-day regarded as one of the chief means of protecting railways against attacks. Their construction and equipment are dealt with by Major W. D. Connor, of the Corps of Engineers, U.S.A., in "Military Railways" (Professional Papers, No. 32, Corps of Engineers, U.S. Army, Washington, 1910).

PROTECTION OF RAILWAYS IN WAR. 59

Supplementary to the adoption of this block-house system, in time of war, is the practice followed in various Continental countries, in time of peace, of building *permanent fortresses*, in solid masonry, alongside railway bridges crossing important rivers. In some instances the fortress is so constructed that the railway lines pass through the centre of it. Not only, as a rule, are these fortresses extremely solid and substantial, but they may be provided with bomb-proof covers and be stocked with a sufficient supply of provisions to be able to stand, if necessary, a fairly prolonged siege. One can assume, also, that the garrison would have under its control facilities arranged in advance for the destruction of the bridge, as a last resort, in case of need.

The theory is that such fortresses and their garrisons should be of especial advantage, on the outbreak of war, in checking any sudden invasion and allowing time for the completion of defensive measures. Their construction in connection with all the principal railway bridges crossing the Rhine was especially favoured in Prussia after the war of 1870-1.

Similar fortresses, or "interrupting forts," as the Germans call them, are also built for the protection of important tunnels, junctions, locomotive and carriage works, etc.

Another method adopted for the safeguarding of railway lines in war is the use of *armoured trains ;* though in practice these are also employed for the purposes of independent attacks on the enemy, apart altogether from any question of ensuring the safety of rail communication.[1]

For the *protection of locomotives and rolling stock*, and to prevent not only their capture but their use by the enemy, the most efficacious method to adopt is, of course, that of removing them to some locality where the enemy is not likely to come.

When, in 1866, Austria saw that she could not hold back the Prussian invader, she took off into Hungary no fewer than 1,000 locomotives and 16,000 wagons from the railways in Bohemia and Saxony. Similar tactics were adopted by

[1] The subject of armoured trains will be dealt with more fully in Chapters VII and XVI.

the Boers as against ourselves in the war in South Africa. On the British troops crossing into the Orange Free State, from Cape Colony, they found that the retreating enemy had withdrawn all their rolling stock, as well as all their staffs from the railway stations, leaving behind only a more or less damaged line of railway. Subsequently, when the forces occupied Pretoria, they certainly did find there sixteen locomotives and 400 trucks; but the station books showed that in the previous forty-eight hours no fewer than seventy trains, many of them drawn by two engines, had been sent east in the direction of Delagoa Bay.

When it is not practicable to withdraw locomotives and rolling stock which it is desired the enemy shall not be able to use, the obvious alternative is that measures should be taken either to remove vital parts or to ensure their destruction. Certain of the methods adopted during the Civil War in America were especially efficacious in attaining the latter result. In some instances trains were started running and then—driver and fireman leaping off the engine—were left to go into a river, or to fall through a broken viaduct. In other instances two trains, after having had a good supply of explosives put in them, would be allowed to dash into one another at full speed. Many locomotives had their boilers burst, and wagons were set on fire after having been filled up with combustibles.

Still another method which has been adopted with a view to preventing an enemy from using the railways he might succeed in capturing is that of constructing them with a *different gauge*. The standard gauge of the main-line railways in France, Germany, Holland, Belgium, Denmark, Austria-Hungary, Italy, Switzerland, Roumania and Turkey (like that, also, of railways in Great Britain, Canada and the United States), is 4ft. 8½in., allowing trains to pass readily from one country to the other with the same rolling stock; but the gauge of the Russian railways is 5ft., necessitating a transshipment from one train to another when the frontier is reached. Similar conditions are found in Spain and Portugal, where the standard gauge is 5ft. 6in.[1]

---

[1] See "Field Service Pocket Book, 1914," pp. 151-2.

PROTECTION OF RAILWAYS IN WAR.

Russia adopted her broader gauge so that, in case of invasion, the invader should not be able to run his rolling-stock over her lines, as Germany, for instance, would be able to do in the case of the railways of Belgium and France. Thus far, therefore, Russia strengthened her position from the point of view of defence; but she weakened it as regards attack, since if she should herself want, either to become the invader or to send troop trains over neighbouring territory to some point beyond, she would be at a disadvantage. In the Russo-Turkish War of 1877-78, when the Russian forces passed through Roumania on their way to Turkey, the difference in gauge between the Russian and the Roumanian railways caused great delay and inconvenience by reason of the necessary transfer of troops, stores, guns, ammunition, torpedo boats, etc., at the frontier.

It should, also, be remembered that the reduction of a broad gauge to a narrow one is a much simpler matter, from an engineering point of view, than the widening of a narrower gauge into a broad one. In the former case the existing sleepers, bridges, tunnels, platforms, etc., would still serve their purpose. In the latter case fresh sleepers might have to be laid, bridges and tunnels widened or enlarged, and platforms and stations altered, use of the broader-gauge rolling stock thus involving an almost complete reconstruction of the railway lines. To this extent, therefore, the balance of advantage would seem to be against the country having the broader gauge. The conclusion may, at least, be formed that such a country is far more bent on protecting her own territory than on invading that of her neighbours.

The course adopted by Germany for overcoming the difficulty which, in the event of her seeking to invade Russia, the difference of railway gauge in that country would present, will be told in Chapter XVIII.

CHAPTER VI

Troops and Supplies

In the earlier controversies as to the use of railways in war, attention was almost entirely concentrated on questions relating to the movement of large masses of troops, the saving of time to be effected, and the strategic advantages to be gained. These considerations quickly passed from the theoretical to the practical, and when the results attained were put against such facts as, for instance, the one that in 1805 Napoleon's Grand Army of 200,000 men took forty-two days to march the 700 kilometres (435 miles) between Ulm on the Danube and the French camp at Boulogne, there was no longer any possibility of doubt as to the services that railways might render from these particular points of view.

Quicker transport was, however, only one consideration. There was the further important detail that the movement of troops by rail would bring them to their point of concentration, not only sooner, but in *more complete numbers*, than if they had to endure the fatigues of prolonged marches by road.

According to German authorities, the falling-out of infantry and cavalry when marching along good roads under conditions of well-maintained discipline and adequate food supplies averages three per cent. in cool and dry weather, and six per cent. in hot or wet weather; while in unfavourable conditions as regards roads, weather and supplies, the diminution may be enormous. When, in the autumn of 1799, Suvóroff made his famous march over the St. Gothard, he lost, in eleven days, no fewer than 10,000 men owing to the hardships of the journey. In his invasion of Russia, in 1812, Napoleon's losses in men who succumbed to the

TROOPS AND SUPPLIES

fatigues and trials they experienced on the road were out of all proportion to the casualties due to actual fighting. It was, too, a saying of Blücher's that "he feared night marches worse than the enemy."

An English authority, Lieut.-Col. R. Home, C.B., R.E., wrote in a paper on "The Organisation of the Communications, including Railways," published in Vol XIX. of the Journal of the Royal United Service Institution (1875):—

If an army of moderate size, say 50,000 men, simply marches one hundred miles without firing one shot or seeing an enemy the number of sick to be got rid of is very great.

Experience has shown that in a good climate, with abundant food, easy marches, and fair weather, the waste from ordinary causes in a ten days' march of such a force would be between 2,000 and 2,500 men, while the number of galled, footsore or worn-out horses would also be very large. A few wet days or a sharp engagement would raise the number of both very considerably. An inefficient man or horse at the front is a positive disadvantage.

Another equally important detail relates to the *provision of supplies* for the troops and animals thus transported by rail both more quickly and with less fatigue.

In all ages the feeding of his troops in an enemy's country has been one of the gravest problems a military commander has had to solve; and though, in some instances, vast armies have succeeded in drawing sufficient support from the land they have invaded, there have been others in which an army intending to "live upon the country" has failed to get the food it needed, and has had its numbers depleted to the extent of thousands as the result of sheer starvation. This was the experience of Darius, King of Persia, who, in 513 B.C., crossed the Bosporus, on a bridge of boats, with an army of 700,000, followed the retreating Scythians, and lost 80,000 of his men in wild steppes where no means existed for feeding them. When, also, Alexander the Great was withdrawing from India, in 325 B.C., two-thirds of his force died on the desert plains of Beluchistan from thirst or hunger. Lack of the supplies from which he found himself entirely cut off was, again, a main cause of the disaster that overtook Napoleon in his Russian campaign. Even fertile or comparatively fertile lands, satisfying the needs of their inhabitants in time of peace, may fail to afford provisions for an invading army, either because of the great number of the latter or because the retreating population have destroyed the food supplies they could not take with them into the interior whether for their own sustenance or with a view to starving the invaders.

Should the invading army succeed in "living on the country," the effect of leaving the troops to their own resources, in the way of collecting food, may still be not only subversive of discipline but of strategic disadvantage through their being scattered on marauding expeditions at a time when, possibly, it would be preferable to keep them concentrated.

General Friron, chief of the staff of Marshal Masséna, wrote concerning Napoleon's campaign in Portugal :—

The day the soldier became convinced that, for the future, he would have to depend on himself, discipline disappeared from the ranks of the army. The officer became powerless in the presence of want; he was no longer disposed to reprimand the soldier who brought him the nourishment essential to his existence, and who shared with him, in brotherly goodwill, a prey which may have cost him incalculable dangers and fatigues.

The extent to which a combination of physical fatigue and shortness of supplies in an inhospitable country may interfere with the efficiency of an army is well shown by Thiers (" Histoire du Consulat et de l'Empire ") in regard to the conditions at the very outset of Napoleon's Russian campaign. The French troops arriving on the Niemen—at which point they were merely on the frontiers of Russia—were already overcome by the long marches they had made. They had no bread, no salt, and no spirits; their craving for food could no longer be satisfied by meat without salt and meal mixed with water. The horses, too, were out of condition for want of proper food. Behind the army a great number of soldiers dropped out of the ranks and had lost their way, while the few people they met in a scantily-populated district could speak nothing but Polish, which the wearied and famished men were unable to understand. Yet, under the

TROOPS AND SUPPLIES.

conditions of former days, it was by troops thus exhausted by marches of hundreds of miles, done on, possibly, a starvation diet, that battles involving the severest strain on human energy were fought.

When " living on the country " is no longer practicable, the only alternative for an army is, of course, that of sending supplies after it for the feeding of the troops; but when, or where, this has had to be done by means of ordinary road services, it has involved—together with the transport of artillery, ammunition and stores—(1) the employment of an enormous number of vehicles and animals, greatly complicating the movements of the army; and (2) a limitation of the distance within which a campaign can be waged by an army depending entirely on its own resources.

The latter of these conditions was the direct consequence of the former; and the reason for this was shown by General W. T. Sherman in an article contributed by him to the *Century Magazine* for February, 1888 (pp. 595-6), in the course of which he says:—

According to the Duke of Wellington, an army moves upon its belly, not upon its legs; and no army dependent on wagons can operate more than a hundred miles from its base because the teams going and returning consume the contents of their wagons, leaving little or nothing for the maintenance of men and animals at the front who are fully employed in fighting.

There was, again, the risk when food supplies followed the army by road either of perishables going bad *en route*, owing to the time taken in their transport by wagon, or of their suffering deterioration as the result of exposure to weather, the consequence in either case being a diminution in the amount of provisions available for feeding the army.

All these various conditions have been changed by the railway, the use of which for the purposes of war has, in regard to the forwarding of supplies, introduced innovations which are quite as important as those relating to the movement of troops—if, indeed, the former advantages are not of even greater importance than the latter.

Thanks to the railway, an army can now draw its supplies from the whole of the interior of the home country—provided that the lines of communication can be kept open; and, with the help not only of regular rail services but of stores and magazines *en route* those supplies can be forwarded to rail-head in just such quantities as they may be wanted. Under these conditions the feeding of an army in the field should be assured regardless alike of the possible scanty resources of the country in which it is engaged and of its own distance from the base of supplies.

CHAPTER VII

ARMOURED TRAINS

IN the issue of the now defunct London periodical, *Once a Week*, for August 13, 1859, there was published an article on " English Railway Artillery : A Cheap Defence against Invasion," in which it was said, among other things :—

We have hitherto regarded the rail merely as a vehicle of transport, to carry materials which are not to be set in work till off the rails. If we look at the rail as part of an instrument of warfare, we shall be startled at the enormous means we have at hand, instantly available, from mercantile purposes, to convert to engines of war.

The writer was William Bridges Adams (1797–1872), an authority on railways who had grown up with them, had introduced into their operation many inventions and improvements (including the fish-joint still used for connecting rails), and was the author of various books and papers on railways, transport, and other subjects. His new idea, as set forth in the article in question, was specially directed to the utilisation of railways for defending the shores of Great Britain against an invader ; and in developing this idea he was, also, as far as can be traced, the first to suggest the employment of armoured trains.

The immediate reason alike for the writing of the article and for the making of the suggestion was that in 1859 Great Britain appeared to be faced by the prospect of invasion by France,—a prospect which, in view of the then admittedly defective condition of the national defences, led to the creation of the Volunteer Corps, to the appointment of a Royal Commission to inquire into the question of coast defence, and to suggestions being put forward by many different authorities as to what should be done. Among those suggestions was one by the writer in question for supplementing any system of coast defence that might be adopted by the mounting of guns on railway trucks protected by armour, such trucks being moved from point to point along the coast railways to meet, as far as possible, the needs of the military situation.

Heavy artillery, wrote Adams, though the most formidable implement of modern warfare, had the disadvantage of requiring many horses to draw it. So the problem arose as to how the horses could be dispensed with. This could best be done, he thought, by putting artillery on "our true line of defence,—our rails," and having it drawn, or propelled, by a locomotive. "Mount," he said, "a gun of twenty tons weight on a railway truck, with a circular traversing platform, and capable of throwing a shot or shell weighing one hundred to one and a half a distance of five miles. A truck on eight wheels would carry this very easily, and there would be no recoil." Such a battery would be "practically a moving fortress," and, used on the coast railways, which he regarded as constituting lines of defence, would be "the cheapest of all possible fortresses—absolutely a continuous fortress along the whole coast." Communication with coast railways at all strategical points should, however, be facilitated by the placing of rails along the ordinary highways. After giving some technical details as to the construction alike of coast railways and road tramways, he proceeded :—

With these roads communicating with the railroads, the whole railway system becomes applicable to military purposes.

The railway system is so especially adapted for defence, and so little adapted to invaders, that it should become at once a matter of experiment how best to adapt Armstrong or other guns to its uses. The process of fitting the engines with shot-proof walls to protect the drivers against riflemen would be very easy. . . . Nothing but artillery could damage the engines or moving batteries, and artillery could not get near them if it were desirable to keep out of the way.

One gun transportable would do the work of ten which are fixtures in forts, and there would be no men to take prisoners, for no forts would be captured.

ARMOURED TRAINS.

The more this system is thought of the more the conviction will grow that it is the simplest mode of rendering the country impenetrable to invaders at a comparatively trifling cost.

It will be seen that the scheme here proposed included three separate propositions—(1) the use of railways, as "engines of war," for coast defence; (2) the mounting of Armstrong or other guns on railway trucks from which they could be discharged for the purposes of such defence; and (3) the providing of the engines with "shot-proof walls" for the protection of the drivers. A similar protection for the men operating the guns on the trucks was not then, apparently, considered necessary; but we have here what was clearly the germ of the "armoured train."

Among the other suggestions advanced on the same occasion were some for the employment of railways in general for strategical purposes, and more especially for the defence of London; and here, again, the employment of armoured trains was advocated.

"A Staff Officer," writing in *The Times* of July 16, 1860, declared that the most efficacious and the most economical line of defence which London could have would be a circular railway forming a complete cordon around the Metropolis at a distance of fifteen miles from the centre, and having for its interior lines of operation the numerous railways already existing within that radius. On this circular railway there should be "Armstrong and Whitworth ordnance mounted on large iron-plated trucks" fitted with traversing platforms in the way already recommended by W. Bridges Adams, the trucks themselves, however, and not only the locomotives, being protected by "shot-proof shields." The circular railway was to be constructed primarily for strategical purposes; but during peace the line would be available for ordinary traffic, and in this way it could be made to yield at least some return on the capital expenditure.

The writer of this letter, Lieut. Arthur Walker, then an officer of the 79th Highlanders and the holder of a staff appointment at the School of Musketry, Fleetwood, followed up the subject by reading a paper on "Coast Railways and Railway Artillery" at a meeting of the Royal

United Service Institution on January 30, 1865.[1] On this occasion he specially advocated the use of "moveable batteries" for coast defence in conjunction with railways constructed more or less within a short parallel distance of the entire coast line. Field artillery, he recommended, should be mounted on a truck the sides of which would be "encased in a cuirass of sufficient thickness," while the engine and tender would also be "protected by an iron cuirass, and placed between two cupolas for further protection." He considered that "to attempt to land in face of such an engine of war as this would be simply impossible." Moving batteries of this kind would be "the cheapest of all possible fortresses. . . . We have nothing to do but to improvise well-adapted gun-carriages for our rails." At the same meeting Mr. T. Wright, C.E., gave details of a proposed railway train battery for coast, frontier and inland defence which was designed to carry ten, twenty or forty guns or mortars.

Another early advocate of the use of railways as an actual instrument of warfare was Colonel E. R. Wethered, who, in 1872, wrote to the War Office suggesting that heavy ordnance should be mounted on wheeled carriages so constructed that they could be moved along any of the railways, from point to point. In this way the three-fold advantage would be gained of (1) utilising the railway system for purposes of national defence; (2) rendering possible a concentration of artillery with overwhelming force at any given spot, and, (3) by the use of these moveable carriages for the conveyance of the guns, exposing the men to less risk.

Colonel Wethered further communicated to *The Times* of May 25, 1877, a letter on "Portable Batteries" in which he declared that if, before an enemy could effect a landing, we were to provide the means of concentrating, with unerring certainty, on any given points of the coast, a crushing force of artillery, with guns of heavier calibre than even the warships of the invader could command, it would be

[1] *See* the "Journal of the Royal United Service Institution" Vol. IX., pp. 221-31, 1865.

ARMOURED TRAINS.

impossible for the vessels of an invading force to approach near enough to effect the landing of their men. He continued :—

My proposal is to take the full advantage which our railway system, in connection with our insular position, affords, and provide powerful moveable batteries which can be sent fully equipped in fighting order direct by railway to any required point ; and the recent experimental trials of the 81-ton gun have proved that the heaviest ordnance can be moved and fought on railway metals with considerable advantage. . . . In connection with our present main lines of railway, which probably would require strengthening at certain points, I would construct branch lines or sidings leading to every strategical point of our coast and into every fort, as far as possible, with requisite platforms. . . . These branch lines during peace would, doubtless, be of some small commercial value. . . . I would mount as many of our heaviest guns as practicable on railway gun carriages so that they could be moved by rail from one face of a front to another, and from one place to another.

He also recommended that guns thus mounted, fully equipped, and ready for use, should be kept at three large central depôts which might be utilised for the defence of London. At each of them he would station (1) Militia and Volunteer Artillery able not only to work the guns but to construct, repair or destroy railway lines, and (2) a locomotive corps specially trained in the working of traffic under war conditions.

By reading a paper at the Royal United Service Institution on April 24, 1891, on " The Use of Railways for Coast and Harbour Defence," [1] Lieut. E. P. Girouard, R.E. (now Major-General Sir E. Percy C. Girouard, K.C.M.G.), made what was, at that time, an important contribution to a subject on which there was then still much to be learned. Sketching a detailed scheme comprising the employment of all the coastal railways for the purposes of national defence, he emphasised the value of Britain's " enormous railway power " as the strong point of her defensive position, whether regarded from the point of view of (1) railway

[1] " Journal of the Royal United Service Institution," Vol. XXXV., 1891.

mileage open as compared with the square mile of coastal area to be defended, or (2) the length of coast line compared with the railway mileage at or near that coast line, and, therefore, locally available for its defence. "Why," he asked, "should we not turn to account the enormous advantage which our great railway power gives us to concentrate every available gun at a threatened point in the right and the proper time, which the proper utilisation of our railways can and will do, thereby practically doubling or quadrupling our available gun power?"

Whilst the subject had thus been under discussion in the United Kingdom, America, in her *Civil War of 1861–65*, had set the rest of the world an example by actually introducing armoured-protected gun-carrying trucks into modern warfare.

Writing from Washington, under date August 29, 1862, to Colonel Herman Haupt, then Chief of Construction and Transportation in the Department of Rappahannock, Mr. P. H. Watson, Assistant-Secretary of War, said:—"An armour-clad car, bullet proof, and mounting a cannon, has arrived here and will be sent down to Alexandria." A later message, on the same date added:— "After you see the bullet-proof car, let me know what you think of it. I think you ought at once to have a locomotive protected by armour. Can you have the work done expeditiously and well at Alexandria, or shall I get it done at Philadelphia or Wilmington?" The car was duly received; but Haupt's comments in respect to it, as recorded in his "Reminiscences," show that he was not greatly impressed by the innovation. "P. H. Watson, Assistant-Secretary of War, sent me," he says, "an armour-clad, bullet-proof car, mounting a cannon. The kindness was appreciated, but the present was an elephant. I could not use it, and, being in the way, it was finally side-tracked on an old siding in Alexandria."

It would seem, however, that other armour-clad cars were brought into actual use during the course of the Civil War.

In the *Railway Age Gazette* (Chicago) for January 22, 1915,

ARMOURED TRAINS. 73

Mr. Frederick Hobart, associated editor of the New York *Engineer and Mining Journal*, writes, from personal knowledge, of two armoured cars which were in use in the Civil War. One of these, formed by heavy timbers built up on a flat car, was put together in the shops of the Atlantic and North Carolina Railroad Company at Newberne, N.C., in 1862, about two months after the city had been captured by the Burnside expedition. The armour consisted of old rails spiked on the outside of the planking composing the sides and front of the car. Along the sides there were slits for musketry fire, and at the front end there was a port hole covered with a shutter behind which a gun from one of the field batteries was mounted. The second car was similarly constructed, but was armed with a naval howitzer. The cars were run ahead of the engine, and were used in reconnoitring along the railroad line west of Newberne. Mr. Hobart adds that he was quite familiar with the cars, having assisted in the design and construction of both.

In the *Century Magazine* for September, 1887 (page 774), there is given an illustration ("from a photograph") of an armour-clad car described as "the Union Railroad Battery" which was, apparently, used in connection with the springing of the mine in front of Petersburg on July 30, 1864. The car is shown to have consisted of a low truck with, at one end, a sloping armour plate coming down almost to the rails, and having a hole through which the gun placed behind it on the truck could be fired. The sides of the truck were protected from the top of the sloping armour downwards, but the back was open. The car was, of course, designed to be pushed in front of the locomotive.

Mr. L. Lodian, also, contributed to the issue of the American periodical, *Railway and Locomotive Engineering*, for May, 1915, a communication, under the title of "The Origin of Armoured Railroad Cars Unquestionably the Product of the American Civil War," in which, claiming that "our own Civil War" originated those cars, he said :—

Attached is a picture of one in use on the old Philadelphia-Baltimore Railroad. The illustration appeared in Frank Leslie's illustrated periodical on May 18, 1864. No better proof could be furnished of the authenticity of the fact that such a car was in use at that time. . . . There appears to be no great variation even to-day in armoured car design from the initial effort of half a century ago. Pictures are appearing in numerous periodicals, at the period of writing, of those in use by the European belligerents, and in general appearance and outline they are about the same as the original, the chief variation in their use being that the war-going locomotive is also sheathed in armour, whereas that in use in the sixties was entirely unprotected, except in front, and then only by reason of the mailclad car being placed in front to do the fighting.

As against this suggestion, there is the undoubted fact that in the American Civil War the plan was adopted of having the locomotives of ordinary troop or supply trains protected by armour-plating as a precaution against attack when there was no armoured car in front of them. Writing to the Director of Military Railroads on October 8, 1862, Haupt said :—

I have been thinking over the subject of locomotives. It is one which, at the present time, and in view of the future requirements of the service, demands especial attention. Experience has shown that on engines men are targets for the enemy; the cabs where they are usually seated have been riddled by bullets, and they have only escaped by lying on the footboard. It will be necessary to inspire confidence in our men by placing iron cabins (bullet proof) upon all or nearly all our engines, and the necessity will increase as we penetrate further into the enemy's country.

Again, it is desirable that the smaller and more delicate portions of the apparatus should be better protected than at present, and I would be pleased if you would give to the plans, of which I spoke to you recently, a careful consideration. It seems to me that they are peculiarly well adapted to military service.

Haupt adds that " protected locomotives and bullet-proof cabs were soon after provided, as recommended "; and elsewhere in his " Reminiscences " he says, on the same subject :—

The bullet-proof cabs on locomotives were very useful—in fact, indispensable. I had a number of them made and put on engines, and they afforded protection to engineers and firemen against the fire from guerillas from the bushes that lined the road.

ARMOURED TRAINS. 75

In the *Franco-Prussian War of 1870-71* guns mounted on four armour-plated trucks, fitted up in the workshops of the Orléans Company, under the supervision of M. Dupuy de Lorme, Engineer-in-Chief for Naval Construction, were taken into action on four occasions during the siege of Paris, namely, at Choisy-le-Roi, for the sortie preceding the one from Champigny; near Brie-sur-Marne, to support the Champigny sortie; at Le Bourget, for one of the attempts to recapture that position; and at La Malmaison, to support the Montretout sortie. The wagons were protected by a covering which consisted of five plates of wrought iron, each two-fifths of an inch thick, and giving, therefore, a total thickness of two inches. The two engines used were also protected by armour-plating. One or two of the wagons were struck by field-gun shells without, however, sustaining further damage than the denting of their plates. The engines escaped damage altogether. On going into action the armoured wagons were followed by another bullet-proof engine conveying a party of men with tools and materials to repair any interruption of the lines that might interfere with the return of the trains; but the only damage done was so slight that it was remedied in about a quarter of an hour.[1]

Further use was made of armoured trains in the *Egyptian Campaign of 1882*. One that was put together to assist in the defensive works at Alexandria is declared in the official history of the campaign[2] to have " proved most serviceable." Two of the trucks, fitted with iron plating and sand bags as a protecting cover, carried one Nordenfelt and two Gatling guns. A 9-pr. was also placed on one of the trucks, together with a crane by means of which it could be lowered out immediately. Other trucks, rendered bullet proof by sand bags and boiler-plating, and carrying a force

---

[1] For detailed description, with diagrams, of the trains here in question, see "Armour-plated Railway Wagons used during the late Sieges of Paris," by Lieut. Fraser, R.E. Papers of the Corps of Royal Engineers, N.S., Vol. XX, 1872.

[2] "Military History of the Campaign of 1882 in Egypt." Prepared by the Intelligence Branch of the War Office. Revised edition. London, 1908.

of 200 bluejackets, with small arms, completed the fighting force. On July 28, the train took part in a reconnaissance sent out to ascertain the extent of the damage which had been done to the railway lines near Arabi's outpost. Shots were fired at the train by the enemy, but without effect. The reconnaissance was a complete success inasmuch as it enabled such repairs to be done to the railway as gave the use of a second line between Ramleh and Alexandria.

So useful had the train been found that it was now further improved by adding to it a 40-pr. on a truck protected by an iron mantlet. The locomotive was put in the middle of the train and was itself protected by sand bags and railway iron. Thus strengthened, the train went into action in the reconnaissance in force carried out from Alexandria on August 5, and "the most interesting incident of the engagement," according to the official account, "was the good service done by the 40-pr. from the armoured train."

Early in the morning of September 13 the train, consisting of five wagons, and having, on this occasion, one Krupp gun and one Gatling in addition to the 40-pr., was sent to support the attack on Tel el-Kebir. It was followed by another train having 350 yards of permanent-way materials, with all the necessary tools and appliances for the prompt carrying out of any repairs that might be necessary. Owing, however, to the hazy and uncertain light and to the ever-increasing clouds of smoke that hung over the battlefield, it was impossible to fire the 40-pr.

In the futile attempt made in 1885 to construct a railway from Suakin to Berber, in support of the *Nile Expedition of 1884-85*, resort was had to an armoured train for the purpose of protecting the line from the constant attacks to which it was subjected by the enemy. The train carried a 20-pr. B.L., which could be fired only either in prolongation of the line or at a slight angle from it.

At the Camp of Exercise in *Delhi* in January, 1886, some important experiments were carried out with a view to testing the practicability of firing guns at right angles to an ordinary line of railway, the result being to establish the fact that a 40-pr. R.B.L. could be fired with perfect safety broadside from (a) small empty wagons mounted on four wheels; (b) small empty wagons weighted up to four tons; and (c) empty eight-wheel bogies. These experiments were especially successful when account is taken of the fact that no attempt was made to reduce in any way the energy of recoil.

Other experiments, begun in 1885, were successfully conducted during a succession of years both by the French Government and by private firms in *France* in the transport and the firing of guns from railway trucks with a view to obtaining definite data on the subject, more especially in relation to firing at right angles to the line.

In *Italy* a distinguished officer raised the question in the Italian Parliament, in 1891, as to whether Sicily should not be defended by means of a coast railway and armoured trains.

Some experiments carried out at *Newhaven, Sussex*, in 1894, were the more interesting because the results attained were due to the combined efforts of Artillery Volunteers and of the London, Brighton and South Coast Railway Company.

Under the Volunteer mobilization scheme of 1891 there were some 300 members of the 1st Sussex Artillery Volunteers to whom no special duties had been allotted, and there happened to be, at Shoreham, a 40-pr. Armstrong B.L. gun which was then serving no particular purpose. Inspired by these two facts, the Secretary of the Committee for National Defence suggested, in November, 1891, that negotiations should be opened with the London, Brighton and South Coast Railway Company with a view to their mounting the 40-pr. on a specially prepared truck, designed to form part of an armoured train, experiments in firing the gun from the truck—in order to test the efficiency of this expedient for the purposes of coast defence—being afterwards carried out by the Artillery Volunteers whose services were available for the purpose.

On being approached, the directors of the railway company readily consented to the fitting up of the truck being carried out at their engineering and carriage works; they contributed towards the expenses, and members of their staff entered with great cordiality into the scheme, Mr. R. J. Billington, the locomotive superintendent, being the first to suggest the mounting of the gun on a turntable to be fixed on the truck,—a "bold departure," as it was regarded at the time, and one expected to produce excellent results. The railway staff were the more interested, also, in the proposed experiments because a large proportion of the members of the 1st Sussex Artillery Volunteers consisted of men employed at the Brighton Company's works.

In commenting upon these facts, Col. Charles Gervaise Boxall, the commanding officer, said in a paper on "The Armoured Train for Coast Defence," read by him at a meeting of officers and N.C.O's of the Brigade, held at Newhaven Fort, Sussex, on May 14, 1894:—

When one considers that a railway company is neither a philanthropic institution nor a patriotic society, the generous support given to this experiment by so powerful a body as the directors of the London, Brighton and South Coast Railway Company is in itself some considerable evidence of the importance they themselves ascribe to this effort in the direction of the maintenance of coast defence and protection from invasion.

Preliminary experiments with the gun were conducted on May 5, 1894, and they conclusively showed, Col. Boxall said, "that the gun will require no traversing to correct variation caused by the recoil, while the muzzle of the gun can be directed to any part of its circumference by handspike traversing within half a minute." He was evidently proud of the results even of these preliminary trials. They were the first occasion on which a heavy gun had been fired broadside on the permanent way of an English railway, and the truck was the first armour-plated one on which a turntable, a recoil cylinder, and other inventions introduced had been employed. So, he further declared:—

We do confidently submit that, having proved that such a gun as this can be mounted so as to be transportable to any part of our railway system at a moment's notice, brought into action, and fired with accuracy either end on, broadside, or in any other direction, without danger of capsizing, and without injury to the permanent way, we have become pioneers of a new departure in artillery which must lead to results of the highest importance.

This was written prior to the full trials, which took place at Newhaven on May 19, 1894, in the presence of a distinguished company of military men and others. An account of the event will be found in *The Times* of May 21, 1894. The gun and its carriage are described as standing on a turntable platform pivoted on the centre of the truck, and revolving on a central "racer." The gun detachments were protected by a plating six feet high round three sides of the turntable, and the gun was fired through an aperture in the plating. Drawn by an ordinary locomotive, the truck on which the gun was mounted was accompanied by two carriages conveying the Volunteer Artillerymen who were to serve the gun. Several rounds were fired at a target some 2,500 yards distant, and "the armoured train passed through the searching and severe ordeal most successfully, the jar caused being so slight that a stone placed on the rails remained unmoved by the firing." The truck, it is further stated, had been provided with some cross girders which could be run out and supported on blocks in order to secure a broad base when the gun was fired at right angles to the line, and there was a further arrangement for connecting the truck to the rails by strong clips; but the truck remained sufficiently steady without any need for making use of these appliances.

Finally, as will be told more fully in Chapter XVI, the *South African Campaign of 1899–1902* definitely established the usefulness of armoured trains as an "instrument of war," and led both to the creation of an efficient organisation for their employment on the most scientific and most practical lines and to the establishment of certain principles in regard to such important matters of detail as uses and purposes, administration, staff, armament, tactics, etc. Published in the "Detailed History of the Railways in the South African War" which was issued by the Royal Engineers' Institute, Chatham, in 1905, these principles were adopted in the *United States* with modifications to suit American conditions, and, so modified, are reproduced in

Major William D. Connor's handbook on "Military Railways," forming No 32 of the Professional Papers of the Corps of Engineers, U.S. Army. An excellent treatment of the subject, from a technical point of view, will be found in a paper, by Capt. H. O. Nance, on "Armoured Trains," published, with photographs and drawings, in "Papers of the Corps of Royal Engineers," Fourth Series, Vol. I., Paper 4 (Chatham, 1906).

CHAPTER VIII

Railway Ambulance Transport

ACCORDING to statistics which have been compiled in relation to wars alike in ancient and in modern times, for every ten men among the armies in the field who have died from wounds received in battle there have been from thirty-five to forty who died from sickness or disease. Writing in the *Journal des Sciences Militaires*, Dr. Morache, a surgeon in the French Army, has said that while the total number of deaths among combatants taking part in the Crimean War was 95,000, no fewer than 70,000 were due to typhus, scurvy, cholera or other diseases. In the Italian campaign of 1859 the French lost 5,498 men, of whom 2,500 died from sickness. On the conclusion of the Russo-Turkish War the Russians had 51,000 of their troops sick, the ravages of typhus having been especially severe.

These conditions have been materially aggravated by the gathering together of great numbers of sick and wounded into overcrowded hospitals situate on or near to the theatre of war and destined inevitably to become hot-beds of disease and pestilence far more dangerous to human life, under these conditions, than even the most deadly weapons which the art of war had invented for use on the battle-field itself.

Nor was it the armies alone that suffered. Returning troops spread the seeds of disease among the civil population, causing epidemics that lingered, in some instances, for several years and carried off many thousands of non-combatants, in addition to the great number of victims among the combatants themselves. In a volume of 866 pages, published by Dr. E. Gurlt, under the title of " Zur Geschichte der Internationellen und Freiwilligen Krankenpflege im Kriege " (Leipzig, 1873), will be found many terrible details concerning the ravages in France, Germany and Austria of the typhus which Napoleon's troops brought back with them on the occasion of their disastrous retreat from Russia.

The most practicable means of mitigating, if not of avoiding, these various evils is to be found in the prompt removal of the sick and wounded from the theatre of war, and their distribution in smaller units, not simply among a group of neighbouring towns, but over an area extending to considerable distances inland. The adoption of this remedy only became possible, however, with a provision of adequate rail facilities, and even then many years were to elapse before an efficient system of railway ambulance transport was finally evolved.

The objects which the use of the railway in these directions was to attain were alike humanitarian and strategical.

To the sick and wounded among the troops, prompt removal and wide-spread distribution among hospitals in the interior meant (1) that they avoided the risks to which they would have been subjected in the aforesaid overcrowded and pestilential hospitals near the fighting line, where slight injuries might readily develop dangerous symptoms, and contagious disease complete the conditions leading to a fatal issue; (2) that, apart from these considerations, it would be possible to give them a greater degree of individual attention if they were distributed among a large number of hospitals away from the scene of the fighting; (3) that more conservative methods of surgery became practicable when operations of a kind not to be attempted either on the battle-field or in temporary hospitals (from which the inmates might have to be suddenly removed, owing to some change in the strategical position) could be delayed until the sufferer's arrival at some hospital in the interior, where better appliances and better facilities would be available, and where, after the operation, the patient would be able to remain undisturbed until he was cured; (4) that these improved conditions might more especially permit of the avoidance of amputations otherwise imperatively necessary; and (5) that, on the whole, the wounded soldier was afforded a better chance of effecting a speedy recovery

RAILWAY AMBULANCE TRANSPORT. 83

and of saving both life and limb than would be possible if railways were not available.

To the army in the field the innovation meant that with the speedy removal of the sick and wounded it would be relieved of the great source of embarrassment caused by the presence and dependence upon it of so many inefficients ;[1] depôt and intermediate hospitals could be reduced to the smallest proportions, and would thus occasion less inconvenience if, owing to a retreat or a change in the strategical position, they were brought within the sphere of military operations ; with the delegation of so many of the sick and wounded to the care of civil practitioners in the interior, fewer of the divisional, brigade and regimental medical officers would require to be detached from the marching column ; a smaller supplementary medical staff would suffice ; a considerable reduction could be effected in the stocks of ambulance supplies kept on hand at the front ; while important strategical advantages would be gained through (1) the greater freedom of movement which the army would secure ; (2) the decreased risk of the number of efficients being reduced through the outbreak of epidemics ; and (3) the prospect of a large proportion of the sick and wounded being enabled to rejoin the fighting force on their making a speedy recovery from their illness or their wounds.

The earliest occasion on which the railway was made use of for the conveyance of sick and wounded from a scene of actual hostilities to the rear was on the occasion of the *Crimean War*, when the little military line between Balaklava and the camp before Sebastopol, of which an account will be given in Chapter XV, was so employed. The facilities afforded were, however, of the most primitive character. Only the wagons used for the transport of supplies to the front—wagons, that is to say, little better than those known as " contractors' trucks "—were available, and there were no means of adapting them to the conveyance of sufferers who could not be moved otherwise than in a recum-

---

[1] A saying attributed to Napoleon is that he preferred a dead soldier to a wounded one.

bent position. Sitting-up cases could, therefore, alone be carried ; but what was to develop into a revolution in the conditions of warfare was thus introduced, all the same.

In the *Italian war of 1859* both the French and the Austrians made use of the railways for the withdrawal of their sick and wounded, and, in his " Souvenir de Solferino," Jean Henri Dumant, the " Father " of the Red Cross Movement, speaks of the transportation of wounded from Brescia to Milan by train to the extent of about 1,000 a night. No arrangements for their comfort on the journey had been made in advance, and the changes in the military situation were so rapid, when hostilities broke out, that no special facilities could be provided then. All that was done was to lay down straw on the floor of the goods or cattle trucks used for the conveyance of some of the more serious cases. The remainder travelled in ordinary third-class carriages, and their sufferings on the journey, before they reached the long and narrow sheds put up along the railway lines at Milan or elsewhere to serve as temporary hospitals, must often have been very great. They may, nevertheless, have escaped the fate of those who died, not from their wounds, but from the fevers quickly generated in the overcrowded hospitals at the front, where there was, besides, a general deficiency of ambulance requirements of all kinds. The good resulting from the removal by train is, indeed, said to have been " immense."

These experiences in the campaign of 1859 led to a recommendation being made in the following year by a *German* medical authority, Dr. E. Gurlt,[1] that railway vehicles should be specially prepared for the conveyance of the sick and wounded in time of war. The plan which he himself suggested for adoption was the placing of the sufferers in hammocks suspended from hooks driven into the roof of the goods van or carriage employed, mattresses being first put on the hammocks, when necessary. By this

---

[1] " Ueber den Transport Schwerverwundeter und Kranker im Kriege, nebst Vorschlägen über die Benutzung der Eisenbahnen dabei." 33 pp. Berlin, 1860.

means, he suggested, the sufferers would travel much more comfortably than when seated in the ordinary passenger carriages, or when lying on straw in the goods wagons or cattle trucks.

Dr. Gurlt's pamphlet served the good purpose of drawing much attention to the subject, and his proposals were duly subjected to the test of experiment. They failed, however, on two grounds,—(1) because the roofs of the goods vans, designed for shelter only, were not sufficiently strong to bear the weight of a number of men carried in the way suggested; and (2) because the motion of the train caused the hammocks to come into frequent contact with the sides of the wagon, to the serious discomfort of the occupants.

In November of the same year (1860) the Prussian War Minister, von Roon, appointed a Commission to enquire into the whole subject of the care of the sick and wounded in time of war, and the question of transport by rail was among the various matters considered. As a result of these investigations, the Minister issued, on July 1, 1861, an order to the effect that in future the less seriously wounded should travel in ordinary first, second or third-class carriages, according to the degree of comfort they required, care being taken to let them have corner seats; while for those who were seriously ill, or badly wounded, there were to be provided sacks of straw having three canvas loops on each side for the insertion of poles by means of which the sacks and the sufferers lying upon them could be readily lifted in or out of the goods wagons set apart for their conveyance. In these wagons they were to be placed on the floor in such a way that each wagon would accommodate either seven or eight. In the event of a deficiency of sacks, loose straw was to be used instead. The door on one side of the truck was to be left open for ventilation. A doctor and attendants were to accompany each train, and they were to have a supply of bandages, medicines and appliances. Of the last-mentioned a list of five articles was appended as obligatory. The medical officer was to visit the wagons during the stoppages, and the attendants on duty in the wagons were to carry flags so that, when necessary, they could signal both for the train to pull up and for the doctor to come to the sufferers.

This was as far as Prussia had got by 1861, when the arrangements stated were regarded as quite sufficient to meet the requirements of the situation. Real progress was to come, rather, from the other side of the Atlantic.

In the early days of the *War of Secession* (1861-65) the arrangements for the conveyance by rail of the sick and wounded from the battle-fields of the Eastern States to the hospitals in the large cities were still distinctly primitive. Those who could sit up in the ordinary cars were conveyed in them. Those who could not sit up, or would be injured by so doing, were carried to the railway, by hand, on the mattresses or stretchers they had occupied in the hospitals to which they had first been taken. At the station the mattresses were placed on thick layers of straw or hay strewn over the floors of the freight cars in which supplies had been brought to the front. Large window spaces were cut in the sides or ends of the cars to provide for ventilation. On some occasions, when hay or straw was not available, pine boughs or leaves were used instead. As only the floor space was occupied no more than about ten patients could be carried comfortably in each car, though as many as twenty were occasionally crowded in. The wide doors of the box cars readily permitted of the beds being lifted in or out. Medical officers, with supplies, accompanied each train. On arrival at New York, Washington, Philadelphia, Harrisburg, or other destination, the sufferers were taken out and carried, still on the same mattresses or stretchers, to the hospitals there.

Large numbers of sick or wounded were conveyed by rail under one or other of these conditions, and the work was done with great expedition. Between the morning of June 12 and the evening of June 14, 1863, over 9,000 wounded, victims of the Federal disaster at Chancellorsville, were taken by the single-track Aquia Creek railroad from Aquia Creek to Washington. Many even of the severely wounded declared they had suffered no inconvenience from the journey. After the battle of Gettysburg, July 1-3, 1863, more than 15,000 wounded had been sent by rail from the field hospitals to Baltimore, New York, Harrisburg or Philadelphia by July 22. An even more rapid distribution was effected after the battles of the Wilderness and Spottsylvania when, with a few exceptions, the transfer to the hospitals in the cities mentioned was effected in the course of a few days. Following on the battle of Olustree (February 20, 1864), the serious cases were removed on the Mobile Railway by freight cars bedded with pine boughs, palmetto leaves and a small quantity of straw, each patient having a blanket, in addition.

As an improvement on these methods of transport, the plan was adopted of fixing rows of upright wooden posts, connecting floor and ceiling, on each side of a car as supports for two or three tiers of rough wooden bunks, a central gangway through the car being left. In this way the available space in the car was much better utilised than with the straw-on-floor system. Next, in place of the bunks, came an arrangement by which the stretchers whereon the patients lay could be securely lashed to the uprights; while this was followed, in turn, by the insertion of wooden pegs into the uprights and the placing on them of large and strong india-rubber rings into which the handles of the stretchers could readily be slipped, and so suspended. The first car so arranged came into use in March, 1863.

Meanwhile the Philadelphia Railroad Company had, at the end of 1862, fitted up an ambulance car on the principle of a sleeping car, but so planned that the stretchers on which the sufferers lay could be made to slide in or out of the wooden supports. This particular car was capable of accommodating fifty-one patients, in addition to a seat at each end for an attendant. Other innovations introduced on the car were (1) a stove at which soups could be warmed or tea made; (2) a water tank, and (3) a locker.

What the introducers of these improvements mainly prided themselves upon was the fact that the patient could remain, throughout the entire journey from field hospital to destination, on the stretcher he had been placed on at the start. The adoption of this principle necessitated, however, uniformity in the dimensions of the stretchers in order that these could always be accommodated on the ambulance-car fittings.

The next important development was reached when the ambulance *car*, run in connection with ordinary trains, and used for exceptionally severe cases, was succeeded by the ambulance *train*. Here came further innovations, the nine or ten " ward-cars," of which such a train mainly consisted in the Eastern States, being supplemented by others fitted up as dispensary and store-room, kitchen, and quarters for surgeon, attendants, and staff of train, besides carrying all necessary appliances and provisions for the journey.

What was now specially aimed at was to make the train as close an approach to an actual hospital on wheels as circumstances would permit. " At present," wrote the Medical Director of the Department of Washington, " the sick and wounded are transferred in cars ill-adapted for the purpose and with difficulty spared from the other pressing demands ; and lives are lost on the route not infrequently which, in all probability, might be saved by a more comfortable and easy method of transportation." The train he caused to be constructed consisted of ten ward-cars, one car for the surgeon and attendants, one as a dispensary and store-room, and one as a kitchen, etc. The ward-cars, arranged on an improved principle, each accommodated thirty recumbent and twenty or thirty seated patients. The train was to run regularly on the Orange and Alexandria Railroad between the theatre of war and the base hospitals at Alexandria and Washington. It was either to supplement or to supersede the freight cars with their bedding of straw, hay or leaves. If only from the point of view of the inadequate supply of rolling stock, a car fitted up to accommodate fifty or sixty patients offered an obvious advantage, in the speedy removal and distribution of sick and wounded, over a car, without fittings, in which the floor space alone could be utilised.

Several complete trains of the type stated were soon running on the Orange and Alexandria Railroad, within the Union lines, and the hospital train thus became an established institution in modern warfare.

It was, however, in connection with the chief army in the West, the Army of the Cumberland, operating under General George H. Thomas, that the useful purposes which could be served by hospital trains became most conspicuous.

The need for them in the West was even greater than in the East, because the distances to be covered were greater and lay, also, to a considerable extent, in enemy country.

In the fall of 1863 and the winter of 1864, as narrated in the "Medical and Surgical History of the War of the Rebellion," the chief army of the West was concentrated principally along the line of railroads leading from Nashville, Tennessee, to the South-west, viâ Chattanooga, Tenn., and onwards towards Atlanta, Georgia. At the outset the sick and wounded who could travel in ordinary passenger cars to points in the North were so taken. Severe cases had to remain in the nearest available hospital depôt. In addition to the discomfort suffered by the former in having to travel in cars not suited to invalids, they were liable to frequent and prolonged delays on the single-track lines by reason of the constant passing of supply trains proceeding to the front; and not unfrequently the detentions were at points where nothing could be obtained for feeding the sufferers or making them comfortable, while even if rations could be drawn the train afforded no means of cooking them. So it was resolved to have a train which would be the equivalent of an ambulating, self-contained hospital, capable of carrying both recumbent and sitting-up patients and supplying all their wants on the journey.

On August 11, 1863, instructions were sent from the Assistant-Surgeon-General's Office to the Medical Officer of the Army of the Cumberland directing him "to take immediate measures to fit up a special train for hospital purposes, with every possible comfort," to run between Nashville, Ten., and Louisville, Ken. General Thomas, in turn, accorded the fullest authority to the Medical Officer to select for the purpose the best locomotives and the best cars to be found among the railway rolling stock, and to have new cars fitted up whenever necessary. He further directed that the most experienced drivers, conductors and other necessary railway employés should be selected for the conduct of the hospital-train service.

Three of these trains were ready by the spring of 1864, and they ran regularly—each taking a section of the journey—between Atlanta and Louisville, a distance of 472 miles. They consisted, apparently, in part of specially-built and in part of adapted rolling stock, the large open American passenger cars, with their greater freedom from internal fittings than ordinary European railway carriages, lending themselves specially to the purpose. In the converted passenger cars the carrying of the stretchers through the end doors was avoided by removing two windows and the panelling underneath them from the side of the car, and making an opening 6 ft. in width which could be closed by a sliding door. Each train provided five ward-cars (converted passenger cars) for lying-down patients; a surgeon's car (a passenger car from which the seats had been removed, with partitions and fittings for the accommodation of the doctor and his helpers); a dispensary car (in which an ample supply of medicines, instruments and appliances was carried); an ordinary passenger car for sitting-up patients or convalescents; a kitchen car (divided into kitchen, dining-room and store-room); and a conductor's car. The kitchen car was supplied with a small cooking range, boilers, and other requisites for the feeding of from 175 to 200 patients. The cars were warmed and lighted in winter, and special attention was paid to ventilation, so that Dr. F. L. Town, of the United States Army, was able to report of them:—" In visiting these hospital trains, the air is found sweet and pure, the wards are neat and inviting; and it may unhesitatingly be said that men on hospital trains are often as comfortable and better fed and attended than in many permanent hospitals." The trains had distinguishing signals which were recognised by the Confederates, and none of them were ever fired on or molested in any way.

One, at least, of the trains was despatched daily from the vicinity of the field hospitals. The services rendered by them during the last eighteen months of the war were of the greatest value. It has been said, indeed, that the combined effect of all the provision made for the care of the sick and wounded and their speedy recovery—including therein, as one of the most important items, their prompt removal and distribution by rail—was to ensure for the Federals the retention of a force equal in itself to an army of 100,000 men. No single fact could show more conclusively the *strategical* as well as the humanitarian value of railway ambulance transport.

These details as to what was accomplished in the American Civil War are the more deserving of record because they show that the evolution of the " hospital on wheels," from the initial conditions of a bedding of straw on the floor of a railway goods wagon, was really carried out, step by step, in all its essential details, in the United States. The hospital train was thus *not* an English invention, as is widely assumed to be the case ; though much was to be done here to improve its construction, equipment and organisation.

Whilst America had been gaining all this very practical experience, the *Danish War of 1864* had given Prussia the opportunity of testing the system approved by her in 1861 for the conveyance of the less severely wounded in ordinary passenger carriages and of the seriously wounded on sacks of straw laid on the floor of goods wagons. The results were found so unsatisfactory that on the conclusion of hostilities a fresh series of investigations and experiments was begun, and matters were still at this stage when war broke out between Prussia and Austria.

The conditions in regard to the care of the sick and wounded in the *campaign of 1866* were deplorably defective. Not only, according to Dr. T. W. Evans [1]—an American medical man, settled in Paris, who visited the battle-field and assisted in the work of relief—was there no advance on what had been done in the United States, but the American example was in no way followed, the combatants having made no attempt whatever to profit from her experience.

[1] " Les Institutions Sanitaires pendant le Conflit Austro-Prussien-Italien." Par Thomas W. Evans. Paris, 1867.

After the battle of Sadowa, thousands of wounded were left on the battle-field, and many remained there three days and three nights before they could be removed in the carts and wagons which were alone available for the purpose. Within five days every village in a radius of four leagues was crowded with wounded. Those taken to Dresden and Prague in ordinary passenger carriages or goods vans were detained for days on the journey owing to the congestion of traffic on the lines. Some of them, also, were in the trains for two days before their wounds were dressed. Then the use of straw, depended on by the Austrians, was found to be unsatisfactory. It failed to afford the sufferers a sufficient protection against the jolting of the wagons, especially when they worked through it to the bare boards; and even then there was not always sufficient straw available to meet requirements. Altogether, it is declared, the wounded suffered "unheard-of tortures."

Shortly after the conclusion of the war there was appointed in *Prussia* a further Commission of medical and military authorities to renew the investigation into the care and transport of sick and wounded. The Commission sat from March 18 to May 5, 1867. In the result it still favoured the use of sacks of straw, with canvas loops, as the simplest and most comfortable method to adopt for the rail transport of recumbent sufferers, though it recommended that the sacks should be made with side pieces, giving them the form of paillasses, as this would afford a greater degree of support to those lying on them. The American system of suspending stretchers in tiers by means of india-rubber rings depending from pegs let into wooden uprights was disapproved of, partly because of the continuous swinging of the stretchers so carried, and partly because of the assumed discomfort to one set of patients of having others just above them. The report also recommended the adoption of the following principles :—(1) Through communication between all the carriages employed in one and the same train for the conveyance of sick and wounded ; (2) provision, for the severely wounded, either of beds with springs or of litters suspended from the roof or the sides of the carriages ; and

(3) extra carriages for the accommodation of doctor, nurses, surgical appliances, medical stores, cooking utensils, etc.

These principles were subjected to various tests, and it was found that in Germany the existing carriages which could best be adapted to the desired purpose were those belonging to the fourth-class, inasmuch as they had no internal divisions or fittings, travellers by them being expected either to stand during the journey or to sit on their luggage. The only structural alteration necessary was the placing of the doors at the end of the carriages instead of at the sides, so that, on opening these end doors, and letting down a small bridge to be provided for the purpose, access could readily be obtained from one carriage to another. Instructions were accordingly given that all fourth-class carriages on the Prussian railways should thenceforward have end doors—an arrangement which had, in fact, already been adopted in South Germany. Steps were also taken in Prussia to adapt goods vans and horse boxes for the conveyance of sick and wounded in the event of the number of fourth-class carriages not being sufficient to meet requirements.

The widespread interest which was being attracted throughout Europe to the subject of the care of the sick and wounded in war led to a series of experimental trials being carried out at the *Paris International Exhibition of 1867*, when, with the help of a short line of railway laid down in the exhibition grounds and of a goods wagon supplied by the Western of France Railway Company, a number of different systems were tested. On this occasion, also, a model of an American car fitted up with india-rubber rings for the handles of stretchers was shown.

At this time, and for many years afterwards, the ideal arrangement was considered, on the Continent of Europe, to be one under which railway vehicles sent to the front with troops, supplies or munitions could be readily adapted for bringing back the sick and wounded on the return journey; and alike in Germany, Russia, France, Austria and Italy the respective merits of a great variety of internal fittings designed to adapt existing rolling stock, whether passenger coaches, luggage vans, Post Office vans or goods wagons, to the serving of these dual purposes formed the subject of much experiment and controversy. Rope cables across the roof of a goods wagon, with dependent loops of rope for the reception of the stretcher handles (as in the Zavodovski method); stretchers laid on springs on the floor, suspended from the roof either by strong springs or by rope, resting on brackets attached to the sides, or partly resting and partly suspended; and collapsible frames of various kinds, each had their respective advocates.[1] The use and equipment of ambulance or hospital trains constituted, also, a regular subject of discussion at all the international congresses of Red Cross Societies which have been held since 1869.

The experimental trials at the Paris Exhibition of 1867 were followed by the appointment in *Prussia* of still another Commission of inquiry, and, acting on the recommendations of this body, the Prussian Government adopted the "Grund" system, under which the stretchers whereon the recumbent sufferers lay in the goods wagons or fourth-class carriages were placed on poles resting in slots over the convexity of laminated springs having one end screwed into the floor while the other, and free, end was provided with a roller designed to respond to the varying conditions of weight by sliding to and fro. This was the system mainly used in the "sanitary trains" of the Germans in the *Franco-Prussian War of 1870–71*. It was criticised on the ground (1) that the sick and wounded were still subject to the same jolts and concussions as ordinary seated passengers; (2) that the number who could be carried per carriage or wagon was very small, since it was still the case that only the floor space was utilised; and (3) that it was inconvenient for the doctor and the attendants to have to kneel down in

---

[1] For "A short consideration and comparison of the regulations for the transport of sick and wounded by rail, as laid down in four of the leading Continental armies (the German, French, Austrian and Italian)," see a paper on "Continental Regulations for the Transport of Sick and Wounded by Rail," by Surg.-Capt. C. H. Melville, A.M.S., *Royal United Service Institution Journal*, vol. 42 (1898), pp. 560–594.

RAILWAY AMBULANCE TRANSPORT.   95

order to attend to the patients.[1] Apart from these disadvantages, the ambulance service of the Germans was well organised during the war. Of ambulance trains, fitted up more or less as complete travelling hospitals, twenty-one were run, and the total number of sufferers removed by rail is said to have been over 89,000.

Owing to traffic congestions, the transport to Berlin of wounded from the army engaged in the investment of Paris occupied no less a period than six days; but these journeys were made in the special ambulance trains which, provided in the later stages of the war, ensured full provision for the feeding, nursing and general comfort of the sufferers. The fact that such journeys could be undertaken at all showed the great advance which had been made since the battle of Sadowa, when most of the wounded could be conveyed no further than to cottages and farm-houses in neighbouring villages.

In the *South-African War of 1899-1902* the system favoured was that of having hospital trains either expressly built for the purpose or adapted from ordinary rolling stock and devoted exclusively, for the duration of the war, to the conveyance of the sick and wounded. The "Princess Christian" hospital train, specially constructed for the British Central Red Cross Committee by the Birmingham Railway Carriage and Wagon Company Ltd., according to the plans of Sir John Furley and Mr. W. J. Fieldhouse, and sent out to South Africa early in 1900, consisted of seven carriages, each about 36 ft. in length, and 8 ft. in width,

---

[1] In an article on "Military Hospital Trains; their Origin and Progress," in *The Railway Gazette* of December 4, 1914, it is said: "The comparatively small loss of the Germans by death from wounds in 1870 was due solely to the fact that they entered upon the war with what were then considered wonderfully elaborate arrangements for removing the wounded. . . . The trains were composed partly of first-class carriages, for the less badly wounded, and partly of covered goods wagons. . . . In these covered vans were placed beds formed of boards laid on springs. Each van would hold four or five men, and a sister rode in the van." One would not, however, consider to-day that there was anything wonderfully elaborate in an arrangement under which no more than four or five sufferers were accommodated in each goods van.

for running on the Cape standard gauge of 3ft. 6in. The carriages were arranged as follows :—I., divided into three compartments for (*a*) linen and other stores, (*b*) two nurses and (*c*) two invalid officers ; II., also divided into three compartments, for (*a*) two medical officers ; (*b*) dining-room and (*c*) dispensary ; III., IV., V., and VI., ward-cars for invalids, carried on beds arranged in three tiers ; VII., kitchen, pantry, and a compartment for the guard. The train carried everything that was necessary for patients and staff even though they might be cut off from other sources of supply for a period of two or three weeks.

Seven other hospital trains, all adapted from existing rolling stock in Cape Colony or Natal, were made available for the transport of sick and wounded in the same war. One of these, No. 4, was arranged and equipped at the cost of the British Central Red Cross Committee, under the direction of Sir John Furley, then acting as the Society's Chief Commissioner in South Africa. The arrangement of the other converted trains was carried out by the Army Medical Service in South Africa, with the co-operation of the Government Railway officials in Cape Town and Natal. A number of specially-fitted carriages, placed at convenient distances on the railways occupied by the British, were made use of to pick up small parties of sick from the various posts along the lines, such carriages being attached to passing trains for the conveyance of the sufferers to the nearest hospital. Many of them had a regular service up and down a particular stretch of railway. Some were provided with iron frames for the support of service stretchers, and others were fitted up similarly to the ward-carriages of the converted hospital trains. Convalescents and "sitting-up" patients for whom no special accommodation was necessary travelled in such ordinary trains as might be available.

In effect, there are four classes of trains by which, under the conditions of to-day, the sick and wounded may be despatched from the seat of war :—(1) Permanent hospital trains, specially constructed for the purpose ; (2) temporary hospital trains, made up either entirely of converted ordinary vehicles or partly of converted and partly of specially-constructed rolling stock, their use for this purpose continuing for the duration of the war; (3) ambulance trains improvised at rail-head out of rolling stock bringing troops, supplies and stores to the front, the internal fittings for "lying-down" cases being of such a kind that they can be readily fixed or dismantled; and (4) ordinary passenger carriages for slightly wounded or convalescents.

The advantages conferred on armies from a strategical point of view, under all these improved conditions, are no less beyond dispute than the benefits conferred on the individual soldiers, and if railways had done no more in regard to the conduct of warfare than ensure these dual results, they would still have rendered a service of incalculable value. While, also, their provision of an efficient ambulance transport system, with its speedy removal of non-effectives, has served the purposes of war, it has, in addition, by its regard for the sick and wounded themselves, further served to relieve warfare of some, at least, of its horrors.

CHAPTER IX

PREPARATION IN PEACE FOR WAR

THE greater the experience gained of the application of rail-power in practice, and the closer the study devoted to its possibilities, in theory, the more obvious it became that the fullest degree of advantage to be derived therefrom could only be assured as the result of preparation and organisation in peace; and this conclusion appeared specially to apply to countries whose geographical and political conditions led them to regard it as expedient that they should always be ready to meet some great national emergency. The Federal Government of the United States certainly did succeed, in the early sixties, in creating an excellent military rail-transport organisation after hostilities had broken out; but the conditions of warfare to-day make it essentially necessary that arrangements for the use of railways for military purposes should, as far as possible, be planned, perfected or provided for long in advance of any possible outbreak of hostilities.

Among other considerations which strengthen this view are the following :—

I. The increasing dependence of armies on rail transport owing to (a) the vastly greater number of troops employed now than in former days; (b) the supreme importance of time as a factor in enabling a Commander-in-Chief to effect, possibly, an earlier concentration than the enemy, and so obtain the power of initiative; and (c) the magnitude of the supplies, munitions and other necessaries wanted to meet the daily wants of the prodigious forces in the field, and only to be assured by the employment of rail transport from a more or less distant base.

PREPARATION IN PEACE FOR WAR.   99

II. The complications, confusion and possible chaos which may result if, without prior preparation, railway lines designed to serve ordinary transport purposes are suddenly required to meet military demands taxing their resources to the utmost extreme.

III. The further troubles that will assuredly arise if, in the absence of efficient control by properly-constituted and responsible intermediaries, railwaymen unfamiliar with military technicalities are left to deal with the possibly conflicting and impracticable orders of individual military officers themselves unfamiliar with the technicalities and limitations of railway working.

IV. The imperative necessity of having an organised and well-regulated system of forwarding military supplies, etc., in order both to avoid congestion of stations and lines and to ensure the punctual arrival of those supplies in the right quantities, at the right spot, and at the right time.

V. The need, in view of the vital importance of the part that railways may play in war, of having organised forces of railway troops and railway workers available, together with stores of materials and appliances, to carry out, speedily and thoroughly, all the work that may be necessary for the repair, construction or destruction of railway lines.

In making the necessary preparations, in time of peace, to ensure the successful realisation of these and other purposes, there is a vast amount of work that requires to be done.

In readiness for the excessive strain that will be thrown on the railways as soon as they pass from a peace footing to a war footing, on the order being given for mobilisation, the military authorities and the railway authorities must needs have at their command the fullest information as to the physical conditions, the resources and the transport capabilities of every line of railway in the country which, directly or indirectly, may be able to render useful service. Details as to double or single track; gradients; number of locomotives, carriages, wagons, horse-boxes and other vehicles available; and facilities afforded by stations in important centres as regards number and length of platforms and sidings, water supply, loading, unloading or storage accommodation, etc., are all carefully compiled and kept up to date. As regards rolling stock, lines not likely to be called upon to carry any military transports at all may still be able to contribute to the supply of carriages and wagons wanted to meet the heavy demands on other railways. By including all lines of railway in the collected data, it will be known exactly where additional rolling stock may be obtained if wanted. The carrying capacity of the different types of carriages, trucks, etc., is also noted. If necessary, arrangements will be made for the reduction of gradients, the improvement of curves, the construction of connecting links between different main lines, the lengthening of station platforms, or the provision of increased loading or unloading facilities.

On the basis of the information collected elaborate calculations are made in regard to such matters as (1) the number of vehicles required for a given number of men, with horses, guns, munitions, stores, road vehicles, etc., so that rolling stock can be used to the best advantage and according as to whether the troops carried belong to the Infantry, Cavalry or the Artillery; (2) the number of vehicles that can be made up into a train going by any one route; (3) the length of time likely to be taken for the entraining and detraining respectively of a given unit; (4) the time intervals at which a succession of troop trains can follow one another on the same line; (5) the speed of troop trains; and (6) the further intervals to be allowed in the arrival at one and the same station, or centre, of a number of trains starting from different points, so as to avoid the risk of congestion and of consequent delays.

Military time-tables, corresponding to those in everyday use, have next to be prepared, showing exactly what trains must run from given stations, at fixed hours, by clearly defined routes, to specified destinations as soon as the occasion arises. The great aim kept in view in the compilation of these time-tables is, not alone preparation in advance, but the most complete utilisation possible of the available transport facilities of the country as a whole.

PREPARATION IN PEACE FOR WAR.

A selection must also be made in advance of the stations at which troops on long journeys can obtain food, as well as of the stations to be used as depôts for stores and supplies, all the necessary arrangements being provided for.

After the initial great strain on the railway resources involved in mobilisation and concentration, there will still be an enormous amount of transport to be done during the campaign. In the one direction there will be a constant despatch of reinforcements, provisions, clothing, munitions and supplies or stores to the front; in the other direction there will be a steady flow of sick and wounded, of prisoners of war, and of materiel not wanted at the front, followed by the final return home of the troops at the end of the campaign.

At each important point along the lines of communication where special services in connection with the rail transport, in either direction, are to be rendered, there must be organisation of such kind as will ensure that whatever is necessary shall be done promptly and efficiently under the control of persons of recognised authority and responsibility, and without any of the friction that would, inevitably, lead to delays, traffic blocks and other complications.

Nor can the same system of organisation apply to the whole line of communication, from the base to the limit of the rail service at the front. A point will be reached therein where the control, if not the actual operation, of the railway lines must needs be transferred from the civil to the military authorities, rendering necessary a scheme of supervision and working different from that which can be followed on the sections not within the actual theatre of war.

Then, if the army should be compelled to retreat before the enemy, there should be available a sufficiency of forces skilled in the art of rapidly and effectively destroying lines, bridges, viaducts, tunnels, or other railway property, with a view to retarding the enemy's movements until, it may be, reinforcements can be brought up in sufficient number to check his further progress. If, alternatively, the army should advance into the enemy's country, there must again be a provision of Railway Troops fully qualified by previous training and experience both to repair quickly the demolitions or the damage which the enemy will have carried out on his own lines and to construct hastily such new lines—light railways or otherwise—as the circumstances of the moment require. These things done, and still further advance being made into the invaded territory, the need will also arise for a staff capable of operating, under war conditions, the lines of which possession has been taken, in order that communications with the advanced front and the forwarding of reinforcements and supplies can still be maintained.

All these and many other things, besides, must needs be thought out and prepared for in time of peace, long in advance of any probable or even any possible war. They are, in fact, made the subject of exhaustive and continuous study alike by military officers specially entrusted with the task and by railway managers commanding all the technical knowledge requisite for making arrangements calculated to ensure the prompt and efficient satisfaction of all such demands for military rail-transport as may, with whatever urgency, and under whatever conditions, some day be put forward.

Still more practical do the preparations in peace for war become when they include the construction of a network of strategical railways expressly designed to facilitate the mobilisation of troops, their speedy concentration on the frontier, or their movement from one point of attack to another at the theatre of war.

CHAPTER X

ORGANISATION IN GERMANY

IN no country in the world was the desirability of preparing in time of peace for military rail-transport in time of war recognised earlier than in Germany. In none has the practice of such preparation in peace been followed up with greater study and persistence.

As shown in Chapter I, the military use of railways led to the proposal and discussion in Germany of definite schemes for such use as early as 1833; and it is not too much to say that, from that date down to the outbreak of the World-War in 1914, the whole subject had received there an ever-increasing degree of attention from the military authorities, and, also, from a large body of writers as a question of the day in its relation more especially to German expansion.

One great mistake, however, made alike by historians, by writers in the Press, and by popular tradition, has been the attributing to Germany of a far higher degree of credit in regard to the alleged perfection of her preparations for the *Franco-Prussian War of 1870-71* than she was really entitled to claim. Nor, indeed, has the fact been sufficiently recognised that the organisation eventually elaborated by Germany for the efficient conduct of her rail-transport in war had been evolved from studies, investigations, trials, experiments and tests (in actual warfare or otherwise) extending over a period of half a century or more, during which time, also, there was issued a bewildering mass of laws, rules and regulations, each more or less modifying those that had gone before and adding still further to the elaborate, if not the extremely complicated, machinery laboriously built up as the result of the universally recognised genius of the German people for organisation.

The final great test of all this machinery was to be applied in 1914. Here, however, it must suffice, for present purposes, to show how the machinery itself was created and the form it finally assumed.

Down to 1861 Prussia had done no more, in the way of organising military transport by rail, than issue a series of Ordinances dealing with the movement of large bodies of troops, such Ordinances being akin to those which all the leading countries of Europe had either compiled or were engaged in compiling. Directly influenced by the developments of the Civil War in America, Prussia took the further step, in 1864, of forming a Railway Section of her General Staff. This new body was actively employed in the furtherance of Prussia's interests in the Danish War of the same year, when confirmatory evidence was given of the advantages to be derived from the use of rail transport for military movements, journeys that would have taken the troops sixteen days by road being done within six days by rail.

The organisation thus applied on a comparatively small scale in 1864 was further developed by Prussia in the *campaign of 1866*.

On that occasion mobilisation and concentration of the Prussian troops were both carried out mainly by rail, under the direction of an Executive Commission consisting of an officer of the General Staff and a representative of the Ministry of Commerce. This Executive Commission sat in Berlin, and was assisted by Line Commissions operating on the different railways utilised for military purposes. Movements of troops by rail were certainly effected in one-third of the time they would have taken by road, while the Prussians, gaining a great advantage, by the rapidity of such movements, over Austria, routed her combined forces within seven days of crossing the frontier, and dictated terms of peace to her within a month.

Some serious faults were nevertheless developed, even in the course of this very short campaign, in Prussia's rail-

ORGANISATION IN GERMANY.   105

transport arrangements, such being especially the case in regard to the forwarding of supplies. These were rushed to the front in excess of immediate requirements, the only concern of contractors or of officers at the base being to get them away, while the railway companies—bound to accept goods for transport and delivery as ordered—dispatched them without regard for any possible deficiency in the unloading and storage arrangements at the other end. The supplies, forwarded in bulk, followed as close up behind the troops as they could be taken; but the provision made for unloading was inadequate, the railway staffs disclaimed responsibility for the work, and, before long, stations and sidings at the front were hopelessly blocked, although elsewhere the shortage of wagons was so great that everything was at a standstill. Even when wagons had been unloaded, they were too often left on the lines, in long trains of empties, instead of being sent where they were most needed. Each railway company disposed of its own rolling stock independently of the other companies, adopting the view that it had no concern with what was happening elsewhere. In some instances special trains were dispatched for the conveyance of a few hundred men or a few hundredweights of stores. Orders which should have gone direct from one responsible person to another went through a variety of channels with the result that serious delays and no less serious blunders occurred. One East Prussian Battalion, for instance, was sent off by train in a direction exactly opposite to that which it should have taken.

All these and other troubles experienced were directly due to the absence of a central controlling body formed on such a basis that it could (1) govern the rail-transport arrangements as a whole; (2) supervise the forwarding of supplies; (3) provide for a proper distribution, and better utilisation, of rolling stock; (3) secure the prompt unloading and return of wagons, and (5) form a direct link between the military authorities and the railway managements and staffs.

Immediately on the close of the war a mixed committee of Staff officers and railway authorities was appointed, under the supervision of von Moltke, to inquire what steps should be taken to organise the Prussian military transport services on such a basis as would avoid a repetition of the faults already experienced, and give a greater guarantee of efficiency on the occasion of the next war in which Prussia might be engaged. The desirability of making such preparations in time of peace doubtless appeared the greater in proportion as it became more and more evident that the trial of strength between Prussia and Austria would inevitably be followed by one between Prussia and France.

The scheme elaborated by the committee in question took the form of a *Route Service Regulation* which was approved by the King on May 2, 1867, and was, also, adopted by most of the other German States, but was kept secret until the time came for applying it in practice, as was done in the war of 1870-71.

The basis of the scheme was the creation of a system of *Route Inspection* ("Etappen Inspektion") constituting a department of the General Staff, and designed—

I. To watch over the replenishing of the operating army with men, horses, provisions, ammunition, and other military stores.

II. To see to the removal into the interior of the country of the sick and wounded, prisoners and trophies of war.

III. With the assistance of the troops appointed for the purpose and the Railway Field Corps, to maintain the line of communication, viz., railway, roads, bridges, telegraphs, and postal arrangements; to undertake the government of the hostile conquered provinces, and other duties.

The preparation of the necessary plans for the attainment of these objects was entrusted to a *Central Commission* composed, partly of officers connected with the General Staff and the Ministry of War, and partly of prominent functionaries on the staffs of the Ministry of Commerce, Industry and Public Works (then in supreme control over the railways), and of the Minister of the Interior. Two of its members—a Staff Officer and a railway expert from the Ministry of Commerce—formed an *Executive Commission* and exercised a general supervision over the arrangements for military transports; though on the removal of the Great Head-quarters from Berlin, the Executive Commission was to be succeeded by an *Auxiliary Executive Commission*, which would supervise the railways in the interior to be made use of for supplying the needs of the army.

In time of war the Central Commission was to be supplemented by *Line Commissions* formed by military officers and railway officers in combination, and operating each in a leading centre of railway traffic. Their function it would be—with the assistance of *District Line Commissions*—not only to communicate to the line or lines of railway in their district such orders as might be necessary for the transport of troops, guns, ammunition, horses, and supplies, but, also, to draw up or make the final arrangements in connection with the time-tables for the running of military trains; to fix the direction in which the trains would go; to decide at what stations the troops should stop for their meals or for their coffee; and, in fact, to arrange everything connected with the said transport down to—as it appeared at the time—the smallest details.

In the forwarding of supplies, each Army Corps was to have its own line of communication, separate and distinct from that of the other Army Corps, the object aimed at being that of avoiding the confusion and disorder which might result from the fact of several Army Corps using the same railway.

Each of such lines of communication would start from some large railway station forming a *Point of Concentration* ("Etappenanfangsort") for the collection and the dispatch therefrom of supplies for the Army Corps it would serve, or for the receipt and further distribution in the interior of persons or commodities coming back from the seat of war.

Along the line of railway, at distances of about 100 or 125 miles, stations were to be selected which would serve as halting-places for the feeding of troops, for the watering of horses, for the reception of sick and wounded unable to continue their journey, for the repair of rolling stock, or for other such purposes. The furthest point to be reached by rail from day to day would constitute *Railhead* ("Etappenhauptort "), whence communication with the fighting line would be carried on by road, being further facilitated by *Halting Places* ("Etappenörter") *en route*.

The whole of this elaborate organisation—and here we come to the weakest point in the system—was to be under the supreme direction and control of an *Inspector-General of Communications*—a sort of Universal Provider of every requirement the Army could possibly need, and responsible for the fulfilment of a long and exceedingly varied list of obligations among which the conduct of military rail-transport became simply one of many items. The special merit of his position was assumed to be that of a superior authority who, having the rank of Commandant of a Division, and being in constant touch both with the Commander-in-Chief of the Army and with the War Minister, would be able to establish harmony in the operations of the different services and corps. The principle itself was sound; but, in practice, such a multiplicity of duties fell upon him, or, through him, on his department, that the break-down which actually occurred in the campaign of 1870–71 should have been foreseen in advance.

On the declaration of war the Inspector-General was to organise the stations for the feeding of the troops and horses proceeding to the front, and was then himself to go to some station one or two marches from the fighting-line, and fix, each day, the Rail-head Station for the time being, moving his own head-quarters as occasion might require. From these head-quarters he was to exercise control and direction over a staff among whose duties—apart from those relating to railways or rail-transport—were the following:—A centralisation of all the services through a Chief of the Staff giving a common impulse to them according to the instructions of the Inspector-General; the forwarding of all troops to the front, special precautions having to be taken that none were left behind; distribution of the troops on arrival at their destination; the forwarding of all supplies; decision of all personal questions that might arise in connection with the troops; the keeping of journals and registers, the drawing up of reports, and the carrying on of

ORGANISATION IN GERMANY.

correspondence with the War Minister and the Chiefs of the army; everything concerned with horses for the troops, transport and distribution of prisoners of war, and maintenance of good order among the troops; assurance of an ample supply of ammunition for the artillery; construction or provision of barracks, huts, or temporary hospitals; maintenance of roads and telegraphs; control of telegraphs and postal services at the seat of war; supervision of road communications; responsibility for the safe and regular delivery to the troops of all supplies and necessaries ordered to meet their requirements, and establishment of hospitals, infirmaries and convalescent homes, with the arrangements for the removal thereto of the sick and wounded.

In regard to railway matters, the Inspector-General was assisted by a *Director of Field Railways* who, in turn, had many duties to perform. Acting in the name and with the authority of the Inspector-General, he gave directions to the Line Commissions concerning the succession in which supplies were to be forwarded, and, in conjunction with the military and railway authorities, drew up the time-tables for military transports, submitting them, however, for the approval of his chief before they were put into operation. The actual transport of troops and material—on the basis of principles the details of which would have been worked out in advance—was also to be conducted under the supervision of the Director of Railways. In the event of any of the lines being destroyed by the enemy, he was to undertake their reconstruction, obtaining through the Inspector-General such helpers—whether soldiers or civilians—as he might require to supplement his own working staff in the accomplishment of the necessary work. On the lines being restored, the Director was further to take control of their operation by means of troops and, also, of railway employés to be furnished by the Minister of Commerce on the requisition of the Inspector-General of Communications.

Such was the elaborate machinery which, constructed alike in peace and in secret by the Great General Staff, under the direct supervision of von Moltke himself, was to be tested in the inevitable war with France for which it had been designed.

According to popular belief, Germany's preparations for that war were so complete that she had only, as it were, to press a button, or pull a lever, in order to ensure the immediate and perfect working of all the plans she had made in advance. Whether or not this was really so in regard to her transport arrangements, at least, is a point to which attention may now be directed.

At the beginning of the war a *Route Inspection*, organised on the basis already detailed, and having its own Inspector-General of Communications in charge of, and responsible for, the efficient working of the entire network of duties and obligations, was called into being for each of the three German armies. Subsequently a fourth, under the Crown Prince of Saxony, was added.

So far as the mobilisation of the German troops and their concentration on the frontier were concerned the plans worked, on the whole, remarkably well; though even in this respect complete success was not attained. There were, in 1870, nine lines of concentration available, namely, six for the Northern and three for the Southern Army; and between July 24 and August 3, there were dispatched by these different routes 1,200 trains, conveying 350,000 men, 87,000 horses, and 8,400 guns or road vehicles. Yet the delays which occurred to some of these trains were alone sufficient to show that the machinery which had been elaborated was not working with perfect smoothness. On, for example, the route known as line " C," the troops sent to Giessen were—as told by Balck, in his " Taktik "—eleven hours late in their arrival. They then had their first warm food after a journey which had lasted twenty-one hours. For the transport to Homburg-in-der-Pfalz and Neunkirchen forty hours had been allowed. The first train did the journey in the time, but the next one took ninety hours.

It was, however, in the forwarding of supplies and in the provisioning of the troops that the greatest difficulties were experienced; and here there certainly appeared to be little real advance on the shortcomings of the campaign of 1866,

ORGANISATION IN GERMANY.

notwithstanding all the preparations which had been made in the meantime.

Comprehensive as it undoubtedly was, the scheme prepared in time of peace included no adequate organisation for regulating the transport of supplies to the front and for ensuring alike their dispatch and their arrival in just such quantities, and under just such conditions, as would provide for the needs of the troops from day to day. Magazines had certainly been set up, but not in sufficient number or always in the right place. The system, too, of operating them was defective. Just as in 1866, so in 1870, army officers, contractors and railway companies, all inspired by zeal for the welfare of the troops, rushed off train-load after train-load of supplies to stations provided with an inadequate supply alike of sidings where the wagons could be accommodated and of labour for the work of unloading. Stores were handed to the railway staffs under the same conditions as in peace time, the idea being, apparently, that if they were only dispatched as soon as possible they would be sure to get to the troops in want of them.

As for the conditions at the other end, it not unfrequently happened that even though the supply-trains might go to stations where the facilities for unloading them were ample, the Commissariat or other officers in charge would follow the example already being set in France by regarding loaded railway trucks as convenient movable magazines which should not be unloaded until their contents were really wanted. This was done regardless of the fact alike that the trucks thus kept standing on the lines impeded the traffic and that they were urgently wanted to meet the shortage of trucks elsewhere. But for the stringent action taken to check it, the evil due to this use of railway trucks for storage purposes would have assumed even graver proportions than was actually the case. Defective, also, as the German arrangements in this respect undoubtedly were, they still did not attain to the same degree of inefficiency as was the case in France.

All the same, the general result of these various conditions was that serious difficulties were experienced on the

German no less than on the French railways. No sooner had the concentration of the Prussian troops been completed than provisions and stores were sent after them in such volume that a hopeless block, extending to Cologne in one direction and Frankfort in the other, was speedily produced on the lines along the left bank of the Rhine, while the feeding of the troops was brought to a temporary standstill. The combined efforts of the Prussian Executive Commission, of the Minister of Commerce and of the Line Commissions failed for a time to overcome the conditions of chaos and confusion thus brought about, and on August 11, 1870, instructions had to be given that thenceforward supplies were to be forwarded only on the express order of the Intendant-General or of an Inspector-General of Communications. Yet on September 5 there were standing, on five different lines, a total of no fewer than 2,322 loaded wagons, containing 16,830 tons of provisions for the Second Army, or sufficient to keep it supplied for a period of twenty-six days. Such blocks on the German lines—though not always on so great a scale—were of frequent occurrence throughout the war.

Trouble arose, also, in getting provisions from the railway to the troops by reason either of the inadequate number of road vehicles or because of the use of these for the conveyance of ammunition or for other purposes, instead. Thus the Inspector-General of the First Army started with 2,000 road vehicles; but on October 17 the total number still at his disposal was only twenty. The position became still worse as the retreating French destroyed the lines behind them, increasing the difficulties of the invaders in maintaining their communications with the Fatherland.

While the food supplies for the German troops were thus blocking the railway lines—or, alternatively, were going bad on account either of the heated conditions of the closed wagons or of exposure to the weather after unloading—many of the German troops were suffering severe privations from lack of adequate nourishment; and they would have suffered still more but for the provision-trains or stores of supplies seized from the French at Metz, For-

ORGANISATION IN GERMANY.

bach, Verdun, Dôle, Le Hans, and elsewhere. If, indeed, the French had only refrained from rushing their own supplies to the extreme front in excessive quantities, or if they had destroyed those they could not remove in time, the invaders would, on various occasions, have found themselves in a condition bordering on starvation. Even as it was, they were often reduced to the necessity of dependence on their " iron " rations.

Difficulty was especially experienced in feeding the army of occupation during the investment of Paris. The supplies received by train from Germany were equal to scarcely one half of the actual requirements; a resort to " requisitions " on the French territory occupied yielded inadequate results; and the making of a regular daily money-allowance to officers and men, so that they could purchase their own supplies in the open market or otherwise, was, at first, far from satisfactory. It was, in fact, only owing to the most strenuous effort on the part of the responsible officers, both during the investment of Paris and in earlier phases of the war, that the German troops were often saved from actual want.[1]

The main reasons for the defects and shortcomings thus developed in a scheme on which so much care and preparation had been bestowed were (1) that, while based on fundamentally sound principles, the scheme in its actual application threw too great a strain on the department of the Inspector-General of Communications, which, as we have seen, was expected to look after, not only rail transport, but route marching, telegraphs, postal arrangements, and a great variety of other things besides; (2) that, owing

[1] In "Der Kriegs-Train des deutschen Heeres," by E. Schäffer, (Berlin, 1883), the author, dealing with the subject of transport in the war of 1870-71, and its effect on the feeding of the German Army, says of the situation in August-September, 1870 : " Immerhin wurden den Truppen damals nicht unerhebliche Entbehrungen auferlegt"; while concerning the position of the army of occupation in France he writes : " Immerhin erforderte es umfassender Massregeln seitens der Intendantur, die Truppen vor wirklichem Mangel zu schützen, namentlich da die Requisitionen wenig ergiebig ausfielen, und anfänglich auch der freihändige Ankauf keinen rechten Erfolg hatte."

to the larger number of Army Corps, it was no longer possible, as had been done in 1866, to place a separate line of railway at the disposal of each, so as to allow the said department to superintend the traffic on the basis of its own organisation; and (3) the absence of a central administration specially designed (a) to act as an intermediary and to ensure co-operation and mutual working between the various Line Commissions and, also, between the individuals and administrations, both military and civil, engaged in the conduct of rail-transport; and (b) to control the traffic as a whole, avoiding difficulties, blocks and delays, assuring a prompt and efficient distribution of supplies, and guaranteeing the utilisation of rolling stock to the best advantage.

With a view to overcoming, as far as possible, the trouble due to the wide extent and the great variety of duties falling on the department of the Inspector-General of Communications, it was arranged, during the latter part of the war, to relieve that department of all responsibility for the railway services and to transfer the control and direction of these to the Executive Commission established at the Royal Head-quarters. In this way it was hoped to utilise the rail-transport facilities to greater advantage, to decrease the risk of collisions and delays, and, through a central organisation, to distribute the transport demands more equally among the various railways concerned. By means of these provisional modifications in the original scheme a better system of operation was obtained during the remainder of the war. But the complete reorganisation that was really necessary was then impracticable, and much friction in the working of the railway services was still experienced, partly because this needful reorganisation could not be carried out, and partly because of the conflicting orders coming from different authorities, each of whom, under the conditions then existing, was perfectly within his right in giving them.[1]

The difficulties due to the attempts to rush supplies in excessive quantities direct to the fighting-line, or as near

[1] "Revue militaire de l'Etranger," 27 Novembre, 1872.

thereto as possible, were also met, to a certain extent, during the course of the war, by the setting up of additional railway magazines or depôts where the forwarding of necessaries could be better controlled ; but it was not until the end of 1870 that any approach to regularity in supplying the wants of the German forces was finally secured.

No sooner had the war come to an end than the work of remedying the defects which had been developed was taken in hand by the Minister of War and the Great General Staff. Following the creation, on October 1, 1871, of a Railway Battalion on a permanent basis came, on July 20, 1872, a new Regulation cancelling the one of May 2, 1867, which had been in operation during the war, and substituting a new basis of organisation in its place.

While retaining the principle of a Central Commission in Berlin, the scheme of 1872 relieved the route authorities of all responsibility for rail transport as well as for railway restoration and operation at the theatre of war, transferring to a new military department all the duties falling under these heads, with the further advantage that such department would be able to control the railways in time of war independently of the civil authorities, and without the disadvantages hitherto resulting from the need to deal, in regard to railway questions, with nine separate Ministries of Commerce and about fifty different railway companies. At the same time the principle of co-ordination was to be maintained by the appointment of an *Inspector-General of Railways and Lines of Communication* who, in each of these departments, would control a far more efficient organisation than had previously existed, and, also, as director-in-chief, would constitute a central authority and an intermediary between the services concerned and the head of the Great General Staff, under whose direction he would himself act.

Another important feature of the new Regulation was that a distinction was now drawn between (1) railways on or near to the theatre of war which could not be worked by their ordinary staffs, and must needs pass under military operation, with a paramount military control; and (2) " home " or other railways, in the rear of the fighting, which might carry ordinary traffic—except so far as the lines were wanted for military purposes—and might still be worked by their own staffs, but in the operation of which there should be a military element in time of war in order to facilitate the transport of troops and military necessaries.

Various other Regulations, and notably a series in 1878 and 1888, followed that of 1872, and eventually the whole scheme of organisation, with its additions and modifications, seeking to provide for every possible contingency, became extremely complicated. Of the multifarious instructions, provisions and orders which had been compiled, some applied to peace only, some to war only, and some to both peace and war; some to "home" railways and some to railways at the seat of war; some to military men and some to railway men, and so on. As an elaborate piece of machinery the organisation was more comprehensive and more complete than ever; but the fear arose that there had again been a failure to take the human element sufficiently into account. Of those in the military and the railway service who should have applied themselves in time of peace to a study of the elaborate and extremely involved provisions which would apply in time of war, comparatively few, it was found, were disposed to devote themselves to so uninviting a task.

So there was issued, on January 18, 1899, still another new Regulation which repealed some of the earlier ones and aimed at amplifying, condensing, rearranging and facilitating reference to the provisions remaining in force, in order that the whole scheme should be made clearer, simpler and easier to grasp. These results were fully attained, and, though still subject to the final test of a great war, such as that which broke out in 1914, the German Regulation of 1899 might certainly be considered a masterpiece of organisation as prepared in time of peace. One especially useful purpose it served was that of defining clearly the duties, responsibilities, and spheres of action of all the authorities, civil or military, concerned in the control and operation of railways for military purposes.

The various Regulations here in question have been supplemented from time to time by *Field Service Regula-*

tions, the first series of which, issued under date May 23, 1887, was designed to take the place of the Ordinances of 1861 relating to the movement by rail of great bodies of troops. These Field Service Regulations of 1887 constituted an epoch in the military history of Germany. They were regarded at the time as offering a resumé of the most advanced ideas of Moltke, if not, also, as the crowning glory of military organisation in the reign of William I ; and they certainly exercised a powerful influence on German military literature. They were, further, the starting-point of a prolonged series of similar Regulations, all amending, modifying, adding to, or abbreviating their predecessors. These changes led to the issue, on January 1, 1900, of a new edition, based on the exhaustive studies of a Commission of fourteen members ; and still later revisions resulted in the publication of a further series on March 22, 1908.[1]

Here, then, we get still further evidence of the keenness with which Germany has followed up, in times of peace, her preparations for war, while the Field Service Regulations, no less than the other Regulations already detailed, show the important place that military rail-transport holds in the view of those responsible in Germany for the making of these arrangements. "Railways," it is declared in the Regulations of 1908, "exercise a decisive influence on the whole conduct of a war. They are of the greatest importance for mobilising and concentrating the army, and for maintaining it in a state of efficiency, and they enable portions of it to be transported from one place to another during the operations." What the Field Service Regulations do is to present in concentrated and compact form the working details, in respect to field service requirements, of those other and fuller Regulations which cover the whole ground of military transport in general.

Taking these various sources of information, the nature of the organisation that Germany has thus effected as the

[1] "Field Service Regulations (Felddienst Ordnung, 1908) of the German Army." Translated by the General Staff, War Office. London, 1908.

result of so many years of study and experience may be summarised as follows :—

In time of peace the authorities entrusted with the task of ensuring, by their preparations in advance, the success of the whole system of military rail-transport include (1) the Minister of War ; the Prussian Chief of the General Staff of the Army ; the members of the Railway Section of the Great General Staff, the Line Commissions and the Station Commissions ; authorities concerned in the forwarding, transport and receiving of supplies, and representatives of the Commissariat department ; and (2) the Imperial Chancellor, the Imperial Railway Bureau, the Imperial Administration of Posts and Telegraphs, and the various railway administrations.

The *Prussian Minister of War* is the chief representative of the interests of the Army in all questions relating to the military use of the railways.

The *Prussian Chief of the General Staff* of the Army has under his orders, in time of peace, the military authorities concerned in rail-transport, and gives them the necessary instructions. He keeps in close relations with the Imperial Railway Bureau, and serves as intermediary between that Bureau and the Prussian Minister of War. It is he who gives the directions according to which the use of the railways in war-time is regulated, and he prescribes all the preparations that are to be made in advance for the facilitating of such use. On mobilisation, he discharges all the duties appertaining to the office of the Inspector-General of Railways and Lines of Communication until that officer has himself taken them in hand. From that time he issues instructions according to circumstances.

The *Railway Section of the Great General Staff* is required, among other duties, to collect, and have always available, the fullest and most complete information as to the powers and facilities of the railways for the transport of troops, etc. To this end it keeps in constant communication with the railway administrations, and, also, with the Imperial Railway Bureau (which centralises all questions affecting railway administration), completing, if necessary, through investigations made by its own officers, the information furnished annually by the Bureau. The Railway Section further takes charge of a wide range of details and preparations concerning military rail-transport in war-time.

On the outbreak of hostilities there is appointed for each theatre of war an *Inspector-General of Railways and Lines of Communication* who, receiving his orders from the Chief of the General Staff, co-ordinates the two groups of services, and ensures harmony in their joint working. For the operation of the railways, as applied to military purposes, there is a *Director of Field Railways* who, acting under the Inspector-General, controls the whole railway service. Through the Line Commissions or Commandants subordinate to him he conveys to the railway authorities the necessary demands or instructions in respect to military transport, and, in concert with his superior officers, he fixes the boundary between the lines to be operated on a peace footing and those that are to be subject to military working. In the discharge of these and other duties he is assisted by a staff composed partly of military men and partly of railwaymen. Each officer concerned in the transport arrangements has a recognised deputy who can act for him in case of need.

Of *Line Commissions*, placed in charge, for military purposes, over the lines of railway in certain districts, and becoming *Line Commandants* on the outbreak of war, there were twenty under the revised Regulation of 1899, the number being increased in 1904 to twenty-one. The headquarters of these Commissions are at such centres of traffic as Berlin, Hanover, Erfurt, Dresden, Cologne, Altona, Breslau, etc. They serve as intermediaries between the higher military authorities and the railway administrations with which they are associated. Each Line Commission consists, normally, of a staff officer of the active army and a prominent railway functionary, the former having a non-commissioned officer, and the latter a railway official, as secretary, with such further assistance as may be needed.

Subordinate, in turn, to the Line Commissions are the *Station Commissions*, which, receiving instructions from the former, see to the carrying out of the necessary transport requirements either at their particular station or on the section of line of which they are placed in charge.

While full provision is thus made for the representation of the military element in the conduct of rail-transport in time of war, with a view to ensuring its efficiency, precautions are no less taken to avoid repetitions of earlier troubles due to questions of responsibility and control, and, more especially, to the interference of military officers in the technical operation of the railway lines. On this subject the Field Service Regulations of 1900 stated (paragraph 496) :—

Railways can only fully accomplish their important and difficult task during war if no serious hindrances to their management are created by the conduct of the troops.

In the later Regulations of 1908 it was said (paragraph 527) :—

The important rôle which railways have to fulfil renders it incumbent on every commander to do all in his power to prevent any interference with the traffic due to delay, etc., on the part of the troops. The railway staff and conducting officers are bound by the transport arrangements made by the railway authorities.

The conducting officer is responsible for the administration of the detachment of troops or consignment of stores under his charge. It is his duty, as regards himself and his charge, to obey the instructions of the railway officials.

Any interference with the service of the railways is forbidden.

At important stations Railway Staff Officers are appointed who act as intermediaries between the conducting officers and the railway officials.

Concerning *Lines of Communication* the Field Service Regulations of 1908 say :—

A railway station, to serve as a Home Base (" Etappenanfangsort ") will be assigned to every Army Corps. From these home bases supplies are sent forward to Collecting Depôts (" Sammelstationen "), which will be established at not too great a distance from the theatre of war.

In the theatre of war a base will be assigned to each Army, the situation of which will change according to the progress of the operations. The Army Corps are connected with the Field Base by lines of communication roads (" Etappenstrassen "), and on these roads posts are formed about $13\frac{1}{2}$ miles apart.

As for the mass of working details also included in the various Regulations, these may well appear to provide in advance for every possible requirement in regard to military transport by rail, from the movement of entire armies down to the supply of drinking water at stations and the taking of carrier pigeons in the troop trains.

CHAPTER XI

RAILWAY TROOPS IN GERMANY

THE innovation introduced into modern warfare by the Federal Government of the United States, in the organisation on a comprehensive scale of a Construction Corps for the combined purposes of repairing, destroying and operating the railways on which so much might depend in the conduct of war, attracted great attention in Europe, and more especially so in Germany, which was the first country on this side of the Atlantic to follow the American precedent, since adopted more or less completely by all nations possessed alike of railways and a standing army.

Down to the time of the War of Secession the need for such a corps had not been realised in Europe; but the advantages which might be gained therefrom had been shown in so unmistakable a form that when, in 1866, there was the certainty of an early conflict between Prussia and Austria, one of the first steps taken by the former country was to provide, under a decree of May 6, 1866, for a *Field Railway Section*, ("Feldeisenbahnabteilung,") to be formed, and designed to operate, on a basis closely approximating to that which had applied to the corresponding American corps. The special purposes to be served were defined as those of rapidly repairing lines of railway destroyed by the enemy and of destroying railways it might be thought expedient to prevent the enemy from using. The section was to be under the orders of the General Staff either of the Army or of an Army Corps. It was, however, not to come into being until its services were really required, and it was then to act for the duration of the war only.

On the outbreak of hostilities three divisions of the corps

RAILWAY TROOPS IN GERMANY. 123

were mobilised, under Cabinet Orders of May 25 and June 1, one division being allotted to each of the three Prussian armies operating in different parts of the theatre of war. The composition of the corps was partly military and partly civil. The military element was supplied by officers of the Engineers (one of whom acted as chief), non-commissioned officers, and a detachment of Pioneers, the last-mentioned being either carpenters or smiths. The civil element comprised railway engineers, thoroughly acquainted with the construction and repair of permanent way, bridges, etc.; assistant railway engineers, performing the duties of clerks of the works; head platelayers, foremen, locomotive drivers, machinists (for the repair of engines, rolling-stock, water pumps and water tanks), and others. The members of the civil section were chosen from the staff of the Prussian State railways by the Minister of Commerce, their services being placed by him at the disposal of the War Minister. Each of the three divisions constituted a complete unit.

On the side of the Austrians there was at that time no similar force available. Three years before there had been published in Vienna a book, by Oberst. von Panz, entitled " Das Eisenbahnwesen, vom militärischen Standpuncte," in which the author expressed the view that details on the following points, among others, concerning railways should be collected in time of peace and classified for reference in case of need :—Permanent way : system and construction ; gauge and number of lines ; whether lines single or double. Stations : size and construction ; which of them best fitted to serve as depôts. Bridges : underground works, etc. ; which of these could be the most easily destroyed, or soonest repaired if destroyed, and if prepared beforehand for destruction. Embankments : size ; how made ; slope ; if provided with culverts and size of these. Cuttings : length and depth ; slopes ; nature of ground ; whether much or little water, and whether danger of landslips. Tunnels : dimensions and construction ; if lined or cut in rock ; nature of cuttings at end and whether they can be blocked. Large bridges and viaducts : system of construction ; span of arches ; whether or not the piers are mined.[1] Where men, tools, stores and materials can be obtained, and to what extent.

These recommendations attracted much attention at the time. They were quoted by H. L. Westphalen in his book on " Die Kriegführung unter Benutzung der Eisenbahnen " (Leipzig, 1868), of which a French translation was published under the title of " De l'Emploi des Chemins de Fer en Temps de Guerre " (Paris, 1869) ; yet when, just before the outbreak of war with Prussia, the Commander-in-Chief of the Austrian Northern Army recommended that a Construction Corps should be formed, the Minister of War replied that " the repair of railways was work which should be done by the railway companies concerned."

All the same, the retarding of the Prussian advance by interrupting the rail communications became an important phase of Austrian tactics and was followed up with great activity. Bridges and viaducts were destroyed, rails torn up, sleepers burned, points and turn-tables carried away, tunnels obstructed and water cranes and pumps rendered useless. At one place (between Libenau and Sichrau), where the railway passed through a deep cutting, the explosion of mines along the top of each bank detached great masses of rock which, falling on the lines, filled up the cutting to a height of six or eight feet for a distance of about 250 ft., and could not be removed until, by means of blasting, they had been broken up into pieces sufficiently small to be carried away in ballast trucks.

The arrangements made by the Prussians were, however, so complete as to permit, in most instances, of a speedy restoration. Even in the instance just mentioned, fifty Pioneers, aided by twenty labourers, had the line clear for traffic again before midnight of the day the destruction was caused.

Each division of the Construction Corps had at its disposal two locomotives and thirty closed wagons or open

[1] Captain A. de Formanoir states in his book, "Des Chemins de Fer en Temps de Guerre " (Conférences militaires belges. Bruxelles, 1870), that in France and Austria all the railway bridges have mine-chambers so that they can be readily destroyed when the occasion arises.

trucks, provision thus being made for the transport of, among other things, six light covered carts (for use on the roads in the country to be invaded, horses being requisitioned therein as necessary); tools; supplies of blasting powder or gun-cotton; and rails, sleepers, bolts, etc., for 250 yards of railway, reserve materials for a further quarter of a mile of track being left at intermediate depôts, supplemented by an unlimited supply at the base of operations. The construction trains also carried timber, ropes, nails, scaffolding, clamps, etc., for the prompt repair of small bridges. Materials for larger bridges or viaducts were stored at convenient centres.

How the reconnaissance of a line which might have been subjected to the enemy's destructive tactics was carried out is thus told by Captain C. E. Webber, R.E., in his " Notes on the Campaign in Bohemia in 1866 ":—

> The reconnaissance starts with, and, until interrupted, keeps up with, the advance guard, the movement being covered by cavalry scouts on each side of the line.
>
> The greater portion of the train in charge of the department, with one engine in front and another behind, advances slowly, preceded at a distance of about 500 paces by a trolley carrying one of the officers, four men to work it, and a bugler. On arriving at any obstruction the trolley signals to the train by bugle and extra caution is used in advancing towards it. If in presence of the enemy, the scouts give warning to the officer in the trolley, who returns to the train and the whole retires. The second engine can be detached from the rear to send messages or bring up fresh supplies.

But for the successes already gained in the same direction by the Federals in the United States, the speed with which repairs were carried out by the Prussian Construction Corps —then so recently organised—would have been regarded as remarkable. In various instances communication was restored within from one and a half to three days after the destruction even of important bridges.

As it happened, however, whilst the Austrians had shown an excess of zeal in some directions by destroying bridges when the tearing up of the rails would have answered the same purpose, the hesitation of the responsible Austrian officer to fire the mines which had already been laid to the bridge over the Elbe at Lobkowitz was of great advantage to the Prussians, leaving them the use of the line from Turnau to Prague, Pardubitz and Brünn between July 18 and July 27, on which latter date the bridge was at last destroyed by order of the governor of Theresienstadt. This particular bridge was one of exceptional strategical importance, and, according to Captain Webber, the construction even of a temporary substitute—had the Austrians blown up the bridge before the Prussians could cross it—would have taken no less than six weeks. The omission, also, of the Austrians to remove or to destroy the railway rolling stock they left behind at Prague, on their retirement from that city, conferred a further benefit on the Prussians. These examples would seem to show that promptness in carrying out destruction at a critical moment may be no less important on the one side than efficient organisation on the other for accomplishing the work of restoration in the shortest possible time.

While the Construction Corps had thus fully justified its existence, the sudden creation of such a corps for the purposes of a particular war, and for the period of the war only, was considered inadequate for a country where a large standing Army had to be maintained in readiness for action at any moment, in case of need. Hence it was thought desirable that Prussia should have a Field Railway Section established on a permanent and well-organised footing. There was the further reason for adopting this course because the Pioneers, composed almost exclusively of reservists, had received no special training in railway work, while the railway men themselves, accustomed to building lines in a solid way for public use, were at a disadvantage when called on to carry out, with great rapidity, and in a rough and ready manner, work that was wanted only to serve the temporary purposes of the Army with which they were associated.

It was found, also, that the corps, comprising so large a civil element, had escaped the supervision and control of the Executive Commission at Berlin which had for its function the regulation of all matters concerning military rail-transport. Nor did the Construction *and* Destruction Corps constitute, as well, an Operation Corps, providing for the working of railways at the theatre of war, and especially of railways taken from the enemy. The Prussians had, indeed, been able to command the services of Austrian railwaymen in working the railways seized in that country; but there was no certainty that the adoption of a like expedient would be possible in any future war.

By this time the whole subject of the destruction and restoration of railway lines as an important element in modern warfare was attracting attention among military authorities and writers in Germany. A translation of McCallum's report was published, and the issue was begun of what was to develop into a long series of technical papers, pamphlets or books—such as, for example, Wilhelm Basson's " Die Eisenbahnen im Kriege, nach den Erfahrungen des letzten Feldzuges" (Ratibor, 1867)—dealing with the art of rapidly destroying and restoring railways in time of war and the most effective measures to be adopted in the attainment of either end.

These various considerations and developments were, no doubt, the reason for the issuing, on August 10, 1869, of a Prussian Royal Decree which created a permanent cadre of *Railway Troops* to be constituted of Pioneers who were to undergo regular instruction in everything relating to the construction, destruction and operation of railways. A new Battalion of Pioneers was to be raised for the purpose, and the whole scheme was to be carried into effect in the course of 1871.

When, in 1870, the war with France broke out, the preparations for the creation of this permanent corps were still proceeding; but the Prussians were, nevertheless, able to enter on the campaign with four sections of Railway Troops, subsequently increased to six, including one Bavarian section. Each section comprised Engineers, Pioneers, railwaymen and auxiliary helpers, all of whom wore a uniform having the letter " E " (" Eisenbahntruppen ") on the shoulder, and carried rifles. Prussia, in fact, once more started, as in 1866, with such advantage over her enemy as might result from her control of a Railway Construction Corps. At the outset France had no similar body, and though, during the progress of the war, she hurriedly set about the creation of a Construction Corps of her own, that corps did not do very much beyond collecting at Metz and Strasburg a great store of railway materials which was afterwards to fall into the hands of the Prussians, and assist them in their own operations.

Notwithstanding the advantage thus gained, the practical benefits secured by the Germans, although important in their effect on the final issue, were far from being as great as the Army leaders may have anticipated or desired. The destruction work carried out by the French on their own railways, on their retirement, was much more serious than anything experienced in the Prussian campaign in Austria. Thus the works for the re-establishment of the Paris—Strasburg line (of primary importance to the Germans for the siege of Paris) extended from September 17 to November 22. The French had blocked the tunnel of Nanteuil by the explosion therein of six mines which brought down the walls and filled the western end of the tunnel with about 4,000 square yards of sand. Attempts to clear away the obstruction were a failure, owing to the occurrence of fresh slips due to the wet weather, and eventually the Construction Corps built a loop line which avoided the tunnel, and so restored communication. The defence of some of the principal lines by fortresses also contributed to the difficulties of the invaders; though, on the other hand, these difficulties would have been greater still if the French had always adopted the best and most scientific methods of interrupting rail communications, as, presumably, they would have done if they had had the advantage of a well-organised corps prepared in advance for the work that required to be done.

At Fontenoy-sur-Moselle, between Nancy and Toul, there was, for example, a bridge of seven arches, effective destruction of which would have made a very serious check in the communications along the principal line between Germany and Paris; but, instead of blowing up the bridge in the

RAILWAY TROOPS IN GERMANY.

middle, the men entrusted with the work (in January, 1871) brought down two arches at the side of the bridge, causing a break which the Germans were able to fill in with stones and earth, restoring communication in about seventeen days. Then, although several of the tunnels in the Vosges mountains were mined, the mines had not been charged, and before instructions to blow up the tunnels had been received by those awaiting them, the Germans were on the spot and took possession.

On the other hand the absence on the side of the French of an organised corps for destruction as well as construction did not prevent the carrying out of some very bold and highly successful work by parties of *franc tireurs*, who showed alike their appreciation of the importance of rail communications and their skill in impeding them.

One especially striking feat in this direction was accomplished by a company known as the "Franc Tireurs of the Meuse."

Learning that a Prussian troop train was to pass through Lanois (on the line between Reims and Mons) on October 26, 1870, they resolved to effect its destruction. How they operated is told by Lieutenant Fraser, R.E.,[1] who arrived on the spot shortly afterwards, and heard the story from some of the men engaged on the work.

Any obstruction placed on the line would have been seen. Hence a different course had to be adopted. Selecting a spot where the line ran along a 12-ft. high embankment, to which a well-wooded slope came down on one side, the *franc tireurs* took up a pair of rails, removed the sleepers, cut a deep trench across the line, laid some pieces of iron at the bottom of the trench, placed on the iron a box containing thirty kilos (2 qrs. 10 lbs.) of powder, and fixed into the lid of the box a French field shell in such a way that, when the rail was replaced over the box, the head of the fuse would be just below the lower flange of the rail. In restoring the line again in order that there should be nothing to

---

[1] "Account of a Torpedo used for the Destruction of a Railway Train on the 26th of October, 1870." By Lieut. Fraser, R.E. Papers of the Corps of Royal Engineers, N.S., Vol. XX. Woolwich, 1872.

attract attention, the *franc tireurs* omitted one sleeper so that the weight of the locomotive should in passing press the rail down on to the head of the fuse. The party—some seventy-five strong—then withdrew to the shelter of the woods to await developments.

In due time the train of forty coaches approached at the ordinary speed, the driver not suspecting any danger. When the engine reached the spot where the "torpedo" had been placed, an explosion occurred which tore up a mass of earth, rails and sleepers, threw the engine and several carriages down the embankment, and wrecked the train. Those of the Prussian troops who got clear from the wreckage were shot down by the *franc tireurs* under the protection of their cover. The number of the enemy thus disposed of was said to be about 400.

Altogether the French, in their efforts to impede the rail movements of the invader, destroyed many miles of line, together with no fewer than seventy-eight large bridges and tunnels, apart from minor interruptions. The repairs and reconstruction thus rendered necessary threw a great amount of labour on the Prussian Railway Troops, and much trouble arose from time to time on account, not only of the inadequate supply of materials even for temporary constructions, but, also, by reason of the shortcomings of the workers themselves. The sections of Railway Troops had been so recently formed that the men were still without adequate training. In 1870–71, as in 1866, military members and civilian members of the Construction Corps were alike unfamiliar with the special class of work called for in the repair or the rebuilding of railways under the emergency conditions of actual warfare. This instruction had, in fact, to be completed at the theatre of war at a time when the Corps should have been prepared to show the greatest efficiency.

Difficulties arose, also, on the side of the Germans in operating the 2,500 miles of French railway lines of which they took possession.

There was, in the first place, a deficiency both of locomotives and of rolling stock. So far as circumstances would

RAILWAY TROOPS IN GERMANY.   131

permit, the French, as they retreated, either took their railway rolling stock with them or destroyed it, in order that it should not be used by the enemy. Attempts were made to meet the difficulty by obtaining constant reinforcements of engines and wagons from Germany; but even then the organisation for controlling the use of rolling stock, among other transport details, was still so defective that commanders who wanted to ensure the movement of their own troops by rail did not hesitate to take possession of engines and carriages set aside for the regular services of the line. There were, in fact, occasions when, for this reason, the regular services had to be stopped altogether.

In the next place troubles with the *personnel* were no less acute than those with the *matériel*. In proportion as the Germans advanced towards Paris the bulk of the French population retired, while threats and offers of liberal pay alike failed to secure from those who remained assistance either in repairing or in operating the lines of which the invaders had taken possession. In these circumstances not only engines, carriages and wagons, but no fewer than 3,500 railwaymen—in addition to the German Railway Troops already in France—had to be brought from Germany. Yet even the resort to this expedient started a fresh lot of troubles. The railwaymen so imported had been in the service of different German railway companies whose equipment and methods of operation varied considerably; so that when the men were required to work together—and that, also, on the lines of a foreign country, with the accompaniment of much laxity in discipline as well as of much mutual misunderstanding—a vast amount of friction arose.

All these experiences emphasised and strengthened the conclusion arrived at even before the campaign of 1870–71—that the real efficiency of Railway Troops can only be obtained by organising them in time of peace in readiness for times of war. Such conclusion being now beyond all possible dispute, action was taken by Prussia with characteristic promptness.

In accordance with a Royal Order of May 19, 1871, there was added to the Prussian Army, on October 1 of the same year, a *Railway Battalion* ("Eisenbahnbataillon"), the special purposes of which were (1) to afford to those constituting it the means of obtaining, in time of peace, such technical training as would enable them to construct any railway works necessary in time of war, to repair promptly any damage done to railways, and to undertake the entire railway traffic along lines of communication; (2) to procure, or prepare, in time of peace, all plant, materials, tools, etc., likely to be required in time of war; and (3) to constitute the nucleus of all necessary railway formations in war. The Battalion was formed of non-commissioned officers and men of the now disbanded sections of Railway Troops who were still liable to military service, supplemented by three-year volunteers and recruits from all parts of the territory subject to the Prussian Minister of War, only those being accepted, however, whose previous occupations fitted them for one or other of the various grades of railway work. The officers were obtained mainly, though not exclusively, from the Engineers. Members of that corps, together with others who were mechanical engineers by profession, were accepted as one-year volunteers.

On a peace footing the Battalion was composed of a Staff and four Companies, each of 100 or 125 men, with a depôt, and provided with its own means of transport. One of the Companies consisted exclusively of platelayers and watchmen. On mobilisation each Company was to be enlarged into two Construction Companies and one Traffic Company, giving a total, on a war footing, of eight Construction and four Traffic Companies. The Corps also had a reserve division consisting of a Staff, two Companies and a section of railway employés. All officers having railway experience who had served in the war of 1870–71 were included in the reserve.

The training of the Battalion was under the direction of the Inspector-General of the Engineers Corps. It comprised (1) theoretical and scientific instruction of the officers in all branches of railway construction, repair and destruction, coupled with the study of every branch of railway science likely to be of advantage in military transport, while special importance was attached to a close and constant intercourse with the staffs of the various railways, and (2) practical experience of railway construction and operation. This experience was afforded (*a*) on the Battalion's practice grounds, where instruction was more especially given in the art of rapidly destroying railway track ; (*b*) through the employment of the men—subject to the continued maintenance among them of the principle of a military organisation—on many of the private as well as on the State railways in Germany, such employment including the repair of bridges, the laying of track, the enlargement of stations, etc., and (*c*) by the construction, operation and management of a short line of railway which, on completion, was devoted to the public service. The period of training was for either one or three years and the Battalion was kept up to a normal standard of about 500 men by a succession of recruits. These recruits were generally men of a good type, admission to the Battalion being regarded with the greater favour inasmuch as the experience gained was found to be of advantage to the men in obtaining railway employment on their return to civil life.

In the giving of this practical instruction the purpose specially kept in view was that of anticipating as far as possible actual war conditions, and providing for them accordingly. Thus in the laying of rails for any new line built by the Railway Troops great importance was attached to the speed with which the work could be done, the records of the time taken being very closely watched.

To one group of officers was allocated the duty of studying all developments in railway science and operation at home or abroad and conveying information thereon to those under instruction. A further important feature of the scheme included the publication of a series of text-books on railway subjects regarded from a military standpoint. A beginning was also made with the collection of large supplies of rails, bridge materials, etc., for use as required.

In December, 1872, Bavaria created a similar Battalion, comprising a single Company attached to the 1st Bavarian Corps. The constitution and the operations of this Battalion followed closely the precedents established by Prussia.

Such was the importance attached by the highest military authorities in Germany to the formation of these Railway Troops that the Chief of the Great General Staff was their Inspector-General from the time of the first Prussian Battalion being created down to the year 1899.

In December 30, 1875, came the conversion of the Railway Battalion into a *Railway Regiment*. It was felt that the cadres of the former did not respond sufficiently to the needs of the military rail-transport situation, and they were accordingly enlarged into a Regiment of two Battalions, with a regimental Staff of forty-eight, and 502 men in each Battalion. In 1887 the Prussian Regiment was increased from two Battalions to four, and the Bavarian Battalion expanded to the extent of two companies in place of one. In 1890 the Prussian Regiment further became a *Brigade* of two Regiments, each of two Battalions, the number of units thus remaining the same as before; though in 1893 the Prussian Brigade was augmented by two more Battalions, increasing its force to three Regiments, each of two Battalions with four Companies in each Battalion, or a total of twenty-four Companies, of which one was a Würtemberg Company and two were Saxon Companies, while the Bavarian Battalion acquired three Companies in the place of two.

In 1899 Prussia took a further new departure by grouping together, as *Communication Troops* ("Verkerstrüppen"), all the technical units concerned in the railway, the telegraphic and the air-craft services. This new arm was put under the control of an officer holding the rank of a General of Division and receiving his orders direct from the Emperor. A change was also effected in regard to the Berlin-Juterbog railway—a single-track line, 70 km. (44 miles) in length, which, originally constructed mainly by the Railway Troops, was operated by them as a means of acquiring experience in railway working. Prior to the passing of the law of March 25, 1899, troops for the working staff were supplied by the Brigade, and the frequent changes were a cause of some inconvenience. Under the new law a section constituted of three Prussian Companies and a Saxon detachment,

RAILWAY TROOPS IN GERMANY.   135

with a Lieutenant-Colonel as director, was specially created for the operation of the line.

Altogether the Railway Troops comprised a total of thirty-one Companies, having 180 officers and 4,500 non-commissioned officers and men ; but these figures were irrespective of carefully-compiled lists (subjected to frequent revision) of all reservists possessing railway experience and still liable for military service. Brigade, Battalions and Companies thus formed only the cadres of a small army of men considered qualified to undertake railway work of one kind or another in time of war.

Even in Germany itself the need for having so large a body of Railway Troops was called into question some years ago, on the ground, partly, that it was desirable to keep to the lowest practicable minimum the number of non-combatants closely associated with the Army ; and, partly, because of the view—favoured by Von der Goltz, in his " Kriegführung "—that much of the construction work which the Railway Troops would carry out might be left to contractors, without hampering the Army with further bodies of new troops for special purposes.

To these suggestions it was replied, in effect, (1) that in any future war the movement of large bodies of troops would be directly associated with the provision and the maintenance of adequate railway facilities ; (2) that Railway Troops, constituted in time of peace, would alone be capable of ensuring the rapid renovation of damaged lines, or the construction of new ones, in time of war ; (3) that works of this kind, done under great pressure, and serving temporary purposes only, would differ essentially from railway works undertaken in peace by ordinary contractors ; and (4) that Germany required a large body of Railway Troops on account of her geographical position, inasmuch as she might have to face an enemy on either, or both, of two fronts—France and Russia ; while if, in the event of a war with Russia, she should want to send her forces into that country by rail, she would require to have a large body of Railway Troops available either for the conversion of the Russian 5 ft. gauge into the 4 ft. $8\frac{1}{2}$ in. gauge of the German lines (in order that the engines and rolling stock of the latter could be utilised on Russian territory), or for the construction of special military railways as substitutes for the Russian lines.

Whatever the merits of these respective arguments, the fact remains that the Railway Troops of Germany, created under the circumstances and conditions here detailed, have been maintained in steadily increasing numbers, and, also, in constantly expanding efficiency thanks to what is, in effect, their School of Railway Instruction and to the great amount of practical work they have been called upon to do, whether in the building of strategical lines or in other departments of railway construction, destruction or working in which they could gain experience likely to be of advantage in time of war.

There was, also, according to M. Paul Lanoir, as related by him in his book on "The German Spy System," a still further purpose that these Army railwaymen might be called on to serve. He tells how in 1880, the chief of the system, the notorious Stieber, conceived the idea of securing the appointment in every portion of the national railway system of France (and more especially at important junctions or strategical centres) of German spies who, competent to act as railway workers, would, in the event of any future war between Germany and France, and on receiving the necessary instructions, destroy or block the railway lines at those points in such a manner—as planned, of course, in advance—that great delay would occur in the mobilisation of the French troops owing to the traffic being paralysed for the time being; the Germans, in the meantime, rushing their own forces to the frontier. "The extremely important rôle which would devolve on our railwaymen," adds M. Lanoir, "at the moment of the declaration of war, in fulfilling their functions as indispensable auxiliaries to the combatant army, was already thoroughly appreciated at this period."

Submitted to Prince Bismarck, Stieber's scheme was approved by him, and, so far as the obtaining of appointments on the French railways by Stieber's agents was concerned, the plan had been quietly carried into effect by the end of 1883; but a casual incident then led to the discovery of the conspiracy by M. Lanoir himself. Within a week, as the result of his communications with General Campenau, Minister of War, the railway companies received a confidential circular requiring that they should call upon every foreigner employed by them in any capacity whatever to become naturalised without delay. Those who would not adopt this course were to be immediately dismissed. The number of foreigners then in the employ of the railway companies was 1,641, and, although 1,459 of them agreed to become naturalised, there were 182 Germans who refused so to do. These 182 were at once discharged—the assumption being that they were the spies, qualified to act as railway workers, by whom the dislocation of traffic was to have been ensured whenever they might receive word to that effect.

CHAPTER XII

France and the War of 1870-71

WHEN France went to war with Germany in 1870-71, her military rail-transport was still governed by regulations which, adopted as far back as 1851 and 1855, related only to such matters of detail as the financial arrangements between the Army and the railway companies, the length of troop trains, etc., without making any provision for an organisation controlling the transport of large bodies of men in time of war. It certainly had been under these regulations that the French troops were conveyed to Italy when they took part in the campaign of 1859; but the defects then developed, coupled with the further lessons taught by the Austro-Prussian War of 1866, had shown the need for bringing these early French regulations into harmony with the conditions and requirements of modern warfare.

Impressed by these considerations, and realising the disadvantages and dangers of the position into which his country had drifted, the French Minister of War, Marshal Niel, appointed in March, 1869, a " Commission Centrale des Chemins de Fer," composed of representatives of the Army, the Ministry of Public Works, and the principal railway companies, for the purpose not only of revising the existing regulations on military transports but of preparing a new one to take their place. The Commission held twenty-nine sittings and it drew up a provisional scheme on lines closely following those already adopted in Germany and Austria and based, especially, on the same principle of a co-ordination of the military with the railway technical element. This provisional scheme was subjected to various tests and trials with a view to perfecting it before it was placed on a permanent basis. But Marshal Niel died ; no new regulation was adopted ; the projected scheme was more or less forgotten ; time was against the early completion of the proposed experiments, while political and military developments succeeded one another with such rapidity that, on the outbreak of war in 1870, it was no longer possible to carry out the proposed plans. So the studies of the Commission came to naught, and France embarked on her tremendous conflict with no organisation for military transport apart from the out-of-date and wholly defective regulations under which her troops had already suffered in the Italian war of 1859.

There was an impression that the talent of the French soldier would enable him to " se débrouiller "—to " pull," if not (in the English sense) to " muddle," through. But the conditions were hopeless, and the results speedily brought about were little short of chaos.

So far as the actual conveyance of troops was concerned, the railway companies themselves did marvels. " The numerical superiority of Germany," as Von der Goltz says in his " Nation in Arms," " was known in Paris, and it was thought to neutralise this superiority by boldness and rapidity. The idea was a good one. . . but . . . it was needful that the Germans should be outdone in the rapidity with which the armies were massed." That the railway managements and staffs did their best to secure this result is beyond any possibility of doubt.

On July 15, 1870, the Minister of Public Works directed the Est, Nord and Paris-Lyon Companies to place all their means of transport at the disposal of the War Minister, suspending as far as necessary their ordinary passenger and goods services ; and the Ouest and Orléans Companies were asked to put their rolling stock at the disposal of the three other companies. The Est, to which the heaviest part in the work involved was to fall, had already taken various measures in anticipation of an outbreak of war ; and such was the energy shown by the companies, as a whole, that the first troop train was started from Paris at 5.45 p.m. on July 16, within, that is to say, twenty-four hours of the receipt of the notice from the Minister of Public Works. Between July 16 and July 26 there were despatched 594 troop trains, conveying 186,620 men, 32,410 horses, 3,162 guns and road vehicles, and 995 wagon-loads of ammunition and supplies. In the nineteen days of the whole concentration period (July 16–August 4) the companies carried 300,000 men, 64,700 horses, 6,600 guns and road vehicles, and 4,400 wagon-loads of ammunition and supplies.

All this activity on the part of the railway companies was, however, neutralised more or less by the absence of any adequate organisation for regulating and otherwise dealing with the traffic, so far as concerned the military authorities themselves.

The first regiment to leave Paris, on July 16, arrived at the station at 2 p.m. for the train due to start at 5.45 p.m. The men had been accompanied through the streets by an immense crowd shouting " À Berlin ! " and, with so much time to spare, they either blocked up the station or were taken off by their friends to the neighbouring taverns, where the consumption of liquor was such that, by the time the train started, most of the men were excessively drunk. In addition to this, many had been relieved of their ammunition—taken from them, perhaps, as " souvenirs " of an historic occasion, though destined to reappear and to be put to bad use in the days of the Commune, later on.

If, however, at the beginning, the troops got to the station three hours before there was any need, other occasions were to arise when they kept trains waiting three or four hours before they themselves were ready to start.

Then, in Germany the concentration of the troops at some safe point in the interior, and their transport thence by rail to the frontier in complete units, took place as separate and distinct operations. In France the two movements were conducted simultaneously; and this, in itself, was a prolific source of confusion and disorganisation on the railways. The troops came to the stations on a peace footing and in various strengths. One regiment might have only one-third the strength of another despatched earlier the same day or on the previous day, although the railway company would have provided the same number of vehicles for both. There was thus a choice of evils as between removing two-thirds of the carriages (a procedure which time or the station arrangements did not always permit); sending the train away only partially loaded; or filling up the available space either with men belonging to other corps or with such supplies as might be available at the moment. Some trains did leave nearly empty, but it was the last mentioned of the three courses that was generally adopted. Men of different arms—Infantry, Cavalry and Artillery; mobilised troops, reservists, and individuals, separated, it might be, from their own officers and not willing to show themselves amenable to the discipline of other officers—were thus transported at the same time as, possibly, a miscellaneous collection of horses, material and commissariat supplies. Other trains, again, went away so overcrowded that they could not accommodate all the men who should have gone by them, many being left behind in consequence.

Confusion and delays at the railway stations during the entraining of the troops were rendered the more complete because the railway staffs failed to get an adequate degree of support from the military authorities. According to one of the articles in those regulations of 1855 which were still in force, " officers were responsible for the prescribed movements in connection with the entraining, and should personally co-operate in ensuring observance of the regulations referring thereto "; but, according to Baron Ernouf, (" Histoire des Chemins de Fer Français pendant la Guerre Franco-Prussienne,") there were officers who refused absolutely to concern themselves with the entraining of their men at the Est station in Paris, declaring that this was a matter to be looked after by the railway officials with the help of subordinate officers, if they wanted it.

Under such conditions as these, officers in charge of troops got hopelessly separated from their men, who themselves might have been sent off with no knowledge of their proper destination. One General telegraphed to Paris on

July 21 :—"Have arrived at Belfort. Not found my Brigade. Not found General of Division. What should I do? Don't know where my Regiments are." As for the men, it was not many days before the stations *en route* to the front were occupied by a floating mass of "lost" soldiers, who pretended to be looking for their corps but too often found it much pleasanter to remain in the station buffets, and there enjoy the hospitality of local patriots. Such proportions did this evil assume that in August, 1870, the railway station at Reims had to be protected against a mob of from 4,000 to 5,000 "lost" ones, who wanted to plunder the wagons containing supplies for the front.

Confusion, again, was made still worse confounded by the multiplicity of orders—too often contradictory or impossible to carry out—which bombarded the railway officials, and must have driven them at times almost to distraction. Orders came direct from anybody and everybody possessed of the slightest degree of military authority. They came from the Ministry of War, the General Staff, and the Administrative Staff ; from the Quartermaster-General's Department and the Commissariat ; from officers and non-commissioned officers of Infantry, Artillery and Engineers ; while each individual invariably gave his orders based on the range of his own particular sphere, or the convenience of his own particular troops, without any regard for the situation as a whole, for what might be wanted in other spheres, or for whether or not it was physically possible for the railway staffs to do at all what was asked of them, even if they were not being overwhelmed with those other orders, besides. Commanding officers of different corps especially distinguished themselves by presenting to the railway managements claims for priority in the despatch of Infantry, Artillery or supplies, as the case might be, threatening them with grave consequences if, in each instance, they did not yield such priority at once, though leaving them to meet an obviously impracticable position as best they could. Then it might happen that when all the necessary arrangements—involving much interference with other traffic— had been made, another order would come countermanding the first one, or postponing the execution of it until a later occasion.

As though, again, the orders from all these independent military authorities were not sufficient, the railways were further worried by local authorities who wanted special trains for some such service as the conveyance of detachments of garde mobile a distance of ten or twelve miles to an instruction camp so that the men would not have to march by road. There were even demands from certain of the local authorities that they should be allowed to use railway wagons as barracks for troops.

M. Jacqmin, general manager of the Chemin de Fer de l'Est, relates in his book, " Les Chemins de Fer Pendant la Guerre de 1870–71," that at the moment when the Compagnie de l'Est was providing for the transport of Bourbacki's forces, and preparing for the revictualling of Paris, the préfet of the Rhone demanded the use of railway wagons in which to house the garde nationale mobilised on the plain of Vénissieux, on the left bank of the Rhone, there having been a delay in the delivery of the material for barracks. The company refused the request, and they had with the departmental authorities a lively controversy which was only settled by the decision of the Bordeaux Government that those authorities were in the wrong.

Typical of the general conditions, as they prevailed not only in Paris but elsewhere in France, were the circumstances under which the Nineteenth Army Corps, of 32,000 men, 3,000 horses and 300 guns, was sent from Cherbourg to Alençon. The troops were late in arriving at the station; the officers neglected to look after the men; the men refused to travel in goods trucks; orders and counter-orders succeeded one another in rapid succession; two or three hours were required for the despatch of each train, and delays occurred which must have disorganised the traffic all along the line.

Great as the confusion undoubtedly was at the points of despatch, it was far surpassed by that which prevailed at stations to which trains were sent regardless of any consideration as to whether or not they could be unloaded there with such despatch as to avoid congestion. No transfer stations—constituting the points beyond which only the supplies wanted for immediate or early use at the extreme front should be taken, the remainder being forwarded as wanted—had been arranged, and the consignors, military or civil, had assumed that all supplies should be sent in bulk to places as near to the troops as possible There were, consequently, many stations close to the frontier where the rails leading to them were occupied for miles together by loaded wagons, the number of which was being constantly added to by fresh arrivals. Many of these wagons were, in fact, used as magazines or store-houses on wheels. The same was, also, being done to a certain extent on the German lines, though with this difference—that whereas in Germany there were at the railway stations route commandants whose duty it was to enforce the prompt unloading of wagons, in France there was no corresponding authority. It suited the officers or the military department concerned to keep the supplies in the wagons until they were wanted; and this arrangement may have appeared an especially desirable one from their point of view because if the army moved forward—or backward—the supplies could be more readily moved with it if they were still in the wagons.

For these various reasons, there were officers who gave the most stringent orders that the wagons were not to be unloaded until their contents were actually required. It was evidently a matter of no concern to them that the wagons they were detaining might be wanted elsewhere, and that, for lack of them, other troops might be experiencing a shortage in their own supplies.

When the wagons were not deliberately kept loaded, it might still be impossible for the unloading to be done because of there being no military in attendance to do the work. As for the picking out, from among the large number in waiting, of some one wagon the contents of which were specially wanted, the trouble involved in this operation must often have been far greater than if the wagon had been unloaded and the supplies stored in the first instance.

FRANCE AND THE WAR OF 1870–71. 145

Even the stations themselves got congested, under like conditions. The Commissariat wanted to convert them into depôts, and the Artillery sought to change them into arsenals. There were stations at which no platform was any longer available and troops arriving by any further train had to descend some distance away, several days elapsing before their train could be moved from the place where it had pulled up. At stations not thus blocked trains might be hours late in arriving, or they might bring a squadron of cavalry when arrangements had been made for receiving a battalion of infantry.

In one instance a General refused to allow his men to detrain on arrival at their destination at night, saying they would be more comfortable in the carriages than in the snow. This was, indeed, the case; but so long as the train remained where it was standing no other traffic could pass. Sometimes it was necessary for troop trains to wait on the lines for hours because no camp had been assigned to the men, and there was at least one occasion when a Colonel had to ask the station-master where it was his troops were to go.

Most of the traffic had been directed to Metz and Strasburg, and the state of chaos speedily developed at the former station has become historic.

The station at Metz was a large one; it had eight good depôts and four miles of sidings, and it was equal to the unloading of 930 wagons in twenty-four hours under well-organised conditions. But when the first infantry trains arrived the men were kept at the station four or five hours owing to the absence of orders as to their further destination. The men detrained, and the wagons containing road vehicles, officers' luggage, etc., were left unloaded and sent into the sidings. Other trains followed in rapid succession, bringing troops and supplies, and the block began to assume serious proportions.

The railway officials appealed to the local Commissariat force to unload the wagons so that they could be got out of the way. They were told that this could not be done because no orders had been received. The Commissariat

L

force for the division also declined to unload the wagons, saying it was uncertain whether the troops for whom the supplies were intended would remain at Metz or go further on.

Any unloading at all for several days was next rendered impossible by the higher military authorities. They asked the railway officers to prepare for the transport of an army corps of 30,000 men. This was done, and forty trains were located at various points along the line. An order was then given that the trains should be brought to Metz, to allow of the troops leaving at once. Within four hours every train was ready, and its locomotive was standing with the steam up; but no troops appeared. The order was countermanded. Then it was repeated, and then it was countermanded over again.

All this time fresh train-loads of supplies and ammunition had been arriving at Metz, adding to the collection of unloaded wagons which, having filled up all the sidings began to overflow and block up, first the lines leading to the locomotive sheds and next the main lines themselves. Everything was in inextricable confusion. Nobody knew where any particular commodity was to be found or, if they did, how to get the truck containing it from the consolidated mass of some thousands of vehicles. "In Metz," telegraphed the Commissary-General to Paris, " there is neither coffee, nor sugar; no rice, no brandy, no salt, only a little bacon and biscuit. Send me at least a million rations to Thionville." Yet it was quite possible that the articles specified were already in some or other of the trucks on hand, had the Commissary-General only known where they were and how to get them.

The railway people did what they could. They unloaded some of the consignments and removed them a considerable distance by road—only to have them sent back again to Metz station for re-loading and conveyance elsewhere. Hay unloaded at the station was sent into Metz to some magazines which, in turn, and at the same time, were sending hay to the railway for another destination. Finally, as a last resource, and in order both to reduce the block and to get further use out of the wagons, the railway officials began to unload them and put their contents on the ground alongside. A big capture alike of wagons and of supplies was made by the enemy on his occupation of Metz.

Analogous conditions prevailed in many other places. At Dôle (Dep. Jura) an accumulated stock of loaded wagons not only filled up all the sidings but blocked up a large portion of the main line. When the evacuation was decided on a great waste of time occurred in selecting the wagons to be moved. Orders given one hour were countermanded the next; trains which had been made up were moved forward and backward, instead of being got out of the way at once; and, eventually, a considerable quantity of rolling stock, which might and should have been removed, had to be left behind.

On the Paris-Lyon railway a collection of 7,500 loaded trucks had accumulated at a time when a great truck shortage began to be felt, and the whole of these, together with the provisions and the materials they contained, fell into the hands of the Germans, whose total haul of wagons, including those captured at Metz and other places, numbered no fewer than 16,000. The wagons thus taken were first used by them for their own military transport during the remainder of the war; were then utilised for ordinary traffic on lines in Germany, and were eventually returned to France. Not only, therefore, had the French failed to get from these 16,000 railway wagons the benefit they should have derived from their use but, in blocking their lines with them under such conditions that it was impossible to save them from capture, they conferred a material advantage on the enemy, providing him with supplies, and increasing his own means both of transport and of attack on themselves.

The proportions of the German haul of wagons would, probably, have been larger still had not some of the French railway companies, on seeing the advance the enemy was making, assumed the responsibility of stopping traffic on certain of their lines and sending off their rolling stock to a place of safety. In taking this action they adopted a course based alike on precedent and prudence, and one fully warranted by the principle of keeping railway rolling stock designed for purposes of defence from being utilised by the enemy for his own purposes of attack.

CHAPTER XIII

ORGANISATION IN FRANCE

WHILE, on the conclusion of the Franco-Prussian war, Germany began, as we have seen in Chapter X., to improve her own system of military rail-transport, with a view to remedying the faults developed therein, France applied herself with equal, if not with even greater, determination and perseverance to the task of creating for herself a system which, in her case, had been entirely lacking.

Recognising alike her own shortcomings, the imperative need to prepare for future contingencies, and the still more important part that railways would inevitably play in the next great war in which she might be engaged, France resolved to create, in time of peace, and as an indispensable factor in her scheme of national defence, a system of military transport comprehensive in its scope, complete in its working details, and leaving nothing to chance. Everything was to be foreseen, provided for, and, as far as circumstances would permit, tested in advance.

The Prussian organisation of 1870–71 was, admittedly, and as recommended by Jacqmin, taken as a starting point for what was to be done. From that time, also, every new regulation adopted by Prussia in regard to military transport, and every important alteration made in the Prussian system, was promptly recorded and commended or criticised in the ably-conducted French military papers; though in the actual creation of her own system there was no mere following by France of Prussian examples. What was considered worth adopting certainly was adopted; but the organisation eventually built up, as the result of many years of pertinacious efforts, was, in reality, based on French conditions, French requirements, and the most progressive ideas of French military science. The French were, also, to show that, when they applied themselves to the task, they had a genius for organisation in no way inferior to that of the Germans themselves.

In his review of the events of 1870-71, Jacqmin declared that, while the education of France in the use of railways in time of war had still to be completed, the basis for such education had already been laid down by Marshal Niel's " Commission Centrale " of 1869. The two essential conditions were (1) unification of control in the use of railways for military purposes, whether for the transport of men or of supplies ; and (2) association of the military element and the technical element,—an association which should be permanent in its nature and apply to every phase of the railway service, so that before any order was given there should be a guarantee that it was one possible of achievement, and this, also, without prejudice to other transport orders already given or likely to become necessary.

It was these essential conditions that formed the basis of the organisation which France created.

As early as November, 1872, there was called into existence a *Commission Militaire Superieure des Chemins de Fer* consisting of twelve members, who represented the Ministry of Public Works, the Army, the Navy, and the great railway companies. Attached to the Ministry of War, and charged with the task of studying all questions relating to the use of railways by the Army, the Commission had for its first duty a revision of the proposals made by Marshal Niel's Commission of 1869. Following on this came a succession of laws, decrees and instructions dealing with various aspects of the situation in regard to military transport and the military organization of the railways, the number issued between 1872 and 1883 being no fewer than seventeen. These, however, represented more or less tentative or sectional efforts made in combination with the railway companies, who gave to the Chambers and to the administrative authorities their most earnest support and the full benefit of all their technical knowledge and experi-

ORGANISATION IN FRANCE.

ence in regard to the many problems which had to be solved.

In 1884 there were issued two decrees (July 7 and October 29) which codified, modified or further developed the various legislative or administrative measures already taken, and laid down both the fundamental principles and the leading details of a comprehensive scheme which, after additional modifications or amendments, based on later experiences, was to develop into the system of organised military rail-transport as it exists in France to-day.

These later modifications were more especially effected by three decrees which, based on the law of December 28, 1888, dealt with (1) the composition and powers of the Commission Militaire Superieure des Chemins de Fer; (2) the creation of Field Railway Sections and Railway Troops; and (3) the organisation of the military service of railways.

Since its original formation in 1872, the *Superior Military Commission* had already undergone reconstruction in 1886, and still further changes, in addition to those made by the decree of February 5, 1889, were to follow. In its final form the Commission still retains the principle of representation thereon alike of the military and the technical (railway) element. Presided over by the Chief of the General Staff—who, with the help of a special department of that Staff, exercises the supreme direction of the military transport services, subject to the authority of the War Minister—the Commission is composed of six Generals or other military officers of high rank, three representatives of the Ministry of Public Works, and the members of the Line Commission appointed for each of the great railway systems and, also, for the Chemin de Fer d'État.

All the members of the Commission are nominated by the Minister of War. The function they discharge is a purely consultative one. Their business it is to give to the Minister their views on all such questions as he may submit to them for consideration in regard to the use of the railways by the Army, and more especially in regard to—

1. Preparations for military transports.
2. Examination of all projects for new lines or junctions and alterations of existing lines, as well as all projects which

concern railway facilities (stations, platforms, water supply, locomotive sheds, etc.)

3. The fixing of the conditions to be fulfilled by railway rolling stock in view of military requirements, and the alterations which may be necessary to adapt it thereto.

4. Special instructions to be given to troops of all arms as to their travelling by rail.

5. Agreements to be made between railway companies and the War Department in respect to transport of troops, provisions, etc.

6. Organisation, instruction and employment of special corps of railwaymen (for repairs, etc.).

7. Measures to be taken for ensuring the supervision and protection of railways and their approaches.

8. The means of destroying and of rapidly repairing lines of railway.

Heads of the different services at the Ministry of War can attend meetings of the Commission, in a consultative capacity, in respect to matters coming within their jurisdiction, and the Commission can, in turn, apply to the Minister for the attendance of any person it may desire to hear.

As far as possible, all plans and arrangements concerning the transport of troops and supplies in time of war, from the moment of mobilisation onward, are thus prepared, examined or provided for in advance. In article 8 of the Regulation of December 8, 1913, on Military Transports by Railway (" Réglement sur les transports stratégiques par chemin de fer ") it is, in fact, stated that—

All the arrangements relating to the organisation and carrying out of transport for mobilisation, concentration, revictualling and evacuation are studied and prepared in time of peace. The Minister gives, to this effect, all the necessary instructions to the General Staff, to the commanders of Army Corps, and to the different services. A like course is adopted, in time of peace, with regard to the study of the conditions under which the railways will be operated on the lines of communication.

The creation, under the law of March 13, 1875, of Field Railway Sections and Railway Troops was the outcome of the obvious need of having an organised force able to

ORGANISATION IN FRANCE.

take up the duties of constructing, repairing, destroying or operating railways at the theatre of war, such force being established in time of peace and assured all the experience needed to qualify them for the discharge of those various duties. France, in fact, was now, in this respect, to follow the example of Germany, just as Germany had already been inspired by the example of the United States.

Under a decree of February 5, 1889, *Field Railway Sections* ("Sections de chemins de fer de campagne") were defined as permanent military corps charged, in time of war, and concurrently with the Railway Troops, with the construction, renovation and operation of those railways of which the working could not be assured by the national companies. Their personnel was to be recruited from among the engineers, officials and men employed by the railway companies and by the State Railways Administration, such recruiting being carried out either voluntarily or by reason of liability to render military service; and they were to form a distinct corps, having its own governing body with, as its head, a commandant exercising the functions of a Chef de Corps. In time of peace there were to be nine sections, each designated by a distinctive number according to the particular railway system or systems from which it was formed; though authority was given to the Minister of War to call further sections into being in case of war. The number in peace was increased, in 1906, by the formation of a tenth section from among the staffs of railways in the "secondary" group, including local lines and tramways, in order to assure, or to assist in, the operation of these railways or tramways for military transport in time of war.

In time of peace the sections were to be subject to inspections, musters, reviews and assemblies, as ordered by the Minister of War. A further provision in the decree of 1889 says:—" All the arrangements relative to the mobilisation of each section shall be studied and planned in time of peace. Each section should always be ready, in the most complete manner, to render its services to the Minister of War."

Subsequent decrees or instructions constituted each of the sections a complete unit on the following basis : (1) A central body; (2) three distinct divisions, namely, (a) " movement," (b) " voie," and (c) " traction " ; (3) a central depôt common to the three divisions and the central body ; and (4) complementary territorial subdivisions in the same three classes, and attached to the central depôt of the section. The territorial subdivisions are designed to provide a reserve force of men who can complete or strengthen the existing sections, or, alternatively, be constituted into additional sections, if so desired by the Minister of War. The total strength of each section (including 141 allotted to the central depôt) was fixed as 1,466.

The administration of a section rests with an Administrative Council formed by the president and the heads of the several departments, and meeting at least once in every three months in time of peace, and once a week in time of war. Authority is exercised over the sections by the Field Railway Commissions to which they are attached.[1]

Men in the active divisions of the sections who are liable to military service are excused from taking part in the ordinary military exercises, but may be assembled for inspections, etc., or to undergo courses of instruction in railway work. Men in the territorial subdivisions can be summoned by the Minister of War for " a period of exercises " in railway work in time of peace ; and the fact may be recalled that advantage of this power was taken during the French railway troubles of 1910, when the strikers were required to assume the rôle of soldiers doing railway work under military authority and control.

The *Railway Troops* (" Troupes de chemin de fer ") now constitute a Railway Regiment (" 5ᵉ régiment du génie ") organised under the decree of July 11, 1899, and comprising on a peace footing, three Battalions, each of four Companies.

Recruits for the Railway Regiment come from one or other of the following classes : (1) Young soldiers who were

[1] For details concerning the functions and duties of the various divisions, subdivisions, etc., see "Mouvements et Transports. Sections de chemins de fer de campagne. Volume arrêté à la date du 1er septembre, 1914." Paris : Henri Charles-Lavauzelle.

ORGANISATION IN FRANCE. 155

in the railway service before they joined the Army; (2) an annual contingent of railway employés selected by the Minister of War from lists supplied for this purpose by the administrations of the five great railway companies and of the State railways, the number so selected not to exceed 240, distributed as follows: Compagnie du Nord, 42; Est, 18; P. L. M., 54; Orléans, 42; Midi, 15; État, 69; and (3) soldiers belonging to Infantry Regiments who, after one year of training therein, are sent to the Railway Regiment, those chosen for this purpose being, by preference, men whose previous occupation in life has adapted them for railway work.

The railway administrations are also required to provide from among their officials a certain number of officers and non-commissioned officers to form a reserve for the Regiment.

A most complete and systematic course of instruction is arranged.[1] It is divided into (1) military instruction and (2) technical instruction, the purpose of the latter being defined as that of qualifying the Railway Troops to undertake at the theatre of war, subject to the authority of the Director-General of Railways and Communications, works of repair or destruction of railway lines, or, in case of need, the provisional working of the railways. In time of peace it is the duty of the Superior Military Commission for Railways to advise on all questions concerning the organisation, instruction and employment of the special troops for railway work. To enable it to discharge this function the Commission receives, through the Chief of the General Staff, all programmes, proposals or reports that may be issued in regard to the technical instruction of the troops, giving its views thereon, and making such recommendations as it may consider desirable.

Such technical instruction comprises (a) that which is given to the whole of the troops; (b) instruction in particular branches of railway work given to a limited number of individuals; (c) instruction to groups of men operating in

[1] "Bulletin Officiel du Ministère de la Guerre. Génie. Troupes de chemins de fer. Volume arrêté à la date du 1er décembre, 1912."

companies or otherwise, and (d) instruction obtained on the ordinary railways. It is further divided into (i) theoretical and (ii) practical.

Among the measures adopted for ensuring the success of the general scheme, mention might be made of the issuing of special series of textbooks; the regular working by the Regiment of about forty miles of railway—including an important junction—between Chartres and Orleans, on the State Railway system; and arrangements made with the railway administrations under which (1) a certain number of Companies belonging to the Regiment are attached to the ordinary railway systems every year, for periods of two or three months; and (2) power is given to the railway administrations to engage the services of the Railway Troops in carrying out repairs or construction works on their lines, a mutual advantage thus being obtained.

Finally there is a Railway School (" École de chemins de fer ") which has charge of all the materials, tools, etc., used in the technical instruction of the troops; draws up, under the orders of the Colonel, programmes of practical work and instruction; and provides (1) a library which is supplied with books and periodicals dealing with military, railway, scientific and historical subjects, together with maps, plans, decrees, regulations, etc., relating to the military operation of railways; (2) a collection of tools, instruments and models; (3) photographic and lithographic departments; (4) stores of railway construction material for instruction purposes; (5) other stores of like material for use in case of war; (6) workshops for practical instruction in railway repairs, etc.; and (7) practice grounds reserved exclusively for the Railway Troops.

The fact of these two bodies of Field Railway Sections and Railway Troops being organised on so practical and comprehensive a basis secured to France the control of forces certain to be of the greatest service to her in the next war in which she might be engaged. It would, also, even suffice by itself to prove the earnestness, the vigour and the thoroughness with which, after 1870–71, France entered upon the improvement of her system of military rail-trans-

ORGANISATION IN FRANCE. 157

port for national defence. There was, however, much more to be done, besides, before that system could be considered complete; and here, again, a vast amount of study, foresight and energy was shown.

Following, indeed, the laws, decrees, regulations, orders, and instructions issued down to 1889 came so many others—dealing, in some instances, with even the minutest detail concerning some particular phase of the organisation in course of being perfected—that a collected series of those still in force in 1902 formed a volume of over 700 pages.[1] Since the issue of this somewhat formidable collection, still further changes have been introduced, the general conditions being finally modified by decrees passed on December 8, 1913.

Without attempting to indicate all the successive stages in this prolonged series of legislative and administrative efforts, it may suffice to offer a general sketch of the French organisation of military rail-transport on the basis of the laws, regulations and practices in operation on the outbreak of war in 1914.

Connected with each of the great railway systems there is a permanent *Line Commission* ("Commission de réseau") which consists of (1) a technical member who, in practice, is the general manager of the line; and (2) a military member, who is a member of the General Staff of the Army. The former is chosen by the railway administration, subject to the approval of the War Minister, and the latter by the War Minister himself. Each Line Commission controls the services of a combined technical and military staff, and each Commissioner has a deputy who can take his place and exercise his powers in case of need. While the Military Commissioner is specially responsible for measures adopted from a military point of view, the Railway Commissioner is specially responsible for putting at the command of the Army, as far as may be necessary or practicable, all the

[1] "Transports militaires par chemin de fer. (Guerre et Marine.) Édition mise à jour des textes en vigueur jusqu'en octobre, 1902." For later publications, dealing, in separate issues, with particular departments of the military rail-transport organisation, see Bibliography.

resources of the particular railway system he represents.

The authority of a Line Commission on any one of the great railway systems extends to the smaller, or secondary, lines situate within the same territory; but the smaller companies may themselves claim to be represented on the Commission by a duly credited agent.

Among the duties to be discharged by a Line Commission in time of peace are the following :—

1. Investigation of all matters to which military transport on the line or the system can give rise.

2. Study of all the available resources of the system, in material and men, from the point of view of military requirements.

3. Preparation of plans, estimates, and other data in connection with the movement of troops, etc.

4. Verification of reports concerning extent of lines, rolling stock, and station or traffic facilities.

5. Special instruction of the railway staff.

6. Inspection of lines, bridges, etc.

7. The carrying out of experiments of all kinds with a view to ameliorating or accelerating the facilities offered by the system in respect to military transports.

Should several Line Commissions be interested in some particular question concerning military movements by rail, the Chief of the General Staff can summon them to a joint conference as often as may be necessary. The fact, also, that the members of the Line Commissions are members of the Superior Commission assures co-ordination in the studies carried on as regards the railways in general, and provides a ready means by which the central body can obtain the information it desires concerning any one system or group of systems.

As their district executives, the Line Commissions have such number of *Sub-Line Commissions* as may be found necessary. Each of these is, in turn, composed of a military member, nominated by the Minister, and a technical member, chosen by the Line Commission. Then, also, to discharge the function of local executive, there is at every important centre of traffic a *Station Commission* (" Commis-

ORGANISATION IN FRANCE. 159

sion de gare ") which consists of a military officer and the stationmaster. It receives from the Line or Sub-Line Commission all orders or instructions concerning military transport to, from, or passing through, such station, and is the recognised intermediary for carrying them into effect and seeing that efficiency is ensured and good order maintained.

A staff, formed of military men and railwaymen acting in combination, is allotted to each Line, Sub-Line or Station Commission. Concerning the representation of these two elements, military and civil, on the one body, article 10 of the decree of December 8, 1913, on Military Transports says :—

The special function of each of the agents, military or technical, on the Commissions or Sub-Commissions must, in the operation of the service, be maintained in the most absolute manner. At the same time these agents should not lose from their view the fact that their association is designed to effect harmony between the exigencies alike of military requirements and of rail transport, subordinating those of the one to those of the other, according to circumstances.

From the time that mobilisation begins—or even earlier, on the order of the War Minister—the members of the Superior Commission take up their posts *en permanence* at the War Office, and those of the Line, Sub-Line and Station Commissions locate themselves at the stations which will have been allotted to them in time of peace. Thenceforward each Station Commission is in constant communication by telegraph with the Line or Sub-Line Commission under which it acts, supplementing such communication by daily written reports. Among the duties to be discharged by the Station Commissions are those of superintending the entrainment or detrainment of troops and the loading or unloading of material; seeing that the trains required for transport purposes are provided; preventing congestion of the lines or of the station approaches; and ensuring the security of the station and of the lines within a certain radius thereof.

On the outbreak of war the railway companies must

place at the service of the State either the whole or such of their lines, rolling stock, and other means of transport as may be needed for the conveyance of troops, stores, etc., to any points served by them. Thenceforward the lines so required for "strategic transports"—including therein mobilisation, concentration, reinforcements, supplies and evacuations from the theatre of war—can be used for ordinary passengers and goods only to such extent as the Minister may approve.

Following on the order for mobilisation the Minister, after consultation with the Commander-in-Chief, divides the railways of the country into two zones—the "Zone of the Interior," and the "Zone of the Armies." Of these the former passes under the supreme control of the War Minister, and the latter under that of the Commander-in-Chief. The location of the *Stations of Transition*, dividing the one zone from the other, can be varied from time to time by the Minister, in consultation with the Commander-in-Chief, according to the developments of the military situation.

The *Zone of the Interior* is that part of the railway system which, though not situated at the theatre of war, is subject to military control by reason of the services required of it in the forwarding of troops, supplies, guns, ammunition and other necessaries. Operation by the ordinary staffs of the railway systems is continued, but the transports ordered by the War Minister are regulated by the Chief of the General Staff. The execution of the orders given is entrusted from the day of mobilisation to the Line Commissions, each of which, acting under the authority of the War Minister, takes charge over the whole of the services on the lines comprised in its particular territory.

The *Zone of the Armies* is, in turn, divided into two sections (1) the "Zone de l'avant," in which military operation of the railways is necessary on account of their nearness to the fighting-line; and (2) the "Zone de l'Arrière," in which the railways can still be operated by the ordinary railway staffs, under the direction of Line and Station Commissions, as in the adjoining Zone of the Interior.

ORGANISATION IN FRANCE.

Orders given by the Commander-in-Chief in respect to transport in the Zone of the Armies are carried out under the supreme control of an officer now known as the *Directeur de l'Arrière*. The history of this important functionary affords an excellent example of the way in which the whole scheme of operations has been evolved. The " Règlement général " of July 1, 1874,—one of the earliest attempts to meet the difficulties which had arisen in 1870–71 in respect to military rail-transport—was found to be defective inasmuch as it did not apply, also, to those road and rear services (" Services de l'Arrière ") which are necessarily associated with the rail services and themselves constitute so important a phase of military transport as a whole. In 1878 an attempt was made to meet this defect by the inauguration of a system of " Services des Étapes "; but here, again, the existence of separate organisations for rail service and road service, without any connecting and controlling link, was found to be unsatisfactory. In 1883 a Commission, presided over by General Fay, was appointed to consider what would be the best course to adopt, and, in the result, there was issued, on July 7, 1884, a Decree creating a " Directeur Général des Chemins de Fer et des Étapes," whose duties were more clearly defined under a Decree of February 21, 1900. In 1908 the title of this officer was changed to that of " Directeur de l'Arrière," and, after further revisions, the scope of his authority and responsibility was eventually fixed by the Regulation of December 8, 1913.

Taking up his position at the head-quarters of the Commander-in-Chief, and keeping in close touch, also, with the Minister of War through the Chief of the General Staff, the Directeur de l'Arrière has for his special function that of securing complete co-ordination alike between rail services and road services and between the services in the Zone of the Interior and those in the Zone of the Armies. Both from the Minister and from the Commander-in-Chief he receives information as to operations projected or in progress, and as to the needs of the armies in *personnel* and *matériel*. His business it is to see that these needs, according to their order of urgency—as further communicated to him—are supplied under conditions which shall provide for all contingencies and guard against all possible confusion or delays. He fixes, among other things, the lines of communication; he keeps in close touch with the road services, and—having, within the limit of his instructions, complete control over the railways in the Zone of the Armies—he decides on the conditions to be adopted in respect to all transport alike from the interior to the armies and from the armies to the interior. As between, also, the Minister of War and the Commander-in-Chief, he maintains a constant exchange of information concerning time-tables for military trains and other such matters.

In the discharge of these duties the Directeur de l'Arrière is aided by a staff which comprises both the technical and the military elements; but he is not himself responsible for the actual working of either the rail or the road services.

Railway services in the Zone of the Armies are—subject to the supreme authority of the Directeur de l'Arrière—under the control of a *Director of Railways* who is assisted by (1) a combined military and technical staff; (2) a Line Commission for that section of the zone where the railways can still be worked by their ordinary staffs; and (3) one or more *Field Line Commissions* ("Commissions de chemins de fer de campagne"), together with Railway Troops, for the section where military operation is necessary.

In the interests of that co-ordination to which so much importance is rightly attached, the Director of Railways refers to the Directeur de l'Arrière all demands for transport that concern the railways of both the Zone of the Interior and the Zone of the Armies or involve conveyance by road as well as by rail. He also passes on to the Commissions in charge of either section of the railways included in the Zone of the Armies the orders he himself receives from the Directeur de l'Arrière in respect to such transport requirements as may concern them. Time-tables drawn up, and other arrangements made, by these Commissions are subject to his approval. He further decides as to the distribution, within the Zone of the Armies, of the rolling stock and the

ORGANISATION IN FRANCE.

railway personnel placed at his disposal by the Commander-in-Chief.

The *Field Line Commissions* are the executive agents of the Director of Railways in the discharge of the various duties assigned to him. The number of these Commissions is decided by the Directeur de l'Arrière, and the date of their entering on their functions is fixed by the Director of Railways. Each Commission consists of a staff officer and a railway engineer. Of these the former is military president of the Commission and has the controlling voice. When he considers it necessary that he should accept, in addition to his own responsibility, that of the technical commissioner, the latter must defer to his views and to the orders he gives. The president has an assistant—also a staff officer—who can replace him when necessary, while the Commission has a staff of secretaries and orderlies as approved by the Minister of War. The personnel of the Commissions includes Railway Troops (" Sapeurs de chemins de fer " and " Sections de chemins de fer de campagne ") ; a telegraphy staff ; Station Commissions ; and gendarmerie " to undertake police duties in the stations and on the trains.

In addition to making traffic arrangements and undertaking the operation of those lines at the theatre of war that may pass under full military control, the Field Line Commissions are required to carry out such construction, repair, maintenance or destruction work on the railways as should be found necessary.

On the *Lines of Communication* passing through the two zones and ensuring direct communication between the interior and such accessible points on the railway as may, from time to time, be nearest to the armies in the field, the leading stations *en route* are required to serve a variety of military purposes ; though in each and every such instance the system of organisation is such that the duties to be discharged or the responsibilities to be fulfilled are undertaken by, or are under the control of, a Commission formed on the now established basis of representation thereon of both the military and the technical elements.

For the conveyance of troops, there are, in the first

place, *Mobilisation stations* and *Junction Stations*, whence the men within a certain district are sent to the *Embarkation Stations*, at which complete units for the front are made up. These are followed by *Stations for Meals* ("Stations haltes-repas"), for men and horses; though in this case the "stations" may really be goods or locomotive sheds, able to accommodate a large number of men. At the end of the railway line, so far as it is available for troops, come the *Detraining Stations*.

In regard to supplies and stores, the first link in the chain of organisation is constituted by the *Base Supply Stations* ("gares de rassemblement"). Here the supplies going from a certain district outside the theatre of operations to any one Army Corps must be delivered; and here they are checked, made up into full train loads, or otherwise dealt with in such a way as to simplify and facilitate their further transport.

In certain cases full train-loads arriving at these assembling stations pass through to destination, after being checked; but the general practice is for the consignments forwarded from base supply stations to go to the *Supply Depôts* ("Stations-magasins"), serving the purposes of store-houses from which supplies, whether received from the base or collected locally, can be despatched in just such quantities, and at just such intervals, as circumstances may require. These depôts are organised on a different basis according to the particular service or purpose for which they are designed,—Cavalry, Engineers, Artillery, Medical, Telegraph Corps; provisions, live stock, clothing, camp equipment, etc. Their number, character, and location are decided by the Minister of War in time of peace. On the outbreak of war those in the Zone of the Armies pass under the control of the Commander-in-Chief together with the railway lines within that zone. The situation of the depôts may be changed, or additional depôts may be opened, by the Directeur de l'Arrière, with the consent of the Commander-in-Chief.

Each station depôt is under the charge of the military member of the Station Commission. His special function

ORGANISATION IN FRANCE.

it is to supply therefrom the wants of the Army in accordance with the demands he receives. These demands he distributes among the different departments of the depôt, giving instructions as to the time by which the railway wagons must be loaded. He also takes, with the station-master, all the necessary measures for ensuring the making up, the loading, and the departure of the trains; but he must not interfere with the internal administration of the station or with the technical direction and execution of the railway services.

Provision is also made for the immediate unloading of trains bringing supplies to the station depôts for storage there, the military commissioner being expressly instructed to guard against any block on the lines in or near to the station. Wagons need not be unloaded if they are to be sent on after only a brief detention, or if they contain ammunition forming part of the current needs of the Army.

From the supply depôts the supplies and stores pass on to the *Regulating Station* ("gare regulatrice"). This is located at such point on each line of communication as, while allowing of a final regulation of supplies going to the front, does not—owing to its nearness to the fighting line—permit of any guarantee of a fixed train service beyond that point. The locality of the regulating station is changed from day to day, or from time to time, according to developments in the military situation.

The regulating station is in charge of a *Regulating Commission* ("Commission regulatrice"), constituted on the same basis as a Sub-Line Commission. Receiving orders or instructions as to the nature and quantities of the supplies and stores required by the troops at the front, and drawing these from the supply depôts, the Commission must always have on hand a sufficiency to meet requirements. It is, also, left to the Commission to arrange for the further despatch of the supplies from the regulating station by means of such trains as, in the circumstances of the moment, may be found practicable.

As a matter of daily routine, and without further instructions, the supply depôts send one train of provisions each day to the regulating station, and the latter sends on one train daily to the front, always, however, keeping a further day's supply on hand, at or near the regulating station, to meet further possible requirements. Additional trains, whether from the supply depôts or from the regulating station (where rolling stock is kept available) are made up as needed.

Supplementing these arrangements, the Regulating Commission may, at the request of the Director of Road Services, further keep permanently within its zone of action a certain number of wagons of provisions in readiness to meet contingencies, the wagons so utilised as *Stores on wheels* being known as "en-cas mobiles." Should the Directeur de l'Arrière so desire, railway wagons with ammunition can, in the same way, be kept loaded at any station within the Zone of the Armies, or, by arrangement with the Minister of War, in the Zone of the Interior. It is, however, stipulated that the number of these wagons should be reduced to a minimum, in order to avoid congestion either of the stations or of the railway lines.

Beyond the regulating station comes *Railhead*, which constitutes the furthest limit of possible rail-transport for the time being, and the final point of connection between rail and road services, the latter being left with the responsibility of continuing the line of communication thence to the armies on the field of battle.

It is the duty of the Regulating Commission, as soon as it enters on the discharge of its functions and as often afterwards as may be necessary, to advise both the General in command of the Army served by the line of communication and the Director of Road Services as to the station which can be used as railhead and the facilities offered there for the accommodation, unloading, and loading of wagons. On the basis of the information so given the General-in-Command decides each day, or as the occasion requires, on the particular station which shall be regarded as railhead for the purposes of transport. He advises the Regulating Commission and the Director of Road Services accordingly,

ORGANISATION IN FRANCE. 167

and he further notifies to them his wishes in regard to the forwarding of supplies to the point thus fixed.

These elaborate arrangements for ensuring a maintenance of efficiency along the whole line of communication from the interior to the front equally apply to transport of all kinds from the theatre of war to the interior. In principle, evacuations from the army of sick and wounded, prisoners, surplus stores, and so on, are effected from railhead by means of the daily supply-trains returning thence to the regulating station, where the Regulating Commission takes them in charge, and passes them on by the trains going back to the Depôt Stations, or beyond. Should special trains be necessary for the removal of a large number of wounded, or otherwise, the Director of Road Services communicates with the Regulating Commission, which either makes up the desired specials from the rolling stock it has on hand or, if it cannot do this, itself applies, in turn, to the Director of Railways.

For dealing with the sick and wounded, every possible provision is made under the authority of the Minister of War and the Director-General, the arrangements in advance, as detailed in the decrees relating to this branch of the subject, being on the most comprehensive scale. Among other measures provided for is the setting up of *Evacuation Hospitals* ("hôpitaux d'évacuation") in the immediate neighbourhood of the Regulating Stations, if not, also, at railhead. Elsewhere along the line certain stations become *Infirmary Stations*, ("infirmaries de gare") where, in urgent cases, and under conditions laid down by the War Minister, the sick and wounded *en route* to the interior can receive prompt medical attention in case of need. From the *Distribution Stations* ("gares de répartition"), the sick and wounded are sent to the hospitals in the interior to which they may be assigned.

It will be seen that this comprehensive scheme of organisation aims at preventing the recurrence of any of those defects or deficiencies which characterised the military rail-transport movements of France in the war of 1870–71.

The presence, at every important link in the chain of rail communication, of a Commission designed to secure regularity and efficiency in the traffic arrangements should avoid confusion, congestion and delay.

The association, on each of these Commissions, of the military and technical elements, with a strict definition of their respective powers, duties and responsibilities, should ensure the best use of the available transport facilities under conditions in themselves practicable, and without the risk either of friction between the representatives of the two interests or, alternatively, of any interference with the railway services owing to contradictory or impossible orders being given by individual officers acting on their own responsibility.

The setting up of the supply depôts and regulating stations along the line of communication should prevent (i) the rushing through of supplies in excessive quantities to the extreme front; (ii) the congestion of railway lines and stations; (iii) the undue accumulation of provisions at one point, with a corresponding deficiency elsewhere, and (iv) the possibility of large stocks being eventually seized by the enemy and made use of by him to his own advantage.

The measures adopted both to prevent any excessive employment of railway wagons as storehouses on wheels and to secure their prompt unloading should afford a greater guarantee of the best utilisation of rolling stock under conditions of, possibly, extreme urgency.

Finally, the unification of control, the co-ordination of the many different services involved, and the harmony of working established between all the various sections on the line of communication linking up the interior of the country with the troops in the fighting line should assure, not only the nearest possible approach to complete efficiency in the transport conditions, but the conferring of great advantages on the armies concerned, with a proportionate increase of their strength in the field.

The effect of all these things on the military position of France must needs be great. Had France controlled a rail-transport organisation such as this—instead of none

ORGANISATION IN FRANCE. 169

at all—in 1870-71 ; and had Germany controlled a system no better than what we have seen to be the admittedly imperfect one she put into operation on that occasion, the results of the Franco-German war and the subsequent course of events in Europe might alike have been wholly different.

Tests of what were being planned or projected in France as precautionary measures, for application in war, could not, of course, be carried out exhaustively in peace ; but many parts of the machinery designed came into daily use as a matter of ordinary routine. Full advantage was taken, also, of whatever opportunities did present themselves—in the form of exercises in partial mobilisation, reviews, and other occasions involving the movement by rail of large bodies of troops—to effect such trials as were possible of regulations and instructions already based on exhaustive studies by the military and railway authorities. In 1892 the results attained were so satisfactory that a German authority, Lieutenant Becker, writing in his book on " Der nächste Krieg und die deutschen Bahnverwaltungen," (Hanover, 1893,) concerning the trials in France, in that year, of the new conditions introduced by the law of December 28, 1888, was not only greatly impressed thereby but even appeared disposed to think that the French were becoming superior to the Germans in that very organisation which the latter had regarded as their own particular province. The following passages from his book may be worth recalling :—

Towards the middle of September, 1892, from a military railway station improvised for the occasion, there were sent off in less than eight hours forty-two trains conveying a complete Army Corps of 25,000 men.

In their famous mobilisation test of 1887 the French despatched from the Toulouse station 150 military trains without interrupting the ordinary traffic, and without any accident.

Such figures speak a significant language. They show what enormous masses of troops the railway can carry in the course of a few hours to a given point. . . .

If I have referred to the results obtained by our neighbours on their railway systems, it is not because I have the least fear as to the final issue of the next war. Quite the contrary ; but the fact does not prevent me from asking why the German Army cannot base on the railways of that country the same hopes which neighbouring countries are able to entertain in regard to theirs.

The favourable impression thus given, even to a German critic, by the progress France was making in her creation, not so much *de novo* as *ab ovo*, of a system of organised military rail-transport, were confirmed by many subsequent trials, experiments and experiences, all, in turn, leading to further improvements in matters of detail; but it was, indeed, the " nächste Krieg " concerning which Lieutenant Becker wrote that was to be the real test of the organisation which, during more than forty years of peace, France followed up with a zeal, a pertinacity and a thoroughness fully equal to those of Germany herself.

In any case it would seem that France, though having to make up for the headway gained by Germany, finally created a system of military rail-transport which would be able to stand the fullest comparison with even the now greatly-improved system of her traditional foe; while the organisation she thus elaborated, not for the purposes of aggression but as an arm of her national defence, illustrates in a striking degree the ever-increasing importance of the problem of rail-power, and the comprehensive nature of the measures for its effective exercise which a great Continental nation regards as indispensable under the conditions of modern warfare.

Defensive Railways

The measures adopted included, also, the improvement of the French railway system, since this was no less in need of amendment and additions in order to adapt it to the needs of the military situation.

Whilst, as we have seen in Chapter I, the important part that railways were likely to play in war was recognised in France as early as 1833, and whilst, in 1842, attention was called in that country to the " aggressive lines " which Germany was then already building in the direction of the French frontiers, the French railway system itself was,

ORGANISATION IN FRANCE.

prior to the war of 1870-71, developed on principles which practically ignored strategical considerations, were based mainly on economic, political and local interests, and not only refrained from becoming "aggressive" in turn, but even failed to provide adequately, as they should have done, for the legitimate purposes of national defence.

Apart from the absence of any designs on the part of France against her neighbours' territory, during this period of her history, one of the main reasons for the conditions just mentioned is to be found in the predominant position of Paris as the capital and centre-point of French life and French movement. Germany at this time consisted of a collection of States each of which had its own chief city and built its railways to serve its own particular interests, without much regard for the interests of its sister States, even if it escaped the risk of cherishing more or less jealousy towards them. In France there was but one State and one capital, and Paris was regarded as the common centre from which the main lines were to radiate in all directions. Communication was thus established as between the capital and the principal inland towns or important points on the frontiers or on the coasts of France; but the inadequate number of lateral or transverse lines linking up and connecting these main lines placed great difficulty in the way of communication between the provincial centres themselves otherwise than viâ Paris.

Some of these disadvantages were to have been overcome under a law passed in 1868 which approved the construction of seventeen new lines having a total length of 1,840 km. (1,143 miles). When, however, war broke out in 1870, comparatively little had been done towards the achievement of this programme, and France entered upon the conflict with a railway system which had been even less developed towards her eastern frontiers than towards the north, the west and the south, while for the purposes of concentrating her troops in the first-mentioned direction she had available only three lines, and of these three one alone was provided with double-track throughout. Such were the inadequacies of the system at this time that the important line between Verdun and Metz had not yet been completed.

No sooner had the war come to an end than the French Government started on the improvement of the railway system in order to adapt it to the possible if not prospective military requirements of the future, so that they should never again be taken at a disadvantage ; and in carrying on this work—in addition to the reorganisation of their military-transport system in general—they showed an unexampled energy and thoroughness. Within five years of the restoration of peace the French railway system had already undergone an extension which, according to Captain A. Pernot, as told in his " Aperçu historique sur le service des transports militaires," would have been possible in but few countries in so short a period ; while of the situation at the time he wrote (1894) the same authority declared :—
" One can say that everything is ready in a vast organisation which only awaits the word of command in order to prove the strength of its capacity."

Without attempting to give exhaustive details of all that was done, it may suffice to indicate generally the principles adopted.

One of the most important of these related to an improvement of the conditions in and around Paris.

Here the purposes specially aimed at were (1) to establish further connecting links between the various trunk lines radiating from the capital, and (2) to obviate the necessity for traffic from, for example, the south or the west having to pass through Paris *en route* to the east or the north.

These aims it was sought to effect by means of a series of circular railways, or " rings " of railways, joining up the existing lines, and allowing of the transfer of military transport from one to the other without coming into Paris at all. An " inner " circular railway (" Chemin de Fer de Petite Ceinture ") had already been constructed within the fortifications prior to 1870, and this was followed in 1879 by an " outer " line, (" Chemin de Fer de Grande Ceinture "), which provided a wider circle at an average

ORGANISATION IN FRANCE.

distance of about 20 km. (12½ miles) and established direct rail connection, not only between a large number of the more remote suburbs, together with the different trunk lines at a greater distance from the city, but, also, between the various forts constructed for the defence of Paris.

These circular railways were, in turn, succeeded by a series of connecting links which ensured the provision of a complete ring of rail communication at a still greater distance around Paris, the towns comprised therein including Rouen, Amiens, La Fère, Laon, Reims, Chalons-sur-Marne, Troyes, Sens, Montargis, Orleans, Dreux, and so on back to Rouen. Within, again, this outermost ring there was provided a further series of lines which, by linking up Orleans, Malesherbes, Montereau, Nogent, Epernay, Soissons, Beauvais and Dreux, established additional connections between all the lines from Paris to the north and the east of France, and gave increased facilities for the distribution in those directions of troops arriving at Orleans from the south-west, this being once more done without any need for their entering Paris or even approaching it at a closer distance than about forty miles.

Orleans itself was recognised as a point of great strategical importance in regard to the movement of troops, and it was, accordingly, provided with a number of new lines radiating therefrom, and establishing better connections with other lines. Tours and other centres of military significance, from the same point of view, were strengthened in a like manner. At important junctions, and notably so in the case of Troyes (Champagne), loop lines were built in order that troop trains could be transferred direct from one line to another without stopping, and with no need for shunting or for changing the position of the engine.

In the direction of the eastern frontier the line from Verdun to Metz was completed, and by 1899 the three routes which could alone be made use of in 1870–71 had been increased to ten. Most of them were provided with double-track throughout, and all of them were independent of one another, though having inter-communication by means of cross lines.

Other new railways established connection with or between the forts on both the eastern and the northern frontiers. Others, again, provided direct communication between different harbours or between each of them and strategical points in the interior, thus contributing to the possibilities of their defence in case of attack from the sea. Still others were designed for the defence of the French Alps.

Apart from the provision of all these new lines, much was done in the doubling or even the quadrupling of existing track wherever the question of military transport came into consideration at all. Then at railway stations near to arsenals, and at important strategical centres, specially long platforms were provided to allow of the rapid entraining of men or material in case of need.

While, also, so much was being done for the improvement of the French railway system from an avowedly strategical point of view, there were many additional lines constructed or improvements made which, although designed to further the interests of trade and travel, also added to the sum total of available facilities for military transport.

The advantages specially aimed at were (1) the ensuring of a more rapid mobilisation of troops through the betterment of cross-country connections; (2) the avoidance of congestion of traffic in Paris; (3) the securing of a more rapid concentration on the frontiers, especially when each Army Corps could be assured the independent use of a double-track line of rails for its own use; and (4) the more effective defence of all vital points.

National defence, rather than the building of strategical lines designed to serve "aggressive" purposes, was the fundamental principle on which the policy thus followed since 1870-71 was based; and if, as Captain Pernot wrote in 1894, everything was even then ready for all emergencies, the continuous additions and improvements made since that time, bringing the railway system of the country more and more into harmony with the "perfectionnement" aimed at by France in the organisation of her military transport, must have made the conditions of preparedness still more complete by 1914.

CHAPTER XIV

ORGANISATION IN ENGLAND

THE difference between the geographical conditions of the British Isles and those of the principal countries on the Continent of Europe led to the systematic organisation of rail transport for military purposes being taken in hand at a later date in the United Kingdom than was, more especially, the case in Germany. Here there was no question of building lines of invasion or lines to facilitate the massing of troops on a neighbour's frontiers. The questions that alone seemed to arise in England were—(1) the relations between the State and the companies in regard to the use of the railways for the transport of troops and military necessaries under conditions either of peace or of war; (2) the employment of railways both for resisting invasion and for the conveyance of expeditionary forces to the port of embarkation; (3) the adoption of such means as would ensure the efficient working of the railways under war conditions; and (4) the creation of an Army engineering force providing for the construction, repair, operation or destruction of railways either at home, in case of invasion, or to facilitate operations in overseas expeditions through the building and working of military railways.

With these various considerations it may be convenient to deal in the order as here given.

THE STATE AND THE RAILWAYS

In the Railway Regulation Act, 1842, (5 and 6 Vict., c. 55,) entitled " An Act for the better Regulation of Railways and for the Conveyance of Troops," it was provided, by section 20 :—

Whenever it shall be necessary to move any of the officers or soldiers of her Majesty's forces of the line . . . by any railway, the directors shall permit them, with baggage, stores, arms, ammunition and other necessaries and things, to be conveyed, at the usual hours of starting, at such prices or upon such conditions as may be contracted for between the Secretary at War and such railway companies on the production of a route or order signed by the proper authorities.

This was the first provision made in the United Kingdom in respect to the conveyance of troops by rail. It was succeeded in 1844 by another Act (7 and 8 Vict., c. 85,) by which (sec. 12) railway companies were required to provide conveyances for the transport of troops at fares not exceeding a scale given in the Act, and maximum fares were also prescribed in regard to public baggage, stores, ammunition, (with certain exceptions, applying to gunpowder and explosives,) and other military necessaries. In 1867 these provisions were extended to the Army Reserve. Further revision of the fares and charges took place under the Cheap Trains Act, 1883, (46 and 47 Vict., c. 34,) entitled "An Act to amend the Law Relating to Railway Passenger Duty and to amend and consolidate the law relating to the conveyance of the Queen's forces by railway."

State control of the railways in case of war was provided for under the Regulation of the Forces Act, 1871, (34 and 35 Vict., c. 86,) "An Act for the Regulation of the Regular and Auxiliary Forces of the Crown, and for other purposes relating thereto." Section 16 laid down that—

When her Majesty, by Order in Council, declares that an emergency has arisen in which it is expedient for the public service that her Majesty's Government should have control over the railroads of the United Kingdom, or any of them, the Secretary of State may, by warrant under his hand, empower any person or persons named in such warrant to take possession in the name or on behalf of her Majesty of any railroad in the United Kingdom, and of the plant belonging thereto, or of any part thereof, and may take possession of any plant without taking possession of the railroad itself, and to use the same for her Majesty's service at such times and in such manner as the Secretary of State may direct ; and the directors, officers and servants of any such railroad shall obey the directions of the Secretary of State

ORGANISATION IN ENGLAND.

as to the user of such railroad or plant as aforesaid for her Majesty's service.

Any warrant granted by the said Secretary of State in pursuance of this section shall remain in force for one week only, but may be renewed from week to week so long as, in the opinion of the said Secretary of State, the emergency continues.

Provision was also made for the payment of "full compensation" to the interests concerned.

The powers of control thus acquired by the Government followed, in effect, closely upon the precedent already established in the United States, (see p. 16,) even although they were not defined with the same elaborate detail. On the other hand greater emphasis is laid in the English Act on the provision that the Government "may take possession of any plant without taking possession of the railroad itself." This gives them the right to take over the locomotives and rolling stock of any railway in any part of the United Kingdom, even though the lines in question may not themselves be wanted for the purposes of military transport.

Under the provisions of the National Defence Act, 1888, (51 and 52 Vict., c. 31,) traffic for naval and military purposes is to have precedence over other traffic on the railways of the United Kingdom whenever an Order for the embodiment of the Militia is in force.

It was by virtue of the above section of the Act of 1871 that the Government took control over the railways of Great Britain on the outbreak of war in 1914.

As regards the earlier Acts of 1842 and 1844, these were mainly domestic measures relating to the conveyance of troops in time of peace rather than war. The beginnings of organisation of military rail-transport for the purposes of war followed, rather, on a realisation both of the possibilities of invasion and of the weakness of the position in which England at one time stood from the point of view of national defence.

INVASION PROSPECTS AND HOME DEFENCE

In 1847 the Duke of Wellington, (then Commander-in-

Chief,) addressed to Sir John Burgoyne a letter in which he said he had endeavoured to awaken the attention of different Administrations to the defenceless state of the country. We had, he declared, no defence, or hope of chance of defence, except in our Fleet, and he was especially sensible both of the certainty of failure if we did not, at an early moment, attend to the measures necessary to be taken for our defence and of "the disgrace, the indelible disgrace," of such failure. Then, in words that greatly impressed the country, he added :—

I am bordering upon seventy-seven years of age, passed in honour ; I hope that the Almighty may protect me from being the witness of the tragedy which I cannot persuade my contemporaries to take measures to avert.

As the result alike of this pathetic warning ; of a "Letter on the Defence of England by Volunteer Corps and Militia" issued in pamphlet form by Sir Charles Napier in 1852 ; and of the Indian Mutiny in 1857, which event called attention to the defenceless condition of the Empire as a whole, continuous efforts were made to secure the creation of Volunteer Corps for the purposes of defence. For a period of twelve years these efforts met with persistent discouragement, the Government refusing official recognition to certain corps of riflemen tentatively formed ; but in 1859 the prospect of an early invasion of this country by France aroused public feeling to such an extent that on May 12 the then Secretary of State for War, General Peel, addressed a circular to the Lord-Lieutenants of counties in Great Britain announcing that Volunteer Corps might be formed under an Act passed in 1804, when a like course had been adopted as a precautionary measure against the threatened invasion of England by Napoleon.

The formation of Volunteer Corps was thereupon taken up with the greatest zeal, and by the end of 1860 the number of Volunteers enrolled throughout Great Britain was no fewer than 120,000. Other results of the national awakening in 1859 were the public discussion of the questions of coast defence and armoured trains, (of which mention has been made in Chapter VII,) and the appropriation, in 1860,

ORGANISATION IN ENGLAND.

of a loan of seven and a half millions for the improvement of our coast defences and notably the fortifications of Portsmouth and Plymouth.

ENGINEER AND RAILWAY STAFF CORPS

Already in December, 1859, the necessity for some definite engineering instruction for Volunteers was being pointed out, and in January, 1860, the first corps of Volunteer Engineers was created, under the title of the 1st Middlesex Volunteer Engineers. Similar corps were formed in various parts of the country, and by 1867 the number of Volunteer Engineers enrolled was 6,580.

At the beginning of 1860 a further proposal was made for the formation of a body which, composed of eminent civil engineers, the general managers of leading lines of railway, and the principal railway contractors or other employers of labour, would undertake a variety of duties considered no less essential in the interests of national defence.

There was, in the first place, the question of the transport by rail alike of Volunteers and of the regular forces, either on the occasion of reviews or for the protection of our coasts against an invader. While it was evident that the railways could be efficiently worked only by their own officers, it was no less obvious that plans for the movement of large bodies of men, and especially of troops, with horses, guns, ammunition and stores, should be well considered and prepared long beforehand, and not left for the occasion or the emergency when the need for them would arise.

In the next place it was suggested that the engineering talent of the country should be made available for the purpose of supplementing the services of the Royal Engineers in carrying out various defensive works, such as the destruction of railway lines, bridges and roads, the throwing up of earthworks, or the flooding of the lowland districts, with a view to resisting the advance of a possible invader.

Finally the great contractors were to be brought into the combination so that they could provide the labour necessary for the execution of these defensive works under the direction of the civil engineers, who themselves would act under the direction of the military commanders.

Each of the three groups was to discharge the function for which it was specially adapted, while the co-ordination of the three, for the purpose of strengthening the country's powers of resisting invasion, was expected to add greatly to the value of the proposed organisation.

The author of this scheme was Mr. Charles Manby, F.R.S., (1804–1884,) a distinguished civil engineer who for nearly half a century was secretary of the Institution of Civil Engineers and was closely associated with the leading civil engineers, contractors and railway interests of the country. He submitted his ideas to several members of the Council of his Institution, and though, at first, the scheme was not well received, he was subsequently so far encouraged that in August, 1860, he laid his plan before Mr. Sidney Herbert, then Minister at War in Lord Palmerston's second administration. Mr. Herbert expressed cordial approval of the project, giving the assurance, on behalf of the War Office, that an organisation on the basis suggested could not fail to be of public benefit; but Mr. Manby still met with difficulties alike from several members of the Council, who either offered direct opposition to the scheme or else gave unwilling consent to join, and, also, from the railway companies, who thought that arrangements for rail-transport might very well be left to themselves, and that there was no necessity for the suggested system so far as they, at least, were concerned.

In these circumstances Mr. Manby made, at first, very little progress; but he was unremitting in his efforts to demonstrate alike to civil engineers and to the railway companies the practical benefits from the point of view of public interests that would result from the organisation he advocated, and in 1864 he felt sufficiently encouraged to lay his views once more before the War Office. Earl de Grey, then in charge of that Department, thereupon instructed the Inspector-General of Volunteers, Colonel McMurdo, (afterwards General Sir W. M. McMurdo, C.B.,) to inquire into and report to him on the subject.

ORGANISATION IN ENGLAND. 181

In the result there was created, in January, 1865, a body known as the Engineer and Railway Volunteer Staff Corps, constituted, according to its rules, "for the purpose of directing the application of skilled labour and of railway transport to the purposes of national defence, and for preparing, in time of peace, a system on which such duties should be conducted." The Corps was to consist of officers only, and its members were to be civil engineers and contractors, officers of railway and dock companies, and, under special circumstances, Board of Trade Inspectors of Railways. Civil engineers of standing and experience who had directed the construction of the chief railways and other important works, general managers of railways and commercial docks, and Board of Trade Inspectors of Railways, were alone eligible for the rank of Lieutenant-Colonel. Other civil engineers and contractors connected chiefly with railway works, and, also, railway officers other than general managers, take the rank of Major. Col. McMurdo was appointed Honorary Colonel of the Corps on February 9, 1865.[1] As ultimately constituted, the corps consisted of an Honorary Colonel (now Maj.-Gen. D. A. Scott, C.V.O., C.B., D.S.C.), thirty Lieutenant-Colonels

---

[1] Colonel McMurdo had special qualifications for the post. Becoming a Lieutenant-Colonel in the Army in October, 1853, he was Assistant-Adjutant-General at Dublin from May, 1854, to January, 1855. On February 2, 1855, he was entrusted with the duties of Director-General of the new Land-Transport Corps, and was sent out to the Crimea, with the local rank of Colonel, to reorganize the transport service, then in a deplorably defective condition. He is said to have accomplished this task with great energy and success. Before the close of the campaign his corps numbered 17,000 men, with 28,000 horses, mules, etc. He also took over the working of the pioneer military railway in the Crimea. In 1857 the Land-Transport Corps was converted into the Military Train, with Colonel McMurdo as Colonel-Commandant. Early in 1860, when the Volunteer movement was assuming a permanent character, Colonel McMurdo was appointed Inspector of Volunteers, and in June of the same year he became Inspector-General, a post he retained until January, 1865. He was chosen as Colonel of the Inns of Court Volunteers on January 23, 1865, and his further appointment to the post of Colonel of the newly-formed Engineer and Railway Volunteer Staff Corps followed, as stated above, in February, 1865. He was created K.C.B. in 1881 and G.C.B. in 1893. He died in 1894.

including a Commandant, (now Lieut.-Col. Sir William Forbes, general manager of the London, Brighton and South Coast Railway) and twenty Majors.[1]

FUNCTIONS AND PURPOSES

That the Corps thus created was the direct outcome, first, of the Volunteer movement, and, through that movement, of the state of semi-panic into which the country had drifted in 1859, as the result both of the anticipations of invasion and the admitted weakness, at that time, of our national defences, has thus been clearly established. Writing in 1869, Major-General McMurdo, who had been raised to that rank in 1868, said in a pamphlet he issued under the title of "Rifle Volunteers for Field Service" that the Corps was "prepared to work, not for Volunteers alone, but for the entire defensive forces of the country."

In this same publication Major-General McMurdo gave an account of the functions and purposes the Corps had been designed to serve. Alluding first to the Volunteer movement, he showed how the railway carriage must both carry and shelter the Volunteer when moving from one part of the country to another; and he proceeded :—

I will ask you to look attentively for a moment at a Bradshaw's railway map, and you will see that throughout the network of rails that overspreads the land none of the meshes, so to speak, in any vital parts of the country, exceed fifteen miles across, from rail to rail ; but as the eye approaches the Metropolis, or any of the commercial centres, these meshes are diminished to about one-half the area of the others.

He then dealt with the operations which the movement of troops along these lines of railway would involve, and continued :—

The railway schemes for the accomplishment of such delicate operations would emanate from the Council of the Engineer and Railway Staff Corps. . . .

---

[1] The names of present members of the Corps will be found in "Hart's Army List." Under the Territorial and Reserve Forces Act of 1907 the Corps became part of the Territorial Force, and the designation "Volunteer" was dropped from its title, which since that date has been "The Engineer and Railway Staff Corps."

ORGANISATION IN ENGLAND.

During peace the railway branch of this body is employed in working out hypothetical plans of campaign, in the development of which they manipulate in theory the entire rolling-stock and railway resources of the country, elaborated by special time-tables and technical reports.

The share taken by the civil engineers is not confined to providing merely for the class of railway works contingent on war, whether of construction, demolition, or of reconstruction, but in supplying the military engineers with information, advice and labour. No one, for example, can be more familiar with the features and character of a district than the engineer who has constructed a line of railway through it. No one is so well able to point out the results of *letting in* that which he had been so often employed in *keeping out*, viz., the inundations of the sea. None better acquainted with the existing distribution of labour power throughout the country, and of the means by which it could be concentrated upon given points, for the construction of works of defence. All these elements, in short, by which the gigantic resources of our country may be safely wielded for her defence, are now being silently considered and woven into strategical schemes of operations by these eminent and patriotic men, the value of whose voluntary services will not be fully comprehended or appreciated till the day comes when the discomfiture of the invader shall be accomplished through their instrumentality.

The same distinguished authority wrote concerning the Engineer and Railway Volunteer Staff Corps in an article on " Volunteers " which he contributed to the " Encyclopædia Britannica " (ninth edition) :—

The ready labour power of this useful Corps is estimated at from 12,000 to 20,000 navvies, with tools, barrows and commissariat complete. It has already performed important service in tabulating, and printing at great private cost, complete time-tables and special reports for six general concentrations against possible invasion. A special return was also prepared by the Corps (the first of its kind) of the entire rolling stock of all the railways in Great Britain. This important work—which is corrected and republished annually—shows where the requisite number of carriages of every description can be obtained for the composition of troop trains.

In the official catalogue of books in the War Office Library there is an item which reads :—" Time Tables for Special Troop Trains, etc. Compiled by the Railway Companies. 311 pp. 8vo. London, 1866." This, presumably, refers to the first of the complete time tables mentioned in the "Encyclopædia Britannica" article as having been compiled by the Corps. It is evident, from the date given, that the Corps must have got quickly to work after its formation in 1865.

At one time there was an expectation that the Engineer and Railway Volunteer Staff Corps would develop into a body exercising still wider and more responsible duties than those already mentioned. On this point we have the testimony of the late Sir George Findlay, formerly general manager of the London and North-Western Railway Company, and himself a Lieutenant-Colonel in the Corps.

Col. J. S. Rothwell had written some articles[1] in which, while admitting their practically unlimited resources, he questioned the ability of the British railways, at a few hours notice, to transport to any part of our coasts which might be the scene of a hostile invasion a sufficient body of troops to dispute the advance of an army upon London, and he further suggested that the whole question was one which had not yet received the mature consideration it deserved. Col. Rothwell said, in the course of what he wrote:—

> Though the actual working of our railways must be left in the hands of the proper railway officials, it does not follow that the planning of the arrangements for the military traffic should also be entrusted to them exclusively. This, however, appears to be contemplated, as, under existing circumstances, such arrangements would rest with the members of a body called the "Volunteer Engineer and Railway Staff Corps." . . . Though the efficiency of these gentlemen in their own sphere is undeniable, it appears open to question whether they are likely to have sufficient leisure personally to work out the details of a large concentration of troops by rail, and whether the special requirements of military transport will be fully appreciated by them, or by the subordinates whom they presumably will employ.

Much, he argued, required to be done before the country could be considered ready to meet a possible invader; and he concluded:—

---

[1] "The Conveyance of Troops by Railway." By Col. J. S. Rothwell, R.A., Professor of Military Administration, Staff College, *United Service Magazine*, Dec., 1891, and Jan., 1892.

ORGANISATION IN ENGLAND.   185

If the invasion of England is to be regarded as an event which is within the bounds of possibility, it is surely not unreasonable to ask that those precautionary measures which require time for their elaboration shall be thoroughly worked out before there is any risk of our wanting to employ them. The organisation for the conveyance of our troops by railway is such a measure.

To these criticisms Sir George Findlay replied in an article " On the Use of Railways in the United Kingdom for the Conveyance of Troops," published in the *United Service Magazine* for April, 1892. The complete network of railways covering these islands, admirably equipped and efficiently worked as they were, would, he declared, be found equal to any part they might be called upon to play in a scheme of national defence. As regarded the attention already paid to the question he said :—

The War Office, so far from having in any way neglected the subject, have devoted considerable attention to it, and a complete scheme for the working of our railways for transport purposes in time of war has been elaborated, and would at once be put in operation, if ever the emergency arose.

Passing on to describe the composition and duties of the Engineer and Railway Volunteer Staff Corps, he spoke of its members as meeting in council at their headquarters to discuss from time to time details of railway organisation and other matters delegated to their consideration, afterwards reporting their conclusions to the War Office ; and he went on to say that for the operation of the railways, under State control, on any occasion of national energy or danger—

A draft scheme has been prepared, has been worked out in detail, and would, in all probability, be adopted and put in operation if, unhappily, the necessity should ever arise.

This scheme in its main features provides that, at such time as we are contemplating, the principal railway officials in Great Britain and Ireland would at once become, for the time being, the officers of the State, and in addition to the general managers of the leading railways, who are officers of the Engineer and Railway Volunteer Staff Corps, military rank of some kind would be conferred upon the engineers, locomotive superintendents, chief passenger superintendents and goods managers of the principal railway companies, as well as on the managers of the principal Irish railways.

The railways of the country would be divided into sections, and for each section there would be a committee composed of the general managers of the railways included in the section, together with the principal engineers, locomotive superintendents and other chief officers. The railways would be worked and controlled for military purposes by these committees of sections, each committee having as its president a Lieutenant-Colonel of the Engineer and Railway Volunteer Staff Corps, who would be directly responsible for providing transport for troops and stores over the section of which his committee had charge, while if the operation to be carried out required the co-operation of one or more sections of the railways, the committees of those sections would act in unison. In such a case the Quartermaster-General's requisition for the service to be performed would be made upon the president of the section embracing the point of departure, that officer and his committee taking the initiative and arranging with the other committees for the performance of the service.

For each section, or group, of railways, a military officer of rank would be appointed, with full power to arrange for food, forage and water for the troops and horses *en route*, and having at his disposal a sufficient number of soldiers or labourers to assist in loading and unloading baggage, stores, etc., at the points of entrainment and detrainment within his section. He would also be able to command the services of the Royal or Volunteer Engineers to assist in the erection of temporary platforms or landings, or the laying down of temporary rails, and would be instructed to co-operate with, and assist in every way, the committee of section having charge of his district, but not in any way to attempt to interfere with the working of the line or the movement of the trains or traffic.

The number of sections into which the railways were to be divided for the purposes of this scheme was nine. After defining the various areas, Sir George continued :—

It is contemplated that during any such period of crisis as we are now discussing, the Council of the Engineer and Railway Volunteer Staff Corps would be sitting *en permanence* at its headquarters, and, with a full knowledge of the nature and extent of the operations to be carried out, would have power to regulate the supply and distribution of rolling stock throughout the area affected, all the vehicles in the country being, for the time being, treated as a common stock.

This is a mere outline of the scheme, with the further details of which it is not necessary to trouble the reader, though probably

ORGANISATION IN ENGLAND. 187

enough has been said to show that the subject, far from having been neglected, as Colonel Rothwell appears to assume, has been carefully studied and thought out.

Had the scheme in question been matured and adopted on the lines here stated, a still greater degree of importance would have been attached to the position and proceedings of a Corps then—and still—almost unknown to the world at large, since its chief function was to carry out investigations at the request of the authorities, and prepare reports, statements and statistics which have invariably got no further than the War Office and the Horse Guards, where, alone, the value of the services rendered has been fully understood and appreciated. The scheme was, however, allowed to drop, the policy eventually adopted being based, preferably, (1) on the railways of Great Britain being operated in war time as one group instead of in a series of groups or sections; and (2) on such operation being entrusted to a body specially created for the purpose; though prior to the adoption of the latter course there was to be a fresh development in another direction.

THE WAR RAILWAY COUNCIL

While the Engineer and Railway Volunteer Staff Corps remained, down to 1896, the only organised body which (apart from the individual railway companies) Government departments could consult as to the technical working and traffic facilities of the railways, from the point of view of military transport, it was thought desirable, in the year mentioned, to supplement that Corps by a smaller body known at first as the "Army Railway Council" and afterwards as the "War Railway Council."

Designed to act in a purely advisory capacity, without assuming any administrative or executive functions, this Council was eventually constituted as follows :—The Deputy Quartermaster-General (president); six railway managers, who represented the British railway companies and might or might not already be members of the Engineer and Railway Staff Corps; one Board of Trade Inspector of Railways; two members (not being railway managers) of the Engineer and Railway Staff Corps; the Deputy-Assistant Quartermaster-General; one mobilisation officer; two Naval officers; and one officer of the Royal Engineers, with a representative of the Quartermaster-General's Department as secretary.

The Council approximated closely to the "Commission Militaire Superieure des Chemins de Fer" in France, of which an account has been given in Chapter IX. It also undertook many of the duties which in the case of the German Army would be performed by a special section of the General Staff; though some of these duties it took over from the Engineer and Railway Staff Corps, reducing the functions and the importance of that body proportionately.

In time of peace the Council was (1) generally to advise the Secretary of State for War on matters relating to military rail-transport; (2) to draw up, in conjunction with the different railway companies concerned, and on the basis of data to be supplied to them by the War Office, a detailed scheme for the movement of troops on mobilisation; (3) to arrange in advance as to the composition of the trains which would be required for any such movement; (4) to determine the nature of the data to be asked for from the railway companies,[1] and to prepare the necessary regulations and instructions in regard to the said troop movements; (5) to draw up rules for the organisation of a body of Railway Staff Officers who, located at railway stations to be selected by the Council, would act there as intermediaries between the railway officials and the troops; and (6) to confer with the different railway companies as to the provision of such extra sidings, loading platforms, ramps, barriers, etc., as might be necessary to facilitate military transport, and to decide on the best means by which the provision thereof could be arranged. Information on these subjects was to be carefully compiled, elabor-

[1] Detailed information as to the capacity of British rolling stock; composition of trains required for units at war strength; truck space taken up by Army vehicles; standard forms of reports on existing railways, and other matters, is published in the official publication known as "Railway Manual (War)."

ORGANISATION IN ENGLAND. 189

ated, and, with explanatory maps, placed on record for use as required.

In the event of mobilisation, or of some national emergency, the Council was, also, to advise the Secretary of State for War in regard to matters relating to the movement of troops by rail; to act as a medium of communication between the War Office and the railway companies, and to make all the necessary arrangements in connection with such movements.

Other questions likely to arise, and requiring consideration in time of peace, included the guarding of the railways against possible attack; the prompt repair of any damage that might be done to them; the equipment of armoured trains, and the provision of ambulance trains on lines where they might be required.

All these and various other matters were dealt with at the periodical meetings held by the Council, which, within the range of its limitations as an advisory body, rendered good service to the War Office; though that Department was still left to deal with the individual railway companies in regard to all arrangements and matters of detail directly concerning them.

Railway Transport Officers

In the foregoing statement as to the functions to be discharged by the War Railway Council it is mentioned that these were to include the drawing up of rules for the organisation of a body of Railway Staff Officers who were to act as intermediaries between the troops and the railway station staffs in the conduct of military rail-transport.

We touch here upon those questions of control and organisation of military traffic which had been a fruitful source of trouble in earlier wars, and more especially so on the French railways in the war of 1870–71. There was, indeed, much wisdom in the attempt now being made, as a precautionary measure, to provide well in advance against the risk of similar experiences in regard to movements of British troops by rail, while the course adopted led to the creation of a system which was to ensure excellent results later on.

In the first instance the officers appointed under the system here in question were known as "Railway Control Officers," (R.C.O.'s,) their chief as the "Director of Railways," (D.R.,) and the organisation itself as the "Railway Control Establishment"; but the titles of Railway Transport Officers (R.T.O.'s), Director of Railway Transport (D.R.T.) and Transport Establishments were afterwards substituted.

The functions of the Director of Railway Transport are thus defined in Field Service Regulations, Part II, section 23 (1913):—

Provision of railway transport and administration of railway transport personnel. Control, construction, working and maintenance of all railways. Provision of telegraph operators for railway circuits. Control and working of telephones and telegraphs allotted to the railway service. For the erection and maintenance of all telegraph circuits on railways which are worked by the troops, a representative of the Director of Army Signals will be attached to his headquarters and the necessary signal troops allotted to him as may be ordered by the I.G.C. (Inspector-General of Communications).

As regards the Railway Transport Establishments, the Regulations say (section 62):—

In railway matters, the authority of each member of a railway transport establishment will be paramount on that portion of a railway system where he is posted for duty.

Railway technical officials will always receive the demands of the troops for railway transport through the railway transport establishment.

Except when fighting is imminent or in progress, a member of the railway transport establishment will receive orders from the Director of Railway Transport only, or his representative.

An officer, or officers, of the railway transport establishment, recognized by a badge worn on the left arm marked R.T.O., will be posted for duty at each place where troops are constantly entraining, detraining, or halting *en route*. Their chief duties will be:—

1. To facilitate the transport of troops, animals and material.
2. To act as a channel of communication between the military authorities and the technical railway personnel.
3. To advise the local military authorities as to the capacity and possibilities of the railway.

ORGANISATION IN ENGLAND. 191

4. To bring to the notice of the Director of Railway Transport any means by which the carrying power of the railway may, for military purposes, be increased.

All details as to the entraining and detraining of troops and the loading and unloading of stores will be arranged in conjunction with the technical officials by the railway transport establishment, who will meet all troops arriving to entrain, inform commanders of the times and places of entrainment, and allot trucks and carriages to units in bulk. They will see that the necessary rolling stock is provided by the railway officials, that only the prescribed amount of baggage is loaded, and that no unauthorised person travels by rail. They will meet all troop trains, and see that troops and stores are detrained with the utmost despatch.

It will be observed from these regulations that, whatever his own rank may be, the R. T. O., subject to the instructions he has received from his superior Transport Officer, exercises at the railway station to which he is delegated an authority that not even a General may question or seek to set aside by giving orders direct to the station staff. The R.T.O. alone is the "channel of communication" between the military and the railway elements. He it is who, acting in conjunction with the railway people, must see that all the details in connection with entraining and detraining are properly arranged and efficiently carried out, while the operations of the station staff are, in turn, greatly facilitated alike by his co-operation and by the fact that there is now only one military authority to be dealt with at a station instead, possibly, of several acting more or less independently of one another.

Volunteer Reviews

While all these developments had been proceeding, the railway companies had, since the formation of the Engineer and Railway Volunteer Staff Corps, given repeated evidence of their capacity to move large bodies of Volunteers with complete efficiency. They specially distinguished themselves in this respect on the occasion of the great Volunteer reviews held from time to time. In a book entitled "England's Naval and Military Weakness," (London, 1882,) Major James Walter, of the 4th Lancashire Artillery Volunteers, was highly eulogistic of what was done by the railways on the occasion of the reviews in Edinburgh and Windsor in 1881. In regard to the Windsor review he wrote :—

The broad result has been, so far as the railway part of the business goes, to prove that it is perfectly feasible to concentrate fifty thousand men from all parts of the kingdom in twenty-four hours. . . . The two lines most concerned in the Windsor review—the Great Western and the South Western—carried out this great experiment with . . . the regularity and dispatch of the Scotch mail.

Major Walter seems to have had the idea, rightly or wrongly, that the success of this performance was mainly due to the Engineer and Railway Volunteer Staff Corps. He says concerning that body :—

Not the least valued result of the Windsor and Edinburgh reviews of 1881 is the having introduced with becoming prominence to public knowledge the necessary and indispensable services of the " Engineer and Railway Volunteer Staff Corps." Until these reviews bore testimony to the national importance of this Corps, few knew anything of its duties, or even existence, beyond a list of officers recorded in the Army List. . . . Since the embodiment of the Volunteers the Engineer and Railway Transport Corps has done much service, invariably thorough and without a hitch. . . . These several officers of the Railway Staff Corps set about their transport work of the 1881 reviews in a manner worthy of their vocation. They proved to the country that their Corps was a reality and necessity.

In 1893 the authors of the " Army Book for the British Empire " wrote (p. 531) :—

There is every reason to believe that, in case of the military forces in the United Kingdom being mobilised for the purposes of home defence, and being concentrated in any part or parts of the country for the purpose of guarding against or confronting an invasion, the railway arrangements would work satisfactorily. The remarkable success which has attended the concentration of large bodies of Volunteers gathered from all quarters of the Kingdom for military functions and reviews, on more than one occasion, has shown the extraordinary capabilities of the British railway system for military transport on a great scale. Rolling stock is abundant. The more important lines in England have a double line of rails ; some have four or more rails. Gradients, moreover, as a rule are easy, an important point, since troop trains are very heavy.

THE SOUTH AFRICAN WAR

While no one was likely to dispute these conclusions, it had to be remembered that the transport by rail even of exceptionally large bodies of Volunteers, carrying their rifles only, was a very different matter from the conveyance, under conditions of great pressure, of large forces of troops accompanied by horses, guns, ammunition, road wagons, stores and other necessaries for prospective actual warfare. So the accepted capacity of the British railways had still to stand the test of actual war conditions, with or without the accompaniment of invasion; and this test was applied, to a certain extent, by the South African War.

The bulk of the military traffic on that occasion passed over the lines of the London and South Western Railway Company, troops from all parts of the country being conveyed by different routes and different lines of railway to Southampton, whence they and their stores, etc., were shipped to the Cape. Such was the magnitude of this traffic that between the outbreak of the war, in 1899, and the end of 1900 there were carried on the London and South Western, and despatched from Southampton, 6,160 officers; 229,097 men; 29,500 horses; and 1,085 wheeled vehicles. The conveyance of this traffic involved the running of 1,154 special trains, in addition to a large number of others carrying baggage, stores, etc. At times the pressure was very great. On October 20, 1899, five transports sailed from Southampton with 167 officers and 4,756 men, besides guns horses and wagons. Yet the whole of the operations were conducted with perfect smoothness, there being no overtaxing either of the railway facilities or of the dock accommodation.[1]

Much of this smoothness of working was due to the fact that the War Office had, in accordance with the principle adopted on the appointment of the War Railway Council, stationed at Southampton a Railway Transport Officer who was to act as a connecting link, or intermediary, between

[1] *The Railway Magazine*, May, 1901.

the railway, the docks, the military and the Admiralty authorities, co-ordinating their requirements, superintending the arrivals by train, arranging for and directing the embarkation of the troops and their equipment in the transports allotted to them, and preventing any of that confusion which otherwise might well have arisen. Similar officers had also been stationed by the War Office at leading railway stations throughout the country to ensure co-operation between the military and the railway staffs and, while avoiding the possibility of friction or complications, facilitate the handling of the military traffic.

In the account to be given in Chapter XVI. of " Railways in the Boer War," it will be shown that a like course was pursued in South Africa for the duration of the campaign.

Army Manœuvres of 1912

Further evidence as to what the British railways were capable of accomplishing was afforded by the Army Manœuvres in East Anglia in 1912. This event also constituted a much more severe test than the Volunteer reviews of former days, since it meant not only the assembling, in the manœuvre area, of four divisions of the Army and some thousands of Territorials, but the transport, at short notice, and within a limited period, of many horses, guns, transport wagons, etc., together with considerable quantities of stores. Certain sections of the traffic were dealt with by the Great Northern and the London and North-Western Companies; but the bulk of it was handled by the Great Eastern and was carried in nearly 200 troop trains, consisting in all of about 4,000 vehicles. Of these trains 50 per cent. started before or exactly to time, while the others were only a few minutes late in leaving the station. Such was the regularity and general efficiency with which the work of transportation was carried out that in the course of an address to the Generals, at Cambridge, his Majesty the King referred to the rapid concentration of troops by rail, without dislocating the ordinary civilian traffic, as one of the special features of the manœuvres. The dispersal of the forces on the conclu-

ORGANISATION IN ENGLAND. 195

sion of the manœuvres was effected in a little over two days, and constituted another smart piece of work.[1]

A Railways Executive Committee

In view of all such testimony and of all such actual achievements, there was no reason to doubt that the railway companies, with their great resources in material and personnel, and with the excellence of their own organisation, would themselves be able to respond promptly and effectively to such demands as might be made upon them in a time of national emergency.

There still remained, however, the singular fact that although, so far back as 1871, the Government had acquired power of control over the railways, in the event of an emergency arising, a period of forty years had elapsed without any action being taken to create, even as a precautionary measure, the administrative machinery by which that control would be exercised by the State. Such machinery had been perfected in Germany, France, and other countries, but in England it had still to be provided. Not only had section 16 of the Act of 1871 remained practically a dead letter, but even the fact that it existed did not seem to be known to so prominent a railway manager as Sir George Findlay when he wrote " Working and Management of an English Railway " and the article he contributed to the *United Service Magazine* of April, 1892, his assumption that the State would control the railways in time of war being based, not on the Act of 1871—which he failed to mention

[1] For details as to the nature of the organisation by which these results were effected, see an article on " The Great Eastern Railway and the Army Manœuvres in East Anglia—1912," by H. J. Prytherch, in the *Great Eastern Railway Magazine* for November, 1912. In the *Great Western Railway Magazine* for November, 1909, there are given, under the heading, " The Transport of an Army," some details concerning the military transport on the Great Western system during the Army manœuvres of that year. The traffic conveyed was, approximately, 514 officers, 14,552 men, 208 officers' horses, 2,474 troop horses, 25 guns, 34 limbers, and 581 wagons and carts. " The military authorities and the Army contractors," it is said, " expressed their pleasure at the manner in which the work was performed by the Company's staff."

—but on the Act of 1888, which simply gives a right of priority to military traffic, under certain conditions.

Notwithstanding, too, the draft scheme spoken of by Sir George Findlay, under which the operation of the railways was to be entrusted, in case of emergency, to the Engineer and Railway Staff Corps, that body and, also, the War Railway Council, continued to occupy a purely advisory position.

So it was clearly desirable to supplement the recognized efficiency of the railways themselves by the creation of a central executive body which, whenever the State assumed control of the railways, under the Act of 1871, would (1) secure the necessary co-operation between Government departments and the railway managements; (2) ensure the working of the various railway systems on a national basis; and (3) co-ordinate such various needs as naval and military movements to or from all parts of the Kingdom; coal supply for the Fleet; transport of munitions; the requirements of the civil population, etc.

The necessity for this machinery—which could not possibly be created at a moment's notice—became still more apparent in the autumn of 1911, and steps were taken to provide what was so obviously a missing link in the existing organisation.

Thus it was that in 1912 the War Railway Council was succeeded by a Railways Executive Committee which, constituted of the general managers of leading railway companies, was to prepare plans " with a view to facilitate the working " of the provisions of the Act of 1871, and would, also, in the event of the Government assuming control over the railways of Great Britain, under the provisions of that Act, constitute the executive body for working them on behalf of the State, becoming the recognised intermediary (1) for receiving the instructions of Government departments in respect to military and naval requirements; and (2) for taking the necessary measures in order to give effect to them through the individual companies, each of which, subject to the instructions it received from the Committee, would retain the management of its own line.

ORGANISATION IN ENGLAND.

In accordance with the principle thus adopted, it was through the Railways Executive Committee that the Government, subject to certain financial arrangements which need not be dealt with here, established their control over the railways of Great Britain on the outbreak of war in 1914, the announcement to this effect issued from the War Office, under date August 4, stating :—

An Order in Council has been made under Section 16 of the Regulation of the Forces Act, 1871, declaring that it is expedient that the Government should have control over the railroads in Great Britain. This control will be exercised through an Executive Committee composed of general managers of railways which has been formed for some time, and has prepared plans with a view to facilitating the working of this Act.

In a notification issued by the Executive Committee, of which the official chairman was the President of the Board of Trade and the acting chairman was Mr. (now Sir Herbert A.) Walker, general manager of the London and South Western Railway, it was further stated :—

The control of the railways has been taken over by the Government for the purpose of ensuring that the railways, locomotives rolling stock and staff shall be used as one complete unit in the best interests of the State for the movement of troops, stores and food supplies. . . . The staff on each railway will remain under the same control as heretofore, and will receive their instructions through the same channels as in the past.

As eventually constituted, the Committee consisted of the following general managers :—Mr. D. A. Matheson, Caledonian Railway ; Sir Sam Fay, Great Central Railway ; Mr. C. H. Dent, Great Northern Railway ; Mr. F. Potter, Great Western Railway ; Mr. Guy Calthrop, London and North Western Railway ; Mr. J. A. F. Aspinall, Lancashire and Yorkshire Railway ; Sir Herbert A. Walker, London and South Western Railway ; Sir William Forbes, London, Brighton and South Coast Railway ; Sir Guy Granet, Midland Railway ; Sir A. K. Butterworth, North Eastern Railway, and Mr. F. H. Dent, South Eastern and Chatham Railway, with Mr. Gilbert S. Szlumper as secretary.

1860 AND 1914

Such, then, was the final outcome of a movement which, started in 1860, by individual effort, as the result of an expected invasion of England by France, was, in 1914, and after undergoing gradual though continuous development, to play an important part on behalf of the nation in helping France herself, now England's cherished Ally, to resist the invader of her own fair territory.

With what smoothness the transport of our troops was conducted cannot yet be told in detail; but the facts here narrated will show that the success attained was mainly due to three all-important factors,—(1) the efficiency of the railway organisation; (2) the willingness of the Government, on assuming control of the railways under the Act of 1871, to leave their management in the hands of railway men; and (3) the ready adoption, alike by the railway interests and by State departments, of the fundamental principle enforced by a succession of wars from the American Civil War of 1861–65 downwards,—that in the conduct of military rail transport there should be, in each of its various stages, intermediaries between the military and the railway technical elements, co-ordinating their mutual requirements, constituting the recognised and only channel for orders and instructions, and ensuring, as far as prudence, foresight and human skill can devise, the perfect working of so delicate and complicated an instrument as the railway machine.

RAILWAY TROOPS

While Germany, inspired by the American example, had begun the creation of special bodies of Railway Troops in 1866, it was not until 1882 that a like course was adopted in England. Prior to the last-mentioned year it was, possibly, thought that the labour branch of the Engineer and Railway Volunteer Staff Corps would suffice to meet requirements in regard to the destruction or the re-establishment of railways at home in the event of invasion; but the arrangements of the Corps did not provide for the supply of men

ORGANISATION IN ENGLAND. 199

to take up railway construction and operation on the occasion of military expeditions to other countries.

It was this particular need that led, in the summer of 1882, to the conversion of the 8th Company of Royal Engineers into the 8th (Railway) Company, R.E., the occasion therefor being the dispatch of an expeditionary force under Sir Garnet (afterwards Lord) Wolseley to Egypt, where the necessity for railway work of various kinds was likely to arise. This pioneer corps of British Railway Troops was formed of seven officers, one warrant officer, two buglers, and ninety-seven N.C.O.'s and sappers. So constituted, it was thought better adapted for railway work under conditions of active service than a body of civilian railwaymen would be. There certainly was the disadvantage that those constituting the 8th were not then proficient in railway matters ; but, before they left, both officers and men were given the run of the London, Chatham and Dover Railway lines, and were there enabled to pick up what they could of railway working in the locomotive and traffic departments, while on the London and South Western and the South Eastern Railways they were initiated, as far as could be done in the time, into the art of platelaying. The Corps took out to Egypt four small tank locomotives ; two first-class, two second-class and six third-class carriages ; forty cattle trucks ; four brake vans ; two travelling cranes ; two breakdown vans, and five miles of permanent way, complete, with accessories, tools, etc. Excellent work was done in carrying on regular train services, repairing damaged track, etc., running an armoured train, constructing supplementary short lines, and conveying troops, sick and wounded, and stores, the practical utility of such an addition to the engineering forces of the Army being thus fully assured.

In January, 1885, the 10th Company, Royal Engineers, was converted into the 10th (Railway) Company, and sent to Egypt to assist in the construction of the then contemplated Suakin-Berber line, to which further reference will be made in Chapter XV. Both companies also rendered good service in the South African War.

According to the " Manual of Military Railways," issued

with Army Orders dated March 1st, 1889, the duties likely to be required from the Royal Engineers with regard to railways are as follows :— (1) Laying, working, and maintaining a military line of railway between two places ; (2) restoring an existing line which has been damaged or destroyed by an enemy ; (3) destroying an existing line as much as possible with a given number of men and in a specified time, and (4) working and maintaining an existing line. The "Manual" itself gave much technical information as to the construction, maintenance, destruction and working of railways. It was re-issued by the War Office in 1898 as Part VI of "Instruction in Military Engineering," and was stated to embody a portion of the course of instruction in railways at the school of Military Engineering, Chatham. In the "Manual of Military Engineering," issued by the General Staff of the War Office in 1905, instructions are given (Chap. XVII, pars. 238–244) on the " hasty demolition, without explosives," of railways, stations, buildings, rolling stock, permanent way, water supply, etc. ; and in Chapter XXIII, " Railways and Telegraphs," the statement is made that—

The duties likely to be required of troops in the field with regard to railways (apart from large railway schemes, for which special arrangements would be necessary,) may be considered as either temporary repairs or the laying of short lengths of line to join up breaks, the construction of additional works, such as platforms, etc., to adapt the line for military use, or the demolition of an existing line.

Detailed information is given, for the benefit of R.E. officers, concerning railway construction, repair and reconstruction, and the main principles on which such work should be carried out for military purposes are explained. The best system to adopt for the effecting of rapid repairs is said to be that of establishing construction trains. " The reconstruction staff live in these trains, which rapidly advance along the line as it is being repaired, conveying, also, the necessary material."

The peace training[1] of the Companies includes : recon-

[1] " General Principles, Organisation and Equipment of Roya Engineers," *Royal Engineers Journal*, February, 1910.

ORGANISATION IN ENGLAND.

naissance, survey and final location of a railway; laying out station yards; laying out deviations; rapid laying of narrow-gauge "military" lines; construction of all kinds of railway bridges; signal installation; water supply; repairs to telegraphs and telephones necessary for working construction lines; working of electric block instruments; fitting up armoured trains; construction of temporary platforms, and working and maintenance of construction trains.

Instruction in reconnaissance and survey work is given to officers while at head-quarters, and a certain number of N.C.O.'s and men are also instructed in railway survey work. Parties, each commanded by an officer, are sent to carry out a reconnaissance and final location of a railway between two points about forty miles apart on the assumption that it is an unmapped country, and complete maps and sections are prepared. The Companies have also undertaken the construction and maintenance of the Woolmer Instructional Military Railway,—a 4 ft. 8½ in. gauge military line, about six miles in length, connecting Bordon (London and South Western Railway) with Longmore Camp. All the plant necessary for railway work and workshops for the repair of rolling stock are provided at Longmore.

In time of war the chief duties of a Railway Company, R.E., would be to survey, construct, repair and demolish railways and to work construction and armoured trains.

In the South African campaign, when the military had to operate the railways of which they took possession in the enemy's country, some difficulty was experienced in obtaining from the ranks of the Army a sufficient number of men capable of working the lines. As the result of these conditions, it was arranged, in 1903, between the War Office and certain of the British railway companies that the latter should afford facilities in their locomotive departments and workshops for the training of a number of non-commissioned officers and men as drivers, firemen and mechanics, (capable of carrying out repairs,) in order to qualify them better for railway work in the field, in case of need. This arrangement was carried out down to the outbreak of war in 1914.

The period of training lasted either six or nine months. In order to avoid the raising of any "labour" difficulties, no wages were given during this period to Army men who were already receiving Army pay as soldiers, but a bonus was granted to them by the railway companies, when they left, on their obtaining from the head of the department to which they had been attached a certificate of their efficiency.

Strategical Railways

The subject of strategical railways will be dealt with, both generally and in special reference to their construction in Germany, in Chapter XVIII. In regard to Great Britain it may be said that the position as explained by Sir George Findlay in his article in the *United Service Magazine* for April, 1892, is that whilst Continental countries have been spending large sums of money on the building of strategical lines for the defence of their frontiers, (or, he might have added, for the invasion, in some instances, of their neighbours' territory,) Great Britain, more fortunate, possesses already a system of railways which, though constructed entirely by private enterprise, could not, even if they had been laid out with a view to national defence, "have been better adapted for the purpose, since there are duplicated lines directed from the great centres of population and of military activity upon every point of the coast, while there are lines skirting the coast in every direction, north, east, south and west."

Some years ago there were certain critics who recommended the building of lines, for strategical purposes, along sections of our coast which the ordinary railways did not directly serve; but the real necessity for such lines was questioned, the more so because the transport of troops by rail on such short-distance journeys as those that would have been here in question might, with the marching to and from the railway and the time occupied in entraining and detraining, take longer than if the troops either marched all the way, or (in the event of there being only a small force) if they went by motor vehicles to the coast.

One point that was, indeed, likely to arise in connection

ORGANISATION IN ENGLAND. 203

with the movement of troops was the provision of facilities for their ready transfer from one railway system to another, without change of carriage, when making cross-country journeys or travelling, for instance, from the North or the Midlands to ports in the South.

We have seen that in France many such links were established, subsequent to the war of 1870-71, expressly for strategical reasons; but in Great Britain a like result has been attained, apart from military considerations, from the fact that some years ago the different railway companies established physical connections between their different systems with a view to the ready transfer of ordinary traffic. When, therefore, the necessity arose for a speedy mobilisation, or for the transport of troops from any part of Great Britain to any particular port for an overseas destination, the necessary facilities for through journeys by rail, in the shortest possible time, already existed.

In effect, the nearest approach to purely strategical lines in Great Britain is to be found, perhaps, in those which connect military camps with the ordinary railways; yet, while these particular lines may have been built to serve a military purpose, they approximate less to strategical railways proper, as understood in Germany, than to branch lines and sidings constructed to meet the special needs of some large industrial concern.

Generally speaking, the attitude of Parliament and of British authorities in general has not been sympathetic to suggestions of strategical railways, even when proposals put forward have had the support of the War Office itself.

This tendency was well shown in connection with the Northern Junction Railway scheme which was inquired into by a Select Committee of the House of Commons in 1913. Under the scheme in question, a railway was to be constructed from Brentford, on the west of London, to Wood Green, on the north, passing through Acton, Ealing, Wembley Park, Hampstead and Finchley, and establishing connections with and between several of the existing main-line systems. In this respect it compared with those "outer circle" railway systems which, as a further result of the war of 1870–71, were expressly designed by the French Government for the better defence of Paris.

The Northern Junction scheme was introduced to the Select Committee as one which, among other considerations, "would be important from a military point of view for moving troops from one point to another without taking them through London." Lieut.-General Sir J. S. Cowans, Quartermaster-General, a member of the Army Council responsible for the movement of troops, and deputed by the Secretary for War to give evidence, said:

> The proposed line would be a great advantage in time of emergency if it was constructed in its entirety. The Army Council felt that it would provide important routes between the South of England and East Anglia and the North. At present trains had to come from Aldershot to Clapham Junction by the South-Western line, and be there broken up and sent over congested City lines on to the Great Northern. By the proposed line military trains could be handled without dividing them and be transferred to the Great Northern or Great Eastern without being sent over the congested City lines.

Strong opposition was offered, however, on the ground that the construction of the line would do "irreparable damage" to the amenities of the Hampstead Garden Suburb; and, after a sitting which extended over several days, the Committee threw out the Bill, the Chairman subsequently admitting that "they had been influenced very largely by the objection of the Hampstead Garden Suburb."

In 1914 the scheme was introduced afresh into the House of Commons, with certain modifications, the proposed line of route no longer passing through the Hampstead Garden Suburb, though near to it. One member of the House said he had collaborated in promoting the Bill because "he most earnestly believed this railway was of vital import to the mobilisation of our troops in time of emergency"; but another declared that the alleged military necessity for the railway was "all fudge," while much was now said as to the pernicious effect the line would have on the highly-desirable residential district of Finchley. In the result strategical considerations were again set aside, and the House rejected the Bill by a majority of seventy-seven.

CHAPTER XV

MILITARY RAILWAYS

BY the expression "military railways" is meant lines of railways which, as distinct from commercial lines serving public purposes, have been designed expressly for military use. The fact that any line forming part of the ordinary railway system of the country is employed for the conveyance of troops either direct to the theatre of war or to some port for embarkation therefrom does not constitute that line a "military" railway, in the strict sense of the term, whatever the extent of its use for military transport for the time being. Such line remains a commercial railway, all the same, and the application to it of the designation "military" is erroneous.

Military railways proper fall mainly into two groups—(1) "field" or "siege" railways, constructed on the theatre of war for moving heavy guns, platform materials, etc., to their position; conveying ammunition and supplies to siege batteries, magazines, advanced trenches or bombproofs; bringing up reinforcements rapidly in case of a sortie; conveying working-parties to and from their work; removing sick and wounded to the rear, and other kindred purposes, the loads being generally hauled by animals, by gasoline motor or by men; and (2) "supply" railways, specially constructed to convey troops, stores, etc., from the base to the front, in time of war, or from an ordinary main-line railway to a military camp or depôt in time of peace, where local lines of railway are not available for the purpose.

These two main groups include various types of railways coming under one or the other designation, and ranging from a very light portable tramway, put down at express speed to serve an emergency, and worked by small engines, mules or horses, to substantially built lines, of standard gauge, designed both to be worked by locomotives and to carry the largest possible number of troops or amount of freight.

In any case, the details of construction, equipment and operation of a military railway vary from those of a commercial railway since the one would be intended to serve only a specific and possibly temporary purpose, in the attainment of which the question of speed would be a secondary consideration, whereas the other would require to assume a permanent form, be capable of higher speeds, and afford adequate guarantee of safety for the public, by whom it would be used. The building, also, of a military railway may be, and generally is, carried out by a corps of Railway Troops to which are specially delegated the duties of laying, working, maintaining, repairing, restoring or destroying railways; and, provided the desired lines were built with sufficient dispatch, and answered the desired purpose, the military commanders who would alone be concerned might well be satisfied.

In many different ways the resort to military railways, whatever their particular type, has greatly extended the range of advantages to be gained from the application of rail-power to war. A full record of all that has been accomplished in this direction could hardly be attempted here; but a few typical examples of what has been done in this direction—though not always with conspicuous success—may be offered.

The Crimean War

The earliest instance of a purely military railway being constructed to serve the purpose of a campaign occurred in the Crimean War; and, although the line then made would to-day be regarded as little more than an especially inefficient apology for a railway, it was looked upon at the time as a remarkable innovation in warfare. It further established a precedent destined to be widely followed in later years.

MILITARY RAILWAYS.

Between the camp of the allies at Sebastopol and their base of supplies at Balaklava the distance was only seven or eight miles; yet in the winter of 1854-55 the fatigue parties sent for rations, clothing, fuel, huts, ammunition and other necessaries were frequently no less than twelve hours in doing the return journey. The reason was that during the greater part of that time they were floundering in a sea of mud. The soil of the Crimea is clay impregnated with salt, and, under the combined influence of climatic conditions and heavy traffic, the route between camp and base had been converted into a perfect quagmire. Horses, mules and carts were, at first, alone available for transport purposes; but, although plenty of animals were to be obtained in the surrounding country, only a limited number could be employed by reason of the lack of forage, a totally inadequate supply having been sent out from England. As for the animals that were used, their sufferings, as the result of those terrible journeys, their own shortage of food, and the effect of the intense cold on their half-starved bodies, were terrible. "In the rear of each Division," says General Sir Edward Hamley, in "The War in the Crimea," "a scanty group of miserable ponies and mules, whose backs never knew what it was to be quit of the saddle, shivered, and starved, and daily died." They died, also, on every journey to or from the base. The toil of going through the quagmire even for their own forage, or of bringing it back when they had got it, was too great for them, and the whole line of route was marked by their remains.

As for the troops, they experienced great hardships owing to the inadequate supplies of provisions and fuel at the camp, although there might be plenty of both at the base. Apart from the physical conditions of the roads, or apologies for roads, between the two points, the campaign was begun without transport arrangements of any kind whatever. A transport corps formed for the British Army in 1799, under the title of the Royal Wagon Train, had been disbanded in 1833, and, whether from motives of economy or because the need for war preparations in time of peace was not sufficiently appreciated, no other corps had been created to take its place. Hence the troops sent to the Crimea were required, at the outset, to look after the transport themselves, and in many instances they even had to do the work of mules and horses. It was not until January 24, 1855, that a Land Transport Corps, composed of volunteers from various arms of the service, was raised by Royal Warrant and began to provide for a defect in the military organisation which had, in the meantime, involved the allies, and especially the British, in severe privations owing to the frequent shortage of supplies. The original intention to establish a depôt at head-quarters before Sebastopol had had to be abandoned because of the hopelessness of any attempt to get a sufficient surplus of provisions to form a store.

Such were the conditions that the pioneer military railway was designed to remedy. Built, at a very slow rate, by English contractors, who arrived at the Crimea with their men and material during the month of January, 1855, the line was a single-track one, with a 4 feet $8\frac{1}{2}$ inch gauge. For the first two miles from Balaklava it was worked by a locomotive. Then the trucks were drawn up an incline, eight at a time, by a stationary engine. Six horses next drew two trucks at a time up another incline. After this came a fairly level piece of road, followed by two gullies where each wagon was detached in succession and made to run down one side of the gully and up the other by its own momentum. Then horses were again attached to the trucks and so drew them, finally, to the end of the line on the Upland.

Five locomotives, of from 12 to 18 tons weight, were provided, and there were about forty ordinary side-tip ballast wagons—all entirely unsuitable for use on a military railway.

At first the men belonging to the contractors' staff—navvies and others—were entrusted with the working of the line. The question had been raised as to whether their services should not be made use of in other directions, as well. On their being sent out from England the idea was

MILITARY RAILWAYS. 209

entertained that they might construct trenches and batteries, in addition to building the railway, and there was a suggestion that they should, also, join the siege parties in the attack on Sebastopol. In order to test the question (as recorded by Major-General Whitworth Porter, in his "History of the Corps of Royal Engineers"), Sir John Burgoyne wrote to Mr. Beattie, principal engineer of the Railway Department, asking if he would approve of an invitation being given to the men to undergo such training as would qualify them to defend any position in which they might happen to be. In his answer Mr. Beattie wrote:—

The subject of your letter was very fully and anxiously discussed in London before I left, and it was determined *not* to arm the men. They were considered too valuable to be used as soldiers, and were distinctly told that they would not be called upon to fight.

Their value, however, did not stand the test it underwent when they were called on to work the railway they had built. They were found to be lacking in any sense of discipline; they repeatedly struck work when their services were most urgently needed, and they had to be got rid of accordingly. They were replaced by men from the Army Works Corps and the Land Transport Corps, then in operation in the Crimea, and the members of the new staff—constituting a disciplined force—worked admirably. Major Powell, who became traffic manager of the line in March, 1855, and chief superintendent in the following July, has said concerning them [1]:—

Many lost their lives in the execution of their duty. When I required them to work night and day to throw forward supplies for the great struggle—the capture of Sebastopol—several of them remained seventy-two hours continuously at work.

The quantities of ammunition and stores which could be carried were below the requirements of the troops engaged in the siege operations; but during the last bombardment of Sebastopol—when the line was worked continuously,

[1] See lecture by Capt. C. E. Luard, R.E., on "Field Railways and their general application in war." Journal of the Royal United Service Institution, vol. xvii, 1873.

P

night and day, by a staff increased to about 1,000 men, of whom 400 were Turks—the transport effected rose from 200 tons a day, the limit attained under operation by the undisciplined navvies, to 700 tons. The line also did excellent work on the re-embarkment of the troops at the end of the campaign.

American Civil War

In the American War of Succession, the existing lines of railway were supplemented in various instances by " surface railroads," which consisted of rails and sleepers laid on the ordinary ground without any preparation of a proper road bed, yet serving a useful purpose, notwithstanding the rough and ready way in which they were put together.

The Abyssinian Campaign

How a railway specially constructed for the purpose may assist a military expedition in the prosecution of a " little war " in an uncivilised country, practically devoid of roads, and offering great physical difficulties, was shown on the occasion of the British Campaign in Abyssinia in 1867–68 ; though the circumstances under which the line in question was built were not in themselves creditable to the authorities concerned.

Sent to effect the release of the British prisoners whom King Theodore was keeping in captivity at Magdala, the expedition under Sir Robert Napier (afterwards Lord Napier of Magdala) entered upon what was to be quite as much an engineering as a military exploit. Not only was Magdala 300 miles from Annesley Bay, the base of operations on the Red Sea, but it stood, as a hill fortress, on a plateau more than 9,000 feet above the sea-level. To reach it meant the construction of roads in three sections. The first, which, in parts, had to be cut in the mountain side, rose to a height of 7,400 feet in 63 miles ; the second allowed of no more than a cart road, and the third and final stage was a mere mountain track where the only transport possible was that of mules or elephants.

MILITARY RAILWAYS.

When, in October, 1867, the advance Brigade landed at Zoulla, the port in Annesley Bay from which the advance inland was to be made, they took with them the materials for some tramway lines intended to connect two landing piers with the depôts it was proposed to establish a mile inland. In November these plans were altered in favour of a line of railway, twelve miles in length, from the landing-place to Koomayleh, at the entrance of the Soroo Pass, the route to be taken by the expedition on its journey to the Abyssinian highlands. All the necessary plant was to be supplied by the Government of Bombay, who also undertook to provide the labour ; but it was the middle of January, 1868, before a real start could be made with the work.

Even then, as told by Lieut. Willans, R.E.,[1] who took part in the expedition, the progress made was extremely slow. The rails obtained from different railway companies in India were of five different patterns, of odd lengths, and varying in weight from 30 lb. to 65 lb. a yard. Some of them had been in use many years on the harbour works at Karachi, had been taken up and laid down several times, and had, also, been bent to fit sharp curves or cut to suit the original line. Some single-flanged rails had been fitted in the Government workshops at Bombay with fish-plates and bolts ; but the holes in the plates and rails were not at uniform distances, and the bolts fitted the holes so tightly as to allow of no play. Then, when the rails arrived, no spikes came with them, and without spikes they could not be laid. When the spikes followed, it was found that the augurs for boring holes in the sleepers had been left at Bombay, to come on by another ship ; though this particular difficulty was met by the artisans of the 23rd Punjab Pioneer Regiment making augurs for themselves.

If the rails gave much trouble—and even when they had been laid it was no unusual thing for them to break between two sleepers and throw the engine off the line—the locomotives and rolling stock caused still more.

[1] "The Abyssinian Railway." By Lieut. Willans, R.E. Papers on Subjects Connected with the Duties of the Corps of Royal Engineers. New Series. Vol. xviii. 1870.

Six locomotives were shipped from Bombay; but, owing to the great difficulty in landing and the labour involved in putting them together, only four were used. Of these, one was a tank engine which, although just turned out from the railway workshops at Bombay, required new driving wheels after it had been running a fortnight. Another came with worn-out boiler tubes, and these had to be replaced at Zoulla. The two others, tank engines with only four wheels each, had previously seen many years' service at Karachi. All the engines were very light, weighing with coal and water from 16 to 20 tons each. The best of them could do no more than draw fifteen small loaded trucks up an incline of one in sixty.

The sixty wagons sent were ordinary trolleys having no springs, no spring buffers and no grease boxes. Their axle-boxes were of cast iron, and wore out within a fortnight, owing to the driving sand. As the railway came into use, every truck was loaded to its fullest capacity, and the combination of this weight with the jarring and oscillation on a very rough line led either to the breaking of the coupling chains or to the coupling bars being pulled from the wagons at starting. When fresh coupling chains were asked for it was found that the boxes containing them had either been left behind at Bombay or were buried beneath several hundred tons of other supplies on board ship. At least forty per cent. of the trucks were either constantly under repair or had to be put aside as unfit for use. In May a number of open wagons with springs and spring buffers arrived from Bombay. Some of these were converted into passenger carriages.

Difficulties arose in other directions, besides.

The plant forwarded was adapted to the Indian standard gauge of 5 feet 6 inches, and was heavy and difficult to handle, especially under the troublesome conditions of landing. To-day, of course, a narrow-gauge railway, easily dealt with, would be employed in circumstances such as those of the Abyssinian expedition.

The Indian natives who had been sent in the first instance to construct the line were found unsuitable, and had to be

MILITARY RAILWAYS.

replaced by gangs of Chinese picked up in Bombay. The latter worked well and gave no trouble.

The country through which the line was laid was timberless, if not, also, practically waterless. Wells had to be sunk for the water wanted for the locomotives and the working-parties.

The heat was excessive. The temperature at times was 180 degrees Fahr. in the sun. English navvies could not have made the line at all.

The two piers where the incoming vessels could alone be unloaded got so congested with traffic that it was only with the greatest trouble railway material could be landed.

Use began to be made of the line as soon as any of it was ready, and the traffic at the shore end at once became so heavy that it was difficult to get materials and supplies through to the construction parties at the other end. Officers, also, who should have been superintending the construction had to devote a good deal of time, instead, to details of operation, or to looking after the repairs of rolling stock.

In all these circumstances one cannot be surprised at the slow rate of progress made. One may, rather, wonder that the line got built at all. As it was, four months were spent on eleven miles of railway, or a total of twelve miles including sidings. There remained still another mile or so to be built when, at the end of April, news arrived that the object of the expedition had been attained, and that Magdala had fallen. It was then decided not to complete the line, but to devote all energies to preparing for the heavy traffic to be dealt with in the conveyance of troops, baggage and stores on the return journey.

From the middle of May to the middle of June the resources of the line were severely taxed; but a great improvement had been made in the working arrangements, and a railway which had involved so much trouble in the making was eventually found to be of great practical service. Lieutenant Willans says of it :—

> The Abyssinian railway was a great success, if one may gauge it by the amount of assistance it gave to the expedition, by the

celerity and dispatch with which, by its aid, stores were landed and brought up to the store sheds, and by the rapidity and ease with which the troops and their baggage were brought back and re-embarked at once. . . .

As an auxiliary to the expedition, and as an additional means of transport, no one who had anything to do in connection with it can have doubted its extreme utility.

Faulty, therefore, as had been the conditions under which the line was constructed, the results nevertheless established definitely the principle that, in such campaigns as the one in Abyssinia, military railways might serve an extremely useful purpose in facilitating the transport of troops and supplies.

The Abyssinian experiences did, however, further show the desirability of any country likely to find itself in a position requiring the construction of military railways—as an aid to wars small or great—creating in advance an organisation designed to enable it, as far as possible, to meet promptly whatever emergency might arise, without the risk of having to deal with defective material, unsatisfactory labour, and administrative mismanagement.

The same lesson was to be enforced by other expeditions in which England has taken part, and, down to the period when improvements in our system—or lack of system—began to be effected, there was much scope for criticism as to the way in which military railways, designed to facilitate operations undertaken in countries having a lack of communications, had been either constructed or worked. Writing, in 1882, in the " Professional Papers " of the Royal Engineers (Chatham) on " Railways for Military Communication in the Field," Col. J. P. Maquay, R.E., observed in regard to what had been the experiences to that date :—

In most of the wars that England has undertaken during the past thirty years, attempts have been made to construct railways for the transport of stores and materials from the base of operations. This base must necessarily be on the sea coast for a country situated as England is. These railways have not been successful chiefly because, when war had broken out, such material was hastily got together as seemed most suitable to the occasion ; and, further, the construction of these lines was not carried out on any system. It is not surprising, therefore,

MILITARY RAILWAYS. 215

that our military railways were never completed in time to be of much use to the troops they were intended to serve.

Franco-German War

In the Franco-German War of 1870-71 the Germans constructed two military railways—(1) a line, twenty-two miles in length, connecting Remilly, on the Saarbrück Railway, with Pont à Mousson, on the Metz-Frouard line; and (2) a loop line, three miles long, passing round the tunnel at Nanteuil, blown up by the French.

Special interest attached to these two lines inasmuch as they were the result of construction work done, not in anticipation of a war, or even immediately preceding hostilities, but during the course of an active campaign. In addition to this, they afforded an opportunity for showing what Prussia could do, under pressure, with the Construction Corps she had formed in order, among other things, to meet just such contingencies as those that now arose.

At the beginning of the war the Prussian General Staff had (according to Rüstow) assumed that Metz would offer a prolonged resistance, and that the defenders would be certain to make an attempt to interrupt the rail communication between Germany and her troops in the field. To meet the position which might thus be created, it was decided to build from Pont à Mousson to Remilly a field railway which, avoiding Metz, would link up at Remilly with the line proceeding thence to Saarbrück, and so ensure the maintenance of direct rail communication to and from Germany. On August 14, 1870, the day of the rearguard action at Borny, the survey and the levelling of the ground were begun, and three days later a start was made with the construction. Altogether some 4,200 men were employed on the work, namely, 400 belonging to two Field Railway Companies; 800 forming four Fortress Pioneer Companies, and about 3,000 miners from the colliery districts of Saarbrück who had been thrown out of work owing to the war and accepted employment on the railway. The building corps had at their disposal a park of 330 wagons and other vehicles, and patrol and requisition duties were performed for them by a squadron of Cavalry.

Notwithstanding that so considerable a force was available for the purpose, the work of building the twenty-two miles of railway took forty-eight days, the line not being ready for operation until October 4. This was in no way a great achievement, and it did not compare favourably with much that was done by the Federal Construction Corps employed in the American War of Secession. It is true that the irregularities of the ground were such as to render necessary numerous cuttings and embankments, and that two bridges and two viaducts had to be provided; but the cuttings were only about 3 feet deep, and the embankments were only 5 feet high, except near one of the viaducts, where they were 10 feet high. The viaducts and bridges were of timber, with spans of about 16 feet. The building of the line was, therefore, in no way a formidable undertaking, from an engineering point of view.

Not only, however, did it take over 4,000 men nearly fifty days to make twenty-two miles of line, but the work had been done in such a way that when the autumn rains came on the track settled in many places; traffic on the lines became very dangerous; one of the bridges was washed away by the floods, and almost as many men had to be put on to do repairs as had previously been employed for the construction. Traffic of a very moderate description—each locomotive drawing only four wagons at a time—was carried on for just twenty-six days, and then, happily for the engineers concerned, the developments in and around Metz rendered the line no longer necessary.

How the restoration of the traffic interrupted through the explosion of French mines in the tunnel at Nanteuil occupied from September 17 to November 22 has already been told on page 128.

Russo-Turkish War

In the opinion of one English military critic, what short lines were made in the Franco-German War " were neither

MILITARY RAILWAYS. 217

so speedily constructed nor so successful in result as to encourage the idea that lines of any length could be made during a campaign"; but a different impression is to be derived from the story of what was accomplished in the same direction in the Russo-Turkish War of 1877-78.

Russia planned her campaign against Turkey in the hope and expectation that it would be short, sharp and decisive. She started her mobilisation in good time, that is to say, in November, 1876, although she did not declare war until April 24, 1877. Making the mistake, however, of despising her foe, she anticipated no serious opposition from the Turks, but expected, rather, to paralyse them by a rapid advance, have a triumphal march to Constantinople, secure the desired safeguards for the Christians in Turkey, and see the war over before the end of the summer.

One reason why Russia specially desired to bring the campaign to so early a conclusion lay in the deficient and precarious nature of the rail communication. Under a convention which had been agreed to with Rumania on April 16, 1877, Russia was to have a free passage for her troops through that country. She was, also, to have the use of the Rumanian railways and of all their transport facilities. But the only line then running through Rumania was one that went from Galatz, on the Russo-Rumanian frontier, to Bucharest, and thence (with a branch to Slatina) to Giurgevo, on the Danube, where it connected with a Bulgarian line from Rustchuk, on the south of the river, to Varna, the Turkish base of supplies on the Black Sea. Not only was the Rumanian railway system thus limited in extent, but the lines had been indifferently constructed, they were badly maintained, and they had an inadequate personnel together with an insufficiency both of rolling stock and of terminal facilities. Still further, the fact that the Russian railways had a broader gauge than the railways of Rumania (among other European countries) caused great delay in the transfer, at the frontier, from the one system to the other, not alone of 200,000 men, but of the 850 field and 400 siege guns, of the ammunition, and of much other material the troops required to take with them. The alternative to dependance on the railway was a resort to roads impassable in wet weather.

What really caused the Russian plans to miscarry, however, was the obstinate defence of Plevna by Osman Pasha, who took up his position there on July 19, subjected the Russians to successive repulses, and did not capitulate until December 10, the siege costing the Russians 55,000 men and the Rumanians 10,000.

When it was realised that the check at Plevna rendered certain a prolongation of the campaign, Russia set about the construction of a series of new lines of railway during the course of the war. The principal lines thus taken in hand were:—

1. A line in Russia, from Bender, on the Dniester, to Galatz, establishing direct communication between the Odessa railways and the Rumanian frontier, and affording improved facilities for the sending of reinforcements to the seat of war.

2. A line from Fratesti, on the Bucharest-Giurgevo Railway, to Simnitza, the point on the north bank of the Danube where, on the night of June 26–7, the Russians built the bridge which enabled them to cross the river.

3. A line from Sistova, on the south side of the Danube, to Tirnova (Bulgaria), situate about thirty miles south-east of Plevna, and about twenty-five north of the Shipka Pass.

Of these three lines the construction of the first, 189 miles in length, was begun at the end of July, 1877. The original intention was to build a railway to serve the purposes of the war only; but the conclusion that ulterior strategical and commercial purposes would alike be served by linking up Odessa with the Rumanian frontier led to the building of a railway likely to be of permanent usefulness. The line was a single-track one, with a sufficient number of stations and passing places to allow of the running of seven trains in each direction in the twenty-four hours. The construction, carried out by contract, involved the building of a number of timber bridges and the provision of several embankments, one of which was over three miles in length. Great difficulties were experienced in regard to labour, and especially by reason of the refusal of the men to work either on Sundays or on their numerous saints' days. Trains were, nevertheless, running on the line within 100 days of the construction being started, and this notwithstanding the fact that the number of actual working days had been only fifty-eight. Whereas, therefore, the Germans had, in 1870, with the help of a Construction Corps over 4,000 strong, taken forty-eight days to build twenty-two miles of railway between Pont à Mousson and Remilly, the Russians in 1877 built, by contract, 189 miles of railway in just over double the same period.

A railway from Fratesti to Simnitza had become indispensable inasmuch as the main line of communication for the Russian Army could not be continued for an indefinite period along the forty miles of defective roads—speedily worn out by the heavy traffic—which separated the Bucharest-Giurgevo line from the bridge built across the Danube. The only important earthwork necessary was an embankment a mile and a half long and fourteen feet high. The bridges to be provided included one of 420 feet and two of 210 feet each. In this instance the troubles experienced were due to the difficulty in getting the necessary materials for the work of construction owing partly to the existing Rumanian lines being blocked with military traffic, and partly to the state of the roads and to the use of all available draught horses for Army transport purposes. There could thus be no great celerity shown in construction, and the forty miles of railway, begun in the middle of September, were, in fact, not ready for working until the beginning of December.

Like difficulties were experienced, though to a still more acute degree, in regard to the Sistova-Tirnova line, the length of which was to be seventy-five miles ; and here only the earth-works could be finished before the end of the campaign.

What, however, had been accomplished during the time the war was in progress was (1) the completion of 229 miles of new railway, and the making of the road-bed for another seventy-five miles, together with the carrying out of a number of minor railway works ; (2) the acquisition, by purchase in different countries, of 120 locomotives and 2,150 wagons and trucks, all new, and (3) the provision of a steam railway ferry across the Danube.[1]

So the development of the rail-power principle in warfare was carried still further by this construction, during the course of the Russo-Turkish conflict, of a greater length of railways, designed for military use, than had ever been built under like conditions before. The world gained a fresh lesson as to the importance of the rôle played by railways in war, and it was offered, also, a striking example of what could be done in the way of rapidly providing them in a time of emergency.

On the other hand it had to be remembered that, of the three railways in question, the one which included 189 miles out of the total 229 miles built was constructed on Russian territory where there was no danger of interruption by the enemy, while the delays which occurred with the two other lines, owing to the congestion of traffic, under war conditions, on existing railways depended upon for the supply of materials, seemed to point (1) to the risk that might, from this cause, be run if the building of lines necessary or desirable in the interests of some prospective campaign were left until the outbreak of hostilities, and (2) to the wisdom of constructing all such lines, as far as necessary and practicable, in time of peace.

THE SUDAN

If we turn now to the Sudan, we gain examples of military railways which, designed for the purposes of war, and constructed, in part, during the progress of active hostilities, first rendered great services in facilitating the conquest of a vast area, and then developed into a system of Government

[1] "The Construction of Military Railways during the Russo-Turkish War of 1877-8." By Captain M. T. Sale, R.E. Journal of the Royal United Service Institution, vol. xxiv, 1881. "De la Construction des Chemins de Fer en temps de guerre. Lignes construites par l'armée russe pendant la campagne 1877-78." Par M. P. Lessar, Ingénieur du Gouvernement russe. Traduit du russe par M. L. Avril. Paris, 1879.

MILITARY RAILWAYS. 221

railways operated, in turn, for the purposes of peace, and accomplishing results as conspicuously successful in the latter direction as they had previously done in the former.

During the time that Saïd Pasha was Viceroy of Egypt (1854-63) there was brought forward a scheme for the linking up of Egypt and the Sudan by means of a single line of railway from Cairo to Khartoum, with a branch to Massowa, on the Red Sea. It was an ambitious proposal, and, if it could have been carried into effect, the opening up of the Sudan to civilisation, by means of an iron road, might have altered the whole subsequent history of that much-suffering land. But the cost was regarded as prohibitive, and the scheme was abandoned for a time, to be revived, however, in a modified form in 1871, when Ismail Pasha was Khedive. It was then proposed that the line should start at Wady Halfa and be continued to Matemmeh (Shendy), situate about 100 miles north of Khartoum—a total distance of 558 miles. In 1875 a beginning was made with the building of this railway, which was to consist of a single line, with a gauge of 3 feet 6 inches, and was to be made with 50-lb. rails and 7-ft. sleepers; but when, in 1877, after an expenditure of about £400,000, the railway had been carried no farther than Sarras, thirty-three and a half miles from the starting-point, it was stopped for lack of funds.

In the autumn of 1884 the British expedition to Khartoum, where General Gordon was endeavouring to maintain his position against the Mahdi's followers, was resolved upon, and it was then decided to extend the Sudan Railway beyond the point already reached, at Sarras, in order to facilitate still further the journey of the troops along the valley of the Nile, which had been selected as the route of the expedition.

Plate-laying for the extension was begun in September by a party of English and Egyptian infantry and native labourers, afterwards joined by the 4th Battalion Egyptian Army and the 8th (Railway) Company of the Royal Engineers. While, however, materials previously stored at Sarras were found to be still available, the trucks containing rails, etc., for the extension work had to be pushed by hand from Sarras to railhead owing to the absence of engines; sleepers were carried on the backs of camels, of which 300 were employed for the purpose, and the coolie work was entrusted to 700 native labourers, mainly old men and boys, most of whom had deserted by the end of October, when further plate-laying was discontinued. By that time the extension works had reached the thirty-ninth mile, and the line from Sarras to this point was opened on December 4.

Following on the fall of Khartoum and the death of Gordon in January, 1885, came the decision to extend the line to Firket (103 miles), in view of a then projected further campaign in the autumn of that year. The extension was sanctioned towards the end of February; fifty-two miles of permanent way were ordered from England; 300 platelayers and railway mechanics were obtained from India, to supplement the construction forces already available; and on August 7 the extension was completed as far as Akasha (87 miles).

Meanwhile, however, there had been a change of policy which affected the whole situation. On the return of the expeditionary force to Korti (situate at the southern extremity of the great Nile bend), the whole of the country to the south thereof passed under the control of the Dervishes; and the British Government, reluctant at that time to enter on the formidable task of reconquest, decided that no further military operations should be taken in hand, and that the Sudan must be definitely abandoned. Orders were accordingly given by Lord Wolseley in May, 1885, for the withdrawal of the troops from all stations south of Dongola, which itself was abandoned on June 15, the retreat continuing as far as Akasha. Beyond this point, therefore, plate-laying for the proposed railway extension was not carried, although the formation levels had been completed to Firket.

Subsequently the British retreat was continued to Wady Halfa, which then became the southern frontier of Egypt, the railway extension thence to Akasha, together with all

posts to the south of Wady Halfa, being also abandoned.
Excellent service had, nevertheless, been rendered by the railway, as far as it was carried.

Operation of the line had been taken over by the 8th (Railway) Company, R.E., who, at the outset, had at their disposal only five more or less decrepit locomotives, fifty open trucks, five covered goods vans, and six brake vans. The troops were conveyed in the open trucks, and by the end of 1884 all the stores for the opening of the campaign had been passed up. During the course of 1885 additional locomotives and rolling stock were obtained from the Cape.

Summing up the work done on the Sudan Military Railway for the Nile Expedition of 1884-5, Lieut. M. Nathan, R.E.,[1] says that it included (1) the repair and maintenance of thirty-three and a half miles of existing railway; (2) the construction of fifty-three and a half miles of new line through a nearly waterless desert, with no means of distributing material except the line itself; (3) the transport, for the most part with limited and indifferent stock, of about 9,000 troops round the worst part of the second cataract when going up the river, and round nearly the whole of it when coming down; and (4) the carriage of 40,000 tons for an average distance of thirty-six and a half miles.

As against what had thus been achieved in the Nile Valley must be set a failure on the Red Sea.

When, on the fall of Khartoum in January, 1885, the British Government first decided on an extension of the Nile Valley Railway, they further resolved on the building of a military railway from Suakin to Berber, on the Nile, in order to have a second line of communication available for Lord Wolseley's Army; and an Anglo-Indian force was sent to Suakin, under the command of General Sir Gerald Graham, in order, first, to defeat the Dervishes in the Eastern Sudan, and then to protect the construction of the proposed

[1] "The Sudan Military Railway." By Lieut. M. Nathan, R.E. "Professional Papers of the Corps of Royal Engineers, Occasional Papers," vol. xi, 1885.

railway. Such a line would obviously have been of great strategical value to a Nile expeditionary force; but the attempt to build it broke down owing, in part, to the defective nature of the organisation resorted to, though still more to the active opposition of the enemy.

Sir Andrew Clarke, Inspector-General of Fortifications, had from the first advocated that the line should be supplied and laid by the military engineering strength then available; but he was over-ruled, and the work was given to an English firm of contractors in the expectation, as Major-General Whitworth Porter tells, in volume two of the "History of the Corps of Royal Engineers," "that the necessary material would be supplied more readily, and in shorter time, through civilian agency." It was, however, decided to send the 10th (Railway) Company of Royal Engineers both to carry out some local works in the neighbourhood of Suakin and to assist the contractors in the longer undertaking; and this military element was strengthened, not only by a force of Indian coolies, but, also, by the addition of thirty-nine members of Engineer Volunteer Corps in England who had enlisted for the campaign, all having had experience in trades qualifying them for railway work.[1] There was thus practically a dual system, workable, in the opinion of Sir Andrew Clarke, "only by a species of compromise which was both unscientific and uneconomical."

As for interruptions by the Dervishes, these took the form of constant attacks both on the line under construction and on the workers. Several actions were fought, and at Tofrik, near Suakin, the British sustained a serious loss of life. Posts were erected as the work slowly progressed, and the bullet-proof train mentioned on page 76 was used for patrolling the line at night; but in face of

[1] In his dispatch of May 30, 1885, Sir Gerald Graham said concerning these Volunteers: "Their services would have been of great value had the campaign lasted longer. As it was the Volunteers worked well with their comrades of the Royal Engineers. . . . It may be considered the first experiment in associating the Volunteer force with a combatant branch of the Regular Army on active service."

MILITARY RAILWAYS.

all the difficulties experienced the work was definitely abandoned when only twenty miles of the intended railway had been completed. The troops were recalled in June, 1885, the railway material not used was brought back to England, and a line linking up Suakin (and Port Sudan) with Berber, via Atbara Junction, was not finally opened until 1906.

Reverting to the Nile Valley Railway, it is gratifying to be able to say that the success already spoken of as having been attained in this direction was but a prelude to still more important developments that were to follow.

To prevent the carrying out of schemes which the Dervishes were known to be preparing for an invasion of Egypt, the British Government decided, early in 1896, to allow Egypt to resume occupation of the country along the Nile Valley abandoned at the time of the withdrawal in 1885, and on March 12, 1896, Sir Herbert (now Earl) Kitchener, who had succeeded to the command of the Egyptian army in 1892, received instructions to advance to the south from Wady Halfa. Akasha, the point to which the Nile Valley Railway had been built, was occupied on March 20, the Dervishes retreating to Firket.

As a means towards realising the objects of the expedition, Sir Herbert Kitchener resolved to continue the railway along the Nile Valley to Kerma ; but this meant the construction of practically a new railway, since the Dervishes had torn up over fifty of the eighty-seven miles of the original line between Wady Halfa and Akasha, burning the sleepers and twisting the rails, while the remainder of the line was in such a condition that it required relaying. The work of construction was entrusted to a staff of Royal Engineers operating under Lieut. (now Major-General Sir E. Percy C.) Girouard, and it was pushed forward with great energy, the line being urgently required for the forwarding of stores to the front, and especially so on account of the impediments to navigation along the Nile due to the cataracts.

With the help of the railway, so far as it had then been restored, Sir Herbert Kitchener concentrated a force of

9,000 men at Akasha, and early in June he made a successful advance on Firket. The Dervishes retired to Dongola ; but it was thought prudent, before following them up, to await a further extension of the railway. This was completed as far as Kosha, 116 miles from Wady Halfa, by August 4, 1896. Three weeks later some heavy rains, lasting three days, were the cause of floods which, in a few hours, destroyed twelve miles of the newly-constructed line. The repairs were completed in about a week, but in the same month there was an outbreak of cholera which carried off a large number of the working staff.

Utilising the railway as far as Kosha, Sir Herbert Kitchener concentrated the whole of his force at Fereig, on the north of the Kaibar cataract, and from thence a further advance was made to Dongola, which place the Dervishes made no attempt to defend.

The immediate purpose of the expedition had thus been attained ; but, in the meantime, a further campaign had been resolved upon for the purpose of breaking down the power of the Khalifa and effecting the conquest of Khartoum. To this end the railway was continued another hundred miles, from Kosha to Kerma, which point was reached in May, 1897. Some 216 miles of railway had thus been completed in about thirteen months, notwithstanding interruptions which had led to very little progress being made during five months of this period, and notwithstanding, also, the fact that construction work had to be carried on simultaneously with the transport of troops and stores so far as the line had been completed.

Before, however, Kerma was reached, Sir Herbert Kitchener instructed the staff of the Royal Engineers to make a survey of the Nubian Desert with a view to seeing whether or not it would be practicable to build an alternative line of railway across it from Wady Halfa direct to Abu Hamed (a distance of 232 miles), thus giving a direct route to Khartoum.

A survey carried out at the end of 1896 showed that the work was not likely to present any unsurmountable engineering difficulties, and that the absence of water could

MILITARY RAILWAYS.   227

be overcome by the sinking of wells. The only doubtful point was whether construction could be carried through without interruption by a still active enemy.

It was seen that the proposed desert line was likely to be of far greater importance, both strategically and politically, than a continuation of the Wady Halfa-Kerma line round the remainder of the Nile bend. The cutting off of this bend altogether would confer a great advantage on the Expeditionary Force. It was thus resolved to build the line, to run the risk of attacks by the enemy, and to push construction forward with the greatest energy.

A start was made with the work on May 15, 1897, the staff which had been engaged on the Nile Valley line to Kerma returning to Wady Halfa in order to take the desert line in hand. By the end of July, 115 of the 232 miles of line had been completed, and Sir Herbert Kitchener, utilising the railway which had already been constructed to Kerma, then sent a force along the Nile Valley to effect the capture of Abu Hamed. This was accomplished on August 7, and the constructors of the desert line were thus enabled to resume their work with greater security and even accelerated speed. Abu Hamed was reached on October 31, 1897, the two extreme points of the great Nile bend being thus brought into communication by a direct line of railway. The construction of the 232 miles of track had been accomplished in five and a half months, notwithstanding the fact that the work was carried on during the hottest time of the year. An average length of a mile and a quarter of line was laid per day, while on one day in October a maximum of three and a quarter miles was attained. So well, too, had the work been done that trains carrying 200 tons of stores, drawn by engines weighing, without tender, fifty tons, were taken safely across the desert at a speed of twenty-five miles per hour.

From Abu Hamed the line was at once pushed on in the direction of Berber, and its value from a military point of view was speedily to be proved. Receiving information, towards the end of 1897, that the Dervishes were planning an attack on Berber, Sir Herbert Kitchener sent to Cairo for a Brigade of British troops to join with the Egyptian forces then at Berber in opposing this advance, and the Brigade arrived in January, 1898, having travelled by the desert railway not only to Abu Hamed, but to a point twenty miles farther south, which then constituted railhead. Early in March the Anglo-Egyptian Army was concentrated between Berber and the Atbara river, and the battle of Atbara, fought in the following month, led to the complete annihilation of the forces sent by the Khalifa to drive the Egyptians out of Berber.

There was known to be still an army of 50,000 men in Omdurman, at the command of the Khalifa; but it was considered desirable, before any further advance was made by the Anglo-Egyptian forces, to await not only the completion of the railway to the Atbara but the rise, also, of the Nile, so that the river would be available for the bringing up of steamers and gunboats to take part in the attack on Omdurman.

Once more, therefore, Lieut. Girouard and his staff had to make the most strenuous efforts, and these were again so successful that the line was carried to the Atbara early in July. It was of the greatest service in facilitating the concentration of an Anglo-Egyptian Army, 22,000 strong, at Wad Hamed, and the victory of Omdurman, on September 2, 1898—when 20,000 of the enemy were killed or wounded—followed by the occupation of Khartoum, meant the overthrow of the Mahdi, the final reconquest of the Sudan, and the gaining of a further great triumph in the cause of civilisation.

In the account of these events which he gives in volume three of the "History of the Corps of the Royal Engineers," Colonel Sir Charles M. Watson says concerning this ultimate outcome of a rebellion which had lasted, altogether, for a period of eighteen years :—

> Lord Kitchener, of course, by the skill and determination with which he conducted the operations to a successful termination, deserves the principal credit for the happy conclusion of the campaign. But it must not be forgotten that a large part of the work was carried out by the officers of the Royal

MILITARY RAILWAYS.   229

Engineers, especially those who had charge of the construction and maintenance of that railway without which, it is fair to say, the campaign could not have been conducted at all.

The final triumph was the more gratifying because, although the desert railway had contributed so materially thereto, dependence upon it had not been without an element of serious risk which cannot be told better than in the words of Lord Cromer, in his book on " Modern Egypt ":—

The interval which elapsed between the occupation of Abu Hamed and the final advance on Khartoum was a period of much anxiety. Sir Herbert Kitchener's force depended entirely on the desert railway for its supplies. I was rather haunted with the idea that some European adventurer, of the type familiar in India a century and more ago, might turn up at Khartoum and advise the Dervishes to make frequent raids across the Nile below Abu Hamed with a view to cutting the communication of the Anglo-Egyptian force with Wady Halfa. This was unquestionably the right military operation to have undertaken ; neither, I think, would it have been very difficult of accomplishment. Fortunately the Dervishes . . . failed to take advantage of the opportunity presented to them. To myself it was a great relief when the period of suspense was over. I do not think that the somewhat perilous position in which Sir Herbert Kitchener's army was undoubtedly placed for some time was at all realised by the public in general.

Within about two months of the battle of Omdurman the plans were made for a further extension of the railway from Atbara to Khartoum, and Khartoum North was reached on the last day of 1899. The construction of a bridge over the Blue Nile subsequently allowed of trains running direct into Khartoum.

To-day this same railway has been carried a distance of 430 miles south of Khartoum. It continues along the Blue Nile to Sennah, where it turns to the westward, crosses the White Nile at Kosti, and has its terminus at El Obeid, the capital of Kordofan Province. What this means is that an enormous expanse of territory has been opened up both to civilisation and to commercial development.

Apart from the important gum trade of which El Obeid is the centre, the Sudan is pre-eminently a pastoral country. The number of its cattle, sheep and goats is estimated at "several millions"; it has thousands of square miles available for cotton-growing, already carried on there for centuries, and it has wide possibilities in other directions, besides; though stock-raising and cotton cultivation should alone suffice to ensure for the Sudan a future of great wealth and commercial importance.

Beyond the districts immediately served by the extension there are others which are to be brought into touch with the railway, either direct or via the Nile, by means of a "roads system" linking up towns and villages with a number of highways extending to all the frontiers of the Sudan. On these roads and highways motor traction will, it is hoped, be gradually substituted for transport animals, the troubles caused by the tsetse fly and other pests being thus avoided.

The scheme here in question is certainly an ambitious one, considering that the Sudan covers an area of 1,000,000 square miles, and is equal in extent to the whole of British India; but already the outlook is most promising. For twelve years before its rescue from heathenism by the British and Egyptian forces in 1898, Khartoum, which formerly had a population of 50,000, was represented by the mass of ruins to which it had been reduced by order of the Khalifa. To-day it is a large, beautiful, and well-built city, possessed of a Governor-General's palace, cathedrals, a mosque, schools, hospitals, hotels, broad streets, public gardens, boulevards, imposing business premises, a good water supply, electric light, tramways, ferries, and other essentials of a capital city of the most progressive type. Khartoum itself has now about 30,000 inhabitants; in Khartoum North, on the other side of the Blue Nile, there are 20,000, and in Omdurman 70,000, a total of 120,000 for the three sister cities. Not only, also, have the natives, once living under the terror of their oppressors, settled down to peaceful pursuits, but many thousands of immigrants have come into the Sudan from West Africa (a striking testimony of the confidence felt by native tribes in the justice and security of British rule), while great expansion has taken place in the commercial interests

MILITARY RAILWAYS.

of the Sudan and more especially in the export of cattle and sheep.

In the bringing about of these developments, affecting the peace and prosperity of so huge a country and of so many millions of people, the Sudan Military Railways have played a leading part. They rendered possible, in the first instance, the conquest of the Sudan, and then (save for the now abandoned line from Wady Halfa to Kerma) they became, with their extensions and improvements, the system of "Sudan Government Railways," having their branches to-day both from Atbara to Port Sudan and Suakin, on the Red Sea, and from Abu Hamed to Kareima, on the south side of the great Nile bend, whence there is free communication by water to the third cataract at Kerma. Concurrently, also, with the carrying out of the railway extension schemes, and in order to make greater provision for the prospective increase of traffic, 460 miles of the line north of Khartoum were relaid with 75-lb. rails, in place of the 50-lb. rails originally used, and the whole of the track from Khartoum to El Obeid was also laid with the heavier rails.

So we are enabled to regard military railways from still another point of view—that, namely, in which they may develop into lines of permanent communication and promote the blessings of peace and security no less than afford unquestionable advantages in the prosecution of war. Other examples of a similar kind might be offered from the history of British rule in Africa; but the record of what has been accomplished in the Sudan may suffice to establish the further claim here presented as to the varied purposes that military railways may serve.

CHAPTER XVI

Railways in the Boer War

THE South African campaign of 1899-1902 afforded to Great Britain and to British Imperial interests their greatest, most instructive, and, also, their most anxious experiences, down to that time, not only of the services railways can render in the conduct of war, but of the difficulties and complications which may result from their employment, and especially from dependence on them for the purposes of military transport; though, in the result, the services so rendered were a material factor in the success by which the military operations carried out by the British forces were crowned.

When the Boers declared war in October, 1899, the various railway systems, working in direct communication with one another, in South Africa, had a total length of 4,268 miles, namely, British South Africa, 3,267; the Transvaal, 918; the Orange Free State, 388; and in Portuguese territory, 55. These railways consisted of single-track, narrow-gauge lines (3 feet 6 inches), never designed for such heavy traffic as the transport of an army and all its impedimenta would involve; but it was obvious from the first that they must needs play a part of paramount importance in the campaign. Independently of all that was involved in the conveyance of troops, munitions, supplies, etc., from England to the Cape, there was the consideration that from Cape Town, the principal base of our forces, to Pretoria, their eventual objective, the distance was 1,040 miles. From Port Elizabeth it was 740 miles, and from Durban 511 miles. Journeys such as these could be made only by rail, and there was seen to be an imperative

RAILWAYS IN THE BOER WAR. 233

need, not only for the railways themselves, but for an organisation which would, among other things, superintend military rail-transport in order to ensure efficiency in the movement of troops, stores, etc., and, also, provide for the speedy repair or rebuilding of damaged lines as well as for the operation of lines taken possession of in the captured territory.

In view of the uncertainty of events in the Transvaal, and as a precautionary measure, the 8th (Railway) Company, Royal Engineers, was sent out to the Cape in July, 1899; and when, subsequently, the dispatch of an Army Corps was being arranged by the British Government, it was decided to create a *Department of Military Railways*, of which Major Girouard, R.E. (now Major-General Sir E. Percy C. Girouard, K.C.M.G.), who had rendered such valuable services in connection with military railways in the Sudan, and was then President of the Egyptian Railway Administration, was put in charge as "Director of Railways for the South African Field Force." A number of other Royal Engineer officers who had had experience of railway work in India and other parts of the British Empire were selected to serve as Assistant Directors or staff officers in various capacities, and the 10th (Railway) Company, Royal Engineers, with the 6th, 20th, 31st and 42nd Fortress Companies, were sent to join the 8th (Railway) Company in the carrying out of railway work.

ORGANISATION AND CONTROL

The creation of this Department of Military Railways for South Africa carried still further the development of those questions of organisation and control which, as we have seen, had already raised important issues in the United States, in Germany, and in France.

According to the official "History of the War in South Africa, 1899–1902," the Director and his staff were (1) to be the intermediaries between the Army and the technical working administration of the railway; (2) to see that the ordinary working of the railway was carried on in such a manner as to ensure the greatest military efficiency; and

(3) to satisfy the demands of the Army on the railway without disorganising the working of the railway system as a whole.

"In war," the official "History" further declares, "these services are essential, for the officers of a civil railway administration cannot discriminate between the demands of the various branches and departments of the Army, or class them in the order of urgency." This is perfectly true of the civil railway administration, and it is only what could be expected of railwaymen who, while competent to discharge their ordinary railway duties, might not be well versed in military matters, and ought not to be left with the responsibility of deciding between the possibly conflicting orders of different military commanders.

All the same, there was another side to the question; and this is dealt with by Sir Percy Girouard in his "History of the Railways during the War in South Africa," wherein he says, in regard to rail transport conditions in time of war :—

Military commanders who have not previously studied the working of a railway attempt to seize and work the portion of line nearest to them, regardless of the remainder of the system. They often look upon trucks as another form of commissariat wagon which may be kept loaded for an indefinite period. They expect trains to stop and off-load, or load, on the main line. They like to have a number of trains ready, either loaded or unloaded, in case they should be required. They are apt to give orders for large entrainments and detrainments to be carried out at any part of the line, regardless of the railway facilities at that point, although perhaps a suitable place is within reasonable distance. Frequently they have been known to countermand their orders for entrainments, heedless of the fact that, once arrangements have been made to concentrate rolling stock on a certain place, it takes time to alter these arrangements, and is sure to cause confusion. Many of them expect railway accommodation for troops to be on a liberal scale, and consider that there is no necessity, when close to a railway, to make any effort to cut down baggage and stores. . . .

Commandants of posts on the line, which are very often placed at railway stations, are inclined to think that, because they are called "station commandants," it means that they

RAILWAYS IN THE BOER WAR.

are in charge of the railway station, and can give orders to railway officials as to traffic and other matters. . . .

Civil railway officials have been heard to say that attacks by the enemy are not nearly so disturbing to traffic as the arrival of a friendly General with his force.

It was under these circumstances that Sir Percy Girouard saw from the first the necessity for having in South Africa, for the duration of the war, a staff of officers whose business it would be, as he himself defines their duties, (a) to keep the military commanders fully informed of the capacity and possibilities of the railway, and to convey their orders and requests to the civil railway staff; and (b) to protect the civil railway administration from interference by military commanders and commandants of posts; in fact, to act as intermediaries between the army and the civil railway officials.

In arriving at this conclusion Sir Percy was especially impressed by the rail transport experiences of France in her war with Prussia in 1870-1; and in his Report he gives a digest of Jacqmin's facts and recommendations by way of further justifying the step that he himself took. He thought it absolutely necessary that the staff of the Director of Railways should be paramount on the railway, and that no officer should be able to give any orders to railway staff officers or other railway officials unless fighting was actually proceeding at that spot. "This," he adds, "was the system adopted with great success by the Germans, the want of which caused such chaos on the French railways, and the correctness of which has been entirely established by the experience of this war. It is not too much to say that, unless it had been adopted in South Africa, the chaos would have been past belief."

The *Military Railway Controlling-Staff* created, in accordance with these principles and policy, to co-operate with the technical working staff under the Director of Railways, was constituted as follows:—

I. An *Assistant-Director of Railways* for Cape Colony, who was on the staff both of the Director of Railways and on that of the General Officer Commanding Lines of Communication, Cape Colony. His business it was to co-operate with the General Traffic Manager of the Cape Government Railway, in whose office he was given accommodation. In this dual capacity it was his duty to inform both the General Officer Commanding and the Director as to the traffic capacities of the railways ; to take the orders of the G.O.C. while advising him as to the best method of carrying them out ; to inform the railway officials what was required, and, Sir Percy adds, in giving these details, "to protect them from interference by unauthorised military officers." It was the duty, also, of the Assistant-Director to see that proper regulations were issued to the Army for (a) the efficient conduct of entrainments and detrainments ; (b) the forwarding of stores, and (c) the keeping of financial accounts in respect to the use made of the lines for military purposes. As between the General Officer Commanding and the Chief Traffic Manager, the Assistant-Director of Railways was the sole channel of communication.

II. Four *Deputy-Assistant-Directors*, undertaking similar duties over particular sections of the railway system.

III. *Railway Staff Officers*, located at leading stations to superintend all important movements, and constituting the only means of communication between the Army and the stationmasters. The latter were to take orders in respect to military requirements from no one else, and were, in turn, to be protected by the railway staff officers from interference with by other officers having no authority to give them direct orders.

The defective step in the scheme, as originally planned, was in respect to the railway staff officers, who, of all those constituting the Military Railway Controlling Staff, were, under Army Regulations, on the staff of officers commanding lines of communication and thus not controlled by the Director of Railways. The officers in question, though charged with the duty of looking after entrainments, detrainments, etc., were in no way to interfere with the railway staff in the shunting or marshalling of trains or in regard to the traffic arrangements generally. For this reason the framers of the Army Regulations had assumed that there

RAILWAYS IN THE BOER WAR. 237

was no need for the railway staff officers to have any knowledge of railway operation, or to be under the control of others who did possess such knowledge.

After the annexation of the Orange Free State railways, the Chief of the Staff agreed that the railway staff officers in that State should be under the orders of the Director of Railways through his Deputy-Assistant-Directors; and a like course was adopted shortly afterwards in respect to the railway staff officers in Cape Colony. In this way an undivided chain of responsibility was secured, affording a much greater guarantee of efficiency alike in control and in actual operation.

Concerning the Deputy-Assistant-Directors, Sir Percy Girouard says they were found to be of great benefit to the railway officials, who appreciated their work and laboured in hearty co-operation with them; though they experienced difficulty in establishing their position with the Generals and Staff officers, to whom the arrangement was an entire novelty, and one they did not at first understand.

In the first instance the principle of military control applied specially to the lines in Cape Colony, those in Natal being still operated by the Natal Government Railway Department, with certain assistance in the matter of repairs; though after eighteen months of war, the military transport system first established in Cape Colony became uniform throughout British South Africa.

Transport Conditions

The need for the elaborate organisation thus brought into existence was all the greater because of the difficulties by which those responsible for the conduct of military transport were faced.

In November, 1899, considerable portions of the lines both in Cape Colony and in Natal were in the possession of the Boers, so that, beyond a certain distance, the British would have to fight for every mile of railway before they could make use of it. After, also, regaining possession of the lines on British territory controlled by the Boers, they would require first to capture and then to operate those on the enemy's territory; and in each case they would have to be prepared to repair the damage the enemy would be certain to do to the lines in order to prevent their use by the advancing forces. Meanwhile the traffic must be kept open, as far as possible, for the conveyance of troops and stores to the theatre of war and for the carrying out of such strategic movements as the requirements of the military situation might render necessary, adequate protection of the lines being meanwhile assured. There were, in fact, occasions when the whole issue of the campaign seemed to turn upon the question as to whether or not the British could either secure possession of the railways or, alternatively, repair them as fast, more or less, as the enemy could demolish them.

Although, again, so elaborate a system of organisation had been arranged, there was much that required to be done to adapt it to the conditions of African warfare. Initial mistakes had to be remedied; old evils reappeared in new forms; regulations had to be made or modified according to experiences gained; and, while there was at no time any general failure of transport, there certainly were partial failures. Not only was there an inadequate supply of trucks, partly because of the considerable number in the Boer States at the time of the declaration of war and partly because of the number locked up in Kimberley and Mafeking, but trucks were kept loaded when they should have been promptly unloaded and released for service elsewhere; lines were seriously blocked at critical moments by these loaded trucks, while chaos in certain large troop movements was only avoided owing to the control of Cape Town facilities by the Director's staff and to the fact that the Deputy-Assistant-Directors of Railways were enabled to have special officers at all important points.

How the System Worked

As regards the *operation of the railways* during the war Sir Percy Girouard says:—

Although not, perhaps, so much a matter of railway as of general staff administration, a word should be said as to the

RAILWAYS IN THE BOER WAR. 239

methods whereby the very limited resources of the single line of railway communication were allotted to ensure an equal attention to the requirements of the Army as a whole.

The allocation of railway facilities was reserved strictly to the Chief of Staff, without whose order, in each case, nothing could pass by rail towards the front. The number of trains, or, more accurately, the number of trucks which could be hauled daily in the "up" direction, being communicated by the railway authorities to Lord Kitchener, he placed a number, liable to vary from day to day, at the disposal of the supply and remount departments, either generally for the maintenance of their depôts or for specific traffic.

The number reserved for hospital, ordnance, engineer and special stores was even more closely calculated, and the demands of these departments had to be submitted for approval in the utmost detail. All authorisations were passed to the railway representatives at Headquarters, whose business it was to notify when the total of such orders outstanding for dispatch from the advanced base was exceeding the accommodation which could be provided within a reasonable time under the scheme of proportion in force for the time being. In such case the issue of permits fell temporarily into abeyance, or the outstanding list was revised to accord with the necessities of the moment. No truck could be loaded and no troops dispatched by rail without such authority, with the single exception of details and small parties, who were invariably made to travel upon the loaded supply trucks. Proposed troop movements by rail requiring separate accommodation had to be carefully considered in view of the supply traffic they would displace, and, when time permitted, were generally made by road. It was this system alone which co-ordinated the railway requirements of the various departments and did so much to falsify previously accepted figures as to the limits of the fighting force which could be maintained by a single line of railway.

The Imperial Military Railways

Following the questions which arose as to the working of railways on British territory within the sphere of the military operations came those concerning the *railways taken from the enemy* in the Boer States, and converted into a system of Imperial Military Railways for which the Department also became responsible.

The occupation of Bloemfontein led to that place becoming the base of supplies for an army of 35,000 men, likely to increase to 100,000, while eventually the Imperial Military

Railways included 1,130 miles of line. Efficient operation thus became a matter of grave importance, and the task to be accomplished was one of considerable magnitude, especially considering that a staff for the working of the system had to be created. In the traffic and locomotive departments alone no fewer than 3,000 white workers were needed.

Many of the employés of the Netherlands Railway Company were kept on, even at the risk of their showing hostility to the British; but the number who thus made themselves available was quite inadequate, even if they could all have been trusted. The Cape Government Railways were drawn on to the fullest possible extent for workers; the Railway and the Fortress Companies of the Royal Engineers in South Africa were employed in operating the lines; railwaymen in the Special Railway Reserve in England were sent for, and, of the remaining posts, from 800 to 1,000 were filled—the approval of the Commander-in-Chief being first obtained—by inviting soldiers and reservists serving in the Army who had had experience of railway work in civil life to join the staff of the Imperial Military Railways, pay at Royal Engineer rates being guaranteed to them. Positions of the least importance were filled by men who had had no previous railway experience at all. Railway staff officers were also obtained mainly from among the troops; though many even of these, being unfamiliar with the details of railway operation, had to be taught their special duties before they could attempt to discharge them.

On September 30, 1900, the staff employed on the Imperial Military Railways comprised close on 18,000 officers and men. From the time these railways were brought under the control of the British forces to August 31, 1900, they carried 177,000 passengers, 86,000 animals, and 520,000 tons of goods.

As the moral to be drawn from his experiences in having to create, under circumstances of exceptional difficulty, a staff for the operation of railways captured from the enemy, Sir Percy Girouard says:—

The South African campaign has fully shown the necessity

RAILWAYS IN THE BOER WAR. 241

of having a number of traffic employés registered in peace time, who are paid a small retaining fee which will render them liable to be called out in case of war at home or abroad. The want of this system forced the Director of Railways in South Africa to employ a large number of men who had been employed by the enemy, and who could not be relied on, and also to withdraw from the fighting-line a large number of soldiers with railway experience prior to enlistment; and he was compelled to work the railways with this heterogeneous mass of individuals whose qualifications were unknown. The amount of correspondence entailed over conditions of service, pay, transfer, etc., of all these men, coming from different parts of South Africa and from different units, was tremendous. The registration system would also arrange for the men on the railways being subject to Military Law, the necessity for which has been clearly proved.

Repair of Railways

Whilst all these arrangements in regard to operation and transport were thus being perfected, the need had arisen for an equally complete organisation in another direction, that, namely, of providing for the *repair or restoration of railway lines* damaged or destroyed by the enemy.

Since the American Civil War the art of railway demolition had made considerable advance by reason of the use for this purpose of dynamite—an agency which was now to be employed very freely by the Boers. With dynamite they easily blew up the bridges, or material portions thereof; they destroyed the track for considerable distances by the simple process of exploding dynamite cartridges under alternate rail-joints; they wrecked culverts, pumps and water tanks, and they effectively damaged locomotives which they had not time or opportunity to remove. Then, among other things, they derailed engines and trucks by means of mines; they caused obstructions by throwing down into the railway cuttings boulders of up to two or three tons in weight; they cut telegraph lines; they removed or smashed up instruments and batteries at railway stations; they wrecked the stations; they burned many railway trucks, or otherwise rendered them useless; they set fire to stacks of fuel, and, when dynamite cartridges were not available, they deprived the locomotives of their vital parts and tore up considerable lengths of rails.

By December, 1899, it had become evident that the Railway Companies and the Fortress Companies of the Royal Engineers, sent out to the Cape and brought up to their fullest strength, would be unequal to the requirements of the prospective situation. The Railway Corps thus formed was, accordingly, augmented by a Railway Pioneer Regiment, composed of miners, artisans and labourers who had been employed at Cape Town or Johannesburg, volunteers from the ranks of the Army (preference being given to those already possessed of experience in railway work), and employés of the Orange Free State Railway. Some Field Railway Sections, created to form the nucleus of a staff to take over the working of railways in the enemy's country became construction parties, doing repairs only, and having no control of traffic except at railhead. In addition to all these, a large number of natives were engaged through Native Labour Depôts opened at De Aar, Bloemfontein and Johannesburg, the number so employed at any one time attaining a maximum of about 20,000.

It was in the Orange Free State and the Transvaal that the Boers displayed their greatest activity in the way of railway destruction. At Norval's Pont and Bethulie they broke down the bridges crossing the Orange River, which divided Cape Colony from the Orange Free State. Before leaving Bloemfontein (occupied by the British March 13, 1900), they destroyed all the bridges and all the culverts on the railway in their rear; they blew up miles of the permanent way, and they left the railway itself an almost complete wreck. North of Bloemfontein they pursued similar tactics along 180 miles of track, on which they wrecked more or less completely no fewer than fifty bridges, including the one over the Vaal River—a high structure with seven spans each of 130 feet. No sooner, too, had the line been reopened as far as Johannesburg than Commandant De Wet made a raid on it and undid all that the repairing parties had done over a length of thirty miles. Speedily following the re-establishing of rail communication with

Pretoria, the Boers began a fresh series of guerilla attacks on the lines both in the Transvaal and in the Orange Free State; and they continued these attacks for months—until, in fact, their power for doing further mischief had been finally checked.

In carrying out repairs and reconstruction work of such vital importance to the advance and security of the British forces, the policy adopted by the Director of Railways was that of employing Royal Engineers to do rapid temporary repairs—with a view to having a line of some sort made available with the least possible delay—and leaving permanent or even semi-permanent repairs to the Railway Pioneer Regiment. At convenient sidings on the railways throughout the theatre of war *construction trains* were stationed in charge of permanent-way inspectors and sections of Royal Engineers who had at their disposal, at each of such sidings, a gang of men—whites and natives—varying in number from 300 to 1,000, according to circumstances. Infantry working-parties were also obtained wherever possible.

Gangers began a patrol of the lines at dawn. Information as to any break or alarm was communicated to the nearest military post and telegraphed to the Deputy-Superintendent of Works, who thereupon ordered the dispatch of a construction train to the scene of any reported or prospective break without waiting for confirmation of the news received or of the suspicions aroused.

This well-organised system operated to great advantage. At 2.30 a.m. on January 1, 1901, for instance, information reached the Deputy-Superintendent of Works at Bloemfontein that a break of the line had occurred at Wolvehoek, sixty-three miles distant. The construction train was instantly dispatched, and the repairs were completed by 8 a.m. Rail communication with Johannesburg, notwithstanding the great amount of destruction done by the Boers, was restored within eleven days of the arrival of Lord Roberts at that place. It was restored to Pretoria within sixteen days of the occupation thereof by our troops. On the western side, where the enemy had been no less active than in the Orange Free State, rail communication was reopened within thirteen days of the relief of Mafeking.

In the official report on Field Transport in the South African War, it is said in regard to the Railways Department :—

All temporary repairs in the Cape Colony, Transvaal, and Orange River Colony were carried out, with a few exceptions, by the military railway staff. Up to 31 October, 1900, these temporary repairs included the restoration of seventy-five bridges, ninety-four culverts, and 37 miles of line. A detail of the general advance from Bloemfontein to Johannesburg, a distance of 265 miles, will give some idea of the expedition with which repairs were affected. The period during which the advance was being made was from 3 May to 11 June, 1900, in which space of time the following temporary repairs were executed : Twenty-seven bridges, forty-one culverts, 10 miles of line, including seven deviations, varying in length from 200 yards to 2 miles.

From 6 June to 15 November, 1900, the Imperial Military Railways were more or less seriously damaged by the enemy on 115 occasions, but all such damages were promptly repaired, and did not materially affect the working of the railways, except that the running of trains after dark had to be suspended. During the same period fully 60 per cent. of damaged bridges and culverts were permanently or semi-permanently repaired.

Of *bridges*, over 200, with spans ranging from nine feet to 130 feet, were destroyed wholly or in part during the progress of the war ; but even here the speedy restoration of traffic did not, as a rule, present any very grave difficulty. The course generally adopted, as one suited to South African conditions, was, not to start at once on the repair of the damaged bridge, but, in order to meet the exigencies of the moment, to construct a diversion or deviation line alongside, with small low-level bridges on piers, built of sleepers and rails.[1] These deviation lines offered great disadvantages by reason of their sharp curves, their steep approaches and their liability to be washed away in wet weather. The building even of temporary bridges across deep rivers having

[1] In Vol. II of the "Detailed History of the Railways in the South African War " (Chatham : Royal Engineers Institute, 1904), there is a series of 45 full-page photographs of damaged bridges and of the low-level deviations constructed to take their place.

RAILWAYS IN THE BOER WAR. 245

a considerable volume of water also caused inevitable delays. But the lines in question served their purpose until the reconstruction of the damaged bridges—taken in hand as speedily as possible—could be effected. Anticipating the needs for this more permanent work, the Director of Railways had arranged before leaving England for a supply of girders, similar to those in use in South Africa, to be sent out, together with sufficient timber, of useful dimensions, to rebuild the whole of the railway bridges in the Orange Free State, should it become necessary so to do—as, in point of fact, it did. Of new rails he had available, at one time, a total length of 300 miles.

By October, 1900, the makeshift repairs completed on all the lines taken from the enemy were being gradually converted into permanent or semi-permanent reconstruction by the Works Department of the Imperial Military Railways; but the continuous guerilla raids of the enemy still made it impossible to run trains by night. These conditions led to a resort to the system of *blockhouses* which, first constructed for the defence of railway bridges in Natal during the advance for the relief of Ladysmith, and used extensively when Lord Roberts marched from Bloemfontein into the Transvaal, leaving a long track of railway lines behind him, were subsequently so far extended that the whole of the railway lines in the Transvaal and the Orange River Colony were provided with them.[1] So well did they answer the purpose that by April, 1901, the worst of the trouble involved in maintaining railway communications was over, although another year was to elapse before peace was restored.

Military Traffic

An especially remarkable achievement with which, under the various conditions here narrated, the Department of Military Railways is to be credited was in connection with the concentration of the force with which Lord Roberts

---

[1] For a description of these blockhouses, see vol. iii, pp. 125–6, of the "History of the Corps of the Royal Engineers," by Col. Sir Chas. M. Watson. Royal Engineers Institute, Chatham, 1915.

marched from the Modder River to Bloemfontein. The movement began on January 21, 1900, by which time the repairs of the lines had been completed, and within three weeks no fewer than 20,000 men, 13,590 horses and over 24,000 tons of stores had been conveyed over a single line of railway.

Taking the sum total of the military traffic carried on the Cape Government and the Natal Government Railways respectively during the war period, we get the following substantial figures:—

Cape Government Railways, from October 1, 1899, to March 31, 1901:—Officers, men, and other passengers, 1,247,000; supplies, etc., 1,058,000 tons; horses and other live stock, 540,321, besides many wagons and guns.

Natal Government Railways:—Officers, men, prisoners of war, sick and wounded, women and children (including Boer refugees), natives and Indians, 522,186; baggage and stores, supplies, hay, forage, etc., 861,000 tons; ammunition, 9,784 boxes; guns, 454; vehicles, 6,430; pontoons, 48; traction engines, 84; horses and other live stock, 399,000.

MISCELLANEOUS SERVICES

The figures here given as to the military traffic carried do not represent the full extent of the work that was done by the South African railways during the course of the war. One must also take into account the wide variety of subsidiary services rendered, and these are the more deserving of attention because they show, more than had, perhaps, been the case in any previous war, that railways can afford valuable aid in the conduct of a campaign apart from the achievement of their fundamental purpose in the transport of men and matériel.

If we look at the list of services rendered by the Natal Government Railways we find that the Railway Department—in addition to the transport work represented by the above figures—adapted six armoured trains; prepared special carriages for the 6 in. and 4·7 guns; adapted and equipped three hospital trains, withdrawing for this purpose fully a quarter of the most serviceable carriage stock from the ordinary traffic; wired and lamped the hospitals at four different centres, supplying them, also, with electric current; mounted the electric search-light apparatus with engine, dynamo, etc.; supplied 30,000 troops at Colenso with water; found the plant and fuel at Ladysmith for condensing water from the Klip River for 20,000 persons during the four months' siege; allotted and arranged a portion of the goods-shed as the Base Medical Stores at Durban, and fitted up vans to follow the army with reserve medical supplies.

The Department's Engineering Staff speedily restored, or temporarily provided—either on the Natal system or along 100 miles of the Transvaal railways, when these passed under control of the British forces—72 bridges and culverts, varying in length from 10 to 600 feet; 32 different portions of permanent way; and many water tanks, etc. The Engineering Staff also effected in seven days a clearance through the Lang's Nek Tunnel, blown in by the Boers, and constructed several miles of new lines, sidings and deviations.

The Natal Railway Pioneer Staff advanced with General Buller and worked the Netherlands Railway as far as Greylingstad, 100 miles beyond Charlestown (the point of traffic exchange with the Transvaal system), until the line was taken over by the Imperial authorities on August 15, 1900.

"For nearly six months, up to the relief of Ladysmith," says Mr. C. W. Francis Harrison, from whose official work on "Natal"[1] these details are mainly taken, "the Natal lines were robbed of about 40 per cent. of their total mileage and a quantity of their stock. On the clearance of the enemy from Natal and the south-eastern portion of the Transvaal, large supply depôts were formed at Newcastle, Volksrust, Standerton and intermediate points; and on the joining of the two main portions of the British army at

---

"Natal: An Illustrated Official Railway Guide and Handbook." Compiled and edited by C. W. Francis Harrison. Published by Authority. London, 1903.

Heidelberg, the greater portion of the stores for the forces was conveyed via Natal; and this continued unceasingly until the termination of hostilities."

Armoured Trains

It was, again, in the South African war that armoured trains underwent their greatest development—down to that time—for the purposes alike of line protection and of attack on the enemy, although their real usefulness and the conditions necessary to their efficient operation were not established until after certain early experiences which had tended to throw doubts upon their efficiency, and had even led to their being regarded as of little or no account for the purposes of war.

In view of prospective requirements, five armoured trains had been constructed in advance in the locomotive shops at Cape Town and another at Natal. Others were put together shortly afterwards; but one of the Cape trains was wrecked by the Boers the first night of the war, and two of the Natal trains were locked up in Ladysmith. The remainder were employed on scouting expeditions during the earlier phases of the war. Their use not being then rightly understood, they were often sent considerable distances without any support, with the result that one of the Natal trains was destroyed by the Boers at Chieveley, on November 15, 1899, and the Cape trains had several narrow escapes of sharing the same fate.

On the occupation of Bloemfontein by the British, more armoured trains were constructed at the railway workshops there, and eventually the number available was increased to a fleet of twenty. Under an improved system of control and operation, and converted, by the addition of guns, into what were virtually batteries on wheels, the trains came to be regarded as offering possibilities of much practical usefulness.

In a lecture on " Railways in War," delivered by him at the Royal Engineers' Institute, Chatham, and reported in the " Royal Engineers Journal " for July, 1905, Sir Percy Girouard, said :—

RAILWAYS IN THE BOER WAR. 249

The South African War at one time threatened to produce a siege, that of Pretoria, where fairly modern forts with modern armaments were known to exist. At the same time the enemy at Modder River were giving us some trouble with their heavy artillery. The Navy came to our rescue with heavy B.L. guns mounted on wheels. With a view to trying the use of the railway itself, it was pointed out that the railway department had both the shops and the goodwill to mount heavy guns, if required. This offer was approved, and in a few weeks the two heaviest siege guns ever seen in the field were made ready. The carriages, designed by the combined wit of the machinery officers and the Chief Locomotive Superintendent of the Cape Government Railway, were most creditable achievements, old engine and tender frames being used as a foundation. The guns mounted were a 6-inch B.L., and no less a monster than a 9·2 inch B.L. The 6-inch went into action at Modder River. It was deemed unsafe to fix it at an angle of more than sixteen degrees to either side of the centre line of the railway ; but by placing it on a so-called firing curve a wider field of fire was secured. The gun behaved exceedingly well in every way ; and later on it was fired at right angles to the railway, without any damage either to itself or to the line.

The 9·2-inch gun gave good results in its trials, but, although it was run up to Pretoria on its truck, there was no opportunity of firing it on the enemy.

Sir Percy says in his " History " that—

The experiments demonstrated the possibility of big guns being used in siege operations without any difficulty, the only limit to the size of the gun being the weight which the railway bridges will stand.

Apart from the powers of usefulness offered by these batteries on wheels, there arose, in the early days of the war, the further question whether the usefulness of armoured trains proper might not be marred as the result of a defective system of control.

At the outset the trains were placed entirely under the orders of officers commanding sections of the line ; but the arrangement was found unsatisfactory as the trains were constantly being rushed out regardless of Traffic Department regulations, and sometimes without even a " line clear " message. Having, also, the trains at their disposal, as they considered, officers commanding sections of the line often made use of them to inspect posts between stations, other traffic being stopped while the inspections were being made. On one occasion, when a large mob of cattle was being sent to Pretoria and there were no mounted troops available to convoy them, the expedient was resorted to of employing an armoured train for the purpose. The train had to adapt its speed to the rate of progress of the cattle alongside, and such was the interference with other traffic that the entire length of railway on the Delagoa main line was blocked until the cattle had reached their destination. In fact, instead of assisting traffic by preventing the enemy from interrupting it, the armoured trains caused, Sir Percy Girouard declares, "more interruptions than the enemy themselves."

With a view both to meet these particular difficulties and to ensure a better use of the trains, there was appointed an Assistant-Director of Armoured Trains who was placed on the staff both of the Commander-in-Chief and of the Director of Railways and had under his control all the armoured trains in South Africa. Captain H. C. Nanton, R.E., the officer so appointed, had practical acquaintance alike with railway requirements and regulations and with armoured trains. In touch with Headquarters, and kept informed as to which portions of the line were most threatened by the enemy, it became his duty to order where the trains should be sent. Once despatched to a particular section of the line, an armoured train was to be under the control of the General or other officer commanding that section. The Assistant-Director had power to remove it, however, if he thought it was more urgently required elsewhere. It was his duty, also, to work in harmony with the officers in question; but they, in turn, were not to use a) a private conveyance the train sent to them, and they were not to alter its garrison or equipment, or to give orders to the officer in charge which were contrary to the spirit of the general instructions. The Assistant-Director was himself required to instruct officers in command of the trains as to the proper tactics to adopt, the best methods of patrolling, etc., and to see that they "worked in harmony with

RAILWAYS IN THE BOER WAR. 251

the railway officials, and were an assistance and not a hindrance to traffic."

These improved conditions led to a recognised system for the employment of armoured trains, the purposes and duties of which were eventually defined as follows [1] :—

1. In conjunction with columns in the field, to intercept the enemy whom the columns were driving on to the line.
2. To act on the flank of a column or line of columns, the train being well advanced so as to prevent the enemy breaking to that flank.
3. To reinforce stations and camps on the railway which were threatened by the enemy.
4. To escort ordinary traffic trains.
5. To reconnoitre.
6. To patrol by day and night.
7. To protect traffic routes generally.

The garrison of an armoured train consisted of an Infantry escort and Royal Artillery and Royal Engineer detachments. The R.E. detachment consisted of one N.C.O. and six sappers skilled in railway repairing work and in re-setting derailed engines and trucks; two telegraph linesmen; one telegraph clerk; two engine-drivers and two firemen. When the train was engaged, all counted as effective rifles with the exception of the driver and firemen on the footplate, and even they carried rifles in their engine cab for use against an enemy endeavouring to gain possession of the engine.

Responsibility for the efficiency of the garrisons was placed upon the Assistant-Director of Armoured Trains. Whenever, also, a concentration of the trains had been decided upon, he was to attach himself to one of them, and take charge of the concerted action of the whole.

In reference to the operation of the trains Captain M. H. Grant writes[2] :—

---

[1] "History of the War in South Africa, 1899–1902. Compiled by Direction of His Majesty's Government." Vol. IV, Appendix 10 : "Notes on the Military Railway System in South Africa." London, 1910.

[2] Official "History," Vol. IV, Appendix 10.

It was important that the officer commanding the train should be a man of judgment and strong nerve. He was often called upon to act on his own responsibility. His strong armament and defences enabled him to attack superior forces. Yet his vulnerable points were many. He had ever to be alert that the enemy did not cut the line behind him. In addition to his visible foes and the constant risks of traffic in war time, he had to contend with skilfully-used automatic and observation mines, and had to keep his head even amid the roar which followed the passage of his leading truck over a charge of dynamite, and then to deal with the attack which almost certainly ensued. Officers, therefore, had to be chosen from men of no common stamp. The danger from contact mines was to a certain extent obviated by a standing order that each train should propel a heavily-loaded bogie truck. Such trucks had low sides and ends; they in no way obstructed the view, or fire, from the trains; and they performed the double purpose of exploding contact mines and carrying the railway and telegraph materials. The necessity for this propelled unoccupied bogie was exemplified on several occasions.

As regards their protection of the railway lines, the armoured trains rendered an invaluable service, and this was especially the case when the blockhouse system had been fully developed, and when, concurrently therewith, the enemy's artillery became scarce. In recording this opinion, Sir Percy Girouard further observes :—" There is no doubt, also, that the enemy disliked them intensely, and the presence of an armoured train had a great moral effect."

In addition to the organisation and running of these armoured trains, there was included in every ordinary train, as far as possible, a special gun-truck on which was a pedestal-mounted Q. F. gun, under the charge of an escort. The trains also carried a machine gun at each end, arranged with a lateral sweep, to allow the fires to cross on either side of the train at a distance of from fifty to eighty yards. In addition to this, armour plates were hung on each side of the driver's cab, and the first train run each morning had two or three trucks in front of the engine as a precaution against any mine that might have been laid over-night.

AMBULANCE AND HOSPITAL TRAINS

Supplementing the references already made on pp. 95–6 to the employment of ambulance and hospital trains in the South African War, it may here be stated that three out of the seven adapted from rolling stock already in use on the Cape or the Natal Government lines had been prepared in advance of the outbreak of hostilities, namely, two at the Cape and one in Natal, and these three were, consequently, available for immediate use.

"In Cape Colony," as stated in "*The Times* History of the War in South Africa," "the two hospital trains that had been prepared in September were manned by a complete *personnel* from England, and were kept in constant touch with Lord Methuen's advance. In most cases they were run up almost into the firing line, and during the actions at Belmont, Graspan, Modder River and Magersfontein, they relieved the force of its sick and wounded in an incredibly short time, conveying some to De Aar and Orange River, and others to the general hospitals at Cape Town." The services thus rendered by the hospital trains were greatly facilitated by the fact that during the first three months of the war the fighting was almost entirely on or alongside the railways. It was, therefore, possible to arrange for a speedy evacuation of wounded from the field hospitals.

The same two trains, after working along the line of communication in Cape Colony, reached Bloemfontein early in April, 1900; and here they were of great use in helping to remove the sufferers from the enteric fever which was filling up, not only all the hospitals, but every other available building, as well, and finally attained, by the end of May, a maximum of 4,000 cases. Unable to meet all requirements arising under these exceptional conditions, the two hospital trains were supplemented by a number of locally-prepared or ordinary trains, made available for the transport either of sick or of convalescents.

In regard to Natal, "*The Times* History" says that of all the medical arrangements made in connection with the war, "those during Sir Redvers Buller's operations in Natal presented the most satisfactory features."

The line of communication with the base was short, and it was amply supplied with hospital trains. In addition to the one that had been formed before the outbreak of hostilities, a second and similar train was prepared in November, 1889. The hospital train, "Princess Christian," constructed in England at a cost of £14,000, mainly raised by Her Royal Highness—with a handsome contribution from the town of Windsor—reached Cape Town early in February, 1900. It was sent on in sections to Durban, where it was put together in the Natal Government Railway workshops. Under the charge of Sir John Furley, who had also supervised its reconstruction, the train was the first to cross the temporary trestle bridge provided to take the place of the one across the Tugela, at Colenso, which had been destroyed by the Boers, and it was, also, the first train to enter Ladysmith (March 18, 1900) after the siege. Between this time and September 5, 1901, it made 108 journeys, mainly on the Natal side and on the Pretoria-Koomati Poort line; it ran a total of 42,000 miles, and it carried (in addition to the medical and nursing staff) 321 officers and 7,208 non-commissioned officers and men, a total of 7,529 sick and wounded, of whom only three died *en route*. In June, 1901, the train was formally presented by the Central Red Cross Committee to the Secretary of State for War as a complete hospital train unit for the use of the military forces in South Africa; but, on the assumption, apparently, that no further use for its services as a hospital train was likely to arise, it was subsequently dismantled.

As showing the extent of the work done by the other hospital trains during the course of the war, it may be added that No. 2 ran 114,539 miles, in 226 trips, between November 22, 1898, and the end of August, 1902, conveying 471 officers and 10,325 non-commissioned officers and men, a total of 10,796, of whom only seven died *en route*.

TRANSVAAL RAILWAYS AND THE WAR

To the foregoing account of the British use of railways for

RAILWAYS IN THE BOER WAR. 255

military purposes during the course of the South African War it may be of interest to add a few notes giving the experiences of the Boers, as detailed in a statement on " The Netherlands South African Railway Company and the Transvaal War," drawn up at Pretoria, in April, 1900, by the Secretary of the Company, Mr. Th. Steinnetz, and published in *De Ingenieur* of July 14 and 21, 1900.[1]

Under the terms of the concession granted to the Netherlands South African Railway Company (otherwise the Nederland Zuid Afrikaansche Spoorweg Maatschappij) by the Government of the Transvaal Republic, the latter were, in the event either of war or of danger of war, to have complete control alike over the railway and over everything —and everybody—necessary for its use, subject to certain undertakings as to the payment of compensation to concessionaires. By virtue of these powers the Executive Raad issued a decree on September 13, 1899, establishing Government control over the lines, and stating further :—
" With the view of ensuring that proper use can be made of the railway, the whole of the *personnel* of the company are . . . commandeered to do duty on the railways in the functions they now occupy, and they are placed under the orders of the Commandant-General and the war officers indicated by him, or of other officials." The Government, in effect, took possession of all the lines, rolling stock, workshops and other properties of the railway company for the purposes of military transport, and they assumed control over the staff in order to ensure the working, not only of the company's own lines, but, also, of the lines in such portions of British territory as might be occupied by the forces of the Republic.

Against the possibility of an immediate invasion of the Transvaal—" about which," says the statement, " there was much anxiety on account of the armoured trains, which the English advertised so loudly "—precautions were taken by preparing for demolition some of the bridges on the south-eastern section of the company's lines. Guards were,

[1] For English translation, see " Journal of the Royal United Service Institution," January, 1902.

also, stationed at bridges and other important points throughout the Transvaal in order to protect them against attack or interference by " the great number of Anglophiles " assumed to be still in the Republic ; but the statement seems to suggest that, as shown by the small number of attempts made in this direction, the British rather neglected their opportunities.

In regard to the transport of Transvaal troops, difficulties arose at the outset owing to the absence of data, even of the vaguest character, as to the numbers of burghers, horses and wagons it would be necessary to convey by train. Consequently, no military time-tables could be drawn up, and the traffic demands were met as best they could be when they were made. No more, however, than eleven trains a day, in each direction, could be run on the south-eastern branch—a single-track line, with stations and crossing places about one hour's journey apart. Concerning the amount of traffic carried, Mr. Steinnetz says :—

The total military traffic to the frontier was not so great as one would expect, in spite of only a portion of the burghers having taken up arms. From various districts the commandos marched mounted, with ox-wagons, to the place of assembly, as had been the custom in the past, although the use of the railway would have saved time and trouble to both horses and men. Yet it was not the first time that the Transvaalers had had the opportunity of learning the use of railways in warfare. At the time of the Jameson Raid and the Magato Campaign full use had been made of them.

Among the railway bridges which the Boers had prepared for destruction, in case of need, was an iron one of 116 ft. span, the blowing up of which would have checked the anticipated British invasion of the Transvaal via Lang's Nek ; but the concentration of the British forces at Dundee and Ladysmith allowed the Boers to enter Natal without resistance ; and they took over, in sections, the working of the Natal railway in proportion as they advanced. At various stations in northern Natal long platforms had been specially constructed by the British, and other arrange-

RAILWAYS IN THE BOER WAR.

ments made, to permit of large movements of troops and especially the detraining of cavalry. These improvements, says Mr. Steinnetz, came in very handy for the Federal Army. The *personnel* of the lines had "retired in a great hurry," without attempting any demolitions or doing any damage to the lines beyond what could be easily repaired. The Lang's Nek tunnel was "wholly untouched." Mr. Steinnetz continues :—

> The Boers themselves, however, through fear of being surprised by armoured trains, and for other reasons, gave the breakdown gangs more work to do. The telegraph line was destroyed by them for long distances, the track was broken up and two bridges were damaged. In order to obstruct the retreat of General Yule from Dundee a bridge of two 30-foot spans on the Dundee branch line was blown up by the Irish Brigade with a dynamite charge in the central pier. The damage done was not very great and was easily repaired. The same ineffective measure was applied with greater success to a similar bridge over a small spruit near Waschbank. But even here the repair was not difficult.

These admissions as to the ease with which the work of destruction could, as a rule, readily be put right again are in full accord with Sir Percy Girouard's report, in dealing with the same subject. It is only fair to accept, in turn, the assertion made by Mr. Steinnetz that the damage which the British did to certain of the railway bridges was "speedily repaired."

Some of the later destruction work carried out by the Boers was of a more serious character. The blowing up of the Tugela bridge at Colenso—a structure consisting of five iron lattice girder spans of 100 ft. each on masonry piles—was entrusted by the Boer military authorities to an inspector of the railway company who had served in the Dutch engineers. It was accomplished by the simultaneous detonation of forty dynamite charges all connected by leads to a Siemens and Halske "exploder," the bridge being "thoroughly demolished." In the destruction of the three-span bridge over the Orange River at Norval's Pont the charge employed consisted of about three and a half chests of dynamite, or 198 lbs. Concerning the general destruction of bridges by which the Boers sought to check pursuit after their abandonment of the siege of Ladysmith. Mr. Steinnitz says :—" There was no lack of explosives, and no need to spare them."

The central workshops of the Netherlands Company were made use of by the Government for the repair of guns, rifles, wagons, etc., and for the manufacture of war material. Four complete ambulance trains were also fitted up there for the use of wounded burghers.

All the traffic on the lines was done on Government orders, and all expenses were charged to them. No private traffic at all was carried. There were, consequently, no railway receipts, and the railway company had no responsibility.

Development of Rail Power

In one way or another the South African War of 1899-1902 was concerned in many of the most complicated of the problems that arise in connection with the use of railways for military purposes.[1]

In various ways, also, it advanced to a still further stage the whole question of the nature and possibilities of rail-power in war.

It confirmed under especially remarkable conditions a fact which the American War of Secession had already established, namely, that even single lines of railway, passing through country occupied by or belonging to the enemy, may allow of campaigns being conducted at such distances from the base of supplies as, but for this means of communication, would render war impracticable.

It offered further evidence as to the possibility, in favour-

[1] In the preface of his standard work on "Military Railways," Major W. D. Connor, of the Corps of Engineers, United States Army, says : "On the military side I refer to the reports of Colonel Sir E. P. C. Girouard, K.C.M.G., R.E., of the British Army, whose work in Egypt and South Africa has set a high standard for any engineer who in future may be required to meet and solve railway problems in the theatre of war. These reports give the solution of many points as worked out in the field, and confirm the main lessons to be learned from the history of the military railways in our Civil War." (See "Bibliography.")

RAILWAYS IN THE BOER WAR.

able circumstances, of employing railways for the carrying out of important tactical movements.

It re-established the essential need of organisation for the attainment of efficiency in military transport and especially in so far as such organisation deals with questions of control and co-ordination of the military and the technical elements.

It placed on a recognised and clearly defined basis the uses of armoured trains and the best methods to be adopted for their construction and operation.

It showed still more clearly, perhaps, than any previous war had done, the useful and beneficent purposes served by ambulance and hospital trains, whether constructed for the purpose or adapted from existing railway stock.

It proved that, however apparently insecure a line of rail communication may be, and however active and destructive the attacks made on it by a pertinacious enemy, yet, with a strong and well-organised force of Railway Troops following close on the advancing army, and supplemented by an efficient system of line-protection, repairs and reconstruction can be carried out with such speed that comparatively little material delay will be caused, the final result of the campaign will not necessarily be affected, and the value of rail-power as an instrument of war will suffer no actual reduction.

CHAPTER XVII

THE RUSSO-JAPANESE WAR

THE Russo-Japanese war of 1904-5 was a test not so much of the military strength of the two combatants as of their respective means of communication and concentration.

From Moscow to Port Arthur the distance is 5,300 miles, and, save for the sea journey via the Baltic, the North Sea, the Atlantic and the Indian Ocean, the Russians were dependent for the transport of their troops and stores to Manchuria on such very inadequate railways as they then controlled. Japan, on the other hand, was able to rely on her fleet and her considerably developed mercantile marine ; and, as soon as she had paralysed the Russian fleet and established her own command of the sea—as she did within two days of the outbreak of hostilities—she could land her forces whenever she chose at almost any convenient point on the sea-board of the theatre of war.

The situation recalled, somewhat, the still worse position in which Russia had found herself at the time of the Crimean War when, in the absence of any rail facilities at all, her troops had to march, and their supplies and munitions had to be conveyed, hundreds of miles over dreary steppes—" huge columns that had quitted the far north and east of the interior dwindling to a few broken-down Battalions before they came in sight of Sebastopol "—whereas the allies could send their troops all the way to the Crimea by sea.

While there are many other causes which, rightly or wrongly, have been regarded as contributing to the defeat of Russia by Japan —included therein being personal shortcomings of the Russian officers ; mistakes made by them in strategy and tactics ; defects in the Russian military

THE RUSSO-JAPANESE WAR.

system, and the half-hearted interest of the Russian nation in the struggle—the really decisive factors in the situation were the transport deficiencies of the Siberian and Manchurian railways.

The construction of a *Trans-Siberian Railway* as a great strategic line stretching across Asia, facilitating the development of a vast territory, and, above all, calculated to foster the realisation of Russia's aims in the Far East, first came under discussion about the year 1860. It was made the subject of an exhaustive study by a Committee of Ministers in 1875, but it was not until 1891 that the first sod was turned.

Military and political considerations being paramount, such energy was shown in the work of construction that by 1896 the western section had been carried through Irkutsk to Lake Baikal and from the eastern shores thereof to Strietensk, while the eastern section—known as the Usuri Railway—had been made through Russia's Maritime Province from Vladivostok to Khabarovsk. The original design was that the line should be constructed on Russian territory all the way to Vladivostok; but this meant that from Strietensk it would have to follow the great bend made to the north by the Amur, the southern boundary of Russia, and the Russian Government thought it desirable to secure a more direct route.

Towards the end of 1896, in return for the great services which she considered she had rendered to China in the war between that country and Japan, Russia obtained the concession for a railway which, starting from Chita, Trans-Baikalia, about 200 miles west of Strietensk, would pass through Manchuria to Vladivostok, avoiding the great bend of the Amur, though still offering the disadvantage that one important section of the through route would not be on Russian territory. Under a contract made between the Chinese Government and the Russo-Chinese Bank, a *Chinese Eastern Railway Company* was formed to build and operate the line thus conceded; but the arrangements made were carried out through the Russian Minister of Finance, and the line was directly dependent on the Russian State.

Russia's occupation of Port Arthur in March, 1898, led, in the spring of the following year, to the further construction being begun of a southern branch of the Chinese Eastern Railway from Harbin, a station on the Chita-Vladivostok line, to the extremity of the Liao-tung peninsula.

It was these two railways, the Trans-Siberian and the Chinese Eastern, terminating at Vladivostok in the one direction and at Port Arthur in the other, which came into special consideration in the war of 1904-5. It was on the Trans-Siberian line, more especially, that Russia was mainly dependent (as the German official report on the war points out) not only for the concentration and maintenance of her army but even for the raising and organisation of most of its units.

When the Trans-Siberian was first built, the desire to avoid undue expenditure on a line which must necessarily involve a huge expenditure, with little or no prospect of yielding a return sufficient for the payment of interest thereon, led to the adoption of an economy which was to hamper very materially the transport capacity of the railway. Only a single line of rails was allowed for; a limit was placed on the breadth of the embankments; the curves were greater than considerations of speed and safety should have permitted; the gradients were either dangerously varied or so excessive that divisions of the trains were necessary; the rails used were of no greater weight than from 42 lbs. to 47 lbs. per yard, and they were badly laid, even then; the bridges across the smaller streams were made of wood only; the crossing-places and the railway stations were few and far between, while all the secondary constructions were provided on what was almost the cheapest possible scale.

These conditions necessitated the limitation of the traffic, when the line was first opened, to the running of three trains a day in each direction. The length of the trains was restricted to sixty axles. It was thus impossible to meet the demands even of the ordinary traffic in peace time, apart altogether from any question as to military requirements in time of war. No sooner, therefore, were the main portions

THE RUSSO-JAPANESE WAR. 263

of the line ready, in 1898, than there was set aside, for a railway which was already to cost over £350,000,000, a further sum of £9,130,000 for relaying those portions of the line with a better quality of rails and sleepers, the reconstruction of sections dangerous to traffic, the provision of more stations and more rolling stock, and other improvements. It was expected that this additional work would be completed by 1904, by which time the line was to be equal to the running of thirteen pairs of trains daily.

Reporting on the condition of the Russian railways in 1900 (at which date the Eastern Chinese line was still unfinished), General Kuropatkin, then War Minister, afterwards Commander-in-Chief in Manchuria, did not hesitate to declare that it was still impossible for them to cope with heavy traffic.

Relations between Russia and Japan became strained towards the end of 1903, though the Government of the former country were desirous that any outbreak of hostilities should be avoided until they were better able to undertake them. In his account of "The Russian Army and the Japanese War" General Kuropatkin says concerning the position at this period :—

Our unreadiness was only too plain, and it seemed at that time that we should be able, with two or three years' steady work, so to strengthen our position in the Far East, and improve the railway, the fleet, the land forces, and the fortresses of Port Arthur and Vladivostok that Japan would have small chance of success against us.

Regarding war as inevitable, and disinclined to give Russia an opportunity of first strengthening her position in the directions here suggested, Japan broke off diplomatic relations with Russia on February 6, 1904, this being the immediate prelude to the hostilities that followed.

In anticipation of a possible rupture, Russia had already despatched reinforcements and stores to the Far East by sea; but the rupture, when it did come, found her quite unprepared to send further large reinforcements by land, while her forces in the Far East were scattered over the vast area extending from Lake Baikal to Vladivostok, and from Port Arthur to Nikolaievsk. No orders for mobilisation had been issued ; the army was in the midst of re-armament and re-organisation, and the unreadiness of the railways had prevented the drawing up of time-tables for the concentration of the troops. Ten days after the outbreak of war the Russian Government issued a statement in which they said :—

The distance of the territory now attacked and the desire of the Tsar to maintain peace were the causes of the impossibility of preparations for war being made a long time in advance.

Not only, too, was the seat of war 5,000 miles away, and not only was a single-track ill-equipped line of railway the only practicable means of sending troops and war material there by land, but an exceptionally great obstacle to traffic had to be met owing to the interruption of rail communication by Lake Baikal.

Having a length of 380 miles, a breadth ranging from eighteen miles to fifty-six miles, a mean depth of 850 feet (with a maximum, in parts, of no less than 4,500 ft.), and a total area of over 13,000 square miles, *Lake Baikal* ranks, next to the great lakes of the United States and Central Africa, as the largest fresh-water lake in the world ; though it should, in reality, be regarded less as a lake than as a great inland sea. As it happened, also, this vast expanse of water stood in the direct line of route of the Trans-Siberian railway, and the crossing of it by the Russian reinforcements going to the Far East constituted a seriously defective link in the chain of communication.

At an elevation of 1,360 feet above sea level, the lake is subject alike to severe gales, to heavy fogs, and to frosts so intense that in mid-winter the water may be frozen to a depth of ten feet. From the end of April to the end of December troops and travellers arriving by rail at one side of the lake crossed to the other by passenger steamers. Goods wagons were taken over by ferry-boats which, also, acted as ice-breakers early and late in the winter season, so long as the passage could be kept open. When, in the winter, the ice was strong enough to bear, traffic was conducted by

THE RUSSO-JAPANESE WAR.

transport sledges ; but when there was sufficient ice to stop the ferry-boats, though not sufficient to permit of the sledges being used—conditions which generally prevailed for about six weeks in the year—the traffic had to be discontinued altogether.

The question will naturally be asked,—Why had not the constructors of the line avoided these disadvantages by carrying it round the lake ? The reply is that this had not been done, prior to the outbreak of war, owing to the formidable nature of the work involved from an engineering point of view.

Lake Baikal is bordered, on the south—the route a Circum-Baikal line would have to take—by mountains which rise sheer up from the water's edge to a height of, in places, no less than 4,600 ft. Across the mountains, along the rocky shores, and over the intervening valleys the railway would require to be carried for a distance of 160 miles in order to link up the two sections then divided by the lake. The difficulties of the work were likely to be as great as the cost would certainly be enormous, compared with that of the remainder of the Trans-Siberian railway. So it was that when the war broke out there were still 112 miles of the Circum-Baikal line to be constructed.

So it was, also, that, pending the completion of this line round the lake, Russia's reinforcements from Europe for the Far East had to cross the lake itself ; and the outbreak of hostilities in the month of February placed Russia at an especially great disadvantage in regard to transport.

The combined ferry-steamers and ice-breakers had made their final journey for the winter on January 27, and at first the only way in which the troops could cross the ice was by marching or by sledge. After a day's rest at Irkutsk, they were brought by train to Baikal station, at the lake side, arriving there at about four o'clock in the morning in order that they could complete the journey to Tanchoi station, on the other side of the lake—a distance of about twenty-five miles—in the day. The track was marked out by posts, supplemented by lanterns at night, and it was kept in order by gangs of labourers. Small bridges were placed over cracks in the ice. Shelters, in telephonic communication with one another, were provided at four-mile distances alike for the purpose of rest and for the distribution of food prepared by regimental field kitchens; but the principal meal of the day was taken at a more substantial half-way house, where the cooking arrangements were on a more elaborate scale and better accommodation was provided. Around the half-way house at night petroleum flares were burned, so that it could be seen a long way off. In foggy weather, or during snow storms, bells were rung at all the shelters. Inasmuch as the temperature fell, at times, to 22 deg., Fahr., below zero, the provision of these rest-houses must have been greatly appreciated. Baggage was taken across in sledges, the normal supply of which had been increased by an additional 3,000. Some of the troops also made the journey by this form of conveyance, four men being seated in each sledge. The batteries crossed with their own horses.

As soon as the ice attained a thickness of about $4\frac{1}{2}$ ft., the expedient was adopted of laying a pair of rails along it in order, more especially, that the additional engines and railway wagons urgently needed on the lines east of the lake could be taken across. The rails were laid on sleepers of exceptional length, the weight being thus distributed over a greater surface of ice; but, even with this precaution, it was no easy matter to keep the line in working order owing to the extreme cold, to storms, to the occasional ice movements and cracks, or to the effect of earthquake shocks in destroying lengths of line, sections of which sometimes required to be relaid almost as soon as they had been put down. The line was begun on February 10 and completed by the 29th of the same month. Between March 1 and March 26 there were taken across the lake, by this means, sixty-five dismantled locomotives (re-built on arrival on the eastern side), twenty-five railway carriages, and 2,313 goods wagons. Transport was provided by horses, the number so used being about 1,000.

Constructed to serve an exclusively military purpose, this twenty-five-mile line across Lake Baikal may certainly be regarded as a "military railway," while as a military ice-railway it holds a unique position in the history of warfare.

When, owing to the advancing season, the ice on the lake could no longer be trusted to bear either railway trucks or sledges, and when navigation was again open, dependence had to be placed on the ferry services. There were, however, only two vessels available for the transfer of railway trucks across the lake, and each of these, accommodating twenty-seven trucks at a time, could make no more than three return crossings in the twenty-four hours.

Only in one way could an improvement be effected in these obviously inadequate facilities for getting an army to Manchuria, and that was in carrying the railway round the southern end of the lake, thus avoiding the delay caused by the hitherto unavoidable transshipment and crossing, and ensuring a continuous rail journey. The need for this *Circum-Baikal link* had, in fact, become urgent, and the work was pushed on with the greatest vigour.

Mention has already been made of the engineering difficulties which the construction of the line involved. These will be better understood if it is added that the 160-mile link passes through thirty-four tunnels, having an aggregate length of over six miles; that it is carried across valleys, or open spaces, on two hundred bridges, and that numerous cuttings and many large culverts had also to be provided. The total cost worked out at no less than £52,000 per mile—probably the largest sum per mile ever spent on a railway designed, in the first instance, to serve a distinctly military purpose, and exceeding by £35,000 the average cost per mile, down to that date, of the entire system of Russian railways. Delays occurred, also, through strikes and other causes, and, in the result, it was not until September 25, 1904—more than seven months after the outbreak of war—that the line was ready for use, and that an interruption of the rail journey by the crossing of Lake Baikal became no longer necessary.

Meanwhile, an inadequate supply of engines and rolling stock had been a serious hindrance to traffic alike on the

Trans-Baikal section of the Siberian line and on the Eastern Chinese lines. The locomotives and wagons taken across Lake Baikal either on the ice-railway or on the ferry boats had served a useful purpose, but six months elapsed before the Eastern Chinese lines could be worked to their full efficiency.

There were other directions, as well, in which *traffic hindrances* arose. The freezing, down to the very bottom, of the rivers between the eastern side of Lake Baikal and Harbin (Manchuria) was a cause of serious difficulty in the early part of the year in getting water even for such locomotives as were available. In the western Siberian section the supply of water was impaired by the great percentage of salt in the streams. In Manchuria the fuel reserve was inadequate ; soldiers were the only reliable portion of the subordinate railway staff ; the railway workshops were poorly equipped ; there were not nearly enough engine depôts ; large supplies of rails, fish-plates, sleepers and ballast were needed, and much work had to be done in the construction of additional sidings, etc. All these shortcomings required to be made good whilst the war was in actual progress, though for the transport of most of the necessary materials and appliances there was only a single-track line of railway already overtaxed for the conveyance of troops, munitions and supplies.

The *number of trains* that could be run was extremely limited. The capacity of the line of communication as a whole was fixed by that of the Eastern Chinese Railway between Chita and Harbin ; and after three months of war it was still possible to run from west to east in each twenty-four hours no more than three military trains (conveying troops, supplies, stores and remounts), one light mail train, and, when necessary, one ambulance train ; though these conditions were improved later on.

The *speed* at which the trains ran—allowing for necessary stops in stations or at crossing places on the line—ranged from five to eleven miles an hour, with seven miles an hour as a good average. For the journey from Warsaw to Mukden the military trains took forty days, including one day's rest for the troops at the end of every 600 or 700 miles. In April and May the journey from Wirballen, on the frontier of Russia and Germany, to Liao-yang, situate between Mukden and Port Arthur, took fifty days—an average speed of five and a quarter miles per hour.

What with the transport and other difficulties that arose, it was not for three months after the outbreak of hostilities that the Russian troops in the Far East received reinforcements. It was not until after seven months of war that the three Army Corps sent from European Russia to join the field army were all concentrated in Manchuria.

Under these conditions the Japanese, free to send their own armies by sea to the theatre of war, and able to concentrate them with far greater speed, had all the initial advantage. The Russian reinforcements arrived in driblets, and they were either cut off as they came or, as regards, at least, the fighting from May 14 to October 14, provided only 21,000 men to replace 100,000 killed, wounded or sick; whereas the Japanese were able to maintain a continuous flow of reinforcements to make good their own casualties.

General Kuropatkin is of opinion that if the Russians had been able to command better transport from the outset the whole course of the campaign would have been changed. He thinks that even a single extra through troop train per day would have made a material difference, while the running, from the start, of six trains a day would, he believes, have secured for Russia alike the initiative and the victory. Referring to the Siberian and Eastern Chinese Railways he says :—

If these lines had been more efficient, we could have brought up our troops more rapidly, and, as things turned out, 150,000 men concentrated at first would have been of far more value to us than the 300,000 who were gradually assembled during nine months, only to be sacrificed in detail. . . . If we had had a better railway and had been able to mass at Liao-yang the number specified, we should undoubtedly have won the day in spite of our mistakes.

Kuropatkin himself certainly did all he could to improve the transport conditions. In a statement he submitted to the Tsar on March 7, 1904, he declared that of all urgently pressing questions that of bettering the railway communication between Russia and Siberia was the most important; and he added:—" It must, therefore, be taken up at once, in spite of the enormous cost. The money expended will not be wasted; it will, on the contrary, be in the highest sense productive inasmuch as it will shorten the duration of the war."

On the Trans-Baikal section six new stations were added, and additional crossing places to facilitate the passing of trains were provided elsewhere, so that by May some additional trains per day could be run. In June orders were given by the Government for the execution of extensive works designed to increase the capacity of the Siberian and Eastern Chinese main lines to seven trains per day in each direction, and that of the southern branch to twelve per day. The cost of these improvements was estimated at £4,400,000.

In November, 1904, Kuropatkin submitted to the Tsar a recommendation that the lines should be at once doubled throughout their whole length. The reinforcements, he declared, were even then still coming in driblets. " Supplies despatched in the spring are still on the Siberian side. Waterproofs sent for the summer will arrive when we want fur coats; fur coats will come to hand when waterproofs are wanted."

There was need, also, to provide stores of provisions for the troops. So long as the army was a comparatively small one it could depend mainly on local resources. In proportion as it increased in size it became more and more dependent on supplies from European Russia; but the collection of a sufficiency for a single month meant the running of five extra trains a day for a like period. Even when ample supplies were available at one point, weakness and inefficiency in the transport arrangements might lead to the troops elsewhere suffering privations which should be avoided.

Whether for financial or other reasons, the Russian Government did not adopt the idea of converting the single track of the railway system into double track; but the improve-

THE RUSSO-JAPANESE WAR.

ments made in the traffic facilities (including the provision of sixty-nine additional places for the passing of trains) were such that by the time peace was concluded, on September 5, 1905, the Russians had ten, or even twelve pairs of full-length trains running in the twenty-four hours, as compared with the two per day which could alone be run six months before the outbreak of war and the three per day which were running nine months later. The capacity of the lines had been increased practically fourfold; though the general situation remained such as to evoke the following comment from the writer of the official German account of the war [1]:—

In spite of the efforts made to improve the line, the connection of the Russian forces in East Asia with their home country was, and remained, an unreliable and uncertain factor in the calculations of Army Headquarters. No measures, were they ever so energetic, could be designed to remove this uncertainty, and it was only gradually, as the Manchurian Army itself increased and concentrated, and as the railway works advanced, that greater freedom of action was assured to the Commander-in-Chief; but even then the army as a whole, with all its wants and supplies, remained dependent on the Siberian and Eastern Chinese Railways.

What the railways did was to enable the Russians to collect at the theatre of war, by the time the war itself came to an end, an army of 1,000,000 men—of whom two-thirds had not yet been under fire—together with machine-guns, howitzers, shells, small-arm ammunition, field railways, wireless telegraphy, supplies, and technical stores of all kinds. Kuropatkin says of this achievement:—

The War Department had, with the co-operation of other departments, successfully accomplished a most colossal task. What single authority would have admitted a few years ago the possibility of concentrating an army of a million men 5,400 miles away from its base of supply and equipment by means of a poorly-constructed single-line railway? Wonders were effected; but it was too late. Affairs in the interior of Russia

---

[1] "The Russo-Japanese War. The Ya-Lu. Prepared in the Historical Section of the German General Staff." Authorized Translation by Karl von Donat. London, 1908.

for which the War Department could not be held responsible were the cause of the war being brought to an end at a time when decisive military operations should really have only just been beginning.

Russia, in fact, agreed to make peace at a time when the prospect of her being able to secure a victory was greater than it had been at any time during the earlier phases of the war; but the Japanese failed to attain all they had hoped for, the primary causes of such failure, in spite of their repeated victories, being, as told in the British " Official History " of the war, that " Port Arthur held out longer than had been expected, and the Trans-Siberian Railway enabled Russia to place more men in the field than had been thought possible."[1]

Thus, in respect to rail-power, at least, Russia still achieved a remarkable feat in her transport of an army so great a distance by a single-track line of railway. Such an achievement was unexampled, while, although Fate was against the ultimate success of her efforts, Russia provided the world with a fresh object lesson as to what might have been done, in a campaign waged more than 5,000 miles from the base of supplies, if only the line of rail communication had been equal from the first to the demands it was called upon to meet.

Apart from this main consideration, there were some other phases of the Russo-Japanese War which are of interest from the point of view of the present study.

The *Field railways*, mentioned on the previous page, constituted a network of, altogether, 250 miles of narrow-gauge railways built and operated by the Russian troops—either alone or with the help of Chinese labourers—and designed to act as subsidiary arteries of the broad-gauge Eastern Chinese Railway by (1) providing for the transport therefrom of troops and supplies to the front; (2) conveying guns and munitions to the siege batteries, and (3) bringing back the sick and wounded. Horses, ponies and mules

---

[1] "Official History of the Russo-Japanese War." Prepared by the Historical Section of the Committee of Imperial Defence. London, 1910.

THE RUSSO-JAPANESE WAR. 273

were employed for traction purposes. Each of the three Russian armies in the field had its own group of narrow-gauge lines, and the lines themselves served a most useful purpose in a country of primitive roads and inadequate local means of transport.

In one instance a broad-gauge branch line was built inland, during the course of the war, from the Eastern Chinese Railway for a distance of twenty-five miles. A depôt was set up at its terminus, and thence the supplies were conveyed to the troops by a series of narrow-gauge lines extending to every part of that particular section of the theatre of war.

Construction of the narrow-gauge line serving the Second Army, and extending nineteen miles from a point on the Eastern Chinese Railway near to Port Arthur, necessitated the provision of six bridges and three embankments. Three lines, the building of which was begun in January, 1905, were siege lines specially designed to serve the positions taken up at Liao-yang; but all three were abandoned on the evacuation of Mukden, early in March. It was, however, subsequent to the retreat from Mukden that the greatest degree of energy in constructing narrow-gauge lines was shown by the Russians. In addition to the 250 miles brought into use, there was still another 100 miles completed; but these could not be operated owing to the inadequate supply of wagons—a supply reduced still further through seizures made by the Japanese.

During the course of the war the traffic carried on these military narrow-gauge lines included over 58,000 tons of provisions, stores, etc., 75,132 sick and wounded, and 24,786 other troops.[1]

For the carrying out of all this construction work, and, also, for the operation of the Manchurian and Ussuri railways, Russia had twenty-four companies of *Railway Troops*, the total force of which was estimated at 11,431. In the first part of the war she relied upon her six East Siberian

[1] "Construction et exploitation de chemins de fer à traction animale sur le théâtre de la guerre de 1904-5 en Mandchourie." *Revue du Genie Militaire*, Avril, Mai, Juni, 1909. Paris.

T

Railway Battalions. As the work increased other Battalions were brought from European Russia.

The Japanese were not well provided with Railway Troops; but they were none the less active in endeavouring to destroy the Russian lines of communication, on which so much depended. For instance, the railway to Port Arthur was cut by them near Wa-fang-tien at 11 p.m. on May 6. The Russians repaired the line, and by May 10 a further train-load of ammunition was sent over it into Port Arthur. Three days later the Japanese cut the line at another point, and from that time Port Arthur was isolated.

As regards the *operation* of the Siberian and Eastern Chinese Railways, Colonel W. H. H. Waters says:—[1]

Taking the railway as a whole, from Chelyabinsk, which is the western terminus of the Siberian portion, to Mukden, a distance of close upon 4,000 miles, it has worked better than I expected; but the one great fault connected with it has been, and is, the incapacity of Russian railwaymen, civil or military, to handle heavy station traffic properly. If Russia were to pay a British or American goods-yard foreman, say from Nine Elms station, a salary, no matter how high, and let him import his own staff of assistants, the improvement of the Asiatic lines in question would be remarkable.

Then, again, Captain C. E. Vickers, R.E., writing on "The Siberian Railway in War," in the issue of "The Royal Engineers Journal" (Chatham) for August, 1905, points to the need which was developed for the *control* of the railway during war by a separate staff, as distinct from the staffs concerned in arranging operations, distributing supplies and munitions, and other military duties.

Whether due to the personal incapacity spoken of by the one authority here quoted, or to the lack of a separate organisation alluded to by the other, the fact remains that the operation of the Siberian and Eastern Chinese lines did give rise to a degree of confusion that must have

---

[1] "The Russo-Japanese War. Reports from British Officers attached to the Japanese and Russians Forces in the Field." Vol. III. General Report [dated March, 1905] by Col. W. H. H. Waters. London, 1908.

THE RUSSO-JAPANESE WAR. 275

greatly increased the difficulties of the position in which the Russians were placed.

When, for example, in September, 1904, reservists were urgently wanted at Mukden after the retreat from Liao-yang, the traffic was so mismanaged that it took the troops seven days to do the 337 miles from Harbin—an average speed of two miles per hour. On December 5, Harbin Junction was so blocked in all directions by trains which could neither move in nor go out that traffic had to be suspended for twelve hours until the entanglement was set right. Still further, after the fall of Port Arthur, on January 2, 1905, and the augmentation of the Japanese forces by Nogi's army, the arrival of reinforcements then so greatly needed by the Russians was delayed for over one month to allow of the forwarding of a quantity of stores which had accumulated on the line.

Some, at least, of the difficulties and delays experienced in operation were undoubtedly due to developments of that *interference by individual officers* with the working of the railways of which we have already had striking examples in the case of the American War of Secession and the Franco-German War of 1870–71. Colonel Waters writes on this subject :—

It is interesting to note how the working of the line was interfered with by those who should have been the first to see that no extraneous calls were made upon it when the organisation of the army and the strengthening of Port Arthur were of vital importance.

The chief of the Viceroy's Staff was the intermediary between Admiral Alexeiev and General Kuropatkin, the former being at Mukden and the latter at Liao-yang, thirty-seven miles distant. Frequent conferences took place between Kuropatkin and this officer, who always used to come in a special train to Liao-yang. This necessitated the line being kept clear for indefinite periods of time and dislocated all the other traffic arrangements, as the then chief of the railways himself declared.

In the first days of May, 1904, the Viceroy and the Grand Duke Boris were at Port Arthur, and wished to leave it before they should be cut off. I heard that they actually took three special trains to quit Port Arthur, namely, one for each of them, and one for their baggage and stores. This entirely upset the troop train, supply and ammunition services, at a time, too, when the scarcity of heavy gun munition in the fortress was such that, within a week, Kuropatkin called for volunteers to run a train-load through, which was done a few hours only before the place was definitely invested.

There were, throughout 1904, plenty of other instances of special trains being run for, and siding accommodation occupied by, various individuals, so that the organisation and maintenance of the army was considerably hampered thereby.

These experiences simply confirm the wisdom of the action which other countries had already taken (1) to ensure the efficient operation of railways in time of war by staffs comprising the military and the technical elements in combination, and (2) to prevent the interference of the former in the details of the actual working by the latter.

Russia was, in fact, distinctly behind Western nations in these respects in 1904-5, and the need for placing her military transport system on a sounder basis was among the many lessons she learnt—and acted upon—as the result of her experiences in the war with Japan.

CHAPTER XVIII

STRATEGICAL RAILWAYS: GERMANY

BETWEEN "strategical" and "military" railways there are certain fundamental differences, just as there are, also, between both of them and ordinary commercial railways. While designed partly, mainly, or, it may be, exclusively, to serve military purposes, strategical railways, unlike military railways proper, form part of the ordinary railway system of the country in which they are built. They approximate to commercial lines in construction, equipment and operation, and they are worked in connection with them for the ordinary purposes of trade and travel; though in their case any considerations as to whether the traffic they carry is remunerative does not arise, provided only that they are capable of fulfilling their real purpose—that, namely, of ensuring such military transports as may, sooner or later, be required of them. It is possible that in times of peace the amount of actual traffic passing over them will be comparatively small, if not even practically *nil*, and that many years may elapse before the special facilities they must necessarily offer, —such as extensive siding accommodation and long platforms for the loading and unloading of troop trains—are likely to be employed to the fullest extent; but they nevertheless form an integral part both of the railway system and of the military system of the country, and, having been constructed, they are, at least, available for military purposes whenever wanted.

One must, however, again bear in mind that a railway built to meet the ordinary requirements of trade and travel does not become a "strategical" any more than a "military" railway simply because, in time of war, it is used, to whatever extent, for the conveyance of troops, supplies or war material. The essential factor in each instance is, not the use that is made of the line, but the particular, or, at least, the main object it has been built to serve. Just, also, as a commercial line remains a commercial line notwithstanding its use for military traffic, so, in turn, a strategical line remains a strategical line whatever the amount of civilian traffic it may carry in time of peace.

Yet while the distinction thus drawn between general railways and strategical railways is abundantly warranted, the increase of the former may still have an important bearing on the operation of the latter because of the improvement of transport facilities in the interior, and because of the greater amount of rolling stock which will be made available for war purposes. "From a military point of view," said von Moltke in the Prussian Herrenhaus on March 26, 1876, " every railway is welcome, and two are still more welcome than one "; and he developed this idea in a further speech on December 17, 1879, when, in declaring that the ownership and operation of the leading Prussian railways was desirable from a military standpoint, he said :—[1]

Railways have become, in our time, one of the most essential instruments for the conduct of war. The transport of large bodies of troops to a given point is an extremely complicated and comprehensive piece of work, to which continuous attention must be paid. Every fresh railway junction makes a difference, while, although we may not want to make use of every railway line that has been constructed, we may still want to make use of the whole of the rolling stock that is available.

Another important distinction between military and strategical railways is that whereas the building of the former will be governed primarily by military requirements, that of the latter may be fundamentally due to considerations of State policy. Strategical railways are wanted to serve the purposes of national defence or, alternatively, of national expansion. They are especially provided to ensure

[1] "Gesammelte Schriften." Berlin, 1891, etc.

STRATEGICAL RAILWAYS: GERMANY. 279

the speedy concentration of troops on the frontier, whether to resist invasion by a neighbouring country or to facilitate the invasion either of that country or, it may be, of territory on the other side thereof. The fact that they have been built may, in some cases, even further the interests of peace, should the increased means they offer for military transports render the country concerned a more formidable antagonist than it might otherwise be, and influence the policy of other States or lands accordingly.

In tropical dependencies the building of railways as a practical proof of " effective occupation " is often regarded as preferable to military conquest, being likely, in most cases, to answer the same purpose while offering many other advantages, besides. In West Africa there are not only railways of this class but others that have, in addition, been designed as a precautionary measure against a not impossible invasion, at some future date, by Mohammedan tribes from North Central Africa. All such lines as these belong to the strategical type, though they may, also, serve an important part in furthering the economic development of the territories concerned.

Strategical railways, whether designed for defensive or aggressive purposes, may, in turn, be divided into two main groups, (1) those that constitute a network of lines; and (2) single or individual lines for short or long distances.

A network of strategical railways is generally found in direct association with frontiers. Single or individual strategical lines fall into various groups including (1) short lines or branches running out to some point on or near to a frontier; (2) single lines carried for long distances, and, possibly, crossing entire continents; (3) circular or short lines, connecting different railway systems with one another, in order to facilitate the movement of troops during mobilisation or concentration or for defensive purposes in the event of invasion; (4) lines passing round cities or large towns in order to avoid delay of troop trains; and (5) lines for coast defence.

The ideal conditions for a network of strategical railways

was already a subject of discussion in Germany in 1842, when Pönitz brought forward his proposal that that country should provide herself with such a system. There were, he said, theorists who designed, on paper, strategical railways which, starting from a common centre, radiated in straight lines to different points on the frontier and were connected with one another by parallel or intersecting lines of railway on the principle of a geometrical design, or, he might have added, of a spider's web. Pönitz admitted the excellence of the idea, suggesting that if there were, indeed, a group of lines to the frontier connected by cross lines allowing of a complete interchange of traffic, the enemy would never know at what point a sudden advance in force might not be made, while the linking up of the entire system would greatly facilitate working.

In practice, however, as he proceeded to point out, this ideal system could not be fully adopted, partly because the planning of railways is influenced by the configuration of the country, which may not permit of geometrical designs for iron roads; and partly because the trunk lines of national systems of rail communication had already been laid by private enterprise on the principle of catering for the social and economic needs of the community and of returning interest on capital expenditure, rather than of serving military or political purposes.

In the proposals which Pönitz himself advanced for providing Germany with a complete network of strategical lines he sought to combine, as far as possible, the commercial and the military principle; though the subsequent predominance, in most countries, of the economic element in regard to railways in general strengthened the force of his contention that an ideal system was not necessarily a practicable one. The suggested geometrical design was, nevertheless, not lost sight of, and it continued to be regarded as the plan that should, at least, be followed in respect to strategical railways, as far as circumstances would permit.

Dealing with this particular subject in his "Geschichte und System der Eisenbahnbenutzung im Kriege" (Leipzig,

STRATEGICAL RAILWAYS: GERMANY.

1896), Dr. Josef Joesten included the following among the conditions which, theoretically and practically, should enable a railway system to respond to the necessities of war :—

1. To each of the strategical fronts of the national territory there should be the largest possible number of railway lines, all independent the one of the other.

2. The converging lines terminating at the bases of concentration, and more especially those leading to the coast or to great navigable rivers, should be crossed by numerous transverse lines in order to allow of the rapid passing of troops from any one of the lines of concentration to any other.

3. Positions or localities having a recognised strategical value should be selected as the places where the two types of lines should cross, and these intersection points, when they are near to the frontier, should themselves be protected by fortifications serving as *points d'appui* for movements of advance or retirement.

It is possible that, if the building of railways in Germany had been left entirely to the State from the outset, these principles would have been generally followed there; but in Prussia the private lines taken over as the result of the policy of nationalisation adopted by that country—the total length of those acquired since 1872 being now nearly 10,000 miles—had been originally constructed to serve, not strategic, but economic purposes, and, more especially, the industrial interests of Westphalia and the Rhineland, the Government having been left by private enterprise to provide, not alone the strategical lines, but, also, the lines that were wanted to serve the less promising economic requirements, of Eastern Prussia. To say, therefore, as some writers have done, that the Prussian—if not the German—railways as a whole have been designed to serve military purposes is erroneous. It is none the less true that the adoption of the principle of State ownership conferred alike on Prussia and on other German States a great advantage in enabling them both to build strategical lines as, ostensibly, part of the ordinary railway system and to adapt existing lines to military purposes so far as conditions allowed and occasion might require.

In these circumstances any close adherence to ideal systems has, indeed, not been practicable; yet the activity shown in Germany in providing either new or adapted strategical lines of railway has been beyond all question.

Such activity has been especially manifest since the Franco-German war of 1870-1. It is, indeed, the case that during the last twenty-five years there have been constant representations by Prussian trading interests that the railways in Westphalia and Rhineland, numerous as they might appear to be, were unequal to the industrial needs of those districts. The reasons for these conditions were that the Administration, eager to secure railway "profits," had neglected to provide adequately for improvements, widenings and extensions of line, and for additions to rolling stock. No one, however, is likely to suggest that Prussia has shown any lack of enterprise in the construction of strategical lines which would enable her to concentrate great masses of troops on her frontiers with the utmost dispatch. "The rivalry between neighbouring States," writes von der Goltz in "The Conduct of War," "has had the effect of causing perfectly new lines to be constructed solely for military reasons. Strategical railways constitute a special feature of our time"; and in no country has this fact been recognised more clearly, and acted upon more thoroughly, than in Germany.

It would, nevertheless, be a mistake to attempt to form a reliable estimate of the situation, from a strategical point of view, on the basis of the ordinary German railway maps, and certain reproductions thereof recently offered in the English Press have been wholly misleading. Not only may these maps be hopelessly out of date—one, for instance, that was published in a military journal in the autumn of 1914 contained none of the strategical lines built by Prussia since 1900 for troop movements in the direction of Belgium —but they invariably draw no distinction between State-owned lines which do come into consideration in regard to military transports and agricultural or other lines—including many narrow-gauge ones—which serve local purposes only and are still owned by private companies, the State not having thought it necessary in the general interest to take them over.

A more accurate idea of the real bearings of German railways on the military and strategical situation can be gathered from the large map (" Kartenbeilage I ") which accompanies the " Bericht " presented to the Kaiser, in 1911, by the Prussian Minister of Public Works under the title of " Die Verwaltung der öffentlichen Arbeiten in Preussen, 1900 bis 1910." On this map a clear distinction is drawn between State-owned and company-owned lines, while difference in colouring shows the additions made to the State system during the decade either by construction of new lines or by State acquisition of existing lines.

One especially noticeable feature brought out by this map is the fact that, in addition to the innumerable railway lines built either to the frontiers or establishing intercommunication and exchange of traffic between those lines themselves, there is an almost unbroken series running parallel to the coasts of *Pomerania* and *East Prussia*, and thence southward all along and close to the frontiers of Russia and Russian Poland. In this way troops can be moved, not only by different routes *to* many points along the Baltic coast or the Russian frontier, but, also, *from* one of these coastal or frontier points direct to another, as may be desired.

The strategical significance of this arrangement is sufficiently obvious; but any possible doubt as to the purpose aimed at is removed by some observations thereon made by Joesten, who further says in his " Geschichte und System der Eisenbahnbenutzung im Kriege " :—

If it is true that, generally speaking, the best railways for general purposes constitute excellent lines of communication for armies, it is no less true that good, or very good, strategical lines cannot, and ought not to, in all cases constitute good commercial lines. In support of this assertion one can refer to the immense extent of railway lines on the coasts of Pomerania. These lines, which are of the first importance from a strategical point of view, have only a moderate value from a commercial standpoint, considering that they do not connect the interior of the country with any district providing goods or passenger traffic on a material scale, and only provide means of communication between localities having identical needs.

What is thus admitted in regard to the coastal railways of Pomerania applies no less to many, if not to most, of the frontier lines in East Prussia, West Prussia and Silesia.

Not only, again, is the number of German lines going to the frontiers, and no farther, out of all proportion to the number of those providing for international communication, but the map on which these observations are based shows that between 1900 and 1910 there were added to the Prussian State system many lines which (1) established additional transverse links between those already going to the Russian frontier, (2) provided alternative routes thereto, or (3) supplemented the lines which skirt the frontier, a few miles inland, by branches going therefrom to strategic points actually on the frontier itself.

As against this construction of an elaborate network of strategical lines towards and along *the Russian frontier*, there must be put the fact that although, by this means, Germany acquired the power to effect a great and speedy concentration of troops on the frontier itself, her locomotives and rolling stock would not be able to cross into Russia and run on the railways there because of *the difference in gauge*. On the eastern frontier the question as to how an invasion in large force could be effected was, consequently, quite different from that which would present itself on the western frontiers, where the railway gauges of Belgium, Luxemburg and France were the same as those of Germany.

It was certain that whenever, in the event of war, German troops were able to enter Russian territory, Russia would withdraw into the interior or else destroy such of her locomotives and rolling stock as the enemy might otherwise utilise for his own purpose. If, therefore, the Germans wanted to use the existing Russian lines, they would either have to build, in advance, locomotives and rolling stock capable of running thereon, or they would have to convert the Russian gauge of 5 feet to the German gauge of 4 feet 8

STRATEGICAL RAILWAYS: GERMANY.

inches, so that German trains could run on the other side of the frontier. As already remarked on page 61, the reduction of the broader gauge into a narrower one would involve fewer engineering difficulties than an expansion of the German gauge into the Russian gauge; yet even the former procedure, if carried out over any considerable length of line, would take up a good deal of time, and this would be still more the case if the Russians, when they retreated, destroyed the railway track and bridges behind them, as they might confidently be expected to do.

Dependence, again, on the existing lines across the frontier would, apart from questions of conversion and reconstruction, still give Germany only a very small number of railway routes into Russia, and these, also, at points where the opposition offered might be especially active.

What, in these circumstances, Germany evidently planned to do as soon as her troops crossed the frontier, in the event of a war with Russia, was to supplement the strategical lines on her own side of that frontier by military light railways which, laid on the ordinary roads, or on clearances to be effected, on Russian territory, would render her independent of the ordinary railways there, while offering the further advantage (1) that the laying of these narrow-gauge military lines—in rough and ready fashion, yet in a way that would answer the purposes of the moment—could be effected in shorter time than the gauge-conversion and the reconstruction of the Russian trunk lines would take; and (2) that these military railways could be built from any points along the frontier which were capable of being reached direct from the German strategical lines, and offered either an existing road or the opportunity of making one for the purpose.

In the light of this assumption, one can understand more clearly the reason for those short lines which, branching out from the German strategical railways that run parallel to the Russian frontier though some miles from it, are carried to the frontier and there suddenly stop. It was, presumably, from such terminal points as these that the laying of the military railways on Russian territory would begin.

As regards the type of railways to be employed and the preparations made in advance for supplying and constructing them, we have the testimony of Mr. Roy Norton, an American writer, who says in " The Man of Peace "—one of the " Oxford Pamphlets, 1914-15," published by the Oxford University Press :—

On February 14 of this year (1914) I was in Cologne, and blundered, where I had no business, into what I learned was a military-stores yard. Among other curious things were tiny locomotives loaded on flats which could be run off those cars by an ingenious contrivance of metals, or, as we call them in America, rails. Also there were other flats loaded with sections of tracks fastened on cup ties (sleepers that can be laid on the surface of the earth) and sections of miniature bridges on other flats. I saw how it was possible to lay a line of temporary railway, including bridges, almost anywhere in an incredibly short space of time, if one had the men. . . . Before I could conclude my examination I discovered that I was on *verboten* ground ; but the official who directed me out told me that what I had seen were construction outfits.

Mr. Norton further quotes the following from a letter he had just received from a Hollander who was a refugee in Germany at the outbreak of the war, and reached home on August 30, 1914 :—

Never, I believe, did a country so thoroughly get ready for war. I saw the oddest spectacle, the building of a railway behind a battle-field. They had diminutive little engines and rails in sections, so that they could be bolted together, and even bridges that could be put across ravines in a twinkling. Flat cars that could be carried by hand and dropped on the rails, great strings of them. Up to the nearest point of battle came, on the regular railway, this small one. . . . It seemed to me that hundreds of men had been trained for this task, for in but a few minutes that small portable train was buzzing backward and forward on its own small portable rails, distributing food and supplies. . . . I've an idea that in time of battle it would be possible for those sturdy little trains to shift troops to critical or endangered points at the rate of perhaps twenty miles an hour. . . . A portable railway for a battle-field struck me as coming about as close to making war by machinery as anything I have ever heard of.

One may thus reasonably conclude, in regard to the Russo-

STRATEGICAL RAILWAYS: GERMANY. 287

German frontier, (1) that the broader gauge of the Russian railways would itself offer no real obstacle to the German troops whenever the time came for their invading Russian territory; (2) that in this eventuality the Germans would be able, by reason of the preparations made by them in advance, to lay down along the ordinary Russian roads lines of military light railways already put together in complete sections of combined rails and sleepers, which sections would only require to be fastened the one to the other to be at once ready for use; and (3) that these portable military railways, to be built on Russian territory, were designed both to supplement and to render still more efficient Germany's network of strategical railways along her eastern frontier.

In *southern Silesia* many improvements in the rail communication with Austria were made in 1900-10. New connections were established with the frontier railways, offering alternative routes from interior points, while various lines which stopped short of the frontier were extended to it and linked up with Austrian lines on the other side.

In her relations with *France*, Germany's efforts to improve still further her rail communications to the eastern and north-eastern frontiers of that country have been continuous since the war of 1870-1, on which campaign she started with a great advantage over the French since she was able to concentrate her troops on those frontiers by nine different routes, namely, six in North Germany, and three in South Germany, whereas France herself had then only three available. The course adopted by Germany has been (1) to secure a larger number of routes to the French frontier, South Germany's three lines, for instance, being increased to six; (2) to provide double track, or to substitute double for single track, for lines leading to the frontier and having a strategical importance; (3) to construct lines which cross transversely those proceeding direct to the French frontiers, thus allowing of intercommunication and transfer of traffic from one to another; and (4) improvement of the interior network of lines, with a view to facilitating military transport services in time of war. "Altogether," says Joesten, "we have nineteen points at which our railways cross the Rhine, and sixteen double-track lines for the transport of our troops from east to west, as against the nine which were alone available for concentration in 1870."

While showing all this activity on the immediate frontiers of France, Germany was no less zealous in providing alternative routes for a fresh invasion of French territory, the adoption of this further policy being obviously inspired by the energy that France was herself showing in the strengthening of her north-east frontier against invasion.

One such alternative route was represented by *Luxemburg*. Not only did Germany have lines of her own on the north, south, and east of Luxemburg, but the lines within the Grand Duchy itself had passed under German control; and if Germany thought fit to disregard her treaty obligations, and use the lines for strategical purposes, Luxemburg was powerless to prevent her from so doing.

Another alternative route was by way of *Belgium*; and the various developments of Germany's railway policy on the Belgian frontier since 1908 point in an unmistakable manner to deliberate preparation on her part for an invasion of that country, whether for the purpose of passing through it, as a means of reaching a more vulnerable part of French territory than the strongly fortified north-east corner, or in pursuance of designs against Belgium itself.

The full story of Germany's activity in this direction will be found in a series of articles from the *Fortnightly Review* reproduced by the author, Mr. Demetrius C. Boulger, in " England's Arch-Enemy : A Collection of Essays forming an Indictment of German Policy during the last sixteen years " (London, 1914).[1]

The story opens with the establishment by Germany, about the year 1896, of a camp at Elsenborn, ten miles north-east of Malmédy, a town situate close to the Belgian frontier and four miles from the Belgian town of Stavelot.

---

[1] The articles which here specially come into question are—"The Menace of Elsenborn " (published in the *Fortnightly*, July, 1908); " An Object Lesson in German Plans " (February, 1910) ; and " A Further Object Lesson in German Plans " (February, 1914).

STRATEGICAL RAILWAYS: GERMANY. 289

The camp was begun on a small scale, and at the outset the establishment of it on the site in question was declared by the Prussian authorities to have no strategical significance. It steadily developed, however, in size and importance, and its position, character and surroundings all suggested that it was designed for aggressive rather than defensive purposes.

At first the camp was reached from Hellenthal, a station, fourteen miles away, on a light railway connected with the lines in the Eifel district, between Cologne and Treves (Trier), on the Moselle; but in 1896 a light railway was constructed from Aix-la-Chapelle parallel with the Belgian frontier as far as St. Vith, a distance of fifty miles, the main purpose of this line being stated to be the securing of a better connection, from Sourbrodt, for the camp at Elsenborn. The line was, nevertheless, extended to Trois Vièrges (Ger. Uflingen), where it connected both with the railway system of the Grand Duchy of Luxemburg and with the main lines of the Belgian System from Pepinster, via Spa, Stavelot, Trois Ponts and Gouvy, to Trois Vièrges. From Trois Ponts there is a direct route to Liége, while Gouvy, situate only a few miles from Trois Vièrges, is the junction both for Libramont, on the main line from Brussels to Metz and Alsace, and for the further junction of Beatrix, the central point of a Belgian line running parallel with the French frontier from Dinant to Luxemburg.

The single-track line from Aix-la-Chapelle along the Belgian frontier, supplemented by a light-railway branch from Weismes to Malmédy, met all the traffic requirements of a scantily-populated and primitive district, devoid alike of industries and of local resources, and offering very little traffic; but in 1908 the Prussian Government suddenly decided to double the line, first as far as Weismes, and then to St. Vith, notwithstanding that there was no apparent justification for such a procedure. The widening involved, also, the reconstruction of a high embankment originally designed for one set of metals, a fact which showed that only a few years previously—since when the local traffic had not materially increased—there was no idea that a

U

double-track line would ever be wanted. Still more significant was the fact that, in addition to the second set of metals, sidings were provided on such a scale at the stations *en route*, in localities possessing only a dozen or so of cottages, that, in the aggregate, trains containing a complete Army Corps could have been accommodated on them. At one station three sidings, each about 500 yards long, were supplied, and at another a perfect network of sidings was constructed, including two which were at least half a mile long and were, also, equipped with turntables.[1]

The provision, more especially, of sidings such as these at local stations where the trains were few and far between and the ordinary merchandise was represented by some occasional coal trucks, could have but one purpose. They were obviously designed—in conjunction with the substitution of double for single track—to permit of a large body of troops, whether from Aix-la-Chapelle (an important point of concentration for the Prussian Army, on moblisation), or elsewhere, being assembled in the immediate neighbourhood of Weismes, the junction of the branch line to Malmédy, for an invasion of Belgium. The doubling of the rails as far as Weismes was completed by May, 1909. It was afterwards continued to St. Vith, and so on to Trois Vièrges.

We have thus far, however, got only the first chapter of the story. The second opens with the further attempt of the Prussian Government to secure an extension of the Weismes-Malmédy line as a "light railway" across the frontier to Stavelot, three miles east of Trois Ponts, thus giving a shorter route from Aix-la-Chapelle and the camp at Elsenborn to Liége, Namur, Louvain and Brussels, and a second route to Gouvy for Libramont, Bertrix and the north of France.

As the result of the influence they were able to bring to bear on them, the Germans succeeded in pursuading the Belgian Government, not only to agree to the Weismes-Malmédy branch being continued to Stavelot, but them-

[1] They were "hydraulic turntables," according to Major Stuart-Stephens. See *The English Review* for June, 1915.

selves to build the greater part of this connecting link, and even to cut, on the north of Stavelot, a tunnel without which that town would have remained inaccessible by rail.

Once more there could be no suggestion that this connecting link, opened in October, 1913, was wanted in the interests of the ordinary traffic, the needs of which were adequately met by the diligence running twice a day between Malmédy and Stavelot. What was really aimed at was a rail connection with the Belgian system by means of which the troops concentrated in those extensive sidings on the Aix-la-Chapelle-St. Vith line could be poured into Belgium in a continuous stream for the achievement of designs on Belgium or—operating from either the Belgian or the Luxemburg frontier—on France.

In helping to provide this connection, Belgium, as subsequent events were to show, was in a position akin to that of a man forced to dig the grave in which he is to be buried after being shot; but Belgium, we are told, " yielded in this and other matters because she could not resist without support, and no support was forthcoming." There certainly was an attempt to lull possible suspicions by the designation of the Malmédy-Stavelot link as a " light railway." It was, also, evident that the physical conditions of the Weismes-Malmédy branch, with which it was to connect, would not permit of any heavy traffic along it. But the so-called " light railway " was built with the same gauge as the main-line systems on each side of the frontier; the powers obtained in respect to it allowed of trains being run at a speed of forty miles an hour, as against the recognised speed of sixteen miles an hour on light railways proper; while no sooner had the link been established than Germany discarded the defective Weismes-Malmédy branch for the purposes of military transport, and built a new line from Malmédy to Weywertz, a station to the north or northeast of Weismes. This Malmédy-Weywertz branch would, it was understood, be used exclusively for military traffic, and the station at Weywertz was, in due course, provided with its own extensive platforms and network of sidings for the accommodation of troop trains.

We now come to the third chapter of the story; and here we learn that what was happening in the immediate proximity of the German-Belgian frontier was but part of a much wider scheme, though one still designed to serve the same purpose—that, namely, of ensuring the invasion of Belgium by German troops with the greatest facility and in the least possible time.

From Weywertz, the new junction for Stavelot and the Belgian railways in general, the Germans built a line to Jünkerath, a station north of Gerolstein, on the line from Cologne to Treves. Then from Blankenheim, immediately north of Jünkerath, and from Lissendorf, on the south of the same station, there were opened for traffic, in July, 1912, new double-track lines which, meeting at Dümpelfeld, on the existing Remagen-Adenau line, gave a through route for troops from the Rhine, across the Eifel district to Weywertz, and so on to Stavelot for destinations (in war-time) throughout Belgium, Luxemburg, or along the northern frontier of France.

This direct route to Belgium offered the further advantage that it avoided any necessity for troops from the Rhine to pass through Cologne, where much congestion might otherwise occur. It also left the Aix-la-Chapelle-Weywertz route free for troops from Cologne and Westphalia, while a further improvement of the facilities for crossing the Rhine made Remagen still more accessible for troops from all parts of Central Germany destined for Belgium—and beyond.

Reference to the Prussian State Railways official map shows, also, (1) a new line from Coblenz which joins, at Mayen, the existing railway from Andernach, on the Rhine, to Gerolstein, in the Eifel, whence the Belgian border can be reached either via Jünkerath and Weywertz or via Lammersweiler and the Luxemburg station of Trois-Vièrges; (2) the extension to Daun, also on the Andernach-Gerolstein route, of a short branch on the Coblenz-Treves Railway which previously terminated at Wittlich; and (3) several other small lines in the Eifel district, offering additional facilities for the concentration of troops on the Belgian frontier.

STRATEGICAL RAILWAYS: GERMANY.

So the Malmédy-Stavelot "light railway"—especially in view of this series of new German lines all leading thereto—had become a railway of the greatest strategical importance; and the fourth chapter of the story (though one upon which it is not proposed to enter here) would show how this network of strategical lines, developed with so much energy and thoroughness, was brought into operation in 1914 immediately on the outbreak of war, and, from that time, constituted one of the main arteries for the passage of German troops to and from Belgium and Northern France.

In regard to *Holland*, one finds a new line of railway from Jülich—a station reached from Düren, on the main line between Cologne and Aix-la-Chapelle—to Dalheim, the German frontier station on the direct line from Cologne via Rheydt to Roermond, a Dutch station on the right bank of the Meuse (which is here crossed by two bridges), and thence through the Belgian stations of Moll and Herenthals and across the flat expanse of the Campine to Antwerp.

This line obviously offers an alternative route for the transport of troops from Cologne and Aix-la-Chapelle to Dalheim; but of still greater significance is the information given by the writer of the *Fortnightly Review* articles as to the changes carried out at Dalheim itself, transforming that place from "an unimportant halting-place" into "a point of concentration of great strategical importance" on the frontiers of Holland.

Inasmuch as the line from Dalheim to Roermond and on to Antwerp was already a double one, the alterations made at Dalheim were confined to a liberal provision of railway sidings in order that, as we have seen was done on the Belgian frontier, a large body of troops could be concentrated for a possible invasion, in this instance, either of Holland itself, or of Belgium by the alternative route across the south-eastern corner of Dutch territory.

One of the Dalheim sidings, about a quarter of a mile in length, is situate on a high embankment; and, in order that it could be reached without interfering with other traffic, a bridge over which the main line runs east of Dalheim station was widened to allow of the laying across it of a third pair of rails. Other sidings adjoining Dalheim station have no fewer than ten pairs of parallel rails, and there are still others on the west of the same station, towards the Dutch frontier. At Wegberg and Rheydt, east of Dalheim, further sidings were provided which, like those at Dalheim, would not possibly be required for other than military reasons.

Summing up the situation in regard alike to the Belgian and the Dutch frontiers, Mr. Boulger remarks, in his article of February, 1914 :—

Thus on an arc extending from Treves to Nijmegen (excluding from our purview what is called the main concentration on the Saar, behind Metz), the German War Department has arranged for a simultaneous advance by fourteen separate routes across Holland, Belgium and the Grand Duchy.

In view of all these facts, there is no possible room for doubt as to the prolonged and extensive nature of the preparations made by Germany for the war she instigated in 1914; but the particular consideration with which we are here concerned is that of seeing to what extent those preparations related either to the construction of strategical lines of railway or to the adaptation of existing lines to strategical purposes.

Leaving Belgium and Holland, and looking at the Prussian State lines in *Schleswig-Holstein*, one finds on the official map the indication of a new line (partly built and partly under construction in 1910) which, starting from Holtenau, at the mouth of the Kaiser Wilhelm Canal in the Baltic, continues the short distance to Kiel, then turns to the west, connects with the Neumünster-Vandrup main line to Denmark, crosses the canal, and so on to Husum, a junction on the Altona-Esbjerg west-coast route. This new line would evidently be of strategical advantage in moving troops from Kiel either for the defence of the Kaiser Wilhelm Canal or to resist invasion by sea on the north of the waterway. Then the existing line from Kiel through Eckernförde to Flensburg, on the Neumünster-Vandrup route to Denmark, and giving through connection from

STRATEGICAL RAILWAYS: GERMANY. 295

Kiel to Tondern and Hoyer on the west coast—has been "nationalised," and so added to the Prussian State system; while from two stations just to the north of Flensburg there are short new lines which, meeting at Torsbüll, continue to the Alsener Sund, on the west of the Little Belt, and may—or may not—be of value in improving Prussia's strategical position in this corner of the Baltic, and in immediate proximity to the Danish island of Fünen.

Finally a large number of additions have been made in recent years to the State Railway systems in the interior of Germany; and, although a good proportion of these may have been provided to meet the increased economic and social needs of the German people, many of them must be regarded as strategical lines designed to facilitate (1) the mobilisation of troops on the outbreak of war; (2) their concentration, by routes covering all parts of the Empire, as arranged long in advance; and (3) their speedy transfer across country from one frontier to another, should several campaigns be fought at the same time.

The resort by Germany to strategical railways in Africa and elsewhere, as a means of furthering her Weltpolitik, will be dealt with in the two chapters that follow.

CHAPTER XIX

A German-African Empire

STRATEGICAL railways in South-West Africa were built by Germany as a means towards the achievement of her designs on British South Africa ; but these, in turn, were only part of a still greater plan having for its purpose the transformation of Africa as a whole into a German-African Empire which should compare in value, if not in glory, with that of the Indian Empire itself.

Colonisation societies began to be formed in Germany as early as 1849; though in the first instance the aims of their promotors were directed mainly to such parts of the world as Brazil, Texas, the Mosquito Shore, Chili and Morocco. All such places as these, however, offered the disadvantage that Germans going there could only become foreign settlers under the more or less civilised Powers already in possession.[1] In the 60's and 70's of the nineteenth century attention in Germany began to be diverted, rather, to Africa as a land where vast expanses, possessing great prospects and possibilities, and not yet controlled by any civilised Power, were still available not only for colonisation but for acquisition. So it was that successive German travellers explored many different parts of Africa and published accounts of their journeys designed, not merely as contributions to geographical science, but, also, to impress a then somewhat apathetic German public with the importance of their acquiring a " footing " on the African continent. In 1873 a German Society for the Exploration of Equatorial Africa was founded. This was followed in 1876 by the German African Society, and subse-

[1] See Vol. III. of "The Story of Africa," by Robert Brown. London, 1894.

A GERMAN-AFRICAN EMPIRE. 297

quently these two bodies were combined under the name of the Berlin African Society.

Not long after this, evidence was forthcoming that something far more than the settling of German colonists in Africa and the securing of a " footing " on African soil by Germany was really being kept in view.

In 1880 Sir Bartle Frere, at that time Governor of the Cape and High Commissioner for South Africa, forwarded to Lord Kimberley a translation of an article which had just been contributed to the *Geographische Nachrichten* by Ernst von Weber ; and, in doing so he informed the Colonial Secretary that the article contained " a clear and well-argued statement in favour of the plan for a German colony in South Africa which was much discussed in German commercial and political circles even before the Franco-German War, and is said to have been one of the immediate motives of the German mission of scientific inquiry which visited southern and eastern Africa in 1870-71."

Von Weber's proposals[1] pointed, however, to the creation, not simply of " a German colony " in South Africa, but of a German Empire in Africa. " A new Empire," he wrote, " possibly more valuable and more brilliant than even the Indian Empire, awaits in the newly-discovered Central Africa that Power which shall possess sufficient courage, strength and intelligence to acquire it " ; and he proceeded to show (1) why Germany should be this Power, and (2) the means by which she might eventually secure control of the whole country.

The establishment of trading settlements was to ensure for the Germans a footing in the districts north of the Transvaal, and this was to be followed by the flooding of South Africa generally with German immigrants. The Boers spread throughout South Africa were already allied to the Germans by speech and habits, and they would, he thought, be sure to emigrate to the north and place themselves under the protection of the German colonies there, rather than remain subject to the hated British. In any

[1] "The Germans and Africa," by Evans Lewin, Librarian of the Royal Colonial Institute. London, 1915.

case, "a constant mass-immigration of Germans would gradually bring about a decided numerical preponderance of Germans over the Dutch population, and of itself would effect the Germanisation of the country in a peaceful manner. It was," he continued, "this free, unlimited room for annexation in the north, this open access to the heart of Africa, which principally inspired me with the idea, now more than four years ago, that Germany should try, by the acquisition of Delagoa Bay and the subsequent continued influx of German immigrants into the Transvaal, to secure future dominion over the country, and so pave the way for the foundation of a German-African Empire of the future."

The procedure to be followed was (1) the acquiring of territory in Africa by Germany wherever she could get it, whether in the central or in the coastal districts; (2) co-operation with the Boers as a step towards bringing them and their Republics under German suzerainty; and (3) the overthrow of British influence, with the substitution for it of German supremacy.

These ideas gained wide acceptance in Germany; they became a leading factor in the colonial policy of the Imperial Government, and they reconciled the German people, more or less, to the heavy burdens which the developments of that policy were to involve.

German South-West Africa

The first steps towards the attainment of the aspirations entertained were taken by Herr Adolf Lüderitz, a Bremen merchant who, acting under the auspices of the German Colonial Society, and having received from the Imperial Foreign Office assurances of its protection, established a trading settlement, in April, 1883, in the bay of Angra Pequeña, situate between Namaqualand and Damaraland on the west coast of Africa, and about 150 miles north of Orange River, the northern boundary of Cape Colony. Acquiring from a Hottentot chief a stretch of territory 215 miles in extent in the Hinterland of Angra Pequeña, Lüderitz raised the German flag in the settlement, which thus became Germany's first colony. Further concessions of territory were obtained, and in September, 1884, Germany announced that the west coast of Africa, from 26 degrees S. latitude to Cape Frio, excepting Walfisch Bay (declared British in 1878), had been placed under the protection of the German Emperor. A treaty made between England and Germany in 1890 defined the limits of the German South-West African Protectorate as bounded on the south by the Orange River and Cape Colony, on the north by Portuguese Angola, on the west by the Atlantic, and on the east by British Bechuanaland, with the so-called " Caprivi Strip," giving Germany access from the north-east corner of her Protectorate to a point on the Zambezi River north of Victoria Falls.[1] The total area comprised within these boundaries was about 322,200 square miles.

At the outset, the new Protectorate aroused little enthusiasm in Germany as a colony where her surplus population could hope to settle and prosper under the German flag instead of going to foreign countries, as so many thousands of Germans were then doing. On a coast-line of 900 miles there was no good natural harbour except the one at Walfisch Bay, owned by the British. Swakopmund and Lüderitzbucht, on which the German colonists would have to rely, were then little better than open roadsteads. Considerable expanses of the territory itself consist of drought-stricken desert. The rainfall in Damaraland and Namaqualand averages only about three inches a year. In certain districts a period of five or six years has been known to pass without any rain at all. A record of rainfall on some parts of the coast has shown a total of one-fifth of an inch in the course of twelve months. At Walfisch Bay the British settlement imports its fresh water from Capetown. On the higher of the series of plateaux rising gradually to the Kalahari desert the climatic conditions are more favourable, and the better rainfall in the north-east allows

[1] Under the terms of the treaty of July 1, 1900, Germany was to have "free access" from her South-West Africa Protectorate to the Zambezi River "by a strip which shall at no point be less than twenty English miles in width."

of good crops being grown, while various sections are favourable for stock-raising. In later years, also, various deposits of copper were found in the district of Otavi, some 400 miles from Swakopmund, and diamond fields, which yielded nearly £1,000,000 worth of stones in the first year, were discovered east of Lüderitzbucht in 1908. But in Germany the Protectorate was regarded as a desirable acquisition mainly, if not exclusively, because of the advantages it was expected to afford as a base for the eventual creation of a German-African Empire.

The Herero Rising

The attainment of this higher purpose seemed likely to be furthered as the result of the steps taken to suppress the risings of the Hereros and the Hottentots between the years 1903 and 1907. Not only did the reinforcements sent out from Germany assume such proportions that at one time the Germans are said to have had no fewer than 19,000 men under arms in the Protectorate, but the troops took with them a plentiful supply of pom-poms, mountain guns, field guns and Maxims of various kinds, the *Revue Militaire des Armées Etrangères* being led to remark thereon that " the German columns had an unusually large proportion of artillery, roughly two batteries to three companies of mounted infantry ; and it is difficult to believe that so many guns were necessary, especially as the Hereros had no artillery at all.[1] Probably," the *Revue* continued, " the

[1] The Hereros (Damaras) are not a warlike people, and although, at the time of the rising, many of them were armed with Mausers and Lee-Enfields, it has been said of them that they were not of much account with the rifle, their "natural weapon" being the assegai. A German White Book on the rebellion stated that the cause of the outbreak was the spirit of independence which characterised the Hereros, "to whom the increasing domination of the Germans had become insupportable, and who believed themselves stronger than the whites." According to Mr. H. A. Bryden ("The Conquest of German South-West Africa," *Fortnightly Review*, July, 1915) the real causes were the abuses of the white trader, the brutal methods of certain officials, and the seizure and occupation of tribal lands. The war developed into one of practical extermination for the natives concerned. Of the Hereros between

A GERMAN-AFRICAN EMPIRE. 301

artillery could have been dispensed with altogether ; and had this been done, the columns would have been rendered more mobile."

The military measures taken appeared to be in excess of requirements even when allowance was made for the fact that the campaign was fought in difficult country and that the Germans themselves lost about 5,000 men ; but the real significance of the policy adopted lay in the keeping of a considerable proportion of the German expeditionary force in the colony after the rising had, with German thoroughness, been effectively crushed.

This procedure attracted attention and adverse comment even in Germany, where doubts were already being entertained as to whether good value was being received for the £30,000,000 which the suppression of the troubles had cost. It was, however, made clear that the still considerable body of German troops left in the colony was being kept on hand there in case of the opportunity arising for its employment in another direction—that, namely, of achieving Germany's aspirations in regard to the conquest of British South Africa, and the final elimination of British influence from Africa in general.

Evidence both as to the nature of these continued aspirations and as to the further purpose it was hoped the troops on the spot might effect was forthcoming in various directions.

In a book of 416 pages, published in 1905, under the title of " Das neue Südafrika," Dr. Paul Samassa emphasised the part which the German people had taken in the settlement of South Africa ; pointed to the close relationship and affinity of feeling between Germans and Boers ; encouraged the idea of their mutually looking forward to the opening up of South Africa as " a land of settlement for the German race," and said, further :—

German South-West Africa is, to-day, a strong trump card in our hands, from the point of view of Weltpolitik. In Eng-

---

20,000 and 30,000 were either killed outright or driven into the Kalahari desert to die of starvation. The Hottentots also lost heavily.

land much has been said of late as to what a good thing it would be for that country if our fleet were annihilated before it became dangerous. . . . On our side we might cool these hot-heads, and strengthen the peace party in England, if we reminded them that, whatever the loss to ourselves of a war with that country, England would run a greater risk—that of losing South Africa. We have in German South-West Africa to-day about 12,000 troops, of whom one-half will remain there for a considerable time. In the event of a war between Germany and England the South African coast would naturally be blockaded by England; and there would then be nothing left for our troops to do but to go on to Cape Colony—for their food supplies.

In so doing they could, he argued, count upon the support of the Boers, of whom there were 14,000 opposed to the English at the end of the South African war. As against this possible concentration of German troops and Boers there was the fact that the English garrison in South Africa did not exceed 20,000. So, he added, the people in England could consider " what an incalculable adventure a war with Germany might be, notwithstanding the superiority of the English fleet."

Speaking in the Reichstag in February, 1906, Herr Ledebour called attention to the fact that Major von François, who at one time was in command of German South-West Africa, had declared, in his book, " Nama und Damara," issued three months previously, that fewer than one thousand troops would suffice to maintain order in the colony; and Herr Ledebour added :—" For two years imaginative Pan-German politicians have been disseminating the idea that a large force must be maintained in South-West Africa for the purpose of exercising in the sphere of Weltpolitik pressure upon England, with the eventual object of invading Cape Colony."

There is the testimony, also, of " An Anglo-German," who, in the course of an article on " German Clerks in British Offices," published in *The London Magazine* for November, 1910, tells the following story :—

During a recent stay in Germany I was introduced by a man I know to be one of the chief functionaries of the Commerce

Defence League [1] to a friend of his who had just returned from German South-West Africa. On a subsequent meeting I entered into conversation with this gentleman, and made inquiries about German progress in that part of the world. He answered my questions without reserve. Little headway was being made, and little was looked for. Men and money were being freely expended, without present return. The only good harbour (Walfisch Bay) is a British possession, as likewise are all the islands of any value which are dotted along the coast.

"Why then," was my inevitable query, "do the Germans persist in their occupation of the country?"

He smiled craftily.

"We Germans look far ahead, my friend," he replied. "We foresee a British débâcle in South Africa, and we are on the spot. Thanks to the pioneers of our excellent League, our plans are all matured. The League finances the scheme and the Imperial Government supplies the military forces. By cession—or otherwise—Walfisch Bay will before long be German territory; but in the meantime British Free Trade opposes no obstacle to us, and we can pursue our purpose unmolested."

"But what is that purpose?" I asked, with the object of leading him on.

"Surely you are not so blind as to need enlightment!" was his reply. "Germany has long regarded South Africa as a future possession of her own. When the inevitable happens, and Great Britain finds her hands full elsewhere, we are ready to strike the moment the signal is given, and Cape Colony, Bechuanaland, Rhodesia—all frontier States—will fall like ripe apples into our grasp."

In order, however, that Germany might be prepared thus to take action at a moment's notice, two things were essential, in addition to having troops on the spot, namely, (1) that the colony should possess railways within striking distance alike of the Cape, of Bechuanaland and of Rhodesia; and (2) that the military preparations as a whole should be so complete as to be ready for any emergency.

[1] The Commerce Defence League, as explained by the writer of the article, is an organisation of German traders which gives subsidies to German clerks so that they can take up appointments at nominal salaries in foreign countries, on the understanding that they are to report to the League as to the business methods, etc., of those countries and on openings for German trade or industry therein, the League acting on such information and dividing among its subscribers the profits derived from the agencies opened or the competitive businesses started.

THE RISE OF RAIL-POWER.

Railways in G.S.W. Africa

Railways were indispensable on account, not only of the considerable distances to be covered, but, also, of the sand-belts and stretches of desert across which the transport of troops and stores would be a matter of great difficulty without the help of railways. They were, in fact, a vital part of the whole scheme.

Following on Germany's annexation of Damaraland and Great Namaqualand, and her conversion of them into the Protectorate of German South-West Africa, a party of German engineers and surveyors landed at Swakopmund with the design of planning a line of railway to be constructed from that point to Windhoek, and thence across the Kalahari desert to the Transvaal. About the same time, also, Germans and Boers were alike working to secure as much of Bechuanaland as they could, without attracting too much attention to their proceedings. A realisation of these further aims might have been of great value to Germany in facilitating the attainment of her full programme in respect to Africa ; but the scheme was frustrated by Great Britain's annexation of Bechuanaland in September, 1885, the result of the step thus taken being to drive a wedge of British territory between German South-West Africa and the Boer Republics.

So the railway in question got no further east than Windhoek, the capital of the colony, a distance inland of 237 miles.

Having failed in one direction, Germany tried another. Under a concession granted to them in 1887 by the Government of the Transvaal Republic, a group of Dutch, German and other capitalists, constituting the Netherlands South African Railway Company, built a railway from Delagoa Bay to Pretoria ; and the new aim of Germany was, apparently, to make use of this line, and so get access to the Transvaal—and beyond—from the east coast instead of from the west.

Confirmation of this fact is to be found in " A Brief History of the Transvaal Secret Service System, from its Inception to the Present Time," written by Mr. A. E.

Heyer, and published at Cape Town in 1899. The writer had held a position in the Transvaal which enabled him to learn many interesting facts concerning the working of the system in question. Among other things he tells how, at Lisbon, every effort was made to obtain a port in Delagoa Bay, and how, " aided by Germany, Dr. Leyds approached Lisbon over and over again with a view to get Delagoa Bay ceded to the Transvaal"; though the Doctor got no more from the Portuguese authorities than a reminder that, under the London Convention of 1884, the South African Republic could conclude no treaty or engagement with any foreign State or nation (except the Orange Free State) until such treaty or engagement had been submitted to the Queen of England for her approval.

That Germany, in giving her " aid " in these matters to the Transvaal Republic, was inspired by a regard for the furthering of her own particular schemes is beyond all reasonable doubt ; but Mr. Heyer shows, also, that when the negotiations with Portugal were unsuccessful, there was elaborated a scheme under which Germany and the Transvaal were to get what they wanted by means of a *coup de main*. Mr. Heyer says on this subject :—

I have before me a copy of a document, dated Pretoria, August 24, 1892 (the original of which is still in a certain Government office in Pretoria), wherein a Pretoria-Berlin scheme is detailed, namely, " How a few regiments of Prussian Infantry could be landed at Delagoa Bay and force their way into Transvaal territory, and, ' once in,' defy British suzerainty, and for all time ' hang the annoying question of her paramountcy on the nail.' " The name of Herr von Herff, then German Consul at Pretoria, appears on the document. Any one reading this cleverly-planned " Descent on Delagoa " would be readily convinced as to how very easily a German raid on Delagoa territory could be successfully accomplished.

This project, also, proved abortive, and, in default of Delagoa Bay, Germany had still to regard her South-West African Protectorate, with its railways and its armed forces, as the base from which British interests were to be wiped out—sooner or later—from the Cape to Cairo.

At the time of the outbreak of war in 1914, the principal

railways in German South-West Africa—apart from some minor lines which do not come into consideration—were as follows :—

RAILWAY.	2 ft. GAUGE. Miles.	3 ft. 6 in. GAUGE. Miles.
Northern . . .	121	119½
Otavi	425	—
Southern . . .	—	340½
North-to-South .	—	317
Total .	546	777

Granting that the Northern Railway was needed to afford a means of communication beween Swakopmund and the capital of the colony, and that the original purpose of the Otavi line was to provide an outlet for the copper obtained from the mines in that district, it is, nevertheless, the fact that the Southern and the North-to-South lines were designed to serve what were mainly or exclusively strategical purposes.

When the building of the first section of the Southern line—from Lüderitzbucht to Aus—was under consideration in the Reichstag, one of the members of that body, Herr Lattmann, recommended that the vote should be passed without being referred to a committee ; and in support of his recommendation he said :—

This way of passing the vote would be of particular importance for the whole nation, since the railway would not then have to be regarded from the point of view of provisioning our troops, or with regard to the financially remunerative character of the colony, but because a much more serious question lies behind it, namely, what significance has the railway in the event of complications between Germany and other nations ? Yes, this railway can be employed for other purposes than for transport from the coast to the interior ; our troops can be easily conveyed by it from the interior to the coast and thence to other places. If, for example, a war had broken out with England we could send them into Cape Colony.

A GERMAN-AFRICAN EMPIRE. 307

From Aus the line was extended in 1908 to Keetmanshoop, a distance inland of 230 miles from Lüderitzbucht. Situate in the *Bezirk* (district) of South-West Africa nearest to Cape Province, Keetmanshoop, with the railway as a source of supply from the chief harbour of the colony, developed into the leading military station of German South-West Africa.

At Keetmanshoop all the chief military authorities were stationed. It became the headquarters of the Medical Corps, the Ordnance Department, the Engineer and Railway Corps, and the Intelligence Corps of the Southern Command. It was the point of mobilisation for all the troops in that Command. It had a considerable garrison, and it had, also, an arsenal which a correspondent of the *Transvaal Chronicle*, who visited the town about two years before the outbreak of war in 1914 and gathered much information concerning the military preparations which had then already been made,[1] described as four times as large, and, in regard to its contents, four times as important, as the arsenal at Windhoek. Those contents included—47 gun carriages; fourteen 16-pounders; eighteen ambulances; 82 covered convoy vehicles; 3,287 wheels, mostly for trek ox-wagons; three large transportable marquees used as magazines and containing 28,000 military rifles; huge quantities of bandoliers, kits, etc.; three further magazines for ammunition, and large stores of fodder; while further military supplies were constantly arriving by train from Lüderitzbucht, whither they were brought from Germany by German ships. In the arsenal workshops was a staff of men actively engaged on the making of, among other military requirements, 1,000 saddles and water bags for the Camel Corps kept available for crossing the desert between the furthest limit of the railway and the Cape Province border.

It was, also, in this south-eastern district, and in immediate proximity, therefore, to Cape Province and Bechuanaland, that the military forces kept in the colony had all their principal manœuvres.

[1] See *South Africa*, November 14, 1914.

Of still greater importance, from a strategical standpoint, was the branch of this Southern Railway which, starting from Seeheim, forty miles west of Keetmanshoop, continued in a south-easterly direction to Kalkfontein, eighty miles north of Raman's Drift, on the Orange River, and less than ninety miles from Ukamas, where the Germans had established a military post within five miles of Nakob, situate on the Bechuanaland border, only forty miles from Upington, in Cape Province. From Kalkfontein the branch was to be continued another thirty miles to Warmbad, and so on to Raman's Drift—a convenient point for the passage of the Orange River into Cape Province territory by an attacking force. At Seeheim, the junction of this branch line, a Service Corps was stationed; Kalkfontein was the headquarters of the Camel Corps of 500 men and animals; and at Warmbad there was a military post and a military hospital.

The North-to-South line allowed of an easy movement of troops between the military headquarters at Keetmanshoop and Windhoek, or vice versâ. According to the original estimates this line was not to be completed before 1913. Special reasons for urgency—as to the nature of which it would be easy to speculate—led, however, to the line being opened for traffic on March 8, 1912. From Windhoek, also, troops were supplied to Gobabis, situate 100 miles east of the capital and about forty miles west of the Bechuanaland frontier. Gobabis became a German military station in 1895. Provided with a well-equipped fort, it became the chief strategical position on the eastern border of German South-West Africa. A railway connecting Gobabis with Windhoek was to have been commenced in 1915.

From Windhoek, as already told, there is rail communication with Swakopmund.

Grootfontein, the terminus, on the east, of the Swakopmund-Otavi line, had been a military station since 1899. Its special significance lay in the fact that it was the nearest point of approach by rail to the "Caprivi Strip," along which the German troops, conveyed as far as Grootfontein by rail, were to make their invasion of the adjoining British territory of Rhodesia. Troop movements in this direction would have been further facilitated by a link at Karibib connecting the Swakopmund-Otavi-Grootfontein line with the one to Windhoek and thence to the military headquarters at Keetmanshoop. Karibib was itself a military base, in addition to having large railway offices and workshops.

With, therefore, the minor exceptions, the system of railways in German South-West Africa had been designed or developed in accordance with plans which had for their basis an eventual attack on British territory in three separate directions—(1) Cape Province, (2) Bechuanaland and (3) Rhodesia. The Southern and the North-to-South lines had, also, been built exclusively with the standard Cape gauge of 3 ft. 6 in., so that, when " der Tag " arrived, and German succeeded British supremacy in South Africa, these particular lines could be continued in order to link up with those which the Germans would then expect to take over from Cape Province. Keetmanshoop was eventually to be converted from a terminus to a stopping-place on a through line of German railway from Lüderitzbucht to Kimberley, the effect of which, it was pointed out, would be to shorten the distance from Europe to Bulawayo by 1,300 miles as compared with the journey via the Cape. Surveys had been made for extensions (1) from Keetmanshoop, via Hasuur, to the Union frontier near Rietfontein, and (2) from Kalkfontein, on the southern branch, to Ukamas, also on the frontier and in the direction of Upington, in Union territory. Each of these additions would have carried the original scheme a stage further, though it was not, apparently, thought wise to make them before " der Tag " actually arrived.

On these various railways the Government of German South-West Africa had expended, so far as the available figures show, a total of, approximately, £8,400,000, defrayed in part from Imperial funds and in part from the revenue of the Protectorate. This total includes the amount paid by the Government to the South-West Africa Company for their line from Swakopmund to the Company's mines at Otavi and Tsumeb, but it does not include the cost of the original narrow-gauge Government line from Swakopmund to Windhoek, of which the section between Swakopmund and Karibib was abandoned when the Swakopmund-Otavi line, via Karibib, was taken over, the remaining section from Karibib to Windhoek being then converted into the Cape 3 ft. 6 in. gauge. On most of the open lines no more than two or three trains a week were run, and on some of the branches there was only one train in the week.[1]

MILITARY PREPARATIONS

Further details as to the elaborate nature of the preparations made for the realisation of Germany's dreams of conquest in Africa are supplied by Mr. J. K. O'Connor in a pamphlet published at Capetown, towards the end of 1914, under the title of "The Hun in our Hinterland; or the Menace of G.S.W.A." Mr. O'Connor made a tour through German South-West Africa a few months before the outbreak of the war, assuming the rôle of a journalist in search of data concerning the agricultural resources of the territory. He obtained much information which had other than an agricultural interest.

He ascertained, for instance, that the German troops then in the territory consisted of Mounted Infantry, Field Artillery, Machine Gun Divisions, Intelligence Divisions, an Engineer and Railway Corps, Field Railway Divisions, an Etappen-Formation, a Camel Corps, a Police Force and a Reserve, representing altogether—apart from natives —a trained European force of approximately 10,000 men, whose duties and location in the event of war had all been assigned to them in advance.

He found that the railways had been supplemented by a strong transport service of natives, who had an abundant supply of oxen and mules for their wagons.

[1] "Memorandum on the Country known as German South-West Africa. Compiled from such information as is at present available to the Government of the Union of South Africa." Pretoria, 1915.

A GERMAN-AFRICAN EMPIRE. 311

He tells how (in addition to the military stations already mentioned) the Germans had established throughout the territory a network of block-houses, strengthened by forts at intervals and supplemented by magazines and storehouses at central points; while 1,600 miles of telegraph and telephone wires, together with the " Funken-telegraph," placed all these stations and outposts in touch with one another as well as with the military headquarters and the various towns.[1]

He says concerning Keetmanshoop that its conversion into the chief military station in the territory was " the first move in the German game."

He points to the fact that " Das Koloniale Jahrbuch," published by authority, laid it down that the Boers in British South Africa must be constantly reminded of their Low-German origin; that German ideas must be spread among them by means of German schools and German churches, and he declares :—" For thirty years Teuton ideas have been foisted upon the Boer population of British South Africa. For thirty years, under the guise of friendship, Germany has plotted and planned for the elimination of the Anglo-Saxon element from South Africa."

Mr. O'Connor further writes :—

From what I was able to gather it was evident that the military plans of the Germans were completed for an invasion of the Union territory, and that they were only awaiting the day when Peace would spread her wings and soar from the embassies of Europe. It was not anticipated, however, that that would be in August, 1914.

They were confident of success, and from the conversations that took place between officers and myself it was evident that the possession of the African continent was the greatest desire of the Teutons.

The smashing up of France and Great Britain were only incidents that would lead to the whole continent of Africa becoming a German possession; and it was considered that as Germany would accomplish this, despite her late entrance upon the stage as a Colonial Power, she would have more to show for her thirty years as such a Power than could either England or France, who had started colonising centuries before her.

---

[1] The colony was also in wireless-telegraphic communication, via Togoland, with Berlin.

The great aim became to break France and England, for the purpose of acquiring their African possessions ; and, having broken these Powers, Germany would have turned her attention to the African possessions of smaller Powers who, having neither England nor France to rely upon, would have been compelled to relinquish their possessions, and, by so doing, would have made Germany the supreme Power in Africa.

Summing up the conclusions at which he arrived, as the result of all that he saw for himself and all that he had heard from responsible German officers during the course of his tour, Mr. O'Connor says :—

From the day the Germans set their feet upon South-West African soil they have prepared themselves for a raid into British territory. For years the Reichstag has voted two million pounds per annum for the purpose. Had these millions been spent on the development of South-West Africa it would, to-day, be a colony of which any country might be proud. But what can they show for this expenditure ? Nothing but a military camp.

It is evident, then, that this territory has not been regarded by the Berliners as a colony, but as a jumping-off ground for an invasion of British South Africa.

Here we have simply an amplification of ideas which, as we have seen, had long been entertained in Germany ; though they were ideas it was now being sought to reduce to practice by a resort, in advance, to every step that could possibly be taken for ensuring their realisation. Any suggestion that the system of strategical railways which had been built, and the elaborate military preparations which had been effected, were merely precautions against a further possible rising of the natives would have been absurd.

Rail Connection with Angola

What Mr. O'Connor says in regard to Germany's attitude towards the African possessions of the smaller Powers gives additional significance to a report published in the *Leipziger Neueste Nachrichten* of May 31, 1914, concerning a project for building a line of railway along the coast of German South-West Africa to connect with Portuguese

Angola. This was to be the first of a series of lines which " after lengthy discussions with the Imperial Government," were to be carried out in German South-West Africa by a syndicate of prominent shipping and banking houses in Germany, controlling an initial capital of 50,000,000 marks (£2,500,000). It was further reported that in the early part of 1914 the Governor of German South-West Africa made a tour through the northern part of the Protectorate, going as far as Tiger Bay, in Angola, " in connection with possible railway construction in the near future."

Angola was certainly an item on the German list of desirable acquisitions in Africa. It has been in the occupation of Portugal since the middle of the fifteenth century; but the point of view from which it was regarded by advocates of German expansion may be judged from some remarks made in the *Kölnische Zeitung* by a traveller who returned to Germany from Angola in June, 1914 :—

> The game is worth the candle. An enormous market for industrial products, rich and virgin mineral treasures, a fruitful and healthy country equally suitable for agriculture, cattle-breeding and immigration, and the finest harbours on the west coast—that is the prize that awaits us.

A territory offering these advantages, having an area estimated at 484,000 square miles, and extending inland for a distance of 1,500 miles, might be coveted for its own sake ; but its possession would have been of still greater value to Germany (1) as a continuation, northwards, of German South-West Africa, and (2) as the starting point for a chain of communications, under German control, extending right across the African continent, from west to east.

The coast-railway spoken of by the *Leipziger Neueste Nachrichten* was to link up German South-West Africa with Angola, in which country, also, the Germans hoped to obtain extensive mining and agricultural concessions, thus forwarding their established policy of peaceful penetration by means of commerce and railways, and establishing economic interests which might be expected to lead to political developments in due course, and so prepare the way for an eventual seizure of "the prize that awaits us."

The Germans had also sought to finance the completion eastwards of the Lobito Bay or Benguela Railway, to which reference will be made later on in connection with the development of the Katanga district of the Belgian Congo ; but the condition they advanced, namely that the control of the line should be left in their hands, coupled with their adoption of suspicious lines of policy in other directions,[1] led to their railway proposals being declined by the Portuguese, with thanks.

German East Africa

Then, in order to understand the full scope of the aspirations Germany was cherishing towards the African Continent, one must take into account her railways on the east coast no less than those on the west coast, since these, also, formed an essential part of the general scheme.

The line which stretches right across German East Africa, from Dar-es-Salaam, the capital of the Protectorate, to Kigoma, on Lake Tanganyika, and north of Ujiji, has a total length of 1,439 miles ; and if the economic development of a territory estimated as having a total area of 384,000 square miles had been the sole aim in view, the Tanganyikabahn would have well deserved to rank as a notable enterprise in German colonial expansion, and one calling for commendation rather than criticism. The question arises, however, whether, in addition to the development of German East Africa itself, the railway in question was not intended, also, to facilitate the realisation of Germany's designs against Central Africa as part of her aforesaid scheme for the eventual conquest of the African continent.

The feverish haste with which the second and third sections of the railway were built sufficed, in itself, to give rise to suspicions of ulterior designs. The first section,

---

[1] For details of so-called "invasions" of Portuguese territory by German political agents, posing as engineers and prospectors, see an article on "The Invasion of Angola," by Mr. George Bailey, in the issue of "United Empire : The Royal Colonial Institute Journal," for October, 1915.

A GERMAN-AFRICAN EMPIRE. 315

from Dar-es-Salaam to Morogo (136½ miles), was constructed by a syndicate of German bankers acting under a State guarantee of interest, and the work, begun in February, 1905, was completed in September, 1907. The second section, from Morogo to Tabora (526½ miles), was to have been completed by July 1, 1914; but in 1910, the Reichstag voted a special credit both for the earlier completion of this second section—which was thus finished by February 26, 1912—and for surveys for the third section, from Tabora to Kigoma (776 miles). Such, again, was the celerity with which the work on this third section was pushed forward that, although the date fixed for the completion of the line was April 1, 1915, through rail communication from the Indian Ocean to Lake Tanganyika was established by February 1, 1914—that is to say, one year and two months in advance of time.

We here come to the two-fold question (1) Why was the railway extended at all for the 776 miles from Tabora to Lake Tanganyika, considering that this portion of the German Protectorate offered, in itself, the prospect of no traffic at all for the line [1]; and (2) why was it necessary that such haste should be shown in the completion of the undertaking?

"The Other Side of Tanganyika"

To the first of these questions the reply is (1) that the traffic on which the western section of the Tanganyikabahn was mainly to rely for its receipts was traffic originating in or destined for the Belgian Congo; (2) that the control it was hoped to secure over Belgian trade was, in combination with the strategical advantages offered by the railway, to be the preliminary to an eventual annexation by Germany of the Belgian Congo itself; and (3) that like conditions were to lead, if possible, to the final realisation of von Weber's dream of 1880.

"That we are directing our gaze to the other side of Tan-

[1] "Le Chemin de Fer du Tanganyika et les progrès de l'Afrique orientale allemande." Par Camille Martin. Renseignments coloniaux, No. 3. Supplément de *l'Afrique française*, Mars, 1914. Paris.

ganyika," said the *Kolonial Zeitung* of April 4, 1914, in referring to the completion of the railway to Kigoma—an event which occasioned a great outburst of enthusiasm in Germany—" goes, of course, without saying."

There certainly is much on " the other side of Tanganyika " to which Germany might look with feelings of envy. In regard to mineral wealth, alone, the resources of the South-eastern section of the Belgian Congo could not fail to make a strong appeal to her.

The great copper belt in the Katanga district,[1] commences about 100 miles north-west of the British South African post, Ndola (situate twelve miles south of the Congo border), and extends thence, in a north-westerly direction, for a distance of 180 miles, with an average breadth of twenty-five miles. " In the not far distant future, when the many problems of development are solved, the Katanga copper belt," says Mr. J. B. Thornhill,[2] " will be one of the controlling factors in the copper supply of the world." In the report of the British South Africa Company for the year ending March 31, 1914, it was stated that the copper-mining industry in Katanga had attained to considerable dimensions; that furnaces with a capacity of 1,000 tons of copper per month were at work, and that further large additions to the plant were being made.

Katanga has, also, a tin belt, and coal, gold, iron and other minerals are found there, besides.

In the German territory on the eastern side of Lake Tanganyika there are, indeed, minerals; but they are found in no such abundance as in the Belgian territory on the western side of the lake. German East Africa can, however, produce in great abundance the wheat, the rice and the other food supplies necessary for the workers in Katanga mines, and the German view has been that the eastern and the western sides of the lake should be regarded

---

[1] A region on the Belgian Congo about 115,000 square miles in extent and one of the best watered districts in Africa, lying nearly in the centre of the African continent, and equidistant, therefore, from the Atlantic and Indian Oceans.

[2] " Adventures in Africa under the British, Belgian and Portuguese Flags." London, 1915.

as complementary the one to the other, and that the Tanganyikabahn should convey these food supplies to the lake, for transfer to the other side by steamer, and bring back the products of the mines for distribution, via the German east coast route and the Indian Ocean, among the markets of the world. In the same way it was hoped that all goods and necessaries likely to be imported into the Katanga and Mweru districts from Europe would reach their destination via this German East Africa Central Railway; and German business houses were strongly advised to establish branches in those districts,[1] so that, apparently, Germany would eventually control the trade as well as the transport of " the other side of Tanganyika."

The development of the south-western section of Germany's east-coast Protectorate had, in itself, become a matter of vital importance (" eine Lebensfrage "[2]); but the Belgian Congo was the only quarter to which that section could look for markets for its produce. The possibility of securing sufficient traffic for the Central Railway to ensure its financial success may have been a secondary consideration; but the railway itself was to serve a most important purpose, economically, by helping Germany to capture the Tanganyika and trans-Tanganyika trade, and by making her East Africa colony more prosperous; politically, by strengthening her hold on the Belgian Congo through the increase of her commercial interests there; and strategically, by affording her the means of effecting a speedy concentration of troops in Central Africa, should the occasion for so doing arise.

This last-mentioned purpose was to be further attained by the projected construction of what would have been a purely strategical line from Tabora, on the Tanganyikabahn, to Mwanza, on the southern shores of the Victoria Nyanza, whence German troops would—in case of need—be in a position to make a rear attack on British East Africa.

[1] " Welches Interesse hat Deutschland an der Erschliessung des Congo ? " Von Emil Zimmermann. *Koloniale Rundschau*, Mai, 1911. Berlin.

[2] "Die Eroberung des Tanganyika-Verkehrs." Von Emil Zimmermann. *Koloniale Rundschau*, Jan., 1911. Berlin.

CENTRAL AFRICA

Germany's hopes of thus strengthening her position in Central Africa by means of the Tanganyikabahn received, however, a serious set-back through the activity and enterprise of Belgian and British interests in providing, opening up or projecting alternative transport routes which threatened (1) to divert a large proportion of the traffic she had expected to secure for the East Africa Central line; (2) to diminish greatly the prospect of her achieving the commercial and political aims she cherished in regard to the Belgian Congo; (3) to make it still more difficult for German East Africa to emerge from a position of comparative isolation, and (4) to impede greatly the realisation of Germany's aspirations in regard alike to Central Africa and the African Continent.

It is the more necessary that the bearing of all these facts on the general situation should be understood because they tend to indicate the critical nature of the position into which the said aspirations had drifted, and the imperative necessity by which Germany may, by 1914, have considered she was faced for adopting some bold course of action if she were still to look forward to the possibility of those aspirations being realised.

The principle originally adopted by King Leopold in his efforts to develop the Congo State was that of supplementing navigation on the Congo by railways wherever these were necessary either to overcome the difficulties presented by rapids or to supply missing links in the chain of communication to or from the west coast. The same policy was followed by the Belgian Government when they assumed control, and the last of these links—the line, 165 miles long, from Kabalo to Albertville, connecting the Congo with the Tanganyika—was opened in March, 1915. One reason, in fact, given in Germany for the express speed at which the Tanganyikabahn was completed to Kigoma was an alleged fear that the Belgians might capture the trade and transport of the territory in question by getting to the lake first.

This combined river and rail transport still left it necessary for traffic from the Congo basin to the west coast to

A GERMAN-AFRICAN EMPIRE. 319

follow the winding course of that river, with a number of transhipments; and if the route in question had been the only competitor of the Tanganyikabahn, Germany would have had less cause for uneasiness. Meanwhile, however, the Compagnie du Chemin de Fer du Bas-Congo had built a line—forming a continuation of the Rhodesian Railways—from the boundary of Northern Rhodesia, at Elizabethville, to Kambove (Katanga); and a continuation of this line to Bukama, on the Lualaba, a navigable tributary of the Congo, was (1) to give shorter and better access to the Congo for products from Katanga, and (2) to establish combined rail and water transport between the entire railway system of South Africa and the mouth of the Congo. Already the minerals from Katanga were finding their outlet to the sea on the east coast via the Rhodesian Railways and the Portuguese port of Beira, instead of via the Tanganyikabahn and the German port of Dar-es-Salaam. The former had, indeed, become the recognised route for this important traffic in preference to the latter. The line between Kambove and Bukama had not been completed when war broke out in 1914; but the provision of this through route, and the various facilities it would offer, rendered still more uncertain the prospect of Germany getting control of the trans-Tanganyika traffic for her own lines.

There were other important railway schemes, besides.

From Bukama rail communication is to be continued right across Central Africa to Matadi, to which point the Congo is navigable for large vessels from its mouth, less than a hundred miles distant. This line, in addition to avoiding the great bend of the Congo, will open up and develop the vast and promising territory in the northern districts of the Belgian Congo, south of that river.

Another scheme which is to be carried out is a line from Kambove, in the Southern Katanga, to the south-western boundary of the Belgian Congo, and thence across Portuguese territory to the present eastern terminus of the Lobito Bay Railway. This will give to the mining interests of Katanga direct rail communication, by the shortest possible route, with a port on the west coast, while the connection at Kambove with the Rhodesian and South African systems will make the line a still more important addition to the railways of Africa for the purposes alike of development in the central districts and as a shorter route to and from Europe. German financiers were at one time desirous of undertaking the extension eastward of the Lobito Bay Railway—mainly, as it seemed, with a view to furthering German interests in Portuguese territory (see page 314); but the Kambove-Lobito Bay line is now to be constructed with British capital.

Finally there is the Cape-to-Cairo Railway which, passing through the Katanga mining districts, is likely to divert still more of the traffic Germany had counted upon alike for her Tanganyikabahn and as a means towards the attainment of her political aspirations in Central Africa.

Whilst these various developments were proceeding, there were still others, in the Cameroons, to which attention may now be directed.

THE CAMEROONS, LAKE CHAD AND THE SUDAN

Anticipations of the great results for Germany which would follow from the building of railways in the Cameroons began to be entertained about the year 1897. The main objective of the schemes brought forward seems to have been, however, not simply the internal economic development of an already vast area, but the carrying of lines of communication to the furthest limits of that area in order, apparently, to extend German interests and influence to territories beyond.

One of these schemes was for the building of a line of railway from Duala, the chief port of the Cameroons, to Lake Chad (otherwise Tsâd), a sheet of water some 7,000 square miles in extent which, situate on the western borders of the Sudan, constitutes the extreme northern limits of German territory in this direction, while the shores of the lake are occupied jointly by Germany, England and France.

The proposed line was to have an estimated total length of about 1,000 kilometres (621 miles). In September, 1902,

A GERMAN-AFRICAN EMPIRE.

the German Imperial Government granted to a Kamerun-Eisenbahn-Syndikat a concession for building the line ; an expedition sent out by the syndicate made a survey of the route in 1902-3 ; and a Kamerun-Eisenbahn-Gesellschaft, with a capital of 17,000,000 marks (£850,000), was formed by a group of bankers and others in Germany to build the first section.

In December, 1903, the German Emperor, at his reception of the President of the Reichstag, gave his blessing to all such enterprises by declaring that an essential condition ("eine Lebensbedingung") for the welfare of Germany's colonies in Africa was that the building of railways should be taken earnestly in hand. In 1905 the prospects of the proposed line seemed so hopeful that the early commencement of construction was announced as probable ; but various difficulties arose, including much trouble in regard to labour, and the line did not get beyond the end of its first stage, a distance of only 160 km. (100 miles) from the coast.

Although the scheme was thus not fully carried out, there was no doubt as to the nature of the purposes it had been designed to serve. In his official and detailed account of the proposed undertaking [1]—a book of exceptional merit from the point of view of the clearness and of the exhaustive data with which "the case for the line" is presented—the director of the syndicate says :—

> My opinion is that only a great railway—one that unites the Sudan with the Atlantic, and that extends from Lake Chad to the west coast of Africa—will be in a position both to develop fully the economic interests of the Cameroons and to assure to Germany a means of access to the richest territory that Central Africa possesses.

Had the line been completed as far as Lake Chad, it would have been a powerful competitor of British railways via the Nile or the Red Sea for the traffic of the Sudan,

---

[1] "Kamerun und die Deutsche Tsâdsee-Eisenbahn." Von Carl René, Director des Kamerun-Eisenbahn-Syndikats. 251 pp. Mit 37 Textbildern und 22 Tafeln nach Original-Aufnahmen der Kamerun-Eisenbahn-Expediton, 1902-3. Berlin, 1905.

with its vast commercial possibilities ; and, had it been found the better route, it might have established German commercial supremacy in this part of Central Africa, with the inevitable political developments to follow. " The German Tsâdsee-Eisenbahn," the director of the syndicate further wrote, " will, especially when it has been completed, be for the whole of Central Africa a *Kulturwerk* of the first importance."

The Germanisation of Lake Chad, combined with an eventual acquiring by Germany of French interests in the Sahara and North Africa, would further have permitted the continuation of the Tsâdsee-Eisenbahn from that lake to Algeria along the route already projected in France for a Trans-African line linking up the Mediterranean alike with the Congo and with the Rhodesian and other British railways in South Africa, via Lake Chad—a line which, it is said, would offer no great technical difficulty in construction.[1]

The Cameroons and the Congo

Another ambitious scheme was for the building of a Mittellandbahn which, crossing the Njong, would eventually link up the chief port of the Cameroons with a navigable tributary of the Congo. Here, again, the line as actually constructed has not been carried a greater distance than about 300 km. (186 miles). At one time, in fact, the original project seemed to have been abandoned ; but quite recently it has been brought forward again under conditions which have a distinct bearing on what has already been said concerning Germany and Central Africa.

From the views expressed by Emil Zimmermann in his " Neu-Kamerun," [2] one gathers that in 1913 Germany was regarding with some degree of concern alike the outlook for her Tanganyikabahn, on which over £7,000,000 had been

---

[1] " Bulletin de la Société de Geographie et d'Etudes coloniales de Marseilles." Tome XXXVI, No. 1. Ie Trimestre, 1912.
[2] " Neu-Kamerun ; Reiseerlebnisse und wirtschaftspolitische Untersuchungen." Von Emil Zimmermann. 135 pp. Map. Berlin 1913.

A GERMAN-AFRICAN EMPIRE.   323

spent, and the prospective set-back to her aspirations in regard to the Belgian Congo; and Herr Zimmermann, in giving an account of the additions made to her Cameroons possessions at the expense of France, under the agreement of November 4, 1911, following on the Agadir crisis, makes certain overtures to Belgium, and follows them up with a distinct threat, should she refrain from responding to them.

Belgium and Germany, he says, in effect, are the two dominant Powers in Central Africa; and he is of opinion that it will be to their mutual interest to co-operate in the development of that great territory. Belgium, however, he finds to be faced by the need for a great outlay of money (1) on account of necessary improvements of her Congo rail and river communication, to meet expanding traffic requirements, and (2) in order to develop her Katanga territory. She cannot herself command the necessary capital, but Germany could assist her to raise it, and would do so—provided Belgium undertook that traffic from her Tanganyika and Mweru districts, and, also, from points east of the Middle Congo, should reach the sea by " its natural outlet," that is to say, by the German East African Central Railway.

Should Belgium refuse to agree to these proposals, and should she, by her high tariffs, continue to impede the flow of traffic to German territory, then it would be open to Germany to construct lines of railway from the west coast either to navigable tributaries of the Congo or to the Congo itself, and so divert the traffic from the Belgian Congo at certain important points, to the serious prejudice of Belgian interests.

Apart from what might be done in the way of extending the Duala-Njong line to the said navigable tributaries of the Congo, as originally projected, Herr Zimmermann says that, under the treaty of November 4, 1911, Germany has the right to continue her Cameroons railways across French territory (France having reciprocal rights as regards German territory); and he points out how she could exercise this power, to the detriment of Belgium, should that country not accept her proposals in regard to the Congo basin and Central Africa. He specially mentions the fact that when the boundaries of the 100,000 square miles of territory added, at the expense of France, to the German Cameroons (then already 191,000 square miles in extent), were fixed by virtue of the treaty of 1911, the wedge-like strip on the south of Spanish Muni was so defined as to leave at the eastern point thereof a gap between the Spanish territory and the French Cameroons wide enough for either a road or a railway ; and he emphasises the fact that, by taking advantage of the facilities thus open to her, Germany could, under the treaty of 1911, construct a railway 1,000 km. (621 miles) long from Muni Bay through the said gap and cross French territory to the junction of the Sangha with the Congo. Alternatively, and by arrangement with France, the line could start from Libreville. "What such a railway, tapping the Congo-Sangha-Ubangi traffic at its most favourable point, would mean, can," Herr Zimmermann remarks, " be left to the Belgians themselves to say."

He does not suggest that such schemes as these would in themselves be of great value to Germany ; but he thinks they might have a powerful influence, both politically and economically, on the solution of the Tanganyika problem in Germany's favour. In fact, he considers that since the 1911 treaty Germany has practically controlled the situation in Central Africa ; and from all he says it is a reasonable assumption that the Agadir crisis, the concession of territory exacted from France, and the undertaking as to the carrying of German Cameroon railways across French territory, had far more to do with German designs on the Belgian Congo and Central Africa than is generally supposed.

In another work, published a year later,[1] the same writer, adopting now a distinctly different tone, endeavoured to appease an "Anti-Central Africa agitation" which, he tells us, had developed in Germany and was protesting alike against the "danger" of acquiring any more "Congo-swamps" and against the "boundless German plans" in Africa. He further sought to soothe the suspicions which, he found, had been excited in Belgium and elsewhere as

---

[1] "Was ist uns Zentralafrika ? " Von Emil Zimmermann. 57 pp. Berlin, 1914.

A GERMAN-AFRICAN EMPIRE. 325

to the nature of Germany's plans in Africa. Germany, he declared, had no annexation projects in view. Her aspirations were purely economic. Kamerun, thanks to the German-French treaty of 1911 (which, he reiterated, had changed the whole situation), could now take a considerable share in the development of Central Africa, and was the more entitled so to do since she had, in Duala, " one of the best harbours on the west coast of Africa."

OFFICIAL ADMISSIONS

As against, however, affirmations such as these, there is the undisputable evidence of no less an authority than the German Foreign Minister himself as to the real nature of Germany's designs on the Belgian Congo.

In the second Belgian Grey Book, published in August, 1915, under the title of " Correspondance Diplomatique relative à la Guerre de 1914-15," there is given (pp. 2-3) a letter from the Belgian Minister in Berlin, Baron Beyens, to his Government, recording, under date April 2, 1914, a conversation which the French Ambassador in Berlin informed him he had had quite recently (and, therefore, only about four months before the outbreak of war) with the German Foreign Minister. Herr von Jagow suggested to him that Germany, France and England should arrive at an agreement on the construction and linking up of railways in Africa. M. Gambon replied that in this case Belgium ought to be invited to confer with them, as she was constructing some new railways on the Congo. He also expressed the view that any conference held on the subject should meet at Brussels. To this Herr von Jagow responded, " Oh no ; for it is at the expense of Belgium that our agreement should be made. Do you not think," he added, " that King Leopold placed too heavy a burden on the shoulders of Belgium ? Belgium is not rich enough to develop that vast possession. It is an enterprise beyond her financial resources and her means of expansion." The French Ambassador dissented, but Herr von Jagow went on to affirm that the great Powers were alone in a position to colonise, and that the small Powers were destined to disappear or to gravitate towards the orbit of the large ones. In the words of the Belgian Minister—

Il développa l'opinion que seules les grandes Puissances sont en situation de coloniser. Il dévoila même le fond de sa pensée en soutenant que les petits Etats ne pourraient plus mener, dans la transformation qui s'opérait en Europe au profit des nationalités les plus fortes, par suite du développement des forces économiques et des moyens de communication, l'existence indépendante dont ils avaient joui jusqu'à présent. Ils étaient destinés à disparaître ou à graviter dans l'orbite des grandes Puissances.

"DER TAG" AND ITS PROGRAMME

The story here presented of Germany's aims in Africa has taken us over almost the entire African Continent. It now only remains to be seen how those aims were to be realised, not merely as the outcome of Pan-German dreams and advocacy, but as the result of many years of scheming, plotting and actual preparation, all directed to the wiping out of the influence in Africa of other Powers, great as well as small, and the final realisation of Germany's long-cherished purpose.

According to conversations Mr. O'Connor had with military officers in German South-West Africa just before the outbreak of war in 1914, the programme under which Germany hoped to become "the supreme power in Africa" when "der Tag" so long looked forward to should arrive was, in effect, as follows:—

Belgium was to be disposed of "at one gulp." This would make it an easy matter for Germany to take over the Belgian Congo.

France would be paralysed; and, being paralysed, she would not be able to prevent Germany from succeeding to the whole of her possessions in Africa.

The Dervishes would stir up a rebellion in Egypt,[1] and other rebellions were anticipated in Ireland and India.

[1] How Egypt was to be invaded and captured by the Germans and Turks, in combination, with the help of the railways in Asia Minor, will be told in the following Chapter.

A GERMAN-AFRICAN EMPIRE. 327

While England was fully occupied in these directions the Afrikanders were to rise *en masse* and declare British South Africa an Afrikander Republic.

The forces in German East Africa would make a sudden raid into British East Africa. Having annexed that territory and got possession of the railway, they would next invade Rhodesia from the east, in co-operation with troops from German South-West Africa advancing to the Zambezi, via the Caprivi Strip, from the railway terminus at Grootfontein.

Meanwhile German columns would have moved (1) from the military station at Gobabis into Bechuanaland, crossing the desert of Kalahari, to effect the capture of Vryburg; and (2) from Keetmanshoop, and other points served by the Seeheim branch, into northern Cape Province, via Raman's Drift, Schuit Drift and the south-east corner of the territory.

Rhodesia having been seized, more troops would be available to proceed to the assistance of the Afrikander forces operating in the Cape Province, the Transvaal and the Orange Free State—a " rising " on the part of the Afrikanders as soon as they saw a good opportunity for one being taken for granted. In return for the services thus rendered by her to the Afrikanders in establishing their Republic, Germany would take a portion of the Transvaal, as well as part of the Zululand coast.

With Belgium and France effectively crushed, and the power of Great Britain in South Africa broken down, those countries would no longer be in a position to prevent Germany from annexing Portuguese Angola; and this she was to do next. She would " allow " the Afrikander Republic to take Delagoa Bay; but the Republic itself was to come under the " guardianship " of Germany. The word " suzerainty," Mr. O'Connor says, was not mentioned, " guardianship " being preferred; but, with the exception of Italian Somaliland—about which nothing was said— practically the whole of Africa was either to belong to Germany or to be brought directly or indirectly under her control.

THE OBJECTIVE OF THE WORLD-WAR

Since the outbreak of the World-War in 1914 there has been much speculation as to the real objective and purpose of Germany in bringing it about.

Do the facts stated in the present chapter afford any help towards a solution of this problem?

We have seen the nature of the aims cherished by Germany towards Africa, the practical and persistent efforts she made during a long series of years for their attainment, and the substantial expenditure she incurred in the hope of at last securing the prize she considered was awaiting her.

We have seen how the purpose of Germany in Africa was less to develop colonies for their own sake than to regard them as points from which to absorb or to control neighbouring territories.

We have seen how the development of rival railways in Central Africa had recently threatened the supremacy Germany hoped to gain and may, indeed, have suggested to her the need for early vigorous effort, if she wished still to secure the realisation of her aims.

We have seen what, in the view of the German Foreign Minister, should be the fate of small Powers which stand in the way of the aggrandisement of great ones.

We have seen, also, how, in the opinion of officers serving in German South-West Africa, the real purpose of the war to which they were looking forward, and for which they were preparing, was the German annexation of Africa, and how the " smashing up " of France and Great Britain, the overthrow of Belgium, the seizure of Portuguese possessions, and the virtual absorption of the proposed new Boer Republics were to be the preliminaries to a final transformation of the whole African Continent into a German possession—the " new Empire " which, in the words of von Weber, was to be " possibly more valuable and more brilliant than even the Indian Empire."

May one not conclude, in face of these and of all the other facts which have here been narrated, that one, at least, of the main objectives of Germany (apart from minor ones) in

A GERMAN-AFRICAN EMPIRE.   329

provoking the Great War was no less a prize than the African Continent;[1] and that when she invaded Belgium and France she did so less with the object of annexing the former country, and of creating another Alsace-Lorraine in the latter than of having "something in her hand" with which to "bargain"—in the interests of her projects in Africa—when the time came for discussing the terms of peace, assuming that she had not already attained her purpose at the outset by the sheer force of what she thought would be her irresistible strength?

If this conclusion should seem to be warranted, on the basis of what has already been told, it may certainly be regarded as confirmed by the fact that, down to the moment when these lines are being written, any suggestions coming from German sources as to possible terms of peace have invariably included proposals for the concession to Germany of territory in Africa as "compensation" for the surrender of territory she has herself occupied in Belgium and France.

Thus, in a despatch published in *The Times* of September 4, 1915, a statement was reproduced from the Chicago *Tribune* giving, on the authority of "a writer in close touch with the German Embassy," the terms on which Germany

---

[1] Should there still be any doubt on this point, it will be removed by the frank admission of *Die Neue Zeit*, even whilst the Great War is still in progress, that Germany undertook the war with "the main object of extending her colonial possessions." As quoted in the *Daily Express* of October 8, 1915, *Die Neue Zeit* further said:— "Herr Paul Rohrbach favours the acquisition of the whole of Central Africa, but opines that this territory, vast as it is, will not be adequate to furnish Germany with all the elbow room she may require within the next half-century. Professor Delbrück, while agreeing with Herr Rohrbach, as to the importance of Central Africa, as well as of Angola and the whole of British East Africa, further emphasises the necessity for the acquisition of the Sudan and the southern part of the Sahara, now in the possession of France. We are quite in agreement with these eminent leaders that we must found an "India" of our own, and that the greater part of the African continent must furnish the requisite territory. Once well established in this new empire, we shall link ourselves with Asiatic Turkey, and also with China, reconstructing the political and economic foundations of both on a scientific German basis."

would be prepared to agree to peace. These terms included the following :—

The cession of the Belgian Congo to Germany, as compensation for the evacuation of Belgium.
The cession of African colonial territory to Germany by France, as compensation for the evacuation of Northern France.

Then, also, on October 24, 1915, the *New York American* published a long interview with Professor Hans Delbrück on the terms of peace which Germany hoped to secure if " President Wilson and the Pope " would consent to act as mediators. The interview (which had been approved by the German censor) included the following passage :—

It is quite possible that peace could be secured by ceding to Germany such colonies as Uganda by England and the French and Belgian Congos as a ransom for the evacuation by Germany of Northern France and Belgium.

Such concessions, if one can conceive the possibility of their being made—would still leave Germany far from the attainment of her full African programme ; but the fact of these proposals being put forward at all as " terms of peace " is quite in keeping with the whole course of Germany's policy in Africa, and points clearly to what may, in fact, have been her chief objective in the war itself.

Any moral reflections either on the said policy or on the " programme " by means of which it was to have been carried out would be beyond the scope of the present work.

What we are here concerned in is the fact that Germany's dreams of an African Empire, given expression to by von Weber in 1880, and the subject of such continuous effort ever since, were, in the possibilities of their realisation, based primarily on the extension and utilisation of such facilities for rail-transport as she might be able either to create or to acquire.

CHAPTER XX

DESIGNS ON ASIATIC TURKEY

JUST as avowedly strategical lines in Africa were to lead the way to the creation of a German African Empire, so, in turn, was that system of economic-political-strategical lines comprised within the scheme of what is known as the " Baghdad Railway " designed to ensure the establishment of a German Middle-Asian Empire, bringing under German control the entire region from the Mediterranean to the Persian Gulf, and providing convenient stepping-off places from which an advance might be made on Egypt in the one direction and India in the other.

The conception of this further programme was spread over (1) the period during which Germany's aspirations were limited to the inheritance of Turkey's possessions in Asia ; and (2) the period when such inheritance began to be regarded as a means to the realisation of still greater aims in the domain of Weltpolitik.

For more than half a century Asiatic Turkey has been looked upon as Germany's Land of Promise. Anatolia was thought a most desirable territory for her surplus population. The development, under German influence, of that territory as a whole—especially with a revival of the Babylonian system of irrigation—was considered to offer vast possibilities of commercial prosperity. Wheat, cotton and tobacco, especially, might be raised in prodigious quantities, and there was the prospect, also, of a petroleum industry rivalling that of Baku itself. Turkey was a decadent nation, and as soon as " the Sick Man " succumbed to his apparently inevitable fate—or even before, should circumstances permit—Germany was ready to step into his shoes.

That these aspirations had, indeed, long been cherished is a fact capable of ready proof. In 1848 Wilhelm Roscher, the leading expounder of the historical school of political economy in Germany, selected Asia Minor as Germany's share in the Turkish spoils, whenever the division thereof should take place; and Johann Karl Robertus (1805–1875), the founder of the so-called scientific socialism in Germany, expressed the hope that he would live long enough to see Turkey fall into the hands of Germany, and, also, to see German soldiers on the shores of the Bosporus.

Coming to a more recent period, we find that Dr. Aloys Sprenger, the German orientalist, published, in 1886, a pamphlet on "Babylonia, the richest land in the past, and the most promising field for colonisation in the present," [1] in which, after dealing with the history, physical conditions and resources of Babylonia, he predicted that, before the end of the century, not only Babylonia but Assyria, which was inseparable from it, would, if not formally annexed, at least come under the control of some European Power. Assyria and Syria, he declared, were even better adapted for colonisation than Babylonia. He continued:—

> The Orient is the only territory on earth which has not yet been taken possession of by some aspiring nation. It offers the finest opportunities for colonisation, and if Germany, taking care not to let the opportunity slip, should act before the Cossacks come along, she would, in the division of the world, get the best share. . . . The German Kaiser, as soon as a few hundred thousand armed German colonists bring these promising fields into cultivation, will have in his hand the fate of Asia Minor, and he can—and will—then become the Protector of Peace for the whole of Asia.

Dr. Karl Kaerger, traveller and economist, lamented, in his "Kleinasien; ein deutsches Kolonisationsfeld" (Berlin, 1892), the enormous loss sustained by Germany in the migration of so many of her people and of so much capital to Anglo-Saxon lands; but there were, he affirmed, only

---

[1] "Babylonien, das reichste Land in der Vorzeit und das lohnendste Kolonisationsfeld für die Gegenwart." 128 pp. Heidelberg, 1886.

two countries to which German settlers could go with any hope of retaining alike their nationality and their commercial relations with the *Mutterland*. Those countries were—Africa and Asia Minor. He had been especially impressed, during the course of his travels, by the prospects and possibilities of Anatolia, and he recommended the establishment there of large German companies which would organise schemes of colonisation and land cultivation on a large scale. The colonies so established should be self-governing, free from all taxation for ten years, have the right of duty-free importation of necessaries, and enjoy various other privileges, while Turkey, in return for the concessions she thus made to the settlers, would be assured " the protection of Germany against attack." Not only hundreds of thousands, but millions, of colonists could find a second home on those wide expanses. Germany herself would gain a dual advantage—an economical one, and a political one. Concerning the latter, Dr. Kaerger observed :—

If the German Empire, while maintaining her friendship with Austria and Italy—which, under all circumstances, the political situation in Europe undoubtedly requires—can direct the stream of her emigration to the fertile territories of Turkey, and if she can conclude with that country a closer customs convention, then the entire economic, and with it, also, the political future of Germany will rest on a broader and a firmer basis than if the present streams of hundreds of thousands of her people, and millions of capital, continue to pass in increasing proportions, year by year, to countries which are economically hostile to us.

Dr. Kaerger was especially concerned lest Germany might be anticipated by Russia or England in the realisation of her own designs on Asia Minor. Should, he declared, either of those countries acquire any further territory from Turkey, or increase in any way Turkey's dependence upon them, the result would be the most serious disturbance of the prevailing situation in Europe that had occurred since 1870.

The development of all these ideas went so far that in 1895 the *Alldeutscher Blätter* recommended that Germany should establish a Protectorate over the Turkish possessions in Asia Minor ; and in the following year the *Alldeutscher*

Verband published a manifesto on "German claims to the Inheritance of Turkey" ("Deutschlands Anspruch an das türkische Erbe"), making a formal statement of Germany's alleged rights to the Turkish succession.

Germany had by this time already secured a footing on the soil of Asiatic Turkey by virtue of the *Anatolian Railway*. The first section—a length of about seventy miles, extending from Haidar Pacha (situate on the north-eastern coast of the Sea of Marmara, and opposite Constantinople) to Ismidt—was built in 1875 by German engineers to the order of the Turkish Government. It was transferred in 1888 to a German syndicate, nominees of the Deutsche Bank. Under the powers then conferred upon them, the syndicate opened an extension, on the east, to Angora, in 1892, and another, on the south, to Konia, in 1896, the total length of line being thus increased to 633 miles.

As the result of the visit of the German Emperor to Constantinople in 1898, followed by negotiations between the Porte and the director of the Deutsche Bank, authority was given to a new German Company—the Imperial Ottoman Baghdad Railway Company—under conventions of 1889, 1902 and 1903, to continue the existing Anatolian Railway from Konia to the Persian Gulf, via Adana, Nisibin, Mosul and Baghdad. This extension was to constitute the main line of the *Baghdad Railway* proper ; but the Company also acquired control over most of the branch railways already in operation. One of these was the French Smyrna—Afium Karahissar line, which constitutes the direct trade route between Smyrna and places served by the Anatolian railway, and has, also, a branch to Panderma, on the southern shores of the Sea of Marmara. Another was the short line from Adana to Mersina, giving access to the Mediterranean. This meant the substitution of German for French interests, while the course taken by the Anatolia-Baghdad Railway from the Bosporus to Adana shut off the possibility of an extension of the British line from Smyrna via Aidin to Egerdir (west of Konia) into the interior.

Then in 1911 the Company acquired the right to build a *new port at Alexandretta*, with quays, docks, bonded ware-

DESIGNS ON ASIATIC TURKEY. 335

houses, etc., and to construct thence a short line of railway connecting with the Baghdad main line at Osmanieh, east of Adana. By these means the Germans acquired the control over, if not an actual monopoly of, the traffic between one of the most important ports on the eastern seaboard of the Mediterranean—a port where a trade valued at three and a half million sterling is already being done—and the vast extent of territory in Asia Minor designed to be served by the Baghdad Railway.

From Muslimiyeh, a little town on the north of Aleppo, there is a short branch connecting the Baghdad Railway with the *Hedjaz line* from Damascus to Medina, which is eventually to be carried on to Mecca; while from Rayak, north of Damascus, a branch built in a south-westerly direction was to be carried to within a short distance of the Egyptian frontier.

From the junction for the Aleppo branch, the main line was to continue across the Mesopotamian plain to Baghdad (whence a branch to Khanikin, on the Persian frontier was projected) and so on to Basra, for the Persian Gulf.

Thus the scheme for what passes under the title of the Baghdad Railway embraces three separate and distinct regions of Asiatic Turkey—(1) Anatolia, (2) Syria and (3) Mesopotamia. In other words, whereas in their first phase, German aspirations for Turkish territory were based on the economic advantages of settlement in Anatolia—a region in itself large enough to accommodate all the Germans who were likely to want to settle there—in the second phase those aspirations were based on an extension of the Baghdad Railway towards Egypt in the one direction and the Persian Gulf in the other. This dual extension became the more noticeable, also, inasmuch as for the passage of the Taurus range of mountains a total of nearly 100 miles of blasting and tunnelling would have to be carried out, the cost of construction on certain sections of the line rising to between £35,000 and £40,000 a mile. The extension, therefore, was likely to be a costly business, the total length of the Baghdad Railway proper, apart from the Anatolian system, being, as projected, about 1,350 miles, cf which, however, only about 600 miles were, in June, 1915, available for traffic.[1] Admitting the desirability of opening up Mesopotamia to commercial and agricultural development, it may, nevertheless, be asked, were there other motives—and motives to which still greater weight might have been attached—for this expansion of the earlier designs?

Abdul Hamid's reason for granting the concession is said to have been that the extension of the line to the Persian Gulf would greatly strengthen the military position of Turkey, since it would enable her to effect a speedy transfer of troops between the Bosporus and the Gulf, or intermediate places, as against the many months that might be occupied by marching on foot across plains and mountains

Germany's reasons for seeking to construct the Baghdad Railway, its branches and connections, to the full extent of the programme laid down, were, not simply the development of new trade routes, as certain inspired representations have sought to make the world believe, and not simply the gain of various other economic advantages, but (1) a desire to increase German influence over Turkey; to strengthen her military and other resources with a view to employing them eventually in the advancement of Germany's own interests; and to ensure the realisation of that eventual Protectorate over Turkey which would convert the country into practically a German province; and (2) the furthering of Germany's aims against Great Britain in the belief that she, too, was a decadent country whose possessions, when we could no longer defend them effectively, Germany would be the more likely to secure for herself if, with a concentration of Turkish forces to assist her, she were established within striking distance of some of the most vulnerable points of the British Empire, ready to take instant advantage of any favourable opportunity that might present itself, whether in a prospective break-up of that Empire or otherwise.

Of evidence concerning Germany's efforts to obtain increasing influence over Turkey there is no lack.

We have, in the first place, the fact that in 1882 a German

[1] Important extensions have been carried out since.

DESIGNS ON ASIATIC TURKEY. 337

military mission, of which General the Baron Colmar von der Goltz was the principal member, undertook the training of the Turkish Army according to the principles of German military science, with the result that the Turkish Army became a more efficient instrument for the attainment, not only of her own aims or purposes, but those, also, of Germany herself.

The Kaiser, although the supreme head of the Lutheran Church, and although having no Mohammedan subjects of his own, sought to pose as the champion of Mohammedans in general and the Defender of *their* Faith. During his visit to Damascus in November, 1898, he declared—" May the Sultan, may the three hundred million Mohammedans living who, scattered throughout the earth, honour in his person their Caliph, rest assured that at all times the German Kaiser will be their friend." [1]

Whenever political trouble threatened to fall upon Turkey, as the result of such occurrences as the Armenian and Macedonian atrocities or the insurrection in Crete, it was Germany who became her champion as against the other Powers of Europe.

Everything possible was done to push German trade in Turkey and to establish closer commercial relations with her. There came a time when every city of importance in the Turkish Empire was declared to be " overrun with German bankers, German clerks and German bagmen."

Not only, too, were German engineers active in seeking to get concessions for new railways, and not only were German financiers equally active in endeavouring to control existing ones, but, as Dr. Charles Sarolea points out, in his book on " The Anglo-German Problem," there are, in the agreements between the Baghdad Railway Company and the Porte, financial clauses which must ultimately place Turkey entirely at the mercy of her professed champion. " In Turkey Germany alone would rule supreme " ; and the aspirations for a German Protectorate over Turkey, with the Sultan as a vassal of Germany, would then be realised.

[1] Dr. Dillon, in *The Contemporary Review*, April, 1906.

338 THE RISE OF RAIL-POWER.

Writing on the position as he found it in 1903, M. André Chéradame said in " La Question d'Orient " :—

More and more the Germans seem to regard the land of the Turks as their personal property. All the recent German literature relating to Turkey affords proof of the tendency. An ordinary book of travels is entitled, " In Asia Minor, by German Railways." In his " Pan-Germanic Atlas " Paul Langhams gives a map of " German Railways in Asia Minor." So it is, indeed, a matter of the organised conquest of Turkey. Everywhere and in everything, Turkey is being encircled by the tentacles of the German octopus.

Coming, next, to the nature of *Germany's aims against England* and the part which the Baghdad Railway was to play in their attainment, we have the frank confessions of Dr. Paul Rohrbach, an authority on the subject of Germany's Weltpolitik, and a traveller who has paid four visits to Asia Minor. In " Die Baghdadbahn " (2nd. edition, 1911) he tells us that Ludwig Ross, a professor at Halle who was well acquainted with Anatolia, was the first to point to Asia Minor as a desirable place for German settlement. At the outset economic considerations were alone concerned, and in Bismarck's day Germany's relations to England played only a minor rôle in her foreign politics ; but in proportion as Germany's interests were developed and her soil no longer provided sufficient food for her people or sufficient raw products for her manufactures, she had to look abroad for the supply of her surplus needs. In so doing, however, her interests abroad might be endangered by the British Fleet. Hence the necessity for a German Fleet ; and, although the German sea-power might not be strong enough, by itself, to attack and conquer England, it could bring certain considerations home to English policy. Dr. Rohrbach continues :—

If it came to a matter of war with England, it would be for Germany simply a question of life and death. The possibility of a successful issue for Germany depends exclusively on one consideration, namely, on whether or not we can succeed in bringing England herself into a dangerous position. That end can in no way be obtained by means of a direct attack across the North Sea ; any idea of a German invasion of England being possible is a mere phantasy. One must seek, therefore, another combination in order to assail England at some vulnerable spot ; and here we come to the point where the relations of Germany to Turkey, and the conditions prevailing in Turkey, are found to be of decisive importance for German foreign policy. There is, in fact, only one means possible by which Germany can resist a war of aggression by England, and that is the strengthening of Turkey.

England can, from Europe, be attacked by land and mortally wounded only in one place—Egypt. If England were to lose Egypt she would lose, not only her control over the Suez Canal and her connexions with India and the Far East, but, presumably, also, her possessions in Central and East Africa. The conquest of Egypt by a Mohammedan Power, such as Turkey, might, in addition, have a dangerous effect on her 60,000,000 Mohammedan subjects in India, besides being to her prejudice in Afghanistan and Persia.

Turkey, however, can never dream of recovering Egypt until she controls a fully-developed railway system in Asia Minor and Syria ; until, by the extension of the Anatolian Railway to Baghdad, she can resist an attack by England on Mesopotamia ; until her army has been increased and improved ; and until progress has been made in her general economic and financial conditions. . . . The stronger Turkey becomes, the greater will be the danger for England if, in a German-English conflict, Turkey should be on the side of Germany ; and, with Egypt for a prize, it certainly would be worth the while of Turkey to run the risk of fighting with Germany against England. On the other hand the mere fact that Turkey had increased in military strength, had improved her economic position, and had an adequate railway system, would make England hesitate to attack Germany ; and this is the point at which Germany must aim. The policy of supporting Turkey which is now being followed by Germany has no other purpose than that of effecting a strong measure against the danger of war with England.

From other directions, besides, similar testimony was forthcoming.

The Socialist *Liepziger Volkszeitung* declared in March, 1911, that "the new situation shortly to be created in Asia Minor would hasten the break-up of the British Empire, which was already beginning to totter (schwanken)."

In *Die Neue Zeit* for June 2, 1911, Herr Karl Radek said :—

The strengthening of German Imperialism, the first success of which, attained with so much effort, is the Baghdad Railway; the victory of the revolutionary party in Turkey; the prospect of a modern revolutionary movement in India, which, of course, must be regarded as a very different thing from the earlier scattered risings of individual tribes; the movement towards nationalisation in Egypt; the beginning of reform in Egypt —all this has raised to an extraordinary degree the political significance of the Baghdad Railway question.

The Baghdad Railway being a blow at the interests of English Imperialism, Turkey could only entrust its construction to the German Company because she knew that Germany's army and navy stood behind her, which fact makes it appear to England and Russia inadvisable to exert too sensitive a pressure upon Turkey.

In the *Akademische Blätter* of June 1, 1911, Professor R. Mangelsdorf, another recognised authority on German policy and politics, wrote :—

The political and military power an organised railway system will confer upon Turkey is altogether in the interest of Germany, which can only obtain a share in actual economic developments if Turkey is independent ; and, besides, any attempt to increase the power and ambition of England, in any case oppressively great, is thereby effectively thwarted. To some extent, indeed, Turkey's construction of a railway system is a threat to England, for it means that an attack on the most vulnerable part of the body of England's world-empire, namely Egypt, comes well within the bounds of possibility.

These declarations and admissions render perfectly clear the reasons for Germany's professions of friendship for Turkey and for her desire that that country should become stronger and more powerful. They also leave no doubt as to the real purpose the south-western branch of the Baghdad Railway was designed to effect. The *conquest of Egypt* by a combined German and Turkish force was the first object to be accomplished with the help of the railway extension to the Egyptian frontier in one direction and to Mecca in another; but Dr. Rohrbach's suggestion that the loss of Egypt by England would entail the loss, also, of her possessions in Central and East Africa has a further bearing on what has been told in the previous chapter concerning Germany's designs on Africa as a whole. The strategical

DESIGNS ON ASIATIC TURKEY. 341

railways in German South-West Africa; the projected extensions thereof—when circumstances permitted; the German East African lines, *and* the south-western branch of the Baghdad Railway in the direction of Egypt were all to play their part in the eventual creation of a Cape-to-Cairo German-African Empire.

If we now direct our attention to the south-eastern branch of the Baghdad Railway, we are met by the repeated protests made by Germany that in desiring the construction of a railway to the *Persian Gulf* she was influenced solely by commercial considerations. Against these protests, however, there are to be put various material facts which leave no room for doubt that Germany's aims in this direction were otherwise than exclusively economic, while even the economic purposes which the Baghdad Railway would, undoubtedly, have served must have eventually led to a strengthening of Germany's political position, this, in turn, helping her military and strategical purposes.

As originally planned, the port of Basra (the commercial centre of trade in Mesopotamia, situate, sixty miles from the sea, on the Shat-el-Arab—the great river formed by the junction of the Tigris and the Euphrates—and open to the shipping of the world) was to have been the terminus of the Baghdad Railway; and if commercial considerations had, indeed, been exclusively aimed at, this terminus would have answered all requirements.

No objection was, or could be, raised by the British Government to the construction of the Baghdad Railway, on Turkish territory, as far as Basra. In the later developments of the scheme, however, Germany and her Turkish partner sought to ensure the continuation of the line from its natural commercial terminus, at Basra, to a political and strategical terminus, at Koweit, on the shores of the Persian Gulf. The *Abendpost* (Berlin) voiced the German view when it spoke of Koweit as " the only possible outlet to the Baghdad Railway."

But the extension of an avowedly German line of railway to Koweit would have been a direct challenge to the paramountcy which Great Britain claimed over the Persian

Gulf. It would have come into collision with British policy, interests and prestige in the East. It would have given the German and Turkish allies an excuse for creating at Koweit a harbour, with wharves, docks, warehouses, etc., which might be converted into a naval and military base capable of serving far different purposes than those of trade and commerce—those, namely, of a new line of advance on *India*. It would, in combination with the control already exercised by the Deutsche Bank over the railways in European Turkey, have assured to Germany the means of sending her Naval forces or her troops, together with supplies and ammunition, direct to the Persian Gulf, either to strengthen her fleet or to carry out any further designs she might cherish in the domain of Weltpolitik as affecting the Far East. It would have meant that, as far as the head of the Persian Gulf, at least, rail-power would have rendered her less dependent on the exercise of sea-power, on her own account, and would have enabled her to neutralise, also, as far as the said Gulf, the sea-power of England.

What so fundamental a change in the strategical position might imply was well expressed by so eminent and impartial an authority as A. T. Mahan, when he said, in his " Retrospect and Prospect " (1902) :—

The control of the Persian Gulf by a foreign State of considerable naval potentiality, a " fleet in being " there, based upon a strong military port, would reproduce the relations of Cadiz, Gibraltar and Malta to the Mediterranean. It would flank all the routes to the Farther East, to India and to Australia, the last two actually internal to the Empire, regarded as a political system ; and, although at present Great Britain unquestionably could check such a fleet, it might well require a detachment large enough to affect seriously the general strength of her naval position. . . . Concession in the Persian Gulf, whether by positive formal arrangement, or by simple neglect of the local commercial interests which now underlie political and military control, will imperil Great Britain's naval situation in the Farther East, her political position in India, her commercial interests in both, and the Imperial tie between herself and Australia.

One is thus led to the conclusion that Koweit, as the

terminus of the south-eastern branch of the Baghdad Railway, and within four days of Bombay, would have been as vital a point for British interests as the terminus of the south-western branch within about twelve hours of Egypt; while the possession of this further advantage by Germany would have been in full accord with the proposition laid down by Rohrbach and others as to the line of policy Germany should adopt for "bringing England herself into a dangerous position."

With a view to safeguarding British interests from any possible drifting into this position, as regards the Persian Gulf, the claim was raised, some years ago, that England should have entire control of the railway from Baghdad to Koweit. Germany did not see her way to assent to this proposal; but in 1911 she announced that she would forgo her right to construct the section from Baghdad to Basra on the understanding that this final section would be completed by Turkey. By way of compensation for the concession thus made by her to British views, she secured certain financial advantages and the right both to build the Alexandretta extension and to convert Alexandretta itself into practically a German port on the shores of the Mediterranean.

The precise value of the "concession" thus made by Germany was, however, open to considerable doubt. If she could succeed in her long-cherished aim of establishing a virtual protectorate over Turkey, then the fact that the final section of the Baghdad Railway had been built by Turkey, and not by Germany, would have become a matter of detail not likely to affect the reality of Germany's control. The line to Basra might have been nominally Turkish but the directing policy would have been German; and like conditions would have arisen had Great Britain agreed to allow Turkey—though not Germany—to continue the railway from Basra to Koweit.

In the wide scope of their aggressive purpose, the Baghdad Railway and its associated lines can best be compared with those roads which the Romans, in the days of their pride—the pride that came before their fall—built for the better achievement of their own aims as world-conquerors. Apart from the fact that the roads now in question are iron roads, and that the locomotive has superseded the chariot, the main difference between Roman and German is to be found in the fact that the world which the former sought to conquer was far smaller than the one coveted by the latter.

The programme of Weltpolitik comprised in the German schemes embraced not only countries but continents. In addition to the aspirations cherished as regards Europe, that programme aimed at the eventual annexation to the German Empire of three other Empires—the Turkish, the Indian, and a new one to be known as the German-African. It was further to secure the means of sending troops direct from Germany via Constantinople and the Baghdad Railway to the frontiers of Persia for possible operations against that country in combination with the Turkish military forces, these having first been brought under German control. The Baghdad Railway itself was, in the same way, and with like support, to afford to Germany the means of threatening Russian interests both in Persia and in Trans-Caucasia. It was to nullify England's sea power in the Mediterranean, if not, to a certain extent—through the establishment of a new Power at the gate of India—in the Far East, as well. It would, as Mahan showed, have flanked our communications with Australia, giving Germany an advantage in this direction, also, had Asia and Africa failed to satisfy her aspirations.

Regarded from the point of view of its designed effect on the destinies of nations, on the balance of political power, and on the reconstruction of the world's forces—all for the aggrandisement of a single people—the full programme must be looked upon as the most ambitious and the most unscrupulous project of world-conquest that has yet been placed on record in the history of mankind.

For its attainment, however, it clearly depended no less upon rail-transport than upon force of arms; and in this respect it represented Germany's greatest attempt to apply, in practice, that principle of rail-power to which she had devoted eight decades of inquiry, trial and organisation.

CHAPTER XXI

SUMMARY AND CONCLUSIONS

As will have been gathered from the preceding chapters, a prolonged period of consideration, preparation and application in many different countries throughout the world, prior to the outbreak of the Great War in 1914, had established certain definite facts and fundamental principles in regard to the relations of railways to warfare in general. These may now be brought together and summarised in four groups or divisions, namely, (A) Advantages; (B) Conditions Essential to Efficiency; (C) Limitations in Usefulness; and (D) Drawbacks and Disadvantages.

A.—ADVANTAGES

Assuming (1) the provision, in advance, of a system or systems of railways capable of meeting all the requirements of the military situation on the outbreak of war, or (2) the possibility of constructing military railways during the progress of hostilities, such railways should permit of—

A mobilisation of troops and their concentration at the frontier, or at the seat of war, with a speed that was impossible under earlier conditions.

Simultaneous use of different routes across the national territory for concentration either on the frontier or at a point some distance therefrom where the concentration can be completed without fear of interruption by the enemy.

Sudden invasion of neighbouring territory by troops sent in a succession of rapidly-following trains direct from various points in the interior of the country where they might have been concentrated without the knowledge of the enemy, this procedure being adopted in preference to collecting at the frontier in advance a force on such a scale as would disclose prematurely the intentions entertained.

The possibility of using promptly, for these purposes, the full strength of the country's available resources—the railway lines in the interior having already been adapted thereto, as well as those on or directly connecting with the frontier—with a proportionate increase of the offensive and defensive power of the State.

The supplementing of increased mobility and celerity by decreased strain on the physical powers of the troops and the avoidance of such inevitable reduction in their numbers as would result from the trials and fatigues of prolonged marches by road (in combination with the carrying of kits, etc.), should railway lines not be available.

A further consequent increase in the fighting strength of the army.

The possible attainment of the power of initiative through an early concentration of large forces at points of strategic importance either on national or on enemy's territory.[1]

The carrying out of strategical combinations on a scale or of a character which would formerly have been impracticable.

Employment of railways for tactical purposes during the progress of a war, including therein (a) movement of troops from one part of the theatre of war to another, whether with a view to effecting big changes of front or otherwise ; (b) employment of the same Army Corps on different fronts in succession, their transfer being effected in the briefest possible interval of time ; (c) the rapid bringing up of reinforcements at a critical moment to some position exposed to overpowering attack which might otherwise be lost ; (d) surprise attacks on the enemy ; (e) the throwing of great

[1] Von Moltke is reported to have said on one occasion in the Reichstag : "Our Great General Staff is so much persuaded of the advantages to be derived from obtaining the initiative at the outset of a war that it prefers to construct railways rather than forts. An additional railway, crossing the whole country, makes a difference of two days in the assembling of the army, and advances the operations proportionately." "In the concentration of armies," says von der Goltz in "The Conduct of War," "we reckon almost by hours."

SUMMARY AND CONCLUSIONS. 347

masses of troops on distant points ; (*f*) strengthening weak places in the fighting line ; (*g*) strengthening threatened forts by means of troops, guns, munitions or supplies ; (*h*) relief of invested fortresses, and (*i*) retirement by rail—when circumstances permit—of troops after defeat.

Control of a line of rail communication between the base and the strategic centre of operations, facilitating the enormous amount of transport in both directions which must be kept up in the rear of the army, and for which the elements of speed, safety and regularity may be of vital importance.

The possibility, thanks to railways, of regarding the whole interior of the national territory as a base for the supply of requirements at the front, dependence having no longer to be placed on a base established in one particular district with its restricted range of possible supplies and its collection of magazines, stores, workshops, transport parks, etc., protected by fortresses, entrenched camps, or other means of defence.

The establishment of supplementary, sectional or advanced bases along the line of communication, with railway services so arranged that supplies can be dispatched daily in such regulated quantities, and to such points, as will serve the immediate needs of the army in the field, without risk either of shortage or of excess.

Avoidance, under these conditions, of congestion of the railway lines in the immediate rear of the army by trains or loaded wagons containing a redundancy of supplies which (*a*) cannot be unloaded, (*b*) restrict the use of the lines for other purposes, and (*c*) might have to be abandoned to the enemy in the event of a sudden retreat.

Material benefits from the substitution of rail for road transport of food, etc., by reason of (*a*) greater speed and regularity ; (*b*) less risk of deterioration from exposure to weather, and other causes ; (*c*) decreased cost of transport as compared with earlier conditions involving the employment of a greater number of drivers, escort, guards, horses and road vehicles ; and (*d*) the arrival at destination of the full quantities dispatched, the need for the consumption of an appreciable proportion *en route* by men and animals in a convoying wagon train, carrying supplies for long distances by road, being non-existent.

Reduction in the need for field ovens and other paraphernalia of the army cook, since much of the food required —bread, for example—can be prepared in cities or elsewhere at a distant base and forwarded regularly by rail.

Freedom, more or less complete, from the once prevalent obligation on the part of an advancing army that it should " live upon the country "—a condition which the enormous increase in the size of armies to-day would render impossible of fulfilment, even assuming that the people of the country invaded had not withdrawn live stock, vehicles and food supplies on their retirement before the invader.

In addition to this provision for the wants of an army in its advance into hostile country, the safeguarding of the troops against the risk of their becoming a band of demoralized marauders, wandering over a wide area to seek and appropriate food whenever they can find it—as was the case, for instance, in the Napoleonic wars—the maintenance of discipline and the continued usefulness of the troops as a concentrated body for the military purposes in view being further assured when both men and leaders are relieved of anxiety as to the continuance of their supplies.

The conduct of war at a great distance from the base by reason of the facilities offered for the forwarding alike of troops, reinforcements, supplies and military materials, the value of even a single line of railway in the achievement of this purpose having been incontestably established.

Defence of frontiers by strategical railways which may, also, become available for general use.

Investment of cities or fortresses in occupied territory when, owing to the lack or the deficiency of food supplies in the surrounding country, the troops engaged are mainly if not entirely dependent on those brought to them by rail from their own base.[1]

---

[1] " Without railroads, it is said, the siege of Paris would have been impossible " (Bigelow's " Principles of Strategy "). " During the siege of Paris one railway for some time fed the [German] army

SUMMARY AND CONCLUSIONS. 349

Victualling of cities before, and their revictualling after, investment.[1]

Extension of lines of communication by means of quickly-constructed narrow-gauge siege railways to be operated by motor traction, animal power, or otherwise, including therein trench tramways for (a) removal of wounded men from the trenches ; (b) transport of siege guns to trenches ; and (c) supplying ammunition to battery.

Transport of heavy siege guns, mortars, ammunition and other materials of a size or weight that would render impracticable their conveyance, whether singly or in the aggregate, along ordinary roads, the railway offering, in this respect, facilities for ponderous transport comparable to those of the steamship, with the further advantage of being able, in most instances, to take the guns, etc., to the spot or to the locality where they are wanted.

Material aid given to expeditions to countries otherwise devoid of means of communication, by the construction of military railways.

Employment of armoured trains which, apart from their usefulness in defending railways against attack, may, as movable fortresses, render important service in the operations against the enemy.

Removal of sick and wounded from the theatre of war, and the ensuring of their distribution among hospitals in the rear or throughout the interior, thus (a) avoiding alike the embarrassment to the army and the many dangers and evils that would result from their remaining in overcrowded hospitals on or near the battle-field ; (b) giving the men a

---

of, in round numbers, 200,000 men, brought up the siege materials and reinforcements averaging 2,000 to 3,000 men a day, and even, at one time, fed Prince Frederick Charles' army, as well, with very slight assistance from the exhausted theatre of war " (Hamley's "Operations of War").

[1] During the thirty-five days preceding the investment, Paris received by the Western Railway, alone, 72,442 tons of provisions and 67,716 head of cattle. But for these supplies she could not have endured so long a siege. In the revictualling of Paris, after the siege, the railways, though much restricted by the Germans, brought into the city, in the course of twenty days, 155,955 tons of provisions and 42,580 head of cattle.

better chance of effecting a speedy recovery and returning soon to the ranks ; and (c) adding to the fighting strength of the army by the combination of these two advantages.

Facilities for giving a short leave to officers and men who, though neither sick nor wounded, have been so far affected by their strenuous exertions that they stand in need of a rest, or change, for which they will fight all the better subsequently.

Dispatch of prisoners of war into the interior by trains which have brought reinforcements or supplies, the army thus being speedily relieved of what might otherwise be a hindrance to its operations.

Return of material no longer wanted at the front and constituting impedimenta of which it is desirable to get rid as soon as possible.

Conveyance into the interior of "trophies of war"— including plunder—taken from captured towns or cities.

Retirement of troops from occupied territory on the declaration of peace.

B.—Conditions Essential to Efficiency

In the matter of railway construction there should be—

i. Uniformity of gauge, together with physical connections between the different systems or sections, in order (a) that the locomotives and rolling stock on any one line can be used for military transport on any other ; (b) that mobilisation, concentration and the forwarding of supplies and military material can be facilitated by the running of through trains from any probable or possible point of dispatch ; and (c) that troops can readily be transferred from one front, or from one part of the coast, to another for the purpose either of attack or of defence.

ii. Lines linking up the interior of the country with the frontier, with the coast, or with principal ports by different routes, tranverse lines connecting them, in turn, one with another.

iii. Double track for all lines leading direct to the frontier.

iv. In the case of single-track lines crossing continents or otherwise, a liberal provision of passing places each capable

SUMMARY AND CONCLUSIONS.   351

of accommodating the longest troop train likely to be run.

v. On all lines, and at all important stations, a sufficiency of sidings, with provision of, or the possibility of providing speedily, all such facilities as may be needed for the prompt and efficient handling of military transports whenever the occasion should arise.

Preparations in advance should include—

i. The carrying out of a scheme of organisation based on recognition of the following principles :—(a) That, while the railway is an instrument capable of rendering great and even incalculable services in the conduct of war, the working of it is a highly-skilled business only to be entrusted to those possessed of the necessary experience ; (b) that interference with such working on the part of military officers not possessing the requisite technical knowledge of the details and limitations of railway operation may result in chaos and disaster ; (c) that railwaymen, in turn, are not likely to be fully acquainted with the technicalities of military conditions and requirements, and should not, in any case, be left with the responsibility of having to decide between the possibly conflicting demands of various military authorities ; (d) that, for these reasons, there should be co-ordination of the military and the technical railway elements, operating throughout the whole scheme of organisation in its manifold details, avoiding conflict of authority, ensuring harmony of working, and offering the fullest guarantee that all military requirements will be met so far as the capacity of the railway, together with a due regard for safe and efficient operation, will allow ; and (e) that effect can best be given to these various conditions by the appointment of intermediary bodies which, representing the dual elements, shall alone have power to give directions, or to make demands, in respect to military rail-transport during the continuance of war.

ii. Collection of data concerning the physical character, resources and transport capabilities of the railways both in the national territory and in any other country to which the war operations may extend.

iii. Study of all movements of troops, etc., likely to be

necessary on the outbreak of war ; the preparation of special time-tables for the running of troop trains, etc., and the working out of all essential details respecting military transport in general.

iv. Creation and training of bodies of Railway Troops qualified to undertake the construction, destruction, repair and operation of railways in time of war.

C.—LIMITATIONS IN USEFULNESS

The usefulness of railways in war is limited by the following considerations, among others :—

Railways are "inferior to ships in power of simultaneously transporting heavy loads" (Von der Goltz). For this reason an overland route to India could never compete, in respect to military transport, with the sea route via the Suez Canal. Such overland route, also, passing through foreign countries, would be especially liable to attack and interruption. Where, however, the overland route goes entirely through national territory (as in the case of the Trans-Siberian Railway), and when the questions of time and safety, in regard to an alternative sea route, suggest possible disadvantages, railways will be preferred to ships in spite of the said inferiority.

Railways are inferior to roads in so far as, like rivers and canals, they are on fixed spots. Troops depending on them are thus able to move only in the direction in which lines have been or can quickly be laid, whereas if they went by road they might have a greater choice of alternative routes.

For these reasons the choice of the zone of concentration or of the "decisive points" may depend less to-day on political, military or geographical reasons (as in the Napoleonic wars) than on the direction, extent and capacity of the available railways.

Great masses of troops can be entrained only at stations where facilities for their so doing have been prepared in advance. The provision of these facilities is even more necessary in the case of Cavalry or Artillery than in that of Infantry. Hence the movement of considerable bodies of troops may be restricted to certain lines, and their entrain-

SUMMARY AND CONCLUSIONS. 353

ment or detrainment even to certain large stations. In the case of road marching these restrictions would not apply.

Vehicles specially constructed for the purpose can alone be used on railways. Any deficiency in their supply must needs cause delay.

During the time the troops are travelling by railway their power of resisting attack is much more restricted than it would be if they were marching by road, they can do little or nothing to protect the railway lines, while if the enemy can only get to the railway he may be in a position to prevent the train from continuing its journey, and take the troops in it at a disadvantage.

For these reasons, among others, troop movements by rail at the theatre of war, and especially in the enemy's country, are attended by a degree of risk which may render it desirable to abandon the use of the railway for the time being.

Railways are especially liable to destruction by the enemy, and, although the arrangements made in advance may permit of speedy repairs or reconstruction, the interruption of traffic for even a day or half a day may be a matter of grave importance during the concentration of the army or at some critical moment.

Destructions of line carried out by a retreating force, in order to delay pursuit by the enemy, will be to the disadvantage of that force when, after having driven back the enemy, it would itself make use of the line it had rendered unserviceable.

Dependence on the railway for the transport of considerable bodies of troops on short journeys—say for twenty, twenty-five or thirty miles—is rendered inexpedient by the fact that, when allowance is made for the time likely to be taken, not only on the journey, but in the assembling at the station, in the entraining and detraining (perhaps at some place devoid of adequate platform or siding accommodation), and in the march from the arrival station to destination, it may well be found that the troops could cover the distance in less time by road, apart from the consideration, suggested above, as to their being in a better position, when marching, to resist attack. Experts in all countries have studied this question with a view to deciding, on the basis of their national conditions, within what limit it would be better for troops to march by road in preference to going by rail.

For reasons akin to those here stated, supplemented by the recent great expansion of motor transport, less has been heard of late concerning the proposed construction in this country of strategical railways along a coast-line remarkable for its sinuosities, and presenting, therefore, an exceptional position from the point of view of coast railways for purely defensive purposes.

As regards long-distance journeys, whilst armies marching by road have often been materially reduced in proportions by the number of men falling out owing to lameness, exhaustion, or other causes, those who reached the theatre of war, representing "the survival of the fittest," were better able to endure the trials and fatigues of the subsequent campaign than if they could have made the journey by rail under conditions involving no strain, but affording them no such exercise and strengthening of their physical powers.[1]

Experience has further shown that exceptionally long railway journeys may have a prejudicial effect upon troops

[1] "The railways spare the troops fatigue," remarks Lieut.-Col. Tovey, R.E., in "The Elements of Strategy"; "but it may be that when they have to use their legs afterwards there will be more falling out and lagging behind, in consequence." Balck, in his "Taktik," says: "It is only in respect to the important consideration as to speed that the rail-transport of troops is to be preferred to road-marching. The real advantages of marching on foot—which was formerly the rule, and had the effect of 'separating the chaff from the wheat' and of preparing the men for the toils of fighting—are not counterbalanced by the fact that the troops arrive at the theatre of war in their full numbers. When time permits, marching on foot is preferable because it accustoms the men both to their new equipment and to marching in large bodies. After a long railway journey—on which the feet will have swollen and the new boots will have been especially troublesome—marching becomes particularly irksome, and the falling out of footsore men is very considerable. It is, nevertheless, the almost invariable rule that the troops shall begin their marching immediately they get to the end of the rail journey, since it may be a matter of great importance that the station at which they detrain should be cleared again as soon as possible."

SUMMARY AND CONCLUSIONS. 355

from the point of view, also, of maintenance of discipline.[1]

The services rendered by railways in war relate much more to strategy than to tactics. Great masses of troops and munitions, brought from all parts of the interior, may be conveyed readily and safely by rail to particular points in the theatre of war; but the possibility of effecting their transport by rail from one point to another on the battlefield when the opposing forces are in actual contact is subject to many restrictions and constitutes a much more difficult undertaking.

The imperative need for guarding a long line of railway communications, more especially in occupied territory, may lead to the withdrawal of a considerable number of men from the main army, weakening the strength of the available fighting force proportionately.

D.—Drawbacks and Disadvantages

While, notwithstanding the conditions to be observed and the limitations to be experienced, the balance of advantage conferred by railways on the conduct of war may appear so pronounced, from a military and a political point of view, there is a darker side to the story, as regards the world at large, which must also be taken into account.

If railways have increased the power of defending a country against invasion they have, also, increased enormously the power of aggression at the command of an invader.

They offer vastly greater facilities to military Powers for the making of sudden attacks on neighbouring countries—

[1] In alluding to the conditions under which Russian reinforcements were sent to Manchuria during the Russo-Japanese War, General Kuropatkin writes ("The Russian Army and the Japanese War"): "In former days troops had to make long marches in full service order before they reached the battle-field. If properly conducted these marches hardened the men, and enabled units to settle down; all superfluous luggage was discarded; the weaker men were left behind; the officers and men got to know one another. But, nowadays, with railway transport, the results are very different. Going to the Far East, our men were crowded in railway carriages for as long as forty days at a time, out of the control of their officers, who were in different compartments. In the old and well-diciplined units in particular harm was done; but in the case of newly-formed units . . . it was most harmful."

themselves, it may be, in a state of more or less unpreparedness.

They afford the opportunity for overwhelming weaker Powers by means of armies mobilised and concentrated in the interior and poured on to or across the frontier in an endless succession of trains following one another with such rapidity that the initial movement may, in some instances, be carried out within the short space of twenty-four hours.

They permit of the prosecution of war at distances which, but for the means offered for military transport by rail, would render war impracticable.

They allow of war being carried on between a number of nations at one and the same time, thus spreading the area over which the conflicts of to-day may extend.

They encourage the cherishing of designs of world-power and dreams of universal conquest.

They have added to the horrors of war by facilitating the transport and the employment of the most terrible engines of war.

They have rendered possible the carrying off of plunder from an occupied territory to an extent which would be impossible if the invaders had to depend on ordinary road vehicles for their means of transport.

They have brought fresh risks and dangers upon civil populations, the maintenance of lines of rail communication being a matter of such paramount importance to an invader that the severest measures may be adopted by him towards the community in general as a means of terrorising them and ensuring the security of the railway lines.

What, in effect, count as "advantages" in one direction may be the gravest of disadvantages in another.

Such, for attack or for defence, for good or for evil, is the nature, and such are the possibilities, of that rail-power in warfare which, after eighty years of continuous evolution, was, in the War of the Nations imposed on mankind in 1914, to undergo a development and an application on a wider, more impressive, and more terrible scale than the world had ever seen before.

Appendix

INDIAN FRONTIER RAILWAYS

ON the north-west frontier of India the plains of the Punjab are separated from the great central valley of Afghanistan, from the deserts of Baluchistan, and from the Russian Empire on the north thereof, by ranges of mountains, otherwise " a gridiron of stupendous ridges and furrows," intersected by passes which have always been regarded as the most vulnerable points of the Indian Empire. Through these passes from the earliest days of recorded history there has come a long succession of invasions instigated by that incalculable wealth of India which may well have inspired the envy of dwellers in less favoured lands.[1]

These considerations would alone suffice to establish the need for an effective control of the more important of the said passes by the Power which exercises supremacy in India ; but the obligation thus devolving upon the British people as the present holders of that supremacy has been increased in recent times by two further factors—(1) troubles with frontier tribes ; and (2) the development of that Central Asian Question which, though now no longer acute, was, not so many years ago, a source of great anxiety in England and India. Frontier troubles gave rise to a number of expeditions to Afghanistan from time to time, while the gravity of the general situation was increased by the once steady advance of Russia towards India—whether for the purposes of actual conquest thereof or, alternatively, for the attainment of the aim cherished by Russia during three centuries for an outlet to a southern sea, such outlet being sought via the Persian Gulf on her disappointment in regard to the Dardanelles ; though British interests were concerned in either case.

This combination of circumstances, with the possibility, at one time, that Afghanistan might become the theatre of war

---

[1] Altogether there have been twenty-six invasions of India, dating back to about 2,000 years B.C., and of this number no fewer than twenty-one have ended in conquest.

in a conflict between two great European Powers, invested with special interest and importance the provision on the north-west frontier of India of railway lines which, whether constructed to the more important passes or going actually through them, would form a ready means of concentrating Anglo-Indian troops at such places on the frontier, or beyond, as occasion might require.

From this point of view the Bolan and Khyber passes—the former leading to Quetta and Kandahar and the latter to Kabul—have more especially had importance attached to them as " the two gates of India."

Proposals for constructing railways through them were advanced as early as 1857, when Mr. (afterwards Sir) W. P. Andrew, chairman of the Sind, Punjab and Delhi Railway, acted as spokesman of a deputation which waited on Lord Palmerston in order to urge the construction of (1) a railway down the valley of the Euphrates, improving our communications with India by connecting the Mediterranean and the Persian Gulf; and (2) railways through the Bolan and Khyber passes, not only, as he urged, facilitating the movement of troops to the frontier, but offering alternative routes by means of which the flank or the rear of an enemy operating beyond or between the limits of the two lines might be threatened. Mr. Andrew followed up with great earnestness and perseverance for many years his advocacy of these views, publishing a succession of books and pamphlets, and writing many letters to the Press on the subject.

Such advocacy had, however, no practical issue, and, though the arguments originally advanced in favour of the Euphrates railway lost most of their force on the opening of the Suez Canal, the consequences of the neglect to provide better means of communication with the north-west frontier were well manifested in the troubles of 1878–79–80.

The refusal of the Ameer of Afghanistan—who had already accorded an ostentatious welcome to a Russian Embassy at Kabul—to receive a British mission led, in 1878, to an order being given for the advance of three columns of British forces upon Afghan territory, the routes selected for this purpose being (1) the Khyber Pass, (2) the Kuram Pass, and (3) the Bolan Pass. At this time, however, the system of frontier railways which had been advocated so long scarcely existed except on paper. The nearest point of railway communication with Afghanistan was then at Sukkur, on the Indus. An extension across the Sind desert to the entrance to the Bolan Pass had been surveyed, and a very short section had been laid; but in their advance on Kandahar Sir Donald Stewart and his force had to march all the way from the Indus, experiencing great trials in crossing the intervening desert, where many of the men lost their lives. The work of constructing this desert railway—which presented no engineering difficulty—was now taken actively in hand, and the line was available for the troops on their return.

Success attended the expedition of 1878 so far as it led to the flight of Shere Ali, the occupation of Kandahar by Sir Donald Stewart, the control by the British of the three main highways between India and Afghanistan, and the signing of the treaty of Gandamak ; but the murder of Sir Louis Cavagnari and his staff at Kabul, in September, 1879, rendered necessary the sending of a further expedition, General Sir Frederick (afterwards Lord) Roberts being directed to proceed with a British force by the Kuram route to Kabul.

Thereupon the whole question of transport facilities was revived afresh, and, although the expedition itself was a conspicuous success, delays and commissariat difficulties arose which might have been avoided had better railway facilities been available. The terminus, at that time, of the Punjab State Railway was at Jhelum, seventy miles from Rawal Pindi, 180 from Peshawar, and 260 from Thal, the frontier post of the Kuram pass ; and in spite of the vigorous efforts made, between 1878 and 1880, to extend the line, Jhelum remained the actual railway base throughout, no material assistance being gained from the twenty miles of extension which, owing to the great engineering difficulties presented by innumerable ravines, could alone be carried out during that period. Commenting on the " painfully slow " progress being made by the Khyber column, *The Times* of October 13, 1879, remarked :—

> It is now upwards of a quarter of a century since the chairman of the Sind railway commenced to broach the idea of connecting the Khyber and Bolan passes with the railway system of India. For more than a quarter of a century he has unsparingly advocated these views. . . . Had the views so persistently advocated by Mr. Andrew, and so repeatedly brought forward by us, been adopted at the commencement of the struggle last October, as we then ventured to insist upon, vast sums would have been spared in the hire of transport, and we should have been spared the ignominy of feeling that a British army, nominally on active service, has occupied five weeks in covering less than seventy miles.

Rawal Pindi—one of the most important strategical points in India—was not reached by the railway until October, 1880,

---

[1] It has been stated that the number of camels employed during the expeditions of 1878–80 for transport purposes, in default of better rail communication, was so great as almost to exhaust the supply of the frontier provinces of Sind and Punjab, while from 30,000 to 40,000 of them died owing to the excessive toils and trials of the work they were required to perform, the financial loss resulting therefrom to the Treasury being estimated at £200,000

by which time the Afghan War of 1878-80 had been brought to a close ; and the further extension of the Indian railway system to Peshawar,—another position of the utmost strategic importance, situate ten miles from the entrance to the Khyber Pass, and 190 from Kabul—was effected by May, 1883.

From a military point of view, however, still greater importance was attached, at that time, to the securing of rail communication through the Bolan Pass to Quetta and Pishin in the direction of Kandahar, this being the route by which, it was thought, the Russians would be certain to attempt their invasion of India, —if they should undertake one at all.

Surveys for an extension of the Sukkur-Sibi desert line to Pishin were made whilst that line was under construction, and early in 1880 the Government gave directions that the extension was to be proceeded with ; though they decided that the route to be taken from Sibi should be through the Hurnai Pass in preference to the Bolan route, the former being regarded as preferable for the broad-gauge line (5 ft. 6 in.) with which the " Kandahar State Railway," as it was to be called, would be provided.

Arrangements were at once made for collecting the necessary materials and for carrying through the work with the least possible delay ; but further progress was checked, in July, 1880, by the disaster at Maiwand. In the following October the Gladstone Government, who had succeeded the Beaconsfield Administration and had, apparently, resolved upon a complete reversal of the Indian policy of their predecessors, followed up an earlier announcement of their intention to withdraw from Kandahar by giving orders for the cessation of the work on the Sind-Pishin railway. Maiwand having been avenged, and some refractory tribes subdued, Afghanistan was completely evacuated by the British at the end of April, 1881, and the construction of frontier railways in India was dropped, for the time being.

In the middle of 1883 came a reconsideration of the position. Russia was then showing increased activity in the direction of Merv, and the British Government concluded, apparently, that they had been too hasty in ordering the abandonment of the Kandahar State Railway scheme nearly three years before. So they gave orders that the work should be resumed ; though, in order to render this *volte face* on their part less conspicuous, they directed that the undertaking should now be known only as the " Hurnai Road Improvement Scheme " ; that it should be proceeded with quietly, in order that it might not attract too much attention, and that the suggestion of a " road improvement scheme," instead of a railway, should be kept up by the engineers not being allowed to have even a temporary line of rails for conveying stores, materials for bridges, etc., from the

APPENDIX. 361

base to the passes. This last-mentioned stipulation meant that the stores and materials had to be either transported on the backs of camels or dragged on wheels up stream; and it was estimated that, in addition to the great loss of time, a sum of not less than £1,000,000 was wasted in this way before the order prohibiting the use of temporary rails was rescinded.

A start was made with the work in October, 1883, and the fact that the Russians were then actually approaching Merv, and that a sudden advance by them in force was regarded as probable, led to the laying of great emphasis on the need for construction being pushed on with the utmost vigour. When, in February, 1884, the Russians did occupy Merv, the pressure brought to bear on the Engineer-in-chief became still more acute. Then, in May, the British Government formally announced that, owing to the encroachments of Russia, the line *would* be built. The fiction of a " Hurnai Road Improvement Scheme " was now abandoned. Henceforth the line under construction was to be known as " The Sind-Pishin State Railway."

From the very outset, however, the difficulties which crowded upon Colonel (afterwards Sir James) Browne, R.E., an officer well experienced in railway and engineering work who was entrusted with the carrying out of the scheme, were unfavourable to the prospects of speed in construction. The surveys which had already been made were found not only worthless but misleading. The first members of his staff were unacquainted with railway work and had to be succeeded by men brought from England. The plant and materials previously collected, but disposed of at scrap-iron prices when the line was abandoned in 1880, had now to be replaced at an almost fabulous cost, owing to the urgency of the need for them.

All these were, nevertheless, minor troubles as compared with the physical conditions to be overcome.

Starting from an elevation, at Sibi, of 300 ft., the line was to rise 6,200 ft. in the 120 miles between Sibi and the summit level at Kach.

Then, for the greater part of the 224 miles to which the line was to extend, the country was a wilderness of rocks and stones —a land of barrenness and desolation, where there was no timber, no fuel, scarcely a blade of grass, and, in places, for stretches of several miles, no water. It was a land, too, almost devoid of inhabitants, while those who did dwell there were described as " a savage and blood-thirsty race of robbers," continually engaged in plunder and inter-tribal warfare, and not growing sufficient food even for their own consumption. Almost everything that was wanted—including supplies for from 15,000 to 30,000 workers and materials for the line—had to be imported from a distance.

Still less inviting was this inhospitable region by reason of its range of climatic conditions. The lowlands have the reputation of being one of the hottest corners of the earth's surface. A temperature of 124 deg. Fahr. has been registered in the Nari valley. The highlands, in turn, offer the alternative of Arctic cold, the temperature there falling in winter to 18 deg. below zero. Between the lowlands and the highlands there is a temperate zone; but here the constant pestilence was dreaded no less than the extremes of heat and cold elsewhere.

As the result of these conditions, the work of construction could be carried on in certain districts for part of the year only, and the workers had to be transferred from one section of the line to another according to the season. Such a movement of front involved the transport of everything,—stores, tools, offices and some thousands of men. "The management of this vast exodus," says Captain Scott-Moncrieff, R.E., in his paper on "The Frontier Railways of India,"[1] "was a work of considerable anxiety and difficulty. A sudden influx of people, such as this, into a desolate and barren land naturally caused a famine. Everything was eaten up, and for some days the question of supplies was the burning question of the hour. . . . Nine hundred camel loads of food were consumed daily on the works." The customary load for a camel was 400 lbs., but some of the camels carried loads of 800 lbs. up the pass.

The engineering difficulties fell into four principal groups,— (1) the Nari Gorge; (2) the Gundakin Defile; (3) the Chuppur Rift, and (4) the Mud Gorge.[2]

The Nari Gorge, about fourteen miles in length, beginning just beyond Sibi, has been described as "one of the most weird tracks through which a railway has ever been carried. The hills, absolutely bare, rise above the valley for many thousands of feet in fantastic pinnacles and cliffs. It is a scene of the wildest desolation." The Nari river, running through the gorge, is formed by a combination of three streams having but little water on ordinary occasions, but becoming, in time of flood, a raging torrent which fills up the whole gorge for miles, attains a depth of ten feet, and has a velocity of five feet per second. Over this river the railway had to be carried in five different places. Not alone bridges, but heavy embankments, cuttings and tunnels were needed. At one point there was an especially dangerous tunnel in which so many accidents occurred, owing to roof or sides falling in, that at last no workmen would enter it except at a wage five-fold that of the high rate already being paid. The

[1] "Professional Papers of the Corps of Royal Engineers," Vol xi, 1885.
[2] "Life and Times of General Sir James Browne, R.E., K.C.B., K.C.S.I." by General J. J. McLeod Innes, London, 1905.

APPENDIX. 363

whole work was liable to be stopped for months together, owing to the washing away of half-completed embankments or bridges; though until this portion of the line had been completed no materials could be sent to the sections beyond.

In the Gundakin Defile, eight miles long, two tunnels had to be made through some most treacherous material, and four bridges had to be provided.

The Chuppur Rift is a chasm three miles long in the spurs of a rocky mountain forming an apparently insuperable barrier. In time of floods the river attains a height of from 30 to 40 ft. The running of the railway on a ledge along the side of the mountain being impracticable, owing to the nature of the rock, the engineers cut a line of continuous tunnels partly on one side of the rift and partly on the other, connecting the two series by an iron girder bridge; but, instead of constructing the tunnels in the usual way, from each end—a procedure which would have taken much time—they adopted the expedient of driving openings (adits) into the side of the cliff at various points, and then cutting the tunnel right and left of each of these openings until the various sections met. The only way in which the openings could be made was by lowering men down by ropes several hundred feet from the top of the cliff until they reached the point where the work for an opening was to be started. They then drove crowbars into the perpendicular sides of the cliff in order to gain the necessary support for a platform from which the blasting operations could be carried on. Six of these openings were made on one side of the cliff and six on the other. As a separate gang of men could operate at each it was possible to complete the whole work in the course of a few months. Altogether there is a collective length of 6,400 ft. of tunnels in the rift, in addition to a viaduct 75 ft. high, with seven spans of 40 ft. each, and a bridge having an elevation over the river of 250 ft., and consisting of a central span of 150 ft. and eight spans of 40 ft.

On the summit level, twenty-five miles in length, came the five-mile long Mud Gorge,—a narrow valley, between precipitous mountains, filled with a soil little better than dried mud, and of such a character that several bad slips of road-bed, carrying away the whole of the line, occurred.

One would think that with all these difficulties—physical, climatic and engineering—to face, the constructors of the railway might have been excused any more; but there were others besides.

In August and September, 1884, the troops and native labourers employed on the work on the lower part of the line were visited by an outbreak of fever and scurvy of a virulence almost unprecedented in Indian experience. Large numbers of the men died. In one gang of 200 the average number of deaths was ten a day.

Of those who survived the majority were so prostrated as to be scarcely capable of doing anything. Sixty per cent. of the Sappers were in hospital.

Fresh troops, to the extent of three Battalions of Pioneers, were brought on to the work; but they had scarcely arrived before—in November—there was a severe outbreak of cholera. The Afghans thereupon " bolted to a man "; and they were followed by many skilled artisans who had been collected from various parts of India. Additional labour had to be obtained from the Eastern Punjab, but much time was lost.

Whilst the engineers were struggling to overcome these manifold difficulties, the political situation was steadily becoming still more acute. The climax seemed to be reached by the Penj-deh incident of March 30, 1885, when a Russian force under General Komaroff seized this important strategical position, situate near the junction of the Khushk and Murghab rivers. On April 27, 1885, Mr. Gladstone proposed in the House of Commons a vote of £11,000,000 for the purposes of what then seemed to be an inevitable war with Russia. The money was voted the same night.

So the urgency for completing the line which would now, probably, have been available for use had it not been stopped in 1880, was greater than ever. Orders were sent to India that the work must be continued along all parts of the line regardless of seasons. Within a week or two, however, of the war vote at Westminster, cholera broke out afresh among the construction party in India. By the end of May it was spreading among them " like a raging fire "; while to the cholera itself there was added a heat so intense that even the most willing of workers found it almost unendurable.

Under this combination of cholera and excessive heat, work on the lower sections of the line was stopped altogether for a time—Government orders and Russians notwithstanding. All possible measures were taken to mitigate the severity of the epidemic; but the death-rate increased with frightful rapidity. Some of the best workers, European and Asiatic—men who could least be spared, on account of the responsible positions they held —were carried off. During the month of June no fewer than 2,000 died out of 10,000. Of the remainder large numbers sought safety in flight. Many of the minor Government officials, such as telegraph and Post Office clerks, went off in a body.

Whilst sickness and disease had thus been afflicting the camps, fresh troubles had arisen in another direction. Early in 1885 the district was visited by a succession of floods exceeding in severity anything known there for sixty years. In the course of three months the rainfall amounted to 19.27 inches,—a total six times in excess of the average. Several bridges and many

APPENDIX. 365

miles of temporary roads were washed away; numerous accidents were caused; camping grounds were destroyed; communications were interrupted; food supplies became scarcely obtainable, and great delay resulted in the prosecution of a work for which urgency was being so persistently demanded. The floods did not finally subside until the end of May.

Nature having done so much to impede the progress of the undertaking, it only remained for politicians and officials to do what they could to follow her example.

Mention has already been made of the initial prohibition of temporary lines of rails for the conveyance of stores and materials, and the loss of time and waste of money involved in the use of camels instead; but to this one fact may be added another, namely, that after the Engineer-in-Chief had made his arrangements to obtain sleepers from the juniper forests on the north of the line—this being the only timber available in the whole district—the Government vetoed the arrangement on the ground that it might, possibly, lead to quarrels among the Afghan tribes. The timber had to be procured from India, instead. Hence more delay.

Then the original arrangement with the Engineer-in-Chief, that the work was to be carried out under the Military Department of the Indian Government, and that, in the interests of urgency, he should have a free hand, was changed into one which required that the work should be controlled by a new member of the Public Works Department, who, it is alleged, interfered with many of the working details which should have been left to an Engineer-in-Chief, and, by his " unskilled and unqualified control," caused still further delay, together with much expense and confusion. A good deal of time was lost, for instance, before Col. Browne could get even some indispensable instruments and survey appliances. Especially persistent, also, was Col. Browne's immediate superior in demanding from him " detailed estimates " which, on account of the uncertainties of the engineering work and of the other factors in the situation, it was impossible to prepare whilst the construction of the line was in progress.

Such, however, was the energy which had been shown, in spite of all these difficulties and drawbacks, that the work was completed within the two years and a half fixed by the Engineer-in-Chief at the start as the period in which—" with money freely granted "—it could be done. On March 27, 1887, an engine ran over the line all the way from Sibi to Quetta, and the Hurnai Railway was formally declared open for traffic.

In the meantime the apparent certainty of war with Russia, following, especially, on her seizure of Penj-deh, had led, in April, 1885, to an order being given for the construction of a light railway from Sibi through the Bolan Pass to Quetta, as an alternative, more direct and more quickly constructed route, of which use could be made for a movement of troops to the frontier on the anticipated partial mobilisation of the Indian Army.

The laying of this light railway constituted another notable engineering achievement.

Running through the heart of what has been described as "some of the boldest mountain scenery in India," the Bolan Pass has a length of about sixty miles and a breadth ranging from one mile to a space, in places, of only about twenty yards between the rugged mountain walls which here convert the pass into a mere defile. The pass is, in fact, practically the bed of the Bolan River, and is dry for the greater part of the year, but liable to floods. The temporary narrow-gauge line was to be laid along the river bed without interfering with the military road constructed in 1882–84 as far as Quetta.

For the first forty miles there was a fairly good gradient; but beyond that came a very heavy rise to the top of the pass; and here, at least, anything more than a metre-gauge line would have been impracticable. The possibility of constructing a line of railway through the pass at all had long been the despair of engineers, and this was the reason why the Hurnai route had been decided on in preference to the Bolan for the broad-gauge line to Quetta. Unfortunately, too, the climatic were even greater than the engineering difficulties. The heat in the lower parts of the pass was "beyond all description," and cholera or other diseases carried off thousands of the workers.

With these two lines at their disposal, the Government were, in the spring of 1887, quite prepared for a concentration of British and Indian forces in Afghanistan, had the political condition rendered such a course necessary; but the situation had by then greatly improved, thanks to the negotiations which had been proceeding with Russia for the demarcation of frontiers. In April, 1877, the British and Russian commissioners met at St. Petersburg, and, as the result of still further negotiations, the questions at issue were settled without the appeal to arms which had at one time appeared inevitable.

In 1892 some fifty miles of the Bolan light railway were abandoned in favour of another route which, avoiding the first part of the pass, allowed of a broad-gauge line being laid from Sibi through Quetta to Bostan Junction, where it connects with what is now known as the Hurnai-Pishin Loop. A branch ninety miles in length, from Quetta to Mushki, on the Seistan trade route, was opened in 1905.

To-day the Sind-Pishin railway, with its two sections, via the Bolan and the Hurnai respectively, has its terminus at New Chaman, on the actual frontier of Afghanistan, and within seventy miles of Kandahar. A broad-gauge line throughout, it forms part of the railway system of India, linking up at Ruk junction with the line running thence along the north bank of the Indus to Karachi, and, by means of a bridge across the Indus, with a line on the south of the river which, in one direction provides an alternative route to Karachi, and in the other connects with Calcutta and other leading cities. The Sind-Pishin line affords, in fact, a most valuable means for concentrating on the Afghan frontier, within a short distance of Kandahar, and in the shortest possible time a considerable body of troops collected from all parts of India, together with reinforcements from Europe, landed at Karachi. As a strategical line, therefore, the railway is of exceptional importance to India and to British interests in general; though there can be no suggestion that it would be used otherwise than for purely defensive purposes.

Then, in what, since 1901, has constituted the North-West Frontier Province of India, there has been a considerable extension of frontier railways in recent years,—all serving important strategical purposes. From Peshawar—1,520 miles from Calcutta—there is a broad-gauge extension, twelve miles in length, to Fort Jamrud, at the mouth of the Khyber Pass; from Naushahra, a cantonment twenty-seven miles due east of Peshawar, there is a narrow-gauge line to Dargai, at the foot of the Malakand Pass; while among other lines is one to Thal, a military outpost on the extreme limit of British territory which serves also as a depôt for the trade with Northern Afghanistan passing through the Kurram valley; and one to Banu, a garrison town, seventy-nine miles south of Kohat, built on a site chosen for political reasons by Sir Herbert Edwards in 1848.

A number of other railways on the north-west frontiers of India have been proposed. Whatever may or may not be ultimately done in regard to these further schemes, it is obvious that those already constructed have made an enormous difference in our strategical position in regard to Afghanistan and the lands beyond as compared with the military transport conditions of 1878.

APPENDIX.

THE DEFENCE OF AUSTRALIA

With a total area of 2,948,000 square miles, a population of less than four and a half million, and a coast line of 11,300 miles, the continent of Australia is peculiarly open to attack, and the possibilities of invasion, or of attempts at invasion, have not only been much discussed there of late years, but they have given rise to schemes of land defence in which the building of strategical railways and the adapting of existing lines to strategical purposes form important factors.

Under present conditions Western Australia and the Northern Territory are isolated from the remaining States of the Commonwealth so far as regards rail communication, and are at the mercy of any invader who might be able to land a force there unchallenged by the British Fleet.

Since the autumn of 1912, however, there has been under construction a railway which, starting from Kalgoorlie, the eastern terminus of the Western Australian system, will proceed in a direct line for 1,063 miles to Port Augusta, on the South Australian system, thus establishing through rail connection between Perth (Western Australia) and the farthest limit of the Queensland railway system, a total distance, that is, of about 4,000 miles. When this, the first of Australia's proposed transcontinental lines, is completed, it will be possible to send troops from the Central or the Eastern States to Western Australia, not only by rail, but by a railway laid so far inland that they will be safe from attack from the sea. There would thus be a reasonable certainty of the troops arriving at their destination; whereas if they had to go by water there might be the risk of the vessels in which they were making the journey being captured by the enemy. While, therefore, the Kalgoorlie-Port Augusta line is expected to serve other than purely strategical purposes, it is, in effect, the latter which claim first consideration.

Referring to the Northern Territory, in an article contributed by him to *The Empire Review* for May, 1910, Mr. F. A. W. Gisborne, an authority on Australian questions, wrote :—

> This vast region embraces 523,620 square miles of land, and lies close to Asia, the most populous of the continents. At present it contains, exclusive of the aborigines, barely one thousand white people and about twice as many Chinese. It lacks railway communication with the settled parts of Australia, and is completely isolated from them. Its magnificent harbour, accessible to the largest vessels afloat, and constituting the natural gateway to tropical Australia, lies, save for the British Fleet, absolutely defenceless. Behind it extend millions of acres of fertile plains never yet tilled, and never likely to be cultivated by white hands. Practically no industry

flourishes in a region which could support myriads of agriculturists and operatives.

That some of the peoples of crowded Asia may, sooner or later, seek a settlement for their surplus millions on what, for them, would be so desirable a land as the Northern Territory, with its magnificent opportunities for those capable of working in a tropical climate, is a contingency that has been fully realised in Australia, and the questions have arisen (1) as to whether the presence of a thousand whites in a region half a million square miles in extent constitutes such " effective occupation " thereof as gives them a right to its exclusive possession ; and (2) whether it would be possible either to prevent Asiatics from invading the Northern Territory, if they sought so to do, or to eject them therefrom if they did.

The latter question raises in an especially interesting form the problem as to the respective merits and possibilities of sea-power and rail-power.

Sea-power would, assuredly, have to be relied upon for safeguarding the Northern Territory against invasion, since it would be impossible for the Commonwealth Government to station troops at every prospective landing point along 1,200 miles of a tropical coast-line in sufficient force to keep off any invader who might appear there at some unexpected moment. For the checking, therefore, of such invasion, dependence would have to be placed on the power of the British Fleet (1) to stop the invader, (2) to cut off his connections if he should effect a landing, or (3) to carry war into the invader's own country.

Nor, if any large Asiatic settlement—as distinct from an " invasion " in the ordinary acceptation of that term—did take place in the Northern Territory under conditions that might not call for the intervention of the British Fleet, is it certain that the ejection of the settlers could be ensured with the help even of a trans-continental line of railway. Here the question is not that of the carrying power of a single line of railway. The examples offered by the War of Secession, the South African War and the Russo-Japanese War have well established the great advantages that even single lines, extending for great distances, can confer in the effecting of military transport. The considerations that would arise in Australia are, rather, (1) the fact that troops arriving at Pine Creek or Port Darwin from the south might have to make some very long and very trying marches across the 523,000 square miles comprising the Northern Territory before they reached the settlement of the Asiatics whom they were to eject, while they would be dependent for their supplies on a far-distant railway base ; and (2) the doubt as to whether Australia could spare a sufficiently large body of troops to undertake such an expedition, having regard to the defence requirements of her south-eastern States, the integrity of which would count as of more vital importance than an Asiatic settlement in her Far North. So there are those who think that if such a settlement were eventually effected in the Northern Territory, under conditions not constituting a *casus belli*, Australia would simply have to accept the situation, and reconcile herself to it as best she could.

All these things may seem to reflect on the precise value, from the rail-power point of view, of that direct communication which, more especially for strategical reasons, Australia has hoped eventually to obtain between north and south as well as between west and east. It is, nevertheless, desirable to see what has already been done in this direction.

The construction of a north-to-south trans-continental line, passing through the very centre of the Australian mainland, and linking up the Northern Territory with the southern and eastern States, has been under discussion for a period of about forty years. Progress seemed to be assured by the Acceptance Act of 1910, under which the Government of the Commonwealth, in taking over the Northern Territory from South Australia, agreed to build a trans-continental line connecting Oodnadatta, the northern terminus of the South Australian railway system, and 688 miles from Adelaide, with Pine Creek, the southern terminus of the Northern Territory system, and 145 miles distant from Port Darwin. This connecting link would have a length of 1,063 miles,—the same, by a singular coincidence, as that of the Kalgoorlie–Port Augusta line.

Since this "bargain" between the South Australia and the Commonwealth Governments was made, there have been many advocates of an alternative, or, otherwise, a supplementary route which, instead of going direct from South Australia to the Northern Territory, (passing through the central Australian desert,) would link up—on their west—with the railway systems of Victoria, New South Wales and Queensland, connections with the new line being made by these States where necessary. This "eastern deviation route" would, it is argued, offer a greater strategical advantage, as compared with the other route, because if troops had to be despatched to the north, they could more readily be supplied from Melbourne and Sydney—which, between them, contain over one-fourth of the entire population of Australia—than from Adelaide; while to send troops from Queensland, New South Wales and Victoria to South Australia in order that they might start on their journey to the Northern Territory from Oodnadatta, would involve a material delay under, possibly, urgent conditions. Thus it is estimated that if the eastern route were adopted, troops and travellers from Brisbane to Port Darwin would only travel about 2,234 miles as against 3,691

APPENDIX. 371

miles via Sydney, Melbourne, Adelaide and the central Australian route from Oodnadatta.

How these rival claims and contentions will be eventually settled remains to be seen ; but there has now been added to them a project for the building of other avowedly strategical lines, establishing a more direct connection between the Kalgoorlie-Port Augusta trans-continental line, when it is finished, and the capitals of Victoria, New South Wales and Queensland respectively, facilitating the mutual defence of the eastern, southern and western States in a time of crisis. This further scheme is, however, designed only to supplement the trans-continental lines already mentioned.

As regards the eastern States and the " central " State of South Australia, the question of an Asiatic invasion may be assumed not to arise. It has, however, long been regarded as possible that if Great Britain were at war with some non-Asiatic Power able to challenge her supremacy on the seas, the enemy might make an attack, not on the admittedly vulnerable Northern Territory—which he would not want either as a colony for Europeans or as a " jumping-off " place from which to conquer the remainder of Australia—but on some point along the coast-line of nearly 2,000 miles which, stretching from Rockhampton, in Queensland, to Adelaide, in South Australia, comprises (with a Hinterland of some 200 miles) the most populous, the most wealthy and (for non-Asiatics) the most desirable section of the whole Australian continent.

It is true that Germany—the Power which claims first attention from this point of view—has shown far greater desire to convert Africa into a German Empire than she has to effect the annexation of Australia. Yet that she has recognized the weakness of the Australian situation is suggested by the fact that, in dealing with the defensive power of the Commonwealth, Dr. Rohrbach, one of the exponents of German World-Policy, and author of " Deutschland unter den Weltvölkern," among other works, has declared that Australia could not resist if her four chief towns, all of them near the coast, were occupied by an invader.[1]

Which of these four towns, or which particular point along the said 2,000 miles of coast-line, an invader would select for his main attack—apart from feints elsewhere—must needs be uncertain ; but this very fact only adds to the imperative importance of those responsible for the defence of Australia being able to move troops freely, and within the shortest possible period, either from one State to another or from any place to another within one and the same State, as the defence conditions might require.

[1] See " The Origins of the War " ; by J. Holland Rose, Litt.D. Cambridge, 1914.

APPENDIX.

When we thus pass on to consider the question as to the use of existing lines of railway in Australia for strategical purposes, we find that the most noteworthy expression of opinion on this branch of the subject is contained in the following extract from the "Memorandum" which Lord Kitchener wrote in 1910, as the result of an investigation made by him, at the request of the Commonwealth Government, into the "Defence of Australia":—

Railway construction has, while developing the country, resulted in lines that would appear to be more favourable to an enemy invading Australia than to the defence of the country. Different gauges in most of the States isolate each system, and the want of systematic interior connection makes the present lines running inland of little use for defence, although possibly of considerable value to an enemy who would have temporary command of the sea.

The "different gauges" undoubtedly constitute one of the most serious shortcomings of the existing railways in Australia in regard to those military movements with which we are here alone concerned.

Strategical considerations as applied to rail transport require, not only that troops shall be readily conveyed, when necessary, from one part of a country or one part of a continent to another, but that a mobilisation of the forces shall be followed by a mobilisation of railway rolling stock. Locomotives, carriages and trucks on lines which are not themselves likely to be wanted for military transport should be available for use on the lines that will be so wanted, in order that all the rolling stock of all the railways in all parts of the country or of the States concerned can, at a time of possibly the gravest emergency, be concentrated or employed on whatever lines, or in whatever direction, additional transport facilities may be needed.

The importance of this principle was first recognised by von Moltke ; but when the railways of Australia were originally planned, each State took a more or less parochial view of its own requirements, its own geographical conditions, or its own resources, and adopted the gauge which accorded best therewith, regardless of any future need for a co-ordinated system of rail-transport serving the requirements of the Australian continent as a whole.

So we find that the 3 ft. 6 in. gauge has been adopted in Queensland, South Australia (with a further 600 miles of 5 ft. 3 in. gauge), Western Australia, and the Northern Territory ; the 4 ft. 8½ in. gauge (the standard gauge in Great Britain and, also, of over 65 per cent. of the world's railway mileage,) in New South Wales ; and the 5 ft. 3 in. gauge in Victoria. This means, in most cases, that when the frontier of a State is reached, passen-

APPENDIX. 373

gers, mails, baggage and merchandise must change or be transferred from the trains on the one system to those of the other.

Assuming that the west-to-east trans-continental railway (which is being built with the 4 ft. 8½ in. gauge) were now available for use, a traveller by it from Perth, Western Australia, through South Australia, Victoria, New South Wales, and Queensland would require, on account of the differences in gauge, to change trains at least five times. This may be regarded as an extreme case ; but the evils of the existing conditions are presented to us in a concrete form by an estimate which the Defence Department of the Commonwealth recently made as to the time it would take to move a force of 30,000 mounted troops from Melbourne to Brisbane. It was shown that, with the present break of gauge, this operation would occupy no less a time than sixty-three days ; whereas if there were no break of gauge twenty-three days would suffice. Thus the differences of gauge would mean a loss of forty days in effecting transfers at the frontier. In this time much might happen if the enemy had obtained temporary control of the sea. Under these conditions, in fact, he would be able to move his own forces by sea for the still longer distance from Adelaide to Brisbane in five days. Brisbane might thus be captured by the enemy while the reinforcements it wanted were still changing trains at the State boundaries.

It may be of interest here to recall the fact that at one time there were still greater differences of gauge on the railways in the United States ; that in 1885 the American railway companies resolved upon establishing uniformity as a means of overcoming the great inconveniences due to these conditions ; and that in 1886, after adequate preparation, the conversion of practically the entire system of railways in the United States to the 4 ft. 8½ in. gauge was effected in two days. Strategically, therefore, the United States Federal Government could now, not only send troops by rail from any one part of their vast territory to another, but utilise almost the whole of the available rolling stock for military purposes.[1]

Unification of gauge forms, however, a serious proposition for Australia on account of the prodigious outlay which, owing to the short-sighted policy of the past, it would now involve.[2]

The estimated cost of converting all the 4 ft. 8½ in. gauge in New South Wales and all the 3 ft. 6½ in. gauge in Queensland, South Australia, Western Australia and the Northern Territory

---

[1] In the *New York Sun* of June 18, 1911, there was published an article which had for its heading, "If Troops had to be Rushed, the Railroads in this Country could move 250,000 Men a Day."

[2] The mileage of lines open, under construction, or authorised, in the three gauges, is as follows :—5 ft. 3 in. gauge, 4,979 miles ; 4 ft. 8¼ in. gauge, 6,160 miles ; 3 ft. 6 in. gauge, 11,727 miles.

to the 5 ft. 3½ in. gauge of Victoria is no less than £51,659,000. To convert all the 3 ft. 6 in. and 5 ft. 3 in. railways to the 4 ft. 8½ in. gauge of the New South Wales lines would cost £37,164,000. To convert to the 4 ft. 8½ in. gauge all the trunk lines connecting the capitals—and this without shortening the present circuitous routes or modifying the heavy grades—would alone cost about £12,000,000.

In addition to this still undecided "battle of the gauges" there are in Australia other disadvantages, from a strategical standpoint, in the existing railway system, included therein being (1) an undue preponderance of single over double track, so that any exceptional amount of traffic causes a congestion which is likely only to be aggravated by new lines constructed, or extensions made, before the carrying capacity of the trunk lines has been increased; and (2) the building of lines which either lead nowhere or have been expressly stopped short of the boundaries of a State in order to retain, for the railways of that State, traffic from outlying districts which would pass, by a much shorter journey, to the port of a neighbouring State if, by means of through railway connexion, the residents in the districts concerned were free to avail themselves of their geographical advantage in respect to their nearness to such port.

In addition to the efforts she has already made, or is proposing to make, to effect such improvement both in her railway system and in her military transport facilities as may be practicable, Australia has sought to provide for that effective organisation without which, as experience elsewhere has fully shown, great and even disastrous confusion may arise at a critical moment owing to conflicts of authority and other troubles or difficulties in the working of such railways as may be utilised for military movements.

The action taken in this direction is based on a further recommendation made by Lord Kitchener, who, in the course of his Memorandum to the Commonwealth Government in 1910 said (paragraph 85):—

> Preparation for mobilisation is primarily the work of the General Staff, who recommend the lines to be followed and advise where, and in what quantities, the munitions of war of the various units should be stored. Concentration can only be satisfactorily effected when the railway and military authorities are in the closest touch, and work in absolute harmony. To secure this co-operation, I advise that a War Railway Council be formed, as is the case in the United Kingdom, composed of the Chief Railway Commissioner from each State, under the presidency of the Quartermaster-General of the Citizen Forces, and with an officer of the Headquarters Staff as secretary.

A War Railway Council for the Commonwealth was duly

APPENDIX. 375

constituted in 1911. The Council, which forms an adjunct of the Commonwealth Defence Department, consists of the Quartermaster-General, (president,) the senior officer of the Engineer and Railway Staff Corps also created for the railway system alike of the Commonwealth and of each State (such senior officer being the Chief or the Deputy Commissioner of Railways); the Consulting Military Engineer of the Commonwealth, and two representatives of the naval and military forces, with a military officer as secretary. The duties of the Council in time of peace are, generally, to furnish advice to the Minister of Defence on railway matters, and, particularly (*a*) to determine the method of supplying information to, and obtaining it from, the different railway departments; (*b*) to suggest regulations and instructions for carrying out movement of troops; (*c*) to suggest the method of organising railway staff officers in time of war to act as intermediaries between the various railway authorities and the troops; (*d*) to consider the question of extra sidings, loading platforms, etc.; and proposals for unification of gauges; and (*e*) to suggest the organisation and system of training of railway troops. In time of war the Council further advises the Minister of defence on questions of mobilisation. The organisation for military rail-transport in the several States follows on the lines of the system already adopted in the United Kingdom, as laid down in the Field Service Regulations.

BIBLIOGRAPHY

THE following list of books, pamphlets and articles bearing on the evolution and the development of rail-power down'to the outbreak of the Great War in 1914—this alone being the purpose and the scope of the present work—was originally based on selections from a "List of References on the Use of Railroads in War" prepared by the Bureau of Railway Economics, Washington, D.C., U.S.A., and including items from all the leading libraries of the United States (Library of Congress; the libraries of the principal Universities, Colleges and learned or technical societies; State libraries, public libraries, private railway-libraries, and the library of the Bureau itself), together with various foreign libraries, such as those of the Minister of Public Works in Berlin, the International Railway Congress at Berne, and others besides.

Much valuable help has been derived from the American list; but a large number of its references, and especially those relating to the World-War itself, have not here been reproduced, while so many additions have been gathered in from other sources among which might be mentioned the published catalogue of the War Office Library; the libraries of the British Museum, the Royal Colonial Institute, and the Patent Office; the *Journal* of the Royal United Service Institution, the publications of the Royal Engineers' Institute, and official or other publications in Great Britain, France, etc.), that the Bibliography here presented may, perhaps, be regarded as practically a new compilation, supplementing the excellent purpose which the list of the American Bureau of Railway Economics will undoubtedly serve.

EARLIEST REFERENCES (1833-50).

HARKORT, FRIEDRICH WILHELM. Die Eisenbahn von Minden nach Köln. Hagen, 1833.

[The earliest published work in which the importance and the possibilities of railways from a military standpoint were advocated.]

Ueber die militärische Benutzung der Eisenbahnen. Berlin, 1836.

Darlegung der technischen und Verkehrs-Verhältnisse der Eisenbahnen, nebst darauf gegründeter Erörerung über die militärische Benutzung derselben. Berlin, 1841.

"Pz." (CARL EDUARD POENITZ). Die Eisenbahn als militärische Operationslinien betrachtet und durch Beispiele erläutet. Nebst Entwurf zu einem militärischen Eisenbahnsystem für Deutschland. Adorf [Saxony], 1842.

—— II Aufl. Adorf, 1853.

Essai sur les Chemins de Fer, considérés comme lignes d'opérations militaires. Traduit de l'allemand par L. A. Unger. Paris, 1844.

[A French translation of the above-mentioned work by Poenitz, with an introduction by the translator and a map of Germany and Austria showing railways existing in 1842 and the " system " projected by the German writer.]

Uebersicht des Verkehrs und der Betriebsmittel auf den inländischen und den benachbarten ausländischen Eisenbahnen für militärischen Zwecke ; nach den beim grossen Generalstabe vorhandenen Materialen zusammengestellt. Berlin, 1848-50.

HOFFMANN, C. Amtlich erlassene Vorschriften über Anlage und Betrieb der Eisenbahnen in Preussen. Berlin, 1849.

WARS AND EXPEDITIONS

CRIMEAN WAR (1854-55)

HAMLEY, GEN. SIR EDWARD. The War in the Crimea. London, 1891.

LUARD, R.E., CAPT. C. E. Field Railways and their general application in war. *Journal of the Royal United Service Institution*, Vol. XVII, 1873.

[Refers to military railway built for use in the Crimea.]

ITALIAN WAR (1859)

BARTHOLONY, F. Notice sur les Transports par les Chemins de Fer français vers le théâtre de la guerre d'Italie. 71 pp. Paris, 1859.

—— MILLAR, R.A., MAJOR, Topographical Staff. The Italian Campaign of 1859. *Journal of the Royal United Service Institution*, Vol. V, pp. 269-308. London, 1861.

[Introductory reference to use of railways.]

AMERICAN CIVIL WAR (1861-65)

Abhandlung über die Thätigkeit der amerikanischen Feldeisenbahn-Abtheilungen der Nordstaaten ; bei den Directionen der Staatseisenbahnen. Durch das Königl. Ministerium in Circulation gesetzt. Berlin.

BACON, E. L. How railroads helped save the Union. *Railroadman's Magazine*, July, 1909.
HAUPT, HERMAN. Reminiscences of General Herman Haupt, Chief of the Bureau of United States Military Railroads in the Civil War. 321 pp. Illustrations. Milwaukee, Wis., 1901.
HENDERSON, LIEUT.-COL. G. F. R. Stonewall Jackson and the American Civil War. Second edition. Two vols. London, 1899.
PORTER, W. E. Keeping the Baltimore and Ohio in Repair in War Time was a Task for Hercules. *Book of the Royal Blue*, June, 1907.
United States Military Railroads. Report of Brev.-Brig.-Gen. D. C. McCallum, Director and General Manager, from 1861 to 1866. Executive Documents, 39th Congress, 1st Session. House. Serial number, 1251. Washington, 1866.
VIGO-ROUISSILLON, F. P. Puissance Militaire des États-Unis d'Amerique, d'après la Guerre de la Sécession, 1861–65. III⁰ Partie ; chap. viii, Transports généraux. Paris, 1866.

AUSTRO-PRUSSIAN CAMPAIGN (1866)

COOKE, R.E., LIEUT.-COL. A. C. C. Short Sketch of the Campaign in Austria of 1866. 70 pp. Map. London, 1867.
—— WEBBER, R.E., CAPT. Notes on the Campaign in Bohemia in 1886. Papers of the Corps of the Royal Engineers, N.S., Vol. XVI. Woolwich, 1868.

ABYSSINIAN EXPEDITION (1867–68)

WILLANS, R.E., LIEUT. The Abyssinian Railway. Papers on Subjects Connected with the Duties of the Corps of Royal Engineers. N.S. Vol. XVIII. Woolwich, 1870.

FRANCO-PRUSSIAN WAR (1870–71)

BUDDE, LIEUT. H. Die Französischen Eisenbahnen im Kriege 1870–71 und ihre seitherige Entwicklung in militärische Hinsicht. Mit zwei Karten und zehn Skizzen im Texte. 99 pp. Berlin, 1877.
[Gives maps of the French railway system in 1870 and 1877 respectively.]
—— Die französischen Eisenbahnen im deutschen Kriegsbetriebe, 1870–71. 487 pp. Berlin, 1904.
ERNOUF, LE BARON. Histoire des Chemins de Fer français pendant la Guerre Franco-Prussienne. Paris, 1874.
JACQMIN, F., Ingénieur en Chef des Ponts et Chaussées. Les Chemins de Fer pendant la Guerre de 1870–71. 351 pp. Paris, 1872.
—— 2ᵉ edition. 363 pp. 1874.

MÜLLER-BRESLAU, F. Die Tätigkeit unserer Feldeisenbahn-Abteilung im Kriege 1870-71. Berlin, 1896.
Railway Organisation in the late War. *Edinburgh Review*, January, 1872.

RUSSO-TURKISH WAR (1877-78)

LESSAR, P. De la construction des Chemins de Fer en temps de guerre. Lignes construites par l'armée russe pendant la campagne 1877-78. Traduit du russe par L. Avril. 142 pp. 10 Planches. Paris, 1879.
SALE, R.E., CAPT. M. T. The Construction of Military Railways during the Russo-Turkish War of 1877-78. *Journal of the Royal United Service Institution*, Vol. XXIV. 1880.

EGYPT AND THE SUDAN (1882-99)

History of the Corps of the Royal Engineers. Vol. II. By Maj.-Gen. Whitworth Porter, R.E. The War in Egypt, 1882-85, pp. 64-87. London, 1889.
—— Vol. III. By Col. Sir Chas. M. Watson. The Sudan Campaigns, 1885-99, pp. 53-76. Royal Engineers' Institute, Chatham, 1915.
Military History of the Campaign of 1882 in Egypt. Prepared in the Intelligence Branch of the War Office. Revised edition. London, 1908.
NATHAN, R.E., LIEUT. M. The Sudan Military Railway. Professional Papers of the Corps of Royal Engineers. Occasional Papers, Vol. XI. 1885.
WALLACE, R.E., MAJ. W. A. J. Railway Operations in Egypt during August and September, 1882. Professional Papers of the Corps of Royal Engineers, Chatham. Occasional Papers, Vol. IX.

PHILIPPINE WAR (1898)

COLSON, L. W. Railroading in the Philippine War. *Baltimore and Ohio Employés' Magazine*, Feb., 1913.
Soldiers Running a Railroad. *Railroad Telegrapher*, Sept., 1899.
[Tells how the 20th Kansas Regiment ran four miles of the Manila and Dagupan Railroad during the Philippine insurrection.]

SOUTH AFRICAN WAR (1899-1902)

Detailed History of the Railways in the South African War, 1899-1902. Two vols. Royal Engineers' Institute, Chatham, 1905.
Vol. I.—Organisation, Military Control, Working and Repair of Cape and Natal Government Railways; Management, Engineering and other Departments of Imperial

Military Railways; Railway Pioneer Regiment; Organisation, Equipment and Use of Armoured Trains; Army Labour Depôts. Vol. II.—61 Photographs and 93 Drawings.

GIROUARD, R.E., LIEUT.-COL. E. P. C., Director of Railways, South African Field Force. History of the Railways during the War in South Africa, 1899-1902. 149 pp. Maps. London, 1903.

HARRISON, C. W. FRANCIS. Natal: an Illustrated Official Railway Guide and Handbook. Published by Authority. London, 1903.
[Gives a statement, on pp. 287-290, as to services rendered by Natal Government Railways during South African War.]

History of the War in South Africa, 1899-1902. Compiled by the Direction of His Majesty's Government. Vol. IV, Appendix 10, Notes on the Military Railway System in South Africa. London, 1910.

Netherlands South African Railway Company and the Transvaal War. Account by the Secretary, Th. Steinnetz, dated Pretoria, April, 1900. *De Ingenieur*, July 14 and 21, 1900. English translation in *Journal of the Royal United Service Institution*, Jan., 1902.

The Times History of the War in South Africa, 1899-1902. Vol. VI, Part II, chap. iii, The Railway Work in the War, pp. 297-331. London, 1909.

WATSON, COL. SIR CHAS. M. History of the Corps of the Royal Engineers. Vol. III, chap. iv, The South African War, 1899-1902. Royal Engineers' Institute, Chatham, 1915.

Working of Railways: Duties of Staff Officers. Pamphlet. Published by authority. Pretoria, 1900.

RUSSO-JAPANESE WAR (1904-5)

KUROPATKIN, GENERAL A. N. The Russian Army and the Japanese War. Translated by Captain A. B. Lindsay. Two vols. Maps, Illustrations. London, 1909.

MÉTIN, ALBERT. Le Transsibérien et la Guerre. *Revue Économique Internationale*, Oct., 1904.

Official History of the Russo-Japanese War. Prepared by the Historical Section of the Committee of Imperial Defence. London, 1910.

" P., A." Construction et Exploitation de Chemins de Fer à Traction animale sur le Théâtre de la Guerre de 1904-5 en Mandchourie. *Revue du Génie Militaire*, Avril, Mai, Juin, 1909. Paris.

Russo-Japanese War. Reports from British Officers attached to the Japanese and Russian Forces in the Field. Vol. III.

BIBLIOGRAPHY. 381

General Report (dated March, 1905) by Col. W. H. H. Waters: Section XXXVIII, " Railways," pp. 184-9. London, 1908.
Russo-Japanese War. The Ya-Lu. Prepared in the Historical Section of the German General Staff. Authorised Translation by Karl von Donat. Chaps. ii and iii. London, 1908.
VICKERS, R.E., CAPT. C. E. The Siberian Railway in War. *Royal Engineers' Journal*, Aug., 1905. Chatham.

MEXICAN WAR (1910-13)

HINE, MAJ. CHARLES. War Time Railroading in Mexico. Paper read before the St. Louis Railway Club, Oct. 10, 1913. The Railway Library, 1913. Chicago.
WEEKS, G. E. How Mexican Rebels Destroy Railways and Bridges. *Scientific American*, Sept. 13, 1913.

COUNTRIES

AUSTRALIA.

ELLISON, H. K. Australia's Trans-Continental Railway. *Journal of the Royal United Service Institution*, June, 1912.
KITCHENER OF KHARTOUM, FIELD MARSHAL VISCOUNT. Memorandum on the Defence of Australia. Government of the Commonwealth of Australia, 1910.
Proceedings of the War Railway Council. (1) First and Second Meetings, Feb. 14-16, 1911, and May 19, 1911. (2) Fifth Meeting, Nov. 18 and 19, 1914. Government of the Commonwealth of Australia.

AUSTRIA-HUNGARY

Geschichte der Eisenbahnen der österreichisch-ungarischen Monarchie. Unsere Eisenbahnen im Kriege. Eisenbahnbureau des K. u. K. General-Stabes. Wien, 1898-1908.
HARE, R.E., CAPT. W. A. Organisation of the Austrian Railway and Telegraph Corps. *Journal of the Royal United Service Institution*. Vol. XXIX, pp. 257-79. London, 1885-6.
JESSEP, R.E., LIEUT. H. L. Railway Works in Connection with an Army in the Field; forming the Second Division of the Austrian Guide to Railways. Vienna, 1872 (Translation). Professional Papers of the Royal Engineers. Chatham. Vol. O.II.
JOESTEN, JOSEF. Studien über die heutigen Eisenbahnen im Kriegsfalle. Wien, 1892.
Leitfaden des Eisenbahnwesens, mit besonderer Rücksicht auf den Dienst der Feldeisenbahn-abteilungen. 2 Bände. Wien, 1872.

BIBLIOGRAPHY.

NOSINICH, MAJ. Das österreichisch-ungarische Eisenbahn- und übrige Communications-System. Politisch-militärisch- beleuchtet. 77 pp. Wien, 1871.
OBAUER, H., UND E. R. VON GUTTENBERG. Das Train-Com- munications und Verpflegungswesen, vom operativen Stand- punkte. Wien, 1871.
PANZ, OBERST V. v. Das Eisenbahnwesen, vom militärischen Standpunkte. Two vols. Plates. Wien, 1863.
—— Les Chemins de Fer au point de vue militaire. Traduit de l'Allemand par Costa de Serda. Paris, 1868.
Technischer Unterricht für die K. u. K. Eisenbahn-Truppe. Theil 3 : Strassen, Eisenbahn- und Wasserbau. Theil 7 : Feldmässige Zerstörung von Brücken und Viaducten. Wien, 1898.
TLASKAL, MAJ. L. Uebersichtliche Zusammenstellung der Grundsätze und der wesentlichen Details aus dem Strassen- u. Eisenbahn-Baue, mit Berücksichtigung der Zerstörung und der feldmässigen Wiederherstellung von Eisenbahnen. 90 pp. Plates. Wien, 1877.
ZANANTONI, OBERSTLT. E. Die Eisenbahnen im Dienste des Krieges, und moderne Gesichtspunkte für deren Ausnützung. 33 pp. Wien, 1904.
[See Railways in War and Modern Views as to their Em- ployment. *Royal Engineers' Journal*, March, 1907.]

BELGIUM

BODY, M. Aide-mémoire portatif de campagne pour l'emploi des Chemins de Fer en temps de guerre. 253 pp. Plates. Liége, 1877.
—— Les Chemins de Fer dans leurs Applications militaires. Liége, 1867.
—— Notice sur l'attaque et la defense des Chemins de Fer en temps de guerre. Liége, 1868.
FORMANOIR, A. DE, Capitaine d'État-Major. Des Chemins de Fer en temps de guerre. Conférences Militaires Belges. Bruxelles, 1870.
GRANDVALLET, ANTONIN. La neutralité de la Belgique et les Chemins de Fer français, belges et allemands. 11 pp. Paris, 1889.

FRANCE

ALLIX, G. La Mobilisation des Chemins de Fer français. *Le Journal des Transports*, Jan. 30, 1915. Paris.
BERGÈRE, CAPITAINE C. Les Chemins de Fer et le Service des Étapes, d'après les nouveaux règlements. *Journal des Sciences Militaires*. Neuvième série. Tome vingt- quatrième. Paris, 1886.

BIBLIOGRAPHY.

BRESSON, L. Réorganisation militaire. . . . Chemins de Fer. 50 pp. Paris, 1881.
DANY, JEAN. Le Rôle des Chemins de Fer à la Guerre. *Revue de Paris*, Sept. 15, 1911.
De l'Utilisation des Chemins de Fer dans la prochaine Guerre. Paris, 1899.
EUGÈNE, J. B., Capitaine du Génie. Études sur les Chemins de Fer et les Télegraphes Électriques, considérés au point de vue de la défense du territoire. 2e. édition. Two vols. Paris, 1879.
"G., A." A propos des Réseaux ferrés de la France et de l'Allemagne. 30 pp. Paris, 1884.
GRANDVALLET, ANTONIN. Les Chemins de Fer français au point de vue de la Guerre. 85 pp. Map. Paris, 1889.
JACQMIN, F. Étude sur l'exploitation des Chemins de Fer par l'État. 104 pp. Paris, 1878.
LANOIR, PAUL. Les Chemins de Fer et la Mobilisation. 170 pp. Paris, 1894.
LANTY ——. Exploitation militaire des Chemins de Fer, Opérations executées par le 5e Régiment du Génie à l'occasion des grandes manœuvres de Beance. *Revue de Génie Militaire.* Vol. XX, pp. 345–83. Paris, 1900.
LAPLAICE, A. Notions sur les Chemins de Fer, à l'usage des officiers et sous-officiers de toutes armes. Paris, 1887.
LEROY, A. Cours Pratique de Chemins de Fer, à l'usage de MM. les officiers et sous-officiers de toutes armes, des sections techniques, des ouvriers du génie et des écoles spéciales. 478 pp. Plates and Illustrations. Dijon, 1881.
MARCILLE, CAPT. E. Étude sur l'emploi des Chemins de Fer avant et pendant la guerre. 96 pp. Paris, 1874.
PARTIOT, L. Transport d'un Torpilleur effectué de Toulon à Cherbourg par les Chemins de Fer. Paris, 1891.
PERMEZEL, H. Du Régime des Chemins de Fer en temps de guerre. Paris, 1904.
PERNOT, CAPT. A. Aperçu historique sur le service des transports militaires. Pp. 492. Paris, 1894.
PICARD, ALFRED. Traité des Chemins de Fer. Vol. IV, Part IV, chap. iv, Transports militaires par chemins de fer. Paris, 1887.
PIERRON, GÉN. Les Méthodes de Guerre, etc. Tome I, Part III (Chemins de Fer). Maps and plans. Paris, 1893.
ROVEL, CHEF D'ESCAD. J. J. Manuel des Chemins de Fer, à l'usage des officiers. 122 pp. Plates. Paris, 1882.
WIBROTTE, LIEUT. Construction et destruction des Chemins de Fer en campagne. 2e. edition. 40 pp. Plates. Paris, 1874.
VIGO-ROUISSILLON, F. P. Des Principes de l'Administration des Armées. Paris, 1871.

BIBLIOGRAPHY.

Official Publications

Instruction Speciale pour le Transport des Troupes d'Infanterie et du Génie par des voies ferrées. 6ᵉ édition. Paris, 1899.

Organisation Générale aux Armées. I. Services de l'arrière aux armées. Volume arrêté à la date du 8 Decembre, 1913. 171 pp.

—— II. Transports stratégiques. Tirage Novembre, 1914. 291 pp.

Organisation Générale du Service Militaire des Chemins de Fer. Volume arrêté au 15 Juillet, 1904. 20 pp.

—— Supplement, 31 Décembre, 1912. 8 pp.

Règlements et instructions sur le transport des troupes. Edition annotée . . . jusqu'en Août, 1913. 362 pp.

Reglement Général de 1ʳᵉ Juillet, 1874, pour les transports militaires par chemins de fer. Paris, 1874.

Sections de Chemin de Fer de campagne. Volume arrêté à la date du Sept., 1914. 92 pp.

Transports militaires par Chemin de Fer (Guerre et Marine). Édition mise à jour des textes en vigueur jusqu'en Octobre, 1902. 712 pp. Paris.

Transports ordinaires du matériel de la guerre. 15 Juin, 1912. 270 pp.

Troupes des Chemins de Fer. Volume arrêté à la date du 1er. Décembre, 1912. 106 pp.

GERMANY

A., H. VON. Ueber die militärischen und technischen Grundlagen der Truppentransports auf Eisenbahnen. Darmstadt und Leipzig, 1861.

ALBERT ——. Die Anstellungen im Eisenbahn-Dienst. Handbuch für Unteroffiziere, welche sich dem Eisenbahnfach zu widmen beabsichtigen. 59 pp. Berlin, 1884.

ALLIX, G. L'Organisation Militaire des Chemins de Fer allemands. *Journal des Transports*, 13 Mars., 1915. Paris.

BAUER, HAUPT. Fuhrkolonne . . . und Feldbahn. 31 pp. Plates. Berlin, 1900.

BECK, C. H. Studien über das Etappenwesen. Nordlingen, 1872.

[A detailed account of the rail and road services organised under the Prussian Regulation of May 2, 1867.]

Le Service des Etapes in guerre. *Revue Militaire de l'Etranger.* 1er. Mai, 1872.

[A digest of the facts recorded by C. H. Beck.]

BECKER, LIEUT. Der nächste Krieg und die deutschen Bahnverwaltungen. 62 pp. Hannover, 1893.

Bedeutung der Eisenbahnen für den Krieg. *Jahrbuch für die deutsche Armee und Marine.* Berlin, 1898.

Die Thätigkeit der deutschen Eisenbahntruppen in China, 1900-1. *Annalen für Gewerbe und Bauwesen*, April 15, 1902.

Eisenbahnen im Kriege, Die. *Zeitung des Vereins*, Oct. 18, 1899.

Erste Benutzung der Eisenbahn für Kriegszwecke. *Zeitung des Vereins*, Sept. 2, 1914.

"Ferrarius, Miles" (Dr. jur. Joesten). Die Eisenbahn und die Kriegführung: Eine politisch-militärische Studie. Deutsche Zeit- und Streit Fragen. Heft 66. 30 pp. Hamburg, 1890.

GIESE, OBERST O. v. Provisorische Befestigungen und Festungs-Eisenbahnen. 96 pp. Plans. Berlin, 1882.

JOESTEN, JOSEF. Geschichte und System der Eisenbahnbenutzung im Kriege. Leipzig, 1896.

—— Histoire et Organisation militaires des Chemins de Fer. Traduit de l'allemand par le Lieut.-Colonel B. . . . 226 pp. Paris, 1905.

LANOIR, PAUL. The German Spy System in France. Translated from the French by an English Officer. Pp. viii, 264. London, 1910.

[Chapters on "Designs on French Railways" and "German Strategic Railways."]

SCHAEFFER, EDUARD. Der Kriegs-Train des deutschen Heeres. Berlin, 1883.

SCHMIEDECKE, OBERST. Die Verkehrsmittel im Kriege. (Die Eisenbahnen: die Feld- und Förderbahnen.) Maps and plates. 242 pp. Berlin, 1906.

—— 2te. Auflage. 1911.

STAVENHAGEN, HAUPT. W. Verkehrs- und Nachrichten-Mittel in militärischer Beleuchtung. (Eisenbahnen.) Berlin, 1896.

—— 2te. Auflage, 1905.

W. [WESTPHALEN], HAUPT. H. L. Die Kriegführung, unter Benutzung der Eisenbahnen, und der Kampf um Eisenbahnen. Nach den Erfahrungen des letzen Jahrzents. 290 pp. Leipzig, 1868.

—— II Auflage. Neu bearbeitet von einem deutschen Stabsoffizier. Leipzig, 1882.

De l'emploi des chemins de fer en temps de guerre. Traduit de l'allemand. 241 pp. Paris, 1869.

[A French translation of the 1st edition of Westphalen's work.]

WEBER, BARON M. M. VON. Die Schulung der Eisenbahnen für den Krieg im Frieden. (1870.) Translated into English, under the title of Our Railway System viewed in Reference to Invasion, with Introduction and Notes, by Robert Mallet, M.I.C.E., F.R.S. London, 1871.

WEHBERG, H. Die rechtliche Stellung der Eisenbahnen im Kriege, nach den Beschlüssen der zweiten Haager Friedens-Konferenz. *Archiv für Eisenbahnwesen*, Mai-Juni, 1910. Berlin.

WERNEKKE, REGIERUNGSRAT. Die Mitwirkung der Eisenbahnen an den Kriegen in Mitteleuropa. *Archiv für Eisenbahnwesen*, Juli und August, 1912.

Designs on Africa

BOULGER, DEMETRIUS C. German Designs on the Congo. *Fortnightly Review*, Sept., 1914.
[Republished in England's Arch-Enemy : A Collection of Essays forming an Indictment of German Policy during the last Sixteen Years, by D. C. Boulger. London, 1914.]

BRYDEN, H. A. The Conquest of German South-West Africa. *Fortnightly Review*, July, 1915. London.

CRABTREE, THE REV. W. A. German Colonies in Africa. *Journal of the African Society*, Oct., 1914. London.

LEWIN, EVANS. The Germans and Africa. 317 pp. Map. London, 1915.

MARTIN, CAMILLE. Le Chemin de Fer du Tanganyika et les progrès de l'Afrique orientale allemande. Renseignments coloniaux, No. 3. Supplement à *L'Afrique Française* de Mars, 1914. Paris.

Memorandum on the Country known as German South-West Africa. Section on Railways, pp. 83–88. Pretoria, Government Printing Office, 1915.

O'CONNOR, J. K. The Hun in our Hinterland ; or the Menace of German South-West Africa. 43 pp. Map. Cape Town, 1914.
[Gives details concerning strategical railways in German South-West Africa.]

RENÉ, CARL, Director des Kamerun-Eisenbahn Syndikats. Kamerun und die Deutsche Tsâdsee-Eisenbahn. 251 pp. Mit 37 Textbildern und 22 Tafeln. Berlin, 1905.

South-West African Notes. Republished from the Transvaal Chronicle. *South Africa*, Nov. 14 and Dec. 5, 1914. London.

ZIMMERMANN, EMIL. Neu-Kamerun. Zweiter Teil: Neu Kamerun und das Kongosystem. Deutschland und Zentralafrika. 135 pp. Map. Berlin, 1913.

—— Was ist uns Zentralafrika ? Wirtschafts- und verkehrspolitische Untersuchungen. 57 pp. Maps. Berlin, 1914.

Destruction and Restoration of Railways

Anleitung zur Unterbrechung von Eisenbahnverbindungen,

BIBLIOGRAPHY. 387

resp. Zerstörung, etc., sowie zur Wiederherstellung. Berlin, 1861.

BASSON, WILHELM. Die Eisenbahnen im Kriege, nach den Erfahrungen des letzten Feldzuges. 72 pp. Ratibor, 1867. [A work dealing with the technicalities of railway destruction, restoration and operation on (a) national and (b) occupied territory.]

TAUBERT ——. Zerstörung, Wiederherstellung und Neubau von Vollbahnen und deren Kunstbauten in Feindesland. Leipzig, 1896.

Verhandlungen des Kriegs- und Handelsministeriums über zerstörungen von Eisenbahnen und die Entstehung der Allerhöchsten Instructionen vom Jahre 1859 und vom 31 Juli, 1861. Ungedrucktes Actenstück. Berlin.

Germany and the Baghdad Railway

CHÉRADAME, ANDRÉ. La Question d'Orient. Le Chemin de Fer de Bagdad. Cartes. 397 pp. Paris, 1903.

HAMILTON, ANGUS. Problems of the Middle East, Great Britain, Germany and the Baghdad Railway. Pp. 156–86. London, 1909.

LYNCH, H. F. B. Railways in the Middle East. *Asiatic Quarterly Review*, April, 1911.

—— The Baghdad Railway. *Fortnightly Review*, March, 1911.

—— The Baghdad Railway: Four New Conventions. *Fortnightly Review*, May, 1911.

MAHAN, CAPT. A. T. Retrospect and Prospect. VI: The Persian Gulf and International Relations. Pp. 209–51. London, 1902.

ROHRBACH, DR. PAUL. Die Bagdadbahn. 2. Auflage. 86 pp. Map. Berlin, 1911.

SAROLEA, CHARLES. The Anglo-German Problem. The Baghdad Railway and German Expansion in the Near East. Pp. 247–80. London, 1912.

SCHNEIDER, SIEGMUND. Die Deutsche Bagdadbahn und die projectirte Ueberbrückung des Bosporus, in ihrer Bedeutung für Weltwirthschaft und Weltverkehr. Wien und Leipzig, 1900.

SPRENGER, DR. A. Babylonien, das reichste Land in der Vorzeit und das lohnendste Kolonisationfeld für die Gegenwart. Ein Vorschlag zur Kolonisation des Orients. 128 pp. Map. Heidelburg, 1886.

The Times. Maps of the Baghdad Railway, showing lines open, under construction and projected. Dec. 1, 1914, and Nov. 1, 1915.

"X." The Focus of Asiatic Policy. *National Review*, June, 1901.

Official Publications

Die Verwaltung der öffentlichen Arbeiten in Preussen, 1900 bis 1910. Kartenbeilage I : Die Preussisch-Hessischen Staatseisenbahnen am 1 April, 1900, und Ende März, 1910. Berlin, 1911.

Organisation des Transports grosser Truppenmassen auf Eisenbahnen. Berlin, 1861.

Field Service Regulations (Fielddienst Ordnung, 1908) of the German Army. Translated by the General Staff, War Office. London, 1908.

Railway Troops

Armée allemande. Les troupes de Chemin de Fer. *Revue Militaire de l'Étranger.* Mai, 1898. Paris.

HILLE, MAJ., UND MEURIN, MAJ. Geschichte der preussischen Eisenbahntruppen. Teil I. Von 1859 bis zur Beendigung des deutsch-französischen Krieges. Maps, plans, plates and illustrations. Two vols. Berlin, 1910.

HILLE, MAJ. Geschichte der preussischen Eisenbahntruppen. Teil II, 1871–1911. Portraits, maps, plans, plates and illustrations. Berlin, 1913.

Les troupes allemandes de communications. *Revue Militaire,* Avril, 1900.

RAWSON, R.E., LIEUT. H. E. The German Railway Regiment. *Royal United Service Institution Journal,* Vol. XX, 1877.

—WEBBER, R.E., CAPT. The Field Army Department of the Prussian Army. See Notes on the Campaign in Bohemia in 1866, Papers of the Corps of the Royal Engineers, N.S., Vol. XVI, Woolwich, 1868.

Strategical Railways

LITTLEFIELD, WALTER. Hitherto Unpublished Pages in War's Prelude. Railway Cartography reveals Germany's elaborate Preparations. *New York Times,* Nov. 15, 1914.

NORTON, ROY. The Man of Peace. Oxford Pamphlets, 1914–15. 22 pp. Oxford University Press.

STUART-STEPHENS, MAJOR. How I Discovered the Date of the World War. *The English Review,* June, 1915.

[Deals with the German strategical railways on the Belgian frontier.]

" Y." Object Lesson in German Plans. *Fortnightly Review,* Feb., 1910. London.

—— A Further Object Lesson in German Plans. *Fortnightly Review,* Feb., 1914.

[These two articles were republished in England's

Arch-Enemy: A Collection of Essays forming an Indictment of German Policy during the last Sixteen Years By Demetrius C. Boulger. London, 1914.]
YOXALL, M.P., SIR JAMES. The Kaiser's Iron Web. *The Daily Graphic*, March 9, 1915.

Tactics and Strategy

BALCK, OBERST. Taktik, Band 4. Eisenbahnen, etc. Berlin, 1901.
—— 4te. Auflage, 1909.
Étude sur le Réseau ferré allemand au point de vue de la concentration. 32 pp. Avec une carte des chemins de fer allemands. Paris, 1890.
" FERRARIUS, MILES " (DR. JUR. JOESTEN). Die Anforderungen der Strategie und Taktik an die Eisenbahnen. 48 pp. Berlin, 1895.
GOLTZ, BARON COLMAR VON DER. Das Volk im Waffen. Ein Buch über Heereswesen und Kriegführung unserer Zeit. Berlin, 1883.
—— The Nation in Arms. Translated by Phillip A. Ashworth. New edition. Revised in accordance with the fifth German edition. London, 1906.
—— Kriegführung. Kurze Lehrer ihrer wichtigsten Grundsätze und Formen. Berlin, 1895.
—— The Conduct of War. A Short Treatise on its most important Branches and Guiding Rules. Translated by Major G. F. Leverson. Vol. IV of the Wolseley Series. London, 1899.
LASSMANN, LIEUT. J. C. Der Eisenbahnkrieg. Taktische Studie. 112 pp. Berlin, 1867.
VERDY DU VERNOIS, GEN. J. v. Studien über den Krieg. Theil III. Strategie. Heft 5. (Einfluss der Eisenbahnen operativer Linien auf die Kriegführung). Maps and plans. Berlin, 1906.

GREAT BRITAIN

BURGOYNE, F.R.S., SIR J. Railways in War. A paper read before the British Association at Birmingham. *The Engineer*, Sept. 22, 1865, p. 182. London.
BURNABY, CAPT. F. G. The Practical Instruction of Staff Officers in Foreign Armies. *Royal United Service Institution Journal*, Vol. XVI, pp. 633-44, 1873.
COLLINSON, GEN. T. B. Use of Railways in War. Extracted from three Royal Engineer Prize Essays for 1878 by Captains D. O'Brien and T. J. Willans and Lieut. W. H. Turton. 82 pp. Chatham.

FINDLAY, SIR GEORGE, Assoc. Inst. C.E., Lieut.-Colonel Engineer and Railway Volunteer Staff Corps. Paper on The Transport of Troops by Rail within the United Kingdom, read before the Royal United Service Institution, June 20, 1890, and forming chapter xxiii of Working and Management of an English Railway. London, 5th edition, 1894.
—— The Use of Railways in the United Kingdom for the Conveyance of Troops. *United Service Magazine*, April, 1892.
GIROUARD, 2ND LIEUT. E. P. C. The Use of Railways for Coast and Harbour Defence. *Royal United Service Institution Journal*, Vol. XXXV, 1891.
GIROUARD, R.E., BREV.-LIEUT.-COLONEL SIR E. PERCY C. Railways in War. A lecture delivered at the Royal Engineers' Institute, March 23, 1905. *Royal Engineers' Journal*, July, 1905. Chatham.
HOME, C.B., R.E., LIEUT.-COL. R. On the Organisation of the Communications of an Army, including Railways. *Royal United Service Institution Journal*, Vol. XIX, 1875.
HOPKINS, R.E., CAPT. L. E. Army Railway Organisation. *The Royal Engineers' Journal*, August, 1905. Chatham.
LUARD, R.E., CAPTAIN C. E. Field Railways and their General Application in War. *Royal United Service Institution Journal*, Vol. XVII, 1873.
MALLET, ROBERT, M.I.C.E., F.R.S. See under GERMANY: Weber, Baron M. M.
MAQUAY, R.E., COL. J. P. Railways for Military Communication in the Field. Professional Papers of the Royal Engineers, Chatham, Vol. VIII. 1882.
PHELP, S. M. The Use of our Railways in the Event of Invasion or of a European War. *The Railway Magazine*, May, 1901.
PORTER, R.E., MAJ.-GEN. WHITWORTH. History of the Corps of Royal Engineers. Two vols. London, 1889.
[Vol. III, by Col. Sir Chas. M. Watson, was issued by the Royal Engineers' Institute, Chatham, in 1915.]
PRYTHERCH, H. J. The Great Eastern Railway and the Army Manœuvres in East Anglia, 1912. *Great Eastern Railway Magazine*, Nov., 1912.
ROTHWELL, R.A., COL. J. S., The Conveyance of Troops by Railway. *United Service Magazine*, Dec., 1891, and Jan., 1892.
—— The Reconnaissance of a Railway. Its Utilisation and Destruction in Time of War. *Journal of the Royal United Service Institution*. Vol. XXXVI, pp. 369–89. London, 1892.

Strategical Importance of Railways, The. *The Engineer*, Feb. 16, 1900.
The Part Played by Railways in Modern Warfare. By " A.M.I.C.E." *Land and Water*, Jan. 30 and Feb. 6, 1915. London.
The Transport of an Army. *Great Western Railway Magazine*, Nov., 1909.
[An account of the work done by the Great Western Railway on the occasion of the Army Manœuvres of 1909.]
TOVEY, R.E., LIEUT.-COL. The Elements of Strategy. [1887.] Section on Railways, pp. 42-49. 2nd edition, edited by T. Miller Maguire. London, 1906.
TYLER, R.E., CAPT. H. W., Railway Inspector, Board of Trade. Railways Strategically Considered. *Journal of the Royal United Service Institution*. Vol. VIII, pp. 321-41. Maps. London, 1865.
WILLIAMS, J. A. Our Railway in Time of War. *North-Eastern Railway Magazine*, March, 1912.

Engineer and Railway Staff Corps

Army Book for the British Empire, The. London, 1893.
[References to " Railway Volunteer Staff Corps " on pp. 382 and 531.]
Engineer and Railway Staff Corps. *The Railway News*, Aug. 8, 1914.
JEUNE, C. H. The Engineer and Railway Staff Corps. *Great Eastern Railway Magazine*, July, 1911. London.
MCMURDO, C.B., MAJ.-GEN., Hon. Colonel, Engineer and Railway Staff Corps. Rifle Volunteers for Field Service ; a Letter to Commanding Officers of Rifle Corps. 27 pp. London, 1869.
MCMURDO, GEN. SIR W. M. Article on " Volunteers," Encyclopædia Britannica, 9th edition.
[For references to the " Engineer and Railway Transport Corps," see p. 295.]
WALTER, MAJ. JAMES, 4th Lancashire Artillery Volunteers. England's Naval and Military Weakness. The Volunteer Force. London, 1882.
[References to services rendered by the Engineer and Railway Volunteer Staff Corps in the Volunteer Reviews of 1881. See p. 305.]

Official Publications.

Army Service Corps Training. Part III, Transport. Section VI, Conveyance of War Department Stores. 1—Rail. Appendix III, Acts of Parliament relating to Transport Services. 1911.

BIBLIOGRAPHY.

Field Service Pocket Book. Section 30, Transport by Rail. General Staff, War Office. 1914.
Field Service Regulations. Part I, Operations. 1909. (Reprinted, with amendments, 1914.) Chap. iii, Movements by Rail, pp. 62-6. Part II, Organisation and Administration. 1909. (Reprinted, with amendments, 1913.) Chap. viii, Railway Transport, pp. 91-96. General Staff, War Office.
Instruction in Military Engineering. Part VI, Military Railways. War Office, 1898.
   [Embodies a portion of the course of instruction in railways at the School of Military Engineering, Chatham. Was first issued with Army Orders, dated March 1, 1889, as a Manual of Military Railways, 95 pp.]
Manual of Military Engineering. Chap. xvii : Hasty Demolition of Railways . . . without Explosives. Chap. xxiii : Railways. (Technical details concerning construction, repairs and reconstruction.) 144 pp. General Staff, War Office, 1905.
Manual of Military Law. War Office, 1914.
   [Includes a brief account of the relations of the State to the railways in regard to the conveyance of troops (see pp. 184-5), and gives text of various Parliamentary enactments relating thereto.]
Notes on Reconnaissance and Survey of Military Railways for Officers of R.E. Railway Companies. Compiled in the Quartermaster-General's Department of the War Office. 1910.
Railway Manual (War). 64 pp. 1911. Reprinted, with Amendments, 1914.
Regulations for the Transport of Troops by Railway Quartermaster-General's Office, Horse Guards, Feb. 28, 1867.

HOLLAND

WIJNPERSSE, KAPT. W. J. M. v. D. De voorbereiding van het militair gebruik der spoorwegen in oorlogstijd. 76 pp. Plans and plates. s'Gravenhage, 1905.

INDIA

ANDREW, W. P. Our Scientific Frontier. London, 1880.
INNES, R.E., GEN. J. J. McLEOD. Life and Times of Gen. Sir James Browne, R.E., K.C.B., K.C.S.I. 371 pp. London, 1905.
   [Gives an account of the construction of the Sind-Pishin Railway, of which Sir J. Browne was Chief Engineer.]
LYONS, CAPT. GERVAIS. Afghanistan, the Buffer State. Great

BIBLIOGRAPHY. 393

Britain and Russia in Central Asia. 232 pp. Maps. Madras and London, 1910.
[Gives, in summarised form, much information concerning British Indian frontier and Russian Central Asian Railways.]
Military Railways in India. Précis of Report of the Railway Transport Committee, India, 1876. Professional Papers of the Corps of Royal Engineers. Occasional Papers, Vol. II. Chatham, 1878.
Ross, C.I.E., David. Military Transport by Indian Railways. 109 pp. Maps and plates. Lahore, 1883.
—— Transport by Rail of Troops, Horses, Guns, and War Material in India. A lecture. 24 pp. London, 1879.
Scott-Moncrieff, R.E., Capt. G. K. The Frontier Railways of India. Professional Papers of the Corps of Royal Engineers. Occasional Papers, Vol. XI, 1885. Chatham.

Italy

Allix, G. La Mobilisation des Chemins de Fer Italiens. *Journal des Transports*, 3 Juillet, 1915. Paris.
Aymonino, C. Considérations Militaires et Stratégiques sur les chemins de fer italiens. Traduit de l'Italien par G. Malifaud. 3e. éd. 68 pp. Paris, 1889.
Le Ferrovie dello Stato e le grandi manovre del 1911. *Revista Technica della Ferrovie Italiane*, Nov., 1912.
Zanotti, Mag. B. Impiego dei ferrovieri in guerra. 67 pp. 1902.

Russia

Fendrikh, Col. A. von. The Organisation of a Staff for Military Railway Work and of a Central Management for the Control of Rolling Stock in War Time. Translated from *The Russian Military Magazine*, by Capt. J. Wolfe Murray, R.A., D.A.A.G. *Journal of the Royal United Service Institution*, Vol. XXXII, 1889.
Igel, Gen. von. Russlands Eisenbahnbau an der Westgrenze. *Deutsche Revue*, Dec., 1902. Stuttgart.
K., H. Das russische Eisenbahn-Netz zur deutschen Grenze in seiner Bedeutung für einen Krieg Russlands mit Deutschland. 29 pp. Map. Hannover, 1885.
Nienstädt, Oberstlt. Das russische Eisenbahnnetz zur deutschen-österreichischen Grenze in seiner Bedeutung für einen Krieg. 43 pp. Map. Leipzig, 1895.
Strategical Railways. Translated from the Voïénnyi Sbórnik. *Journal of the Royal United Service Institution*, Oct., 1899.

SPAIN

TAYLOR, TEN. T. L. Los ferrocarriles en la guerra. 288 pp. Plates. Barcelona, 1885.

SWITZERLAND

BLASER, HAUPT. E. Die Zerstörungs- und Wiederherstellungs-Arbeiten von Eisenbahnen. 22 pp. Plates. Basel, 1871.
HOFFMANN-MERIAN, T. Die Eisenbahnen zum Truppen Transport und für den Krieg im Hinblick auf die Schweiz. 2e. Ausg. Basel, 1871.
NOWACKI, KARL. Die Eisenbahnen im Kriege. 160 pp. Zurich, 1906.

UNITED STATES

Are Railroads Neutralising Sea Power? *American Review of Reviews*, June, 1913.
BIGELOW, JOHN, Captain 10th Cavalry, U.S. Army. The Principles of Strategy, illustrated mainly from American Campaigns. 2nd edition. Philadelphia, 1894.
Commerce of the Ohio and Western Rivers. Importance of Railroads in a Military point of view. *DeBow's Commercial Review*, June, 1857.
CONNOR, MAJ. W. D. Military Railways. 192 pp. Illustrations. Professional Papers, No. 32, Corps of Engineers, U.S. Army. Washington, 1910.
―― Operation and Maintenance of the Railroad in a Theatre of War. *Journal of the Military Service Institute*. New York, 1905.
DERR, W. L. The working of railways in Military Operations. *Engineering Magazine*, Oct., 1898.
Great Railroad Feats during War and Flood. *Washington, D.C., Post*, April 25, 1913
GRIMSHAW, ROBERT. War Capacity of United States Railways. *Scientific American*, May 1, 1915.
HAINES, CHARLES O. Our Railroads and National Defence. *The North American Review*, Sept., 1915.
HAUPT, HERMAN. Military Bridges . . . including designs for trestle and truss bridges for military railroads, adapted specially to the wants of the service in the United States. 310 pp. 69 plates. New York, 1864.
Use of Railroads in War. *Journal of the Military Service Institution*. Vol. XXI. New York, 1897.
PALMER, CAPT. JOHN MCAULEY. Railroad Building as a Mode of Warfare. *North American Review*, Dec., 1902.
Railroads, and not Bullets, will feature the next War. *Washington, D.C., Star*, Feb. 11, 1912.

WILSON, W. B. History of the Pennsylvania Railroad Company. Two vols. The Railroad in War Times, Vol. I, pp. 411–18. Philadelphia, 1899.

AMBULANCE AND HOSPITAL TRAINS

FURSE, LIEUT.-COL. G. A. Military Transport. Chap. vii, Railway Ambulance Trains, pp. 185–99. Diagrams and illustrations. London, 1882.

GURLT, DR. E. Ueber den Transport Schwerverwundeter und Kranker im Kriege, nebst Vorschlägen über die Benutzung der Eisenbahnen dabei. 33 pp. Berlin, 1860.
[Contains, so far as can be traced, the earliest recommendations as to the special fitting up of railway rolling stock for the transport of the sick and wounded in war.]

LOEFFLER, DR. F. Das Preussische Militär-Sanitätswesen und seine Reform nach der Kriegserfahrung von 1866. Two parts. Berlin, 1869.
[In the appendix of Part II of this work will be found an "Anleitung zur Ausführung der Beförderung verwundeter und Kranker Militairs auf Eisenbahnen," issued July 1, 1861.]

LONGMORE, SURG.-GEN. SIR T. A Manual of Ambulance Transport. 2nd edition. Edited by Surg.-Capt. W. A. Morris. Chap. vi, Class V, Railway Ambulance Transport, pp. 347–89. Illustrations. London, 1893.
[The 1st edition was published in 1869 under the title of A Treatise on the Transport of Sick and Wounded Troops.]

Medical and Surgical History of the War of the Rebellion. Part III, Vol. II, Surgical History. Railway Transportation, pp. 957–71. Diagrams and illustrations of hospital cars, fittings, etc. U.S.A. Dept. of War. Surgeon-General's Office. Washington, 1883.
[Gives a detailed account of the evolution, in the Civil War, of the hospital train in vogue to-day. A copy of the work will be found in the British Museum Library. Pressmark : 7686 i. 4.]

MELVILLE, A.M.S., SURG.-CAPT. Continental Regulations for the Transport of Sick and Wounded by Rail. *Journal of the Royal United Service Institution.* Vol. XLII, pp. 560–92. London, 1898.

Military Hospital Trains : Their Origin and Progress. *The Railway Gazette*, Dec. 4, 1914. London.

NIEDEN, J. Der Eisenbahn-transport verwundeter und erkrankter Krieger. 2 Aufl. 271 pp. Berlin, 1883.

OTIS, GEORGE A. A Report on a Plan for Transporting Wounded

Soldiers by Railway in Time of War. Surgeon-General's Office, War Department, Washington, 1875.
[The material parts of this work are reproduced in the "Medical and Surgical History of the War of the Rebellion."]
Report by the Central British Red Cross Committee on Voluntary Organisations in aid of the Sick and Wounded during the South African War. Part VII, Hospital Trains, pp. 32–5. London, 1902.
Report on the Medical Arrangements in the South African War. By Surg.-Gen. Sir W. D. Wilson, K.C.M.G., late Principal Medical Officer, South African Field Force. Part IX, Hospital Trains, pp. 213–9. London, 1904.
RIDDELL, J. SCOTT. A Manual of Ambulance. Section on Railway Ambulance Wagons and Ambulance Trains, pp. 168–76. 6th edition. London, 1913.

ARMOURED TRAINS

ADAMS, W. BRIDGES. English Railway Artillery: A Cheap Defence against Invasion. *Once a Week*, Aug. 13, 1859. London.
Armoured Truck ("Union Railroad Battery," Petersburg) used in the American Civil War, 1861–65. See illustration, *Century Magazine*, Sept., 1887, p. 774.
BOXALL, CHARLES GERVAISE, Col. Commanding 1st Sussex Artillery Volunteers. Armoured Train for Coast Defence in Great Britain, The. Paper read at a meeting of Officers and N.C.O.'s of the Brigade at Newhaven Fort, Sussex, May 14, 1894. 11 pp.
—— Railway Batteries and Armoured Trains. *Fortnightly Review*, Aug., 1895.
CONNOR, MAJ. W. D. Military Railways. Section on Armoured Trains, pp. 141–50. Professional Papers, No. 32, Corps of Engineers, U.S. Army. Washington, 1910.
Detailed History of the Railways in the South African War, 1899–1902. Vol. I, Section on Organisation, Equipment and Use of Armoured Trains. Chatham, 1905.
Field Service Regulations. Part I, Operations. 1909. (Reprinted, with amendments, 1914.) Section 40, Defence of Railways. General Staff, War Office, London.
FITZGERALD, W. C. The Armoured Train. *The Four-track News*, March, 1906. New York.
FORBIN, V. Les trains blindés. *Nature*, Dec. 12, 1914. Paris.
FRASER, R.E., LIEUT. T. Armour-plated Railway Wagons used during the late Sieges of Paris in 1870–71. Papers of the Corps of Royal Engineers, N.S., Vol. XX. Woolwich, 1872.

BIBLIOGRAPHY.

GIROUARD, R.E., LIEUT.-COL. E. P. C. History of the Railways during the War in South Africa, 1899–1902. Section V, The Organisation and Use of Armoured Trains. London, 1903.

HOBART, FREDERICK. The first Armoured Train. *Railway Age Gazette*, Jan. 22, 1915. Chicago, U.S.A.

LODIAN, L. The Origin of Armoured Railroad Cars unquestionably the Product of the American Civil War. *Railroad and Locomotive Engineering*, May, 1915. New York.

[Reproduces from *Leslie's Weekly* for May 18, 1864, an illustration of a "Railroad Battery on the Philadelphia and Baltimore Railway," showing a "box" car completely covered with armour plating, with loop-holes at end and side for guns, and placed on the line in front of the locomotive, itself otherwise unprotected.]

Military History of the Campaign of 1882 in Egypt. Prepared in the Intelligence Branch of the War Office. Revised edition. London, 1908.

[References to use of armoured train.]

NANCE, CAPT. H. O. Armoured Trains. Lecture delivered at the Royal Engineers' Institute. 52 pp. Photographs and drawings. Professional Papers, fourth series, Vol. I, Paper 4. Chatham, 1906.

[The subject is dealt with in three sections: (1) Uses of Armoured Trains; (2) Construction, equipment and garrison; (3) Organisation and administration.]

Railway Manual (War). Chapter VI, Section 15, Armoured Trains. London, 1911.

WALKER, LIEUT. ARTHUR. Coast Railways and Railway Artillery. *Journal of the Royal United Service Institution*, Vol. IX, pp. 221–23. Plates. London, 1866.

INDEX

ABYSSINIAN CAMPAIGN : Construction and working of military railway, 210–14.
ADAMS, WILLIAM BRIDGES : 67–9.
ADVANTAGES FROM USE OF RAILWAYS : 345–50.
AFRICA, GERMAN DESIGNS ON : Proposals of von Weber, 297 ; German South-West Africa, 298–300 ; the Herero rising, 300–1 ; railways, 304–10 ; military preparations, 307, 310 –12 ; rail connection with Angola, 312–14 ; German East Africa Central Railway, 314–7 ; Katanga district, 316 ; Central Africa, 318 ; rival railway schemes, 319–20 ; railway schemes in the Cameroons, 320–5 ; official admissions, 325–6 ; "der Tag" and its programme, 326–30.
AGADIR CRISIS, THE : 324.
AGGRESSION, USE OF RAILWAYS FOR : 355–6.
ALEXANDER THE GREAT : 63.
ALEXANDRETTA, GERMANY AND : 334, 343.
ALEXEIEV, ADMIRAL : 275.
AMBULANCE TRAINS : see RAILWAY AMBULANCE TRANSPORT.
AMERICAN CIVIL WAR : What it established, 13 ; railway lines, 15 ; Federal Government and railways, 16 ; mileage taken over, 18 ; gauge of lines, 18 ; condition of lines, 19 ; Transportation Department, 20–1 ; locomotives, 21–2 ; rolling mills, 23 ; movement of troops, 23–5 ; destruction of railways ; 27–8 ; Construction Corps, 29–37 ; control of railways, 43–50 ; protection of, 54–5 ; armoured cars ; 72–4 ; removal of sick and wounded, 86–91 ; American precedents followed in Europe, 104, 122, 153, 177 ; "surface railroads," 210 ; the Civil War and the South African campaign, 258 (*n.*).
ANATOLIA : 331, 335.
ANATOLIAN RAILWAY, THE : 334.
ANGOLA : 299, 312–4, 320.
ARMOURED TRAINS : Protection of railway lines, 59 ; first suggested, 67–9 ; proposals of Lieut. A. Walker, 69–70 ; of Col. Wethered, 70–71 ; of Lieut. E. P. C. Girouard, 71–2; Civil War, 72–4 ; Franco-Prussian War, 75 ; Egyptian Campaign, 75–6, 224 ; Delhi, 76 ; experiments in France, 77; at Newhaven, Sussex, 77–9 ; South African War, 79, 248–52.
ASIA MINOR : Germany's "share" in the Turkish spoils, 332 ; Germany's colonisation field, 332–3 ; proposed German protectorate, 333.
ASPINALL, MR. J. A. F. : 197.
ATLANTIC AND NORTH CAROLINA RAILROAD : 36, 73.
AUSTRALIA AND THE BAGHDAD RAILWAY : 342, 344.
AUSTRIA-HUNGARY : Early troop movements by rail, 8–9 ; scheme for strategical railways, 9 ; Italian campaign of 1859, 11–12 ; Railway Troops, 123 ; German rail communications, 287.
AUSTRO-PRUSSIAN CAMPAIGN : Protection of railways, 55, 59 ; removal of sick and wounded, 91–2 ; Prussian mobilisation, 104 ; defective transport arrangements, 104–5 ; destruction and restoration of railway lines, 124–6.

BABYLONIA, GERMANY AND : 332.

INDEX. 399

BAGHDAD RAILWAY, THE: Concession, 334; branches, 334-5; Germany's aims, 336; the conquest of Egypt, 338-40; the Persian Gulf, 341; India, 342; Capt. Mahan's views, 342; the desired extension to Koweit, 343; what the railway was to accomplish, 344.
BALCK: 110.
BALTIMORE AND OHIO RAILROAD: 29.
BASSON, WILHELM: 127.
BECKER, LIEUT.: 169-70.
BELGIUM: EARLY RAILWAYS IN, 4-5; German strategical lines on Belgian frontier, 288-294; German designs, 323-4, 325-6, 327, 329.
BÉRIGNY, M. DE: 7.
BEYENS, BARON: 325.
BIGELOW, CAPT. J.: 56, 348 (n.)
BILLINGTON, MR. R. J.: 78.
BISMARCK, PRINCE: 136, 338.
BLOCKHOUSES FOR PROTECTION OF RAILWAYS: 54, 58, 245.
BOULGER, MR. D. C.: 288, 294.
BOXALL, COL. C. G.: 78.
BRITISH CENTRAL RED CROSS COMMITTEE: 95, 254.
BRITISH EAST AFRICA: 317, 327.
BRITISH SOUTH AFRICA: German designs on, 301, 302, 303, 308, 312, 327.
BRYDEN, MR. H. A.: 300 (n.).
BUDDE, H.: 51.
BULLER, SIR REDVERS: 254.
BURGOYNE, SIR JOHN: 178, 209.
BUTTERWORTH, SIR A. K.: 197.

CALEDONIAN RLY.: 197.
CALTHROP, MR. GUY: 197.
CAMEROONS, THE: 320-5.
CAMPENAU, GEN.: 137.
CANALS AND TROOPS: 1.
CAPE GOVERNMENT RAILWAYS: 237, 240, 246, 253.
CAPE-TO-CAIRO RAILWAY: 320.
CENTRAL AFRICA: 318-20.
CHÉRADAME, M. ANDRÉ: 338.
CHRISTIAN, PRINCESS: 254.
CLARKE, SIR ANDREW: 224.
COAST DEFENCE: 67, 179.
COMMERCE DEFENCE LEAGUE, THE GERMAN: 303 (n.).
CONGO, THE BELGIAN: 315-320, 322-6.
CONDITIONS ESSENTIAL TO EFFICIENCY: 350-2.

CONNOR, MAJ. W. D.: 58, 80, 258 (n.).
CONSTRUCTION CORPS: U.S.A., 20, 21, 23, 29-37; Prussia, 122-3, 124-8, 132-6, 215-6, 219; Austria, 123-4; Bavaria, 127-133; France, 128, 152-4; England, 198-202; South African War, 242-5; Russo-Japanese War, 273-4.
CONSTRUCTION OF RAILWAYS: Military requirements, 350-1.
CONTROL OF RAILWAYS IN WAR: Conditions of operation, 40-3; American Civil War, 43-50; views of Baron M. M. von. Weber, 50-2; need for intermediaries, 52; organisation in peace, 99; Austro-Prussian War, 104-5; German system in 1870-71, 106-115; new regulations, 115-7; present system, 118-121; inefficient military control in France in 1870-71, 139-147; creation of new organisation, 149-170; State control in England, 176-7; draft scheme for State operation, 185-7; Railway Transport Officers, 189-191; South African War, 233-7, 238-9, 249-52; Russo-Japanese War, 274-5; general, 351.
COWANS, LIEUT.-GEN. SIR J. S.: 204.
CRIMEAN WAR: Deaths from sickness and disease, 81; removal of sick and wounded by railway, 83; transport conditions, 207-8; construction of military railway, 208; operation, 208-10; recalled by Russo-Japanese War, 260.
CROMER, LORD: 229.

DANISH WAR (1864): 91, 104.
DELAGOA BAY: 304-5, 327.
DELBRÜCK, PROF. HANS: 330.
DENT, MR. C. H.: 197.
DENT, MR. F. H.: 197.
DESTRUCTION OF RAILWAYS: Vulnerability, 26-7; early instances, 27; American Civil War, 27-37; Mexican War, 37-9; Austro-Prussian War, 124, 125-6; Franco-German War, 128-30; South African War, 241-5, 256-8; Russo-Japanese War, 274.

INDEX.

DISADVANTAGES OF RAILWAYS: 355–6.
DUFAURE, M.: 7.
DUMANT, JEAN HENRI: 84.

EAST PRUSSIA, STRATEGICAL RAILWAYS IN: 283.
EGYPT: German anticipations of rebellion, 326; aims against Egypt, 338–9; conquest to be facilitated by railways, 340.
EGYPTIAN CAMPAIGNS: Armoured cars, 75–6; Railway Companies, Royal Engineers, 199.
EIFEL DISTRICT: German strategical railways, 289–292.
ELSENBORN, GERMAN CAMP AT: 288–9.
ENGINEER AND RAILWAY STAFF CORPS: Formation, 179–182; constitution, 181–2; functions and work done, 182–7, 192; supplemented by War Railway Council, 187.
ENGLAND, ORGANISATION IN: Early regulation for troop movements, 2; legislative enactments, 175–7; invasion prospects and formation of Volunteer Corps, 178; Engineer and Railway Staff Corps, 179–187; attitude of War Office, 180; War Office and defence scheme, 185–7; War Railway Council, 187–9; Railway Transport Officers, 189–191; Railways Executive Committee, 195–7; Railway Companies, Royal Engineers, 200–2.
ERNOUF, BARON: 141.
EVANS, DR. T. W.: 91.

FAY, SIR SAM: 197.
FIELDHOUSE, Mr. W. J.: 95.
FINDLAY, SIR GEORGE: 184–7, 195, 196, 202.
FORBES, SIR WILLIAM: 182, 197.
FORMANOIR, CAPTAIN A. DE: 124 (*n*.).
FORTRESSES FOR PROTECTION OF RAILWAYS: 59.
FRANCE: Early references in French Chamber, 6–7; complaints in 1842 of German aggressive lines, 7; early railways, 7; railways and the Italian campaign of 1859, 9–11; early regulations, 138; Marshal Niel's Commission, 138–9; experiences in Franco-German War, 139–148; German railway lines on French frontiers, 287–8; Germany's alternative routes, via Luxemburg, 288; via Belgium, 288–93; French possessions in Africa to be seized by Germany, 326; to be demanded as "ransom," 329.
FRANCE, ORGANISATION IN: Early regulations, 138; action taken after the Franco-German War, 149–50; Superior Military Commission, 150, 151–2; Field Railway Sections, 153–4; Railway Troops, 154–6; existing organisation, 157–168; tests, 169; views of German authority, 169; defensive railways, 170–4.
FRANCO-GERMAN WAR: FRANCE: Armoured wagons, 75; rail-transport regulations, 138; the Niel Commission, 138–9; despatches by rail, 139–40; absence of military organisation, 140; confusion and chaos, 140–2; conflicting orders, 142; local authorities, 143; unloading 143–4; congestion at stations, 145–7; seizure of rolling stock by enemy, 147.
FRANCO-GERMAN WAR: GERMANY: Safeguarding of railway lines, 56–8; removal of sick and wounded, 94–5; rail transport conditions, 106–115; Railway Troops, 127–8; destruction of lines, etc., 128–30; operation of French lines by Germans, 130–1; construction of military lines, 215–6.
FRANC-TIREURS AND RAILWAYS: 57, 129–30.
FRASER, R.E., LIEUT.: 129.
FREDERICKSBURG RAILROAD: 29.
FRENCH TRANS-AFRICAN RAILWAY SCHEME: 322.
FRERE, SIR BARTLE: 297.
FRIRON, GEN.: 64.
FURLEY, SIR JOHN: 95, 96, 254.

GAMBON, M.: 325.
GAUGE, RAILWAY: Various countries, 60; Russian policy in respect to, 61; experiences in Russo-Turkish War, 61, 217;

INDEX. 401

Germany and Russian lines, 284–6.
GERMAN EAST AFRICA: 314–5, 316–7.
GERMAN EMPEROR, THE: African railways, 321; visit to Constantinople, 334; to Damascus, 337.
GERMAN SOUTH-WEST AFRICA: 298–312.
GERMANY AND EGYPT: 338–40.
GERMANY: Early proposals for strategical railways, 2–3; early railways constructed, 5; possible attacks on two fronts, 5; "aggressive" lines, 7; early troop transports, 8; control of railways in war, 50–52; railway ambulance transport, 84–6, 91–3, 94; see also GERMANY, ORGANISATION IN.
GERMANY, ORGANISATION IN: Influence of American Civil War, 104, 122; Railway Section of General Staff formed, 104; Danish War (1864), 104; Austro-Prussian War, 104–6; Route Service Regulation, 106–9; Franco-Prussian War, 110–15; further Regulations, 115–6; Field Service Regulations, 117; present basis of organisation, 188–121; Railway Troops, 122–37.
GIROUARD, SIR E. PERCY C.: 71, 225, 228, 233–7, 238–9, 240–1, 248–9, 252, 257, 258 (n.).
GOLTZ, VON DER: 135, 139, 282, 346 (n.), 352.
GORDON, GEN.: 221, 222.
GRAHAM, GEN. SIR G.: 223, 224 (n.).
GRANET, SIR GUY: 197.
GRANT, CAPT. M. H.: 251.
GRANT, GEN.: 22.
GREAT CENTRAL RAILWAY, 197.
GREAT EASTERN RLY.: 194, 204.
GREAT NORTHERN RLY.: 194, 197, 204.
GREAT WESTERN RAILWAY: 192, 195 (n.), 197.
GREY, EARL DE: 180.
GRUND SYSTEM OF RAILWAY FITTINGS: 94.
GURLT, DR. E.: 81, 84, 85.
GYULIA, COUNT: 12.

HALLECK, GEN.: 23–4.
HAMLEY, GEN. SIR E.; 207, 349 (n.).

HARKORT, F. W.: 2–3.
HARRISON, Mr. C. W. F.: 247.
HAUPT, HERMAN: Pioneer of Construction Corps, U.S.A., 29–30; rebuilding of bridges, 31–2; control questions, 43–9; armoured car, 72.
HEDJAZ RAILWAY: 335.
HERBERT, Mr. SIDNEY: 180.
HERFF, HERR VON: 305.
HEYER, Mr. A. E.: 305.
HINE, MAJ. CHARLES.: 37.
HOBART, Mr. F.: 73.
HOLLAND: German strategical lines on Dutch frontier, 293–4.
HOME, R.E., LIEUT.-COL. R.: 63.
HOOD, GEN.: 35.
HOSPITAL TRAINS; see RAILWAY AMBULANCE TRANSPORT.

INDIA: German anticipations of rebellion, 326; the Baghdad railway and India, 342, 344.
INVASION OF ENGLAND: Fears of, 67, 177–8, 182.
ITALIAN CAMPAIGN (1859): Conveyance of troops by rail, 9–13; destruction of railway lines, 27; removal of sick and wounded by rail, 84.

JACQMIN, M.; 143, 148, 235.
JAGOW, HERR VON: 325–6.
JOESTEN, DR. JOSEF: 281, 283.

KAERGER, DR. KARL: 332–3.
KATANGA DISTRICT (Central Africa): 316-20.
KELTON, J. C.: 50.
KITCHENER, LORD: 58, 225, 226, 227, 228, 229, 239.
KUROPATKIN, GEN.: 263, 269–70, 271, 275, 355 (n.)

LAMARQUE, GEN.: 6.
LANCASHIRE AND YORKSHIRE RLY.: 197.
LAND TRANSPORT CORPS (Crimea): 181 (n.), 208, 209.
LANGHAMS, PAUL: 338.
LANOIR, M. PAUL: 136–7.
LATTMANN, HERR: 306.
LEDEBOUR, HERR: 302.
LEOPOLD, KING: 318, 325.
LIMITATIONS IN USEFULNESS OF RAILWAYS: 352–5.
LIVERPOOL AND MANCHESTER RLY.: 1, 8.

D D

INDEX.

LOBITO BAY RLY.: 314, 319–20.
LODIAN, Mr. L.: 73.
LONDON AND NORTH WESTERN RLY.: 194, 197.
LONDON AND SOUTH WESTERN RLY.: 192, 193, 197, 199, 201.
LONDON, BRIGHTON AND SOUTH COAST RLY.: 77–8, 197.
LONDON, CHATHAM AND DOVER RLY.: 199.
LONDON, DEFENCE OF: 71.
LORME, M. DUPUY DE: 75.
LUARD, R.E., CAPT. C. E.: 209.
LÜDERITZ, ADOLF: 298.
LUXEMBURG RAILWAYS: 288, 289, 292.

MCCALLUM, D.G.: Appointed Military Director, etc., U. S. railroads, 17–18; views on situation, 19; creation of Transportation Department and Construction Corps, 20, 32–37; movement of troops, 23–4; question of control, 50; German translation of report, 127.
MCDOWELL, GEN.: 30, 54.
MCMURDO, GEN. SIR W. M.: 180, 181, 182–3.
MAHAN, CAPT. A. T.: 342, 344.
MANASSAS GAP RAILWAY: 55.
MANBY, F.R.S., MR. C.: 180.
MANGELSDORF, PROF. R.: 340.
MAQUAY, R.E., Col. J. P.: 214.
MARSCHALL, M., 7.
MASSENA, MARSHAL: 64.
MATHESON, Mr. D. A.: 197.
MEADE, MAJ.-GEN. G. G.: 54.
MEIGS, Gen.: 48.
MEXICO, RAILWAY DESTRUCTION IN: 37–9.
MIDLAND RAILWAY: 197.
MILITARY OPERATION OF RAILWAYS: Civil War, 20–1; Franco-German War, 130–1; British organisation 175; South African War, 239–41; Russo-Japanese War, 374.
MILITARY RAILWAYS: Description of, 205-6; pioneer military line in Crimean War, 206–10; American Civil War, 210; Abyssinian Campaign, 210–14; Franco-German War, 215–6; Russo-Turkish War, 216–20; the Sudan, 220–231; Russo-Japanese War, 272–3; general, 349.
MILLAR, R.A., MAJ.: 9.

MOLTKE, VON: 8, 106, 109, 278, 346 (n.).
MORACHE, DR.: 81.
MUNI (Spanish): 324.

NANCE, CAPT. H. O.: 80.
NANTON, R.E., CAPT. H. C.: 250.
NAPIER OF MAGDALA, LORD: 210.
NAPIER, SIR CHARLES: 178.
NAPOLEON: 62, 63, 64.
NASHVILLE AND CHATTANOOGA RLY.: 33, 34.
NATAL GOVERNMENT RAILWAYS: 237, 246–8, 253.
NATAL RAILWAY PIONEER STAFF: 247.
NATHAN, R.E., LIEUT. M.: 223.
NATIONAL DEFENCE ACT, 1888: 177, 195.
NETHERLANDS SOUTH AFRICAN RLY.: 240, 254–8.
NIEL, MARSHAL: 138, 139.
NORTON, Mr. ROY: 286.
NORTH EASTERN RLY.: 197.
NORTH MISSOURI RAILROAD: 29.

O'CONNOR, Mr. J. K.: 310–12, 326–7.
ORANGE AND ALEXANDRIA RAILROAD: 46, 55, 88.
OSMAN PASHA: 218.

PANZ, OBERST. VON: 123.
PEEL, GEN.: 176.
PERNOT CAPT. A.: 172, 174.
PHILADELPHIA-BALTIMORE RAILROAD: 73.
PHILADELPHIA RAILROAD: 87.
POMERANIA, STRATEGICAL RAILWAYS IN: 283.
PÖNITZ, C. E.: 4–6, 280.
POPE, GEN.: 43.
PORTER, MAJ.-GEN. WHITWORTH: 209, 224.
POTTER. MR. F.: 197.
POWELL, MAJ.: 209.
PREPARATIONS IN PEACE: Need for, 98–102; 106, 123, 138, 149, 178–180, 184, 351–2.
PROTECTION OF RAILWAYS IN WAR: American Civil War, 54–5; blockhouses, 54, 58; placing of civilians on engines or trains, 55, 57–8; Austro-Prussian War, 55–6; Franco-Prussian War, 56–8; South-African War, 58; permanent fortresses, 59; use of armoured trains, 59; removal of rolling stock,

INDEX. 403

59; destruction of, 60; different gauge, 60-1; terrorising of civil population, 356.

PRUSSIAN RAILWAY TROOPS: Formation of Field Railway Section, 122; operations in Austro-Prussian campaign, 123 124-6; permanent cadre, 127; Franco-Prussian War, 127-8, 130-1; Railway Battalion, 132-4; Railway Regiment, 134; Communication Troops, 134; need for Railway Troops, 135-6; railwaymen as spies, 136-7; construction of military lines, 215-6.

RADEK, HERR KARL: 339-40.

RAILWAY AMBULANCE TRANSPORT: Deaths from disease and sickness, 81; importance of prompt removal of sick and wounded, 82-3; Crimean War, 83; Italian War, 84; recommendations by Dr. Gurlt, 84-5; first Prussian Commission, 85; American Civil War, 86-91; Danish War, 91; Austro-Prussian War, 91-2; second Prussian Commission, 92-3; Paris International Exhibition (1867), 93; third Prussian Commission, 94; Franco-Prussian War, 94-5; South African War, 95-6; 253-4; methods now in vogue, 96-7.

RAILWAY COMPANIES, ROYAL ENGINEERS: Formation, 199; services in Egypt, 199; duties, 200; training 200-2; services in the Sudan, 221-9; South African War, 233, 240, 242, 243, 251.

RAILWAY PIONEER REGIMENT: 242, 243.

RAILWAYS EXECUTIVE COMMITTEE: 195-6.

RAILWAY TRANSPORT OFFICERS: 189-191, 193-4.

RAILWAY WAGONS, UNLOADING OF: American Civil war, 46, 47-8; Austro-Prussian War, 105; Franco-German War, 111-2, 144, 145; South African War, 234, 238, 239.

REGULATION OF THE FORCES ACT, 1871; 176, 177, 195, 196, 197.

RENÉ, CARL: 321-2.

REPRISALS, PRUSSIA AND: 55-6.

RHODESIA: 320, 322, 327.
ROBERTS, LORD: 58, 245.
ROBERTUS, J. K.: 332.
ROHRBACH, DR. PAUL: 338-9, 340.
ROON, VON: 85.
ROSCHER, WILHELM: 332.
ROSS, PROF. LUDWIG: 338.
ROTHWELL, R.A., COL. J. S.: 184.
RUMIGNY, GEN: 3
RUSSIA: Early troop movements by rail, 8; policy in respect to railway gauge, 61, 135-6, 217; military lines built in campaign against Turkey, 216-220; German strategical lines on Russian frontier, 284-7. See also RUSSO-JAPANESE WAR.

RUSSO-JAPANESE WAR: Distances from theatre of war, 260; the Trans-Siberian Railway, 261, 262-3; Chinese Eastern Railway, 261, 262; unreadiness of Russia, 263; Lake Baikal, 263, 264-7; ice railway across the lake, 266-7; circum-Baikal line, 267; traffic hindrances, 268; number of trains, 268; speed, 268; Russian reinforcements in driblets, 269; rail improvements, 270-1; dependence on railway, 271; results accomplished, 271-2; field railways, 272-3; Railway Troops, 273-4; operation, 274; control, 274-6, 355 (*n*.).

RUSSO-TURKISH WAR: Railway gauge, 61; construction of military railways, 216-20.

SAÏD PASHA: 221.
SAMASSA, DR. PAUL: 301-2.
SAROLEA, DR. Charles: 337.
SCHÄFFER, E.: 113 (*n*.).
SCHLESWIG-HOLSTEIN: German strategical lines, 294.
SCHOFIELD, GEN.: 24.
SCOTT, MAJ.-GEN. D. A.: 181.
SHERMAN, GEN. W. T.: 19, 34-6, 54, 65.
SICK AND WOUNDED IN WAR: Evacuation hospitals, 167; infirmary stations, 167; distribution stations, 167; general, 349-50. See also, RAILWAY AMBULANCE TRANSPORT.
SOUTH AFRICAN WAR: Removal of locomotives and rolling stock, 59-60; hospital trains, 95-6, 253-4; transport of troops for

embarkation, 193; South African railways, 232–3; creation of Department of Military Railways, 233; control questions, 233–5; basis of organisation, 235–7; transport conditions, 237–8; how the system worked, 238–9; Imperial Military Railways, 239–40; need for operating staff organised in time of peace, 240–1; destruction and repair of lines, etc., 241–5; Railway Pioneer Regiment, 242; blockhouses, 245; military traffic, 245–6; miscellaneous services, 246–8; armoured trains, 248–52; operation of Netherlands South African Railway by Boers, 254–9; the war and rail-power, 258–9.
SOUTH CAROLINA RAILROAD: 36.
SOUTH EASTERN AND CHATHAM RLY.: 197.
SOUTH EASTERN RLY.: 199.
SPRENGER, DR. A.: 332.
STANTON, MR.: 23, 29.
STAVELOT-MALMÉDY LINE: 288–292.
STEINNETZ, MR. T.: 255–8.
STRATEGICAL MOVEMENTS RY RAIL: 12, 25, 245–6, 346.
STRATEGICAL RAILWAYS: Early proposals in Germany, 2, 5–6, 7; France, 7; Austria, 9; defensive lines in France, 170–4; position in Great Britain, 202; connecting links, 203; attitude of Parliament, 203; Northern Junction line, 203–4; nature of strategical railways, 277–80; ideal conditions, 279–81; position in Germany, 281–4; Pomerania and East Prussia, 283–4; Russian frontier, 284–7; southern Silesia, 287; French frontier, 287–8; Belgian frontier, 288–93; Dutch frontier, 293–4; Schleswig-Holstein, 294; German South-West Africa, 304–9; Angola, 312–4; German East Africa, 314–5; Cameroons, 320–4; Baghdad Railway, 334–344.
STUART-STEPHENS, MAJ.: 290 (*n*.).
STURGIS, GEN.: 44.
SUAKIN-BERBER LINE: 199, 223–5.
SUPPLIES FOR TROOPS: War of Secession, 15–16, 46; "living on the country," 63, 64, 65; conditions in pre-railway days, 63–4; discipline, 64; road transport, 65; advantages of rail transport, 65–6; defective organisation, Austro-Prussian War, 105; new system for Germany, 107; Franco-German War, 110–113, 143–6; present French system, 164–6; general, 347–8.
SURFACE RAILROADS IN THE AMERICAN CIVIL WAR: 210.
SUDAN, THE: Early railway schemes, 221; Wady Halfa-Sarras line, 221; extension for expedition of 1884, 221–2; abandonment, 222; results attained, 223; Suakin-Berber line, 223–5; Nile Valley line, reconstructed and extended, 225–6; Nubian Desert line, 226–7; extension to Atbara, 228; Khartoum, 229; El Obeid, 229; military results, 228; services to civilisation, 230–1; Germany and the Sudan, 321–2.
SUVÓROFF: 62.
SZLUMPER, MR. G. S.: 197.

TACTICAL MOVEMENTS BY RAIL: 346.
THIERS, M.: 64.
THORNHILL, MR. J. B.: 316.
THOMAS, GEN. G. H.: 89.
TOVEY, R.E., LIEUT.-COL.: 354 (*n*.).
TOWN, DR. F. L.: 90.
TRANS-SIBERIAN RLY. *See* RUSSO-JAPANESE WAR.
TRANSVAAL, GERMANY AND THE: 304, 305, 311, 327.
TROOP MOVEMENTS BY RAIL: Early, 8; Italian campaign of 1859, 9–12; Civil War, 23–5; quicker transport, 62; more complete numbers, 62–3; Danish War of 1864, 104; Austro-Prussian War, 104; Franco-Prussian War, 110, 139–140; Volunteer reviews and army manœuvres, 192, 194; South African War, 193, 245–6; Russo-Japanese War, 269, 271; general, 345–6, 352–4.
TURKEY, ASIATIC: Germany's Land of Promise, 331.
TURKEY: Germany's designs against, 331, 336–40.

INDEX.

UNGER, L. A. : 6.

VICKERS, R.E., CAPT. C. E. : 274.
VIGO-ROUISSILLON, M. : 36.
VOLUNTEER CORPS IN GREAT
    BRITAIN ; 67, 178-9, 182, 191-2.

WALKER, LIEUT. ARTHUR : 69.
WALKER, SIR HERBERT A. : 197.
WALTER, MAJ. J. : 191-2.
WAR RAILWAY COUNCIL, THE :
    187-9, 193, 196.
WATERS, COL. W. H. H. : 274, 275.
WATSON, COL. SIR CHARLES, 228.
WATSON, Mr. P. H. : 72.
WEBBER, R.E., CAPT. C. E. : 55,
    125, 126.
WEBER, BARON, M. M. VON : 50-2.

WEBER, ERNST VON : 297, 330.
WEEKS, G. E. : 37-8.
WELLINGTON, DUKE OF : 65, 177.
WELTPOLITIK : 331, 342, 344, 356.
WERNEKKE, REGIERUNGSRAT : 8.
WESTERN AND ATLANTIC RLY. : 34.
WESTPHALEN, H. L. : 124.
WETHERED, COL. E. R. : 70.
WHEELER, GEN. : 34.
WILLANS, R.E., LIEUT. : 211, 213.
WILSON, PRESIDENT : 330.
WOLSELEY, LORD : 199, 222, 223.
WRIGHT, C.E., Mr. T. : 70.

ZAVODOVSKI SYSTEM OF RAILWAY
    FITTINGS : 94.
ZIMMERMANN, EMIL : 322-5.

www.ingramcontent.com/pod-product-compliance
Lightning Source LLC
Chambersburg PA
CBHW061926220426
43662CB00012B/1818